# PSYCHO BUSTERS

# 3

**Story by
Yuya Aoki**

**Manga by
Akinari Nao**

Translated and adapted by
**Stephen Paul**

Lettered by
North Market Street Graphics

Ballantine Books ∗ New York

*Psycho Busters* volume 3 is a work of fiction. Names, characters, places, and incidents are the products of the author's imagination or are used fictitiously. Any resemblance to actual events, locales, or persons, living or dead, is entirely coincidental.

A Del Rey Manga/Kodansha Trade Paperback Original



Published in the United States by Del Rey Books, an imprint of The Random House Publishing Group, a division of Random House, Inc., New York.



Publication rights arranged through Kodansha Ltd.

First published in Japan in 2007 by Kodansha Ltd., Tokyo

ISBN 978-0-345-50408-1

Printed in the United States of America

www.delreymanga.com

9 8 7 6 5 4 3 2 1

Translator/adapter: Stephen Paul
Lettering: North Market Street Graphics

# *Contents*

# Honorifics Explained

Throughout the Del Rey Manga books, you will find Japanese honorifics left intact in the translations. For those not familiar with how the Japanese use honorifics and, more important, how they differ from American honorifics, we present this brief overview.

Politeness has always been a critical facet of Japanese culture. Ever since the feudal era, when Japan was a highly stratified society, use of honorifics—which can be defined as polite speech that indicates relationship or status—has played an essential role in the Japanese language. When addressing someone in Japanese, an honorific usually takes the form of a suffix attached to one's name (example: "Asuna-san"), is used as a title at the end of one's name, or appears in place of the name itself (example: "Negi-sensei," or simply "Sensei!").

Honorifics can be expressions of respect or endearment. In the context of manga and anime, honorifics give insight into the nature of the relationship between characters. Many English translations leave out these important honorifics and therefore distort the feel of the original Japanese. Because Japanese honorifics contain nuances that English honorifics lack, it is our policy at Del Rey not to translate them. Here, instead, is a guide to some of the honorifics you may encounter in Del Rey Manga.

-san:    This is the most common honorific and is equivalent to Mr., Miss, Ms., or Mrs. It is the all-purpose honorific and can be used in any situation where politeness is required.

-sama:   This is one level higher than "-san" and is used to confer great respect.

-dono:   This comes from the word "tono," which means "lord." It is an even higher level than "-sama" and confers utmost respect.

-kun:    This suffix is used at the end of boys' names to express familiarity or endearment. It is also sometimes used by men among friends, or when addressing someone younger or of a lower station.

*-chan:*      This is used to express endearment, mostly toward girls. It is also used for little boys, pets, and even among lovers. It gives a sense of childish cuteness.

*Bozu:*      This is an informal way to refer to a boy, similar to the English terms "kid" and "squirt."

*Sempai/*
*Senpai:*      This title suggests that the addressee is one's senior in a group or organization. It is most often used in a school setting, where underclassmen refer to their upperclassmen as "sempai." It can also be used in the workplace, such as when a newer employee addresses an employee who has seniority in the company.

*Kohai:*      This is the opposite of "sempai" and is used toward underclassmen in school or newcomers in the workplace. It connotes that the addressee is of a lower station.

*Sensei:*      Literally meaning "one who has come before," this title is used for teachers, doctors, or masters of any profession or art.

*[blank]:*      This is usually forgotten in these lists, but it is perhaps the most significant difference between Japanese and English. The lack of honorific means that the speaker has permission to address the person in a very intimate way. Usually, only family, spouses, or very close friends have this kind of permission. Known as *yobisute,* it can be gratifying when someone who has earned the intimacy starts to call one by one's name without an honorific. But when that intimacy hasn't been earned, it can be very insulting.

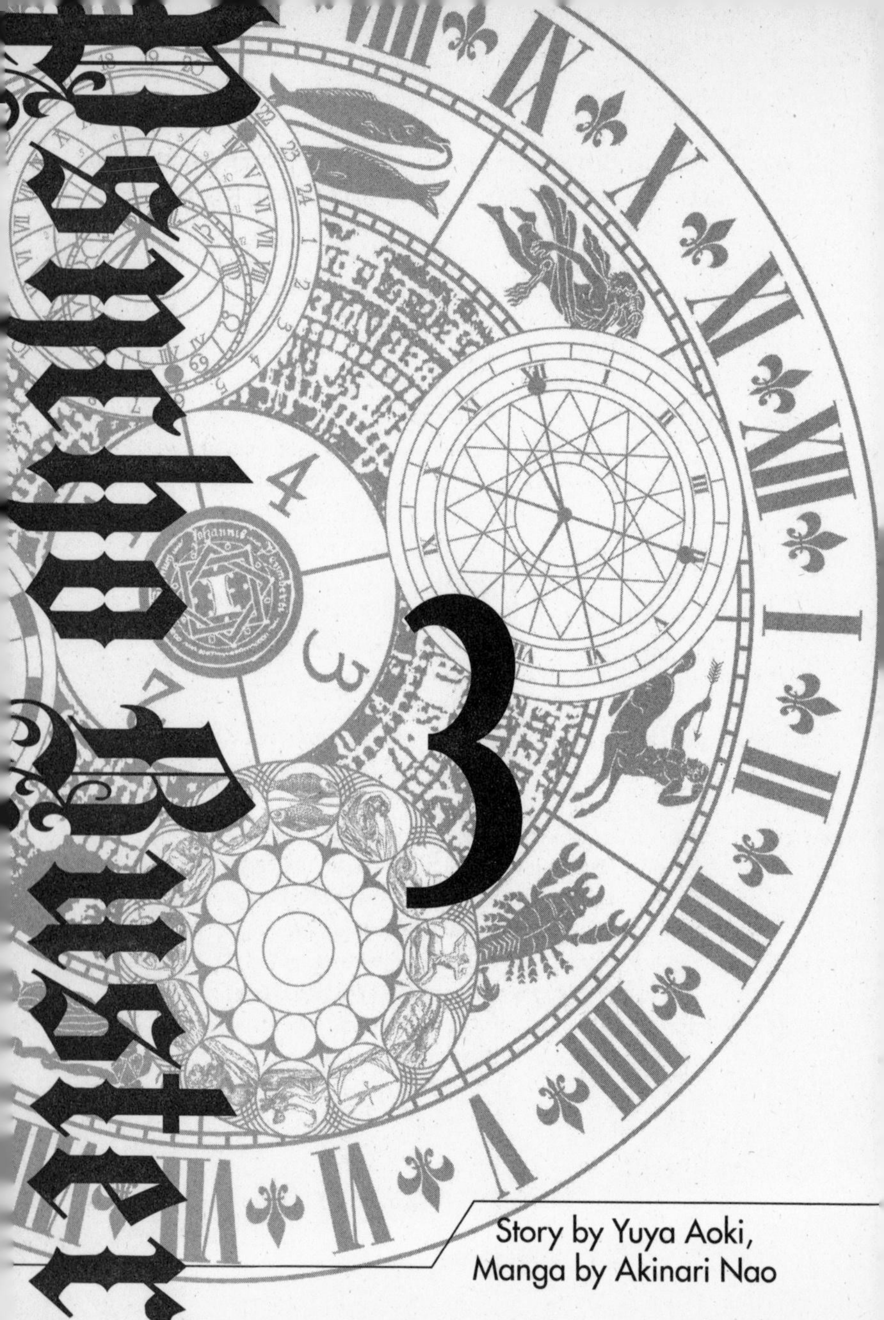

# Psycho Busters

# 3

Story by Yuya Aoki,
Manga by Akinari Nao

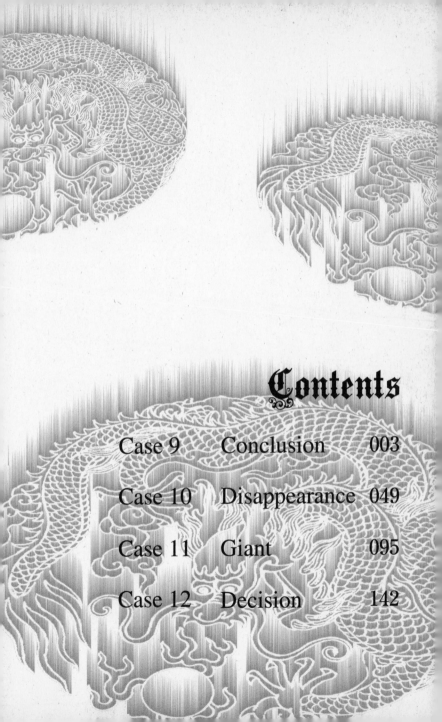

# Contents

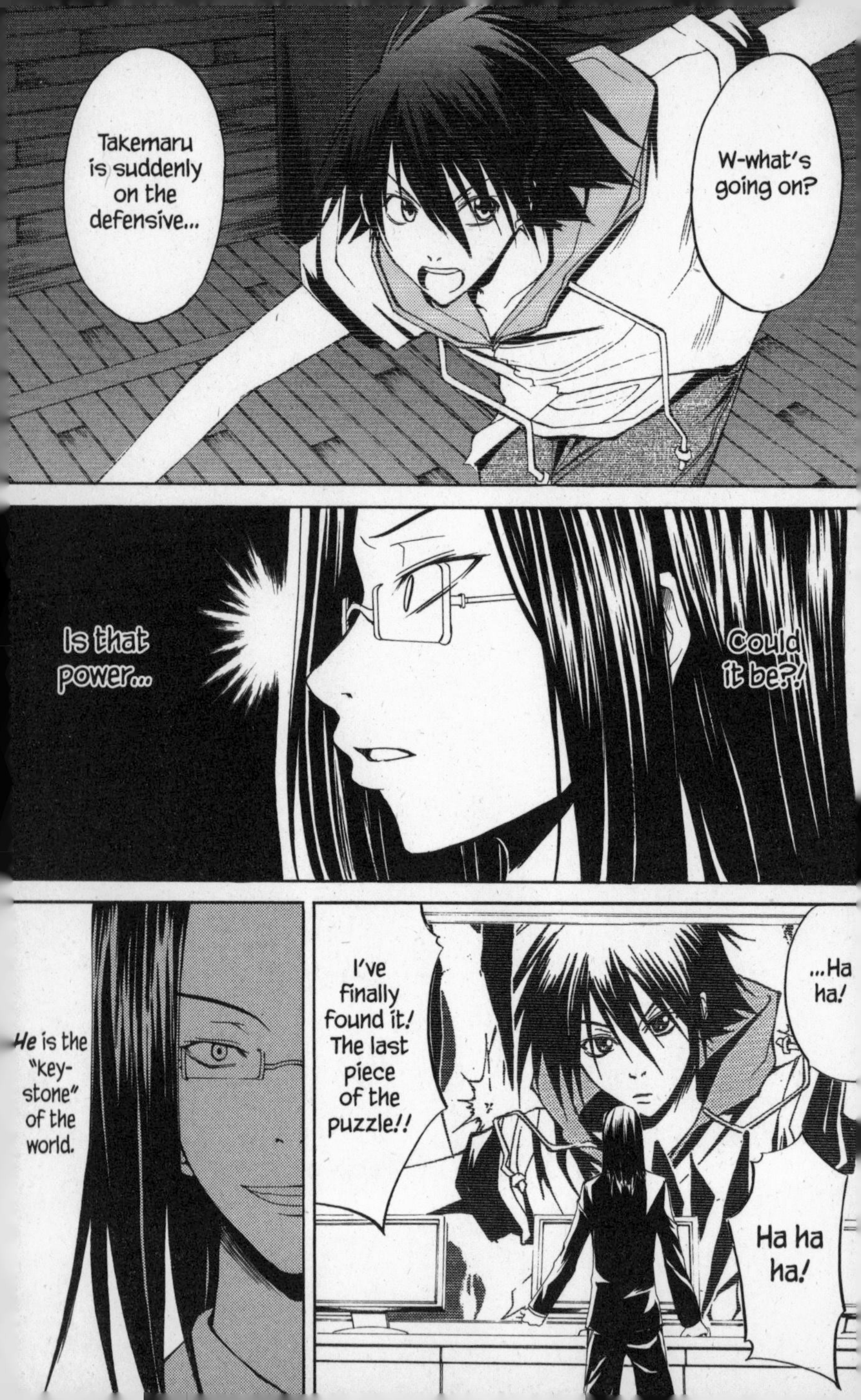
W-what's going on?
Takemaru is suddenly on the defensive...
Could it be?!
Is that power...
...Ha ha!
I've finally found it! The last piece of the puzzle!!
Ha ha ha!
He is the "keystone" of the world.

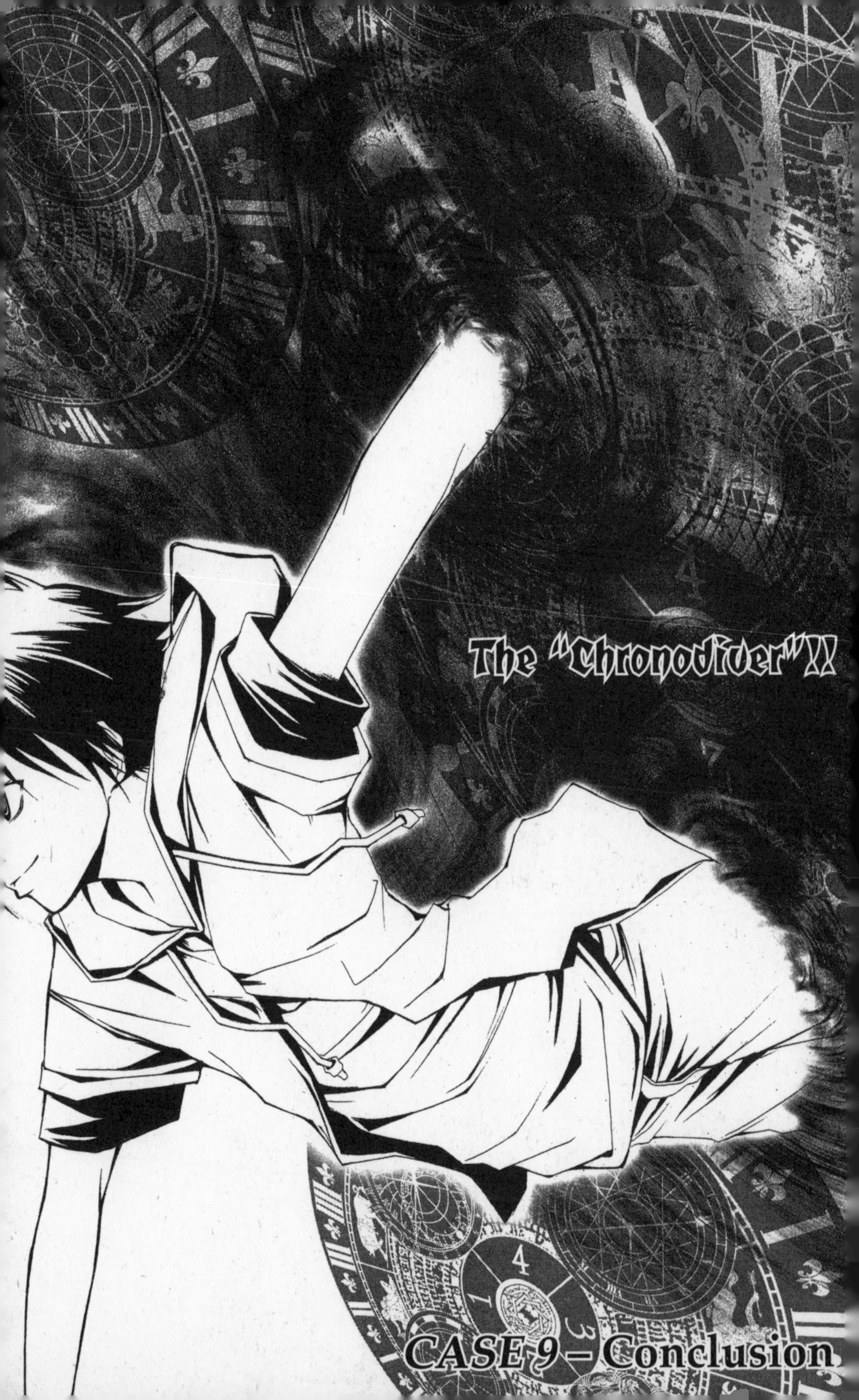
The "Chronodiver"!!
CASE 9 – Conclusion

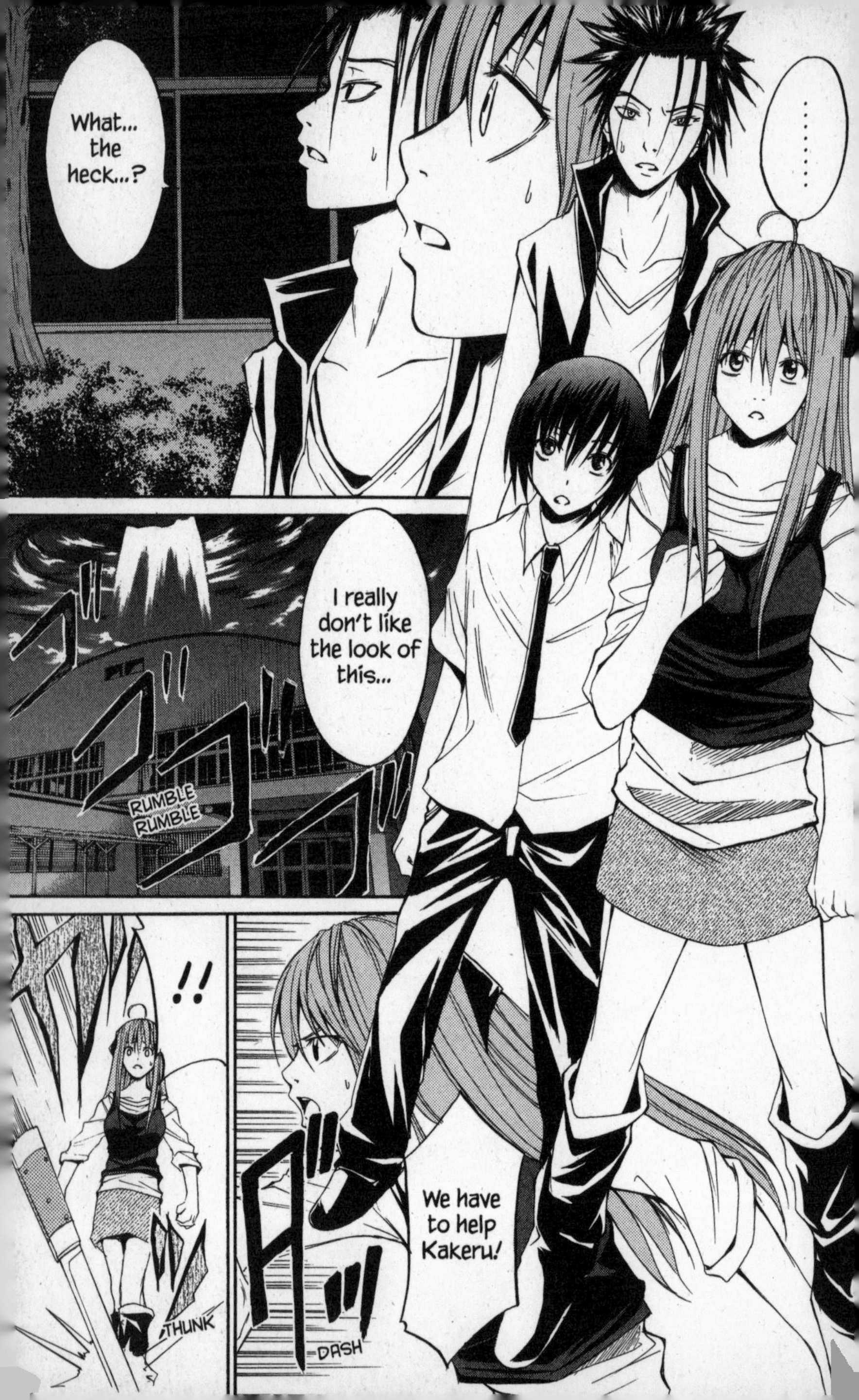
......
What... the heck...?
I really don't like the look of this...
RUMBLE RUMBLE
We have to help Kakeru!
DASH
!!
THUNK

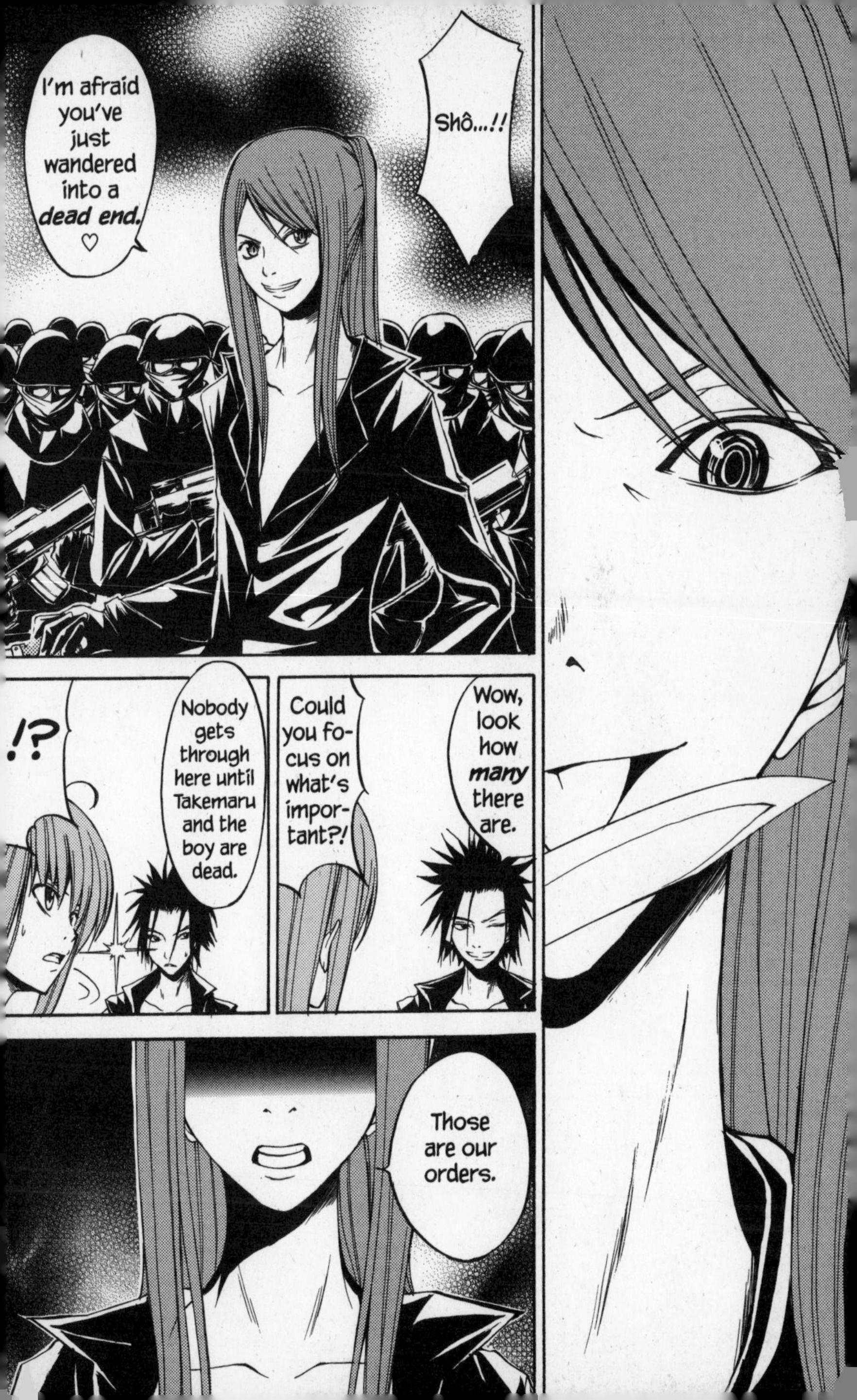

Shô...!!
I'm afraid you've just wandered into a *dead end.* ♡
Wow, look how *many* there are.
Could you focus on what's important?!
Nobody gets through here until Takemaru and the boy are dead.
!?
Those are our orders.

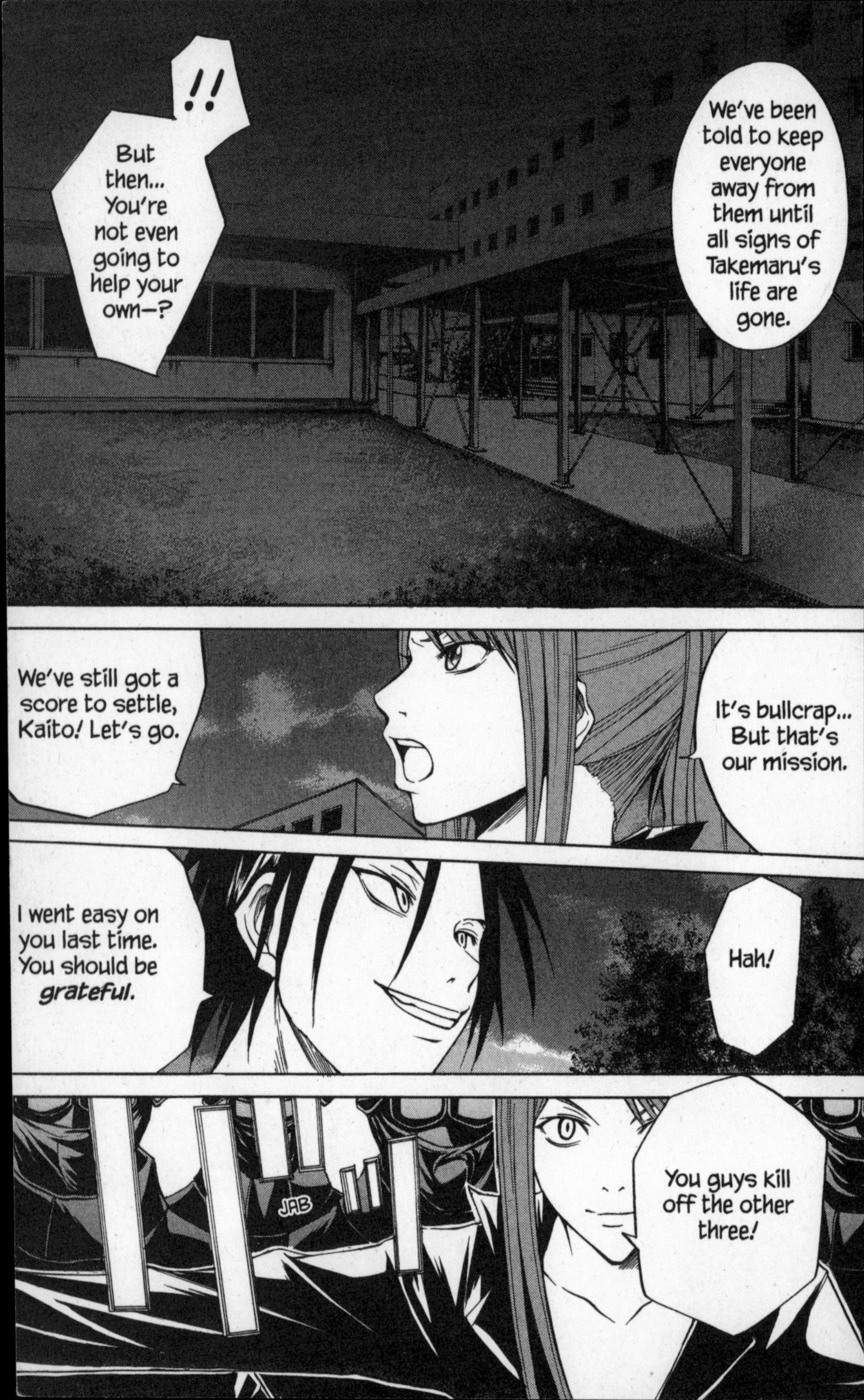
We've been told to keep everyone away from them until all signs of Takemaru's life are gone.
!!
But then... You're not even going to help your own—?
It's bullcrap... But that's our mission.
We've still got a score to settle, Kaito! Let's go.
Hah!
I went easy on you last time. You should be *grateful*.
You guys kill off the other three!
JAB

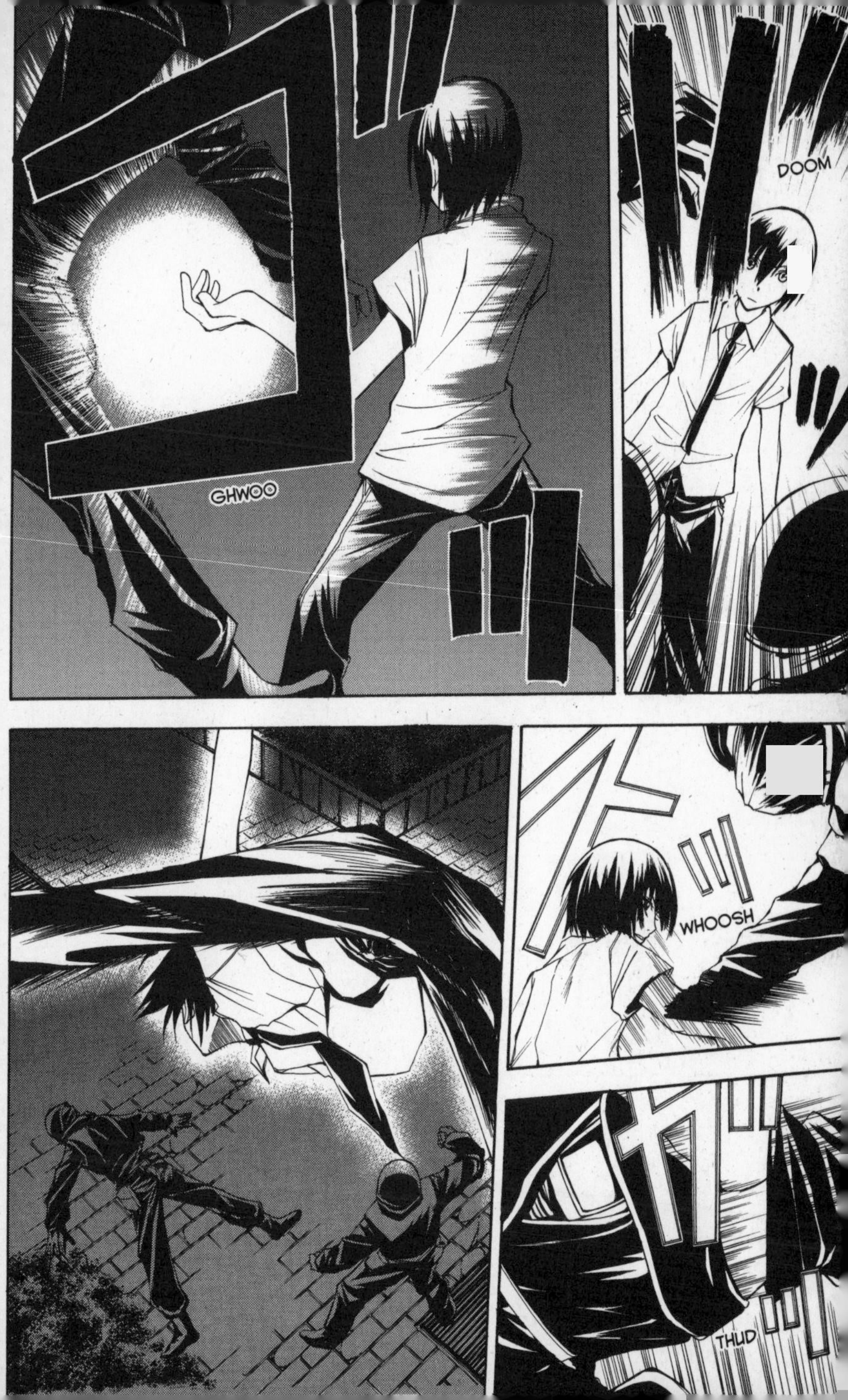
DOOM
GHWOO
WHOOSH
THUD

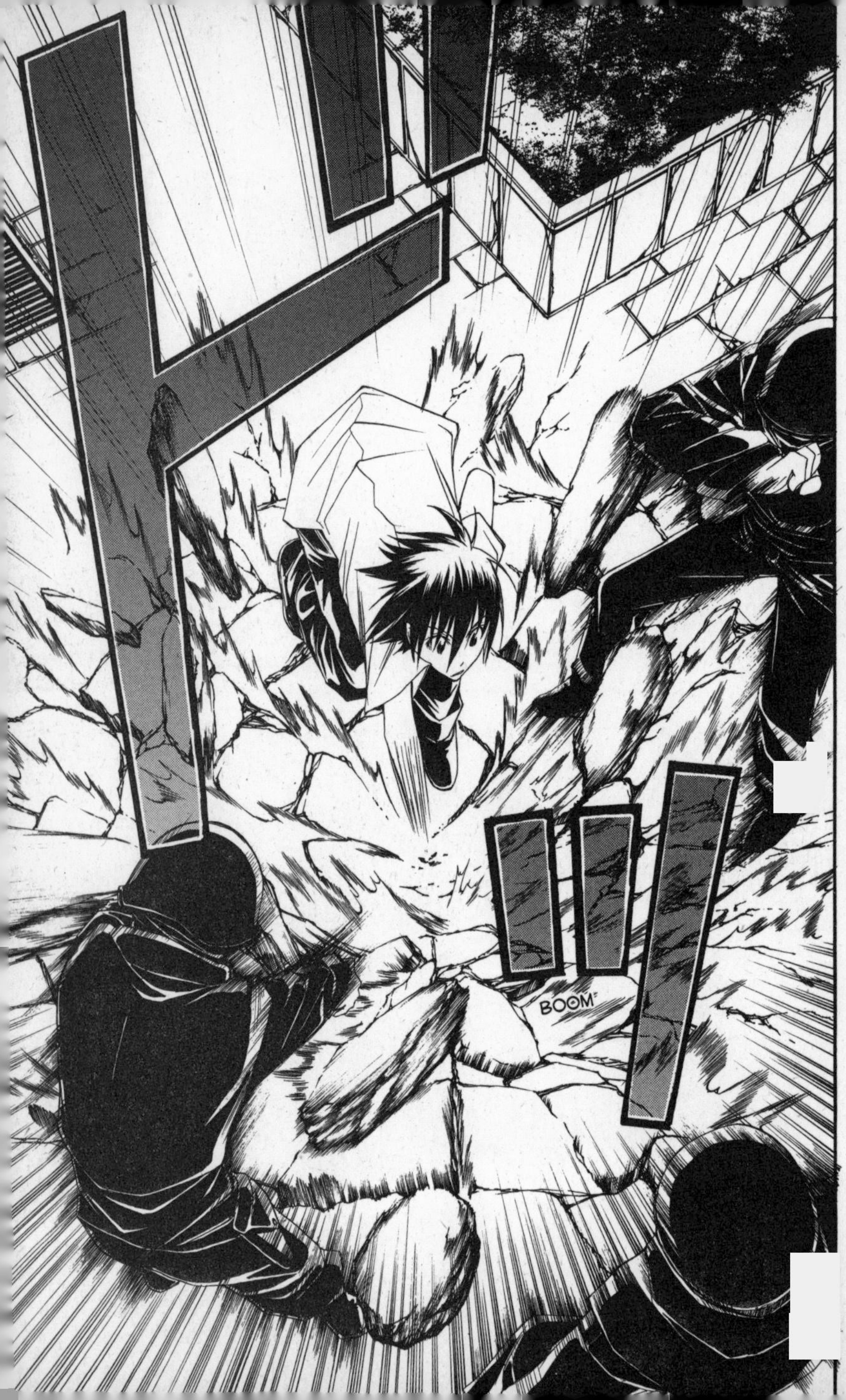
BOOM

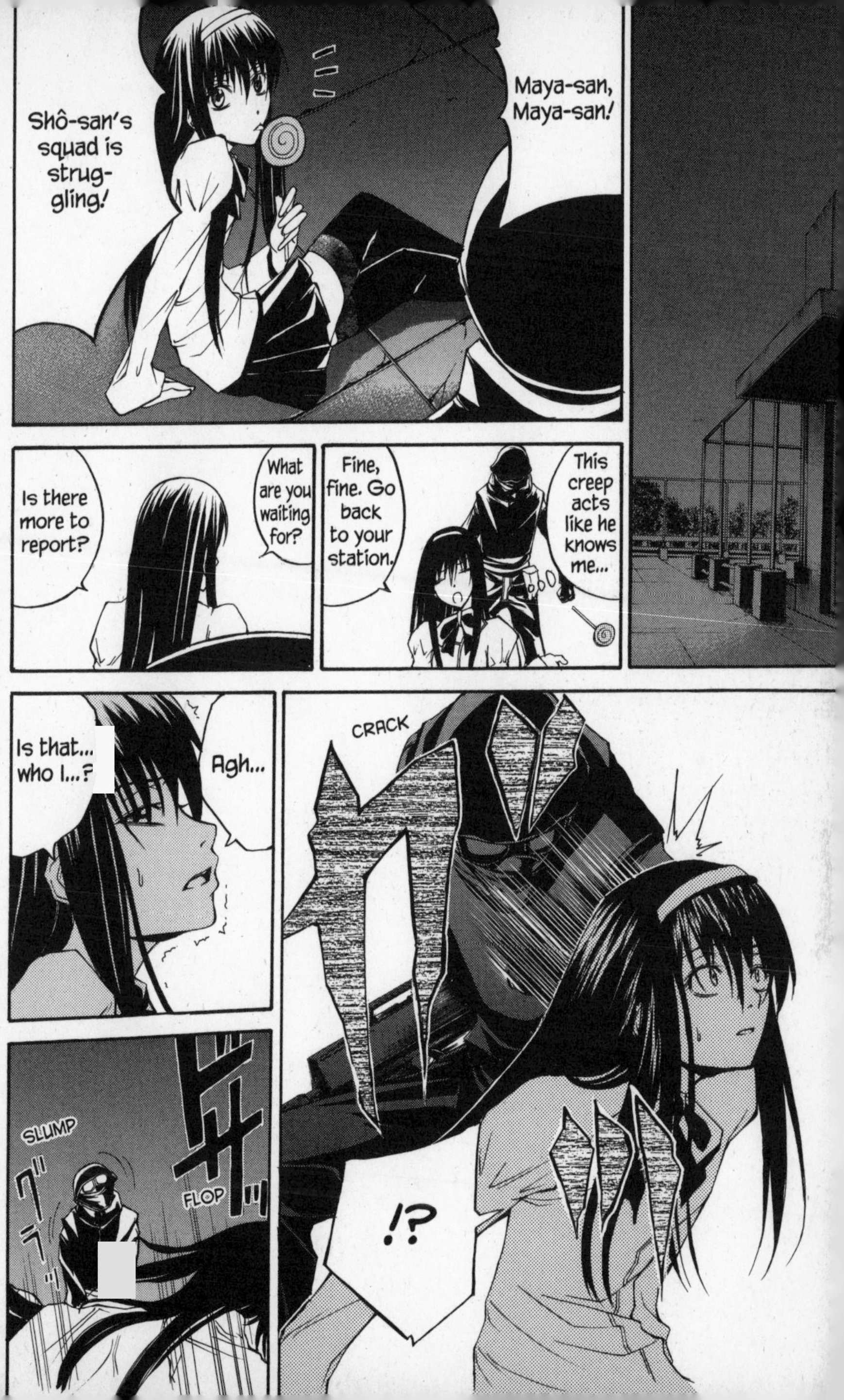
Maya-san, Maya-san!
Shô-san's squad is strug-gling!
This creep acts like he knows me...
Fine, fine. Go back to your station.
What are you waiting for?
Is there more to report?
CRACK
!?
Agh...
Is that... who I...?
SLUMP
FLOP

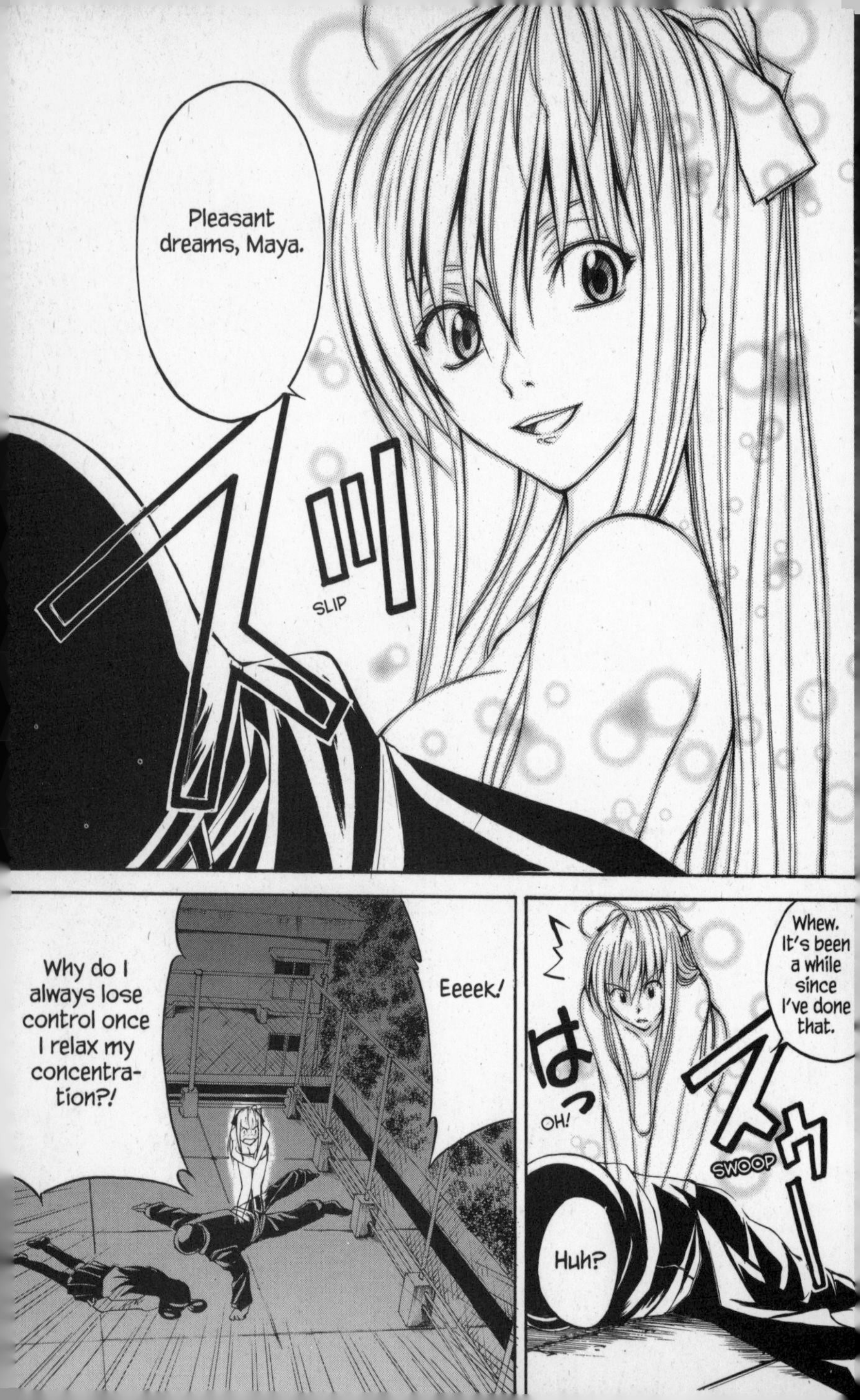
Pleasant dreams, Maya.
SLIP
Whew. It's been a while since I've done that.
SWOOP
OH!
Huh?
Eeeek!
Why do I always lose control once I relax my concentration?!

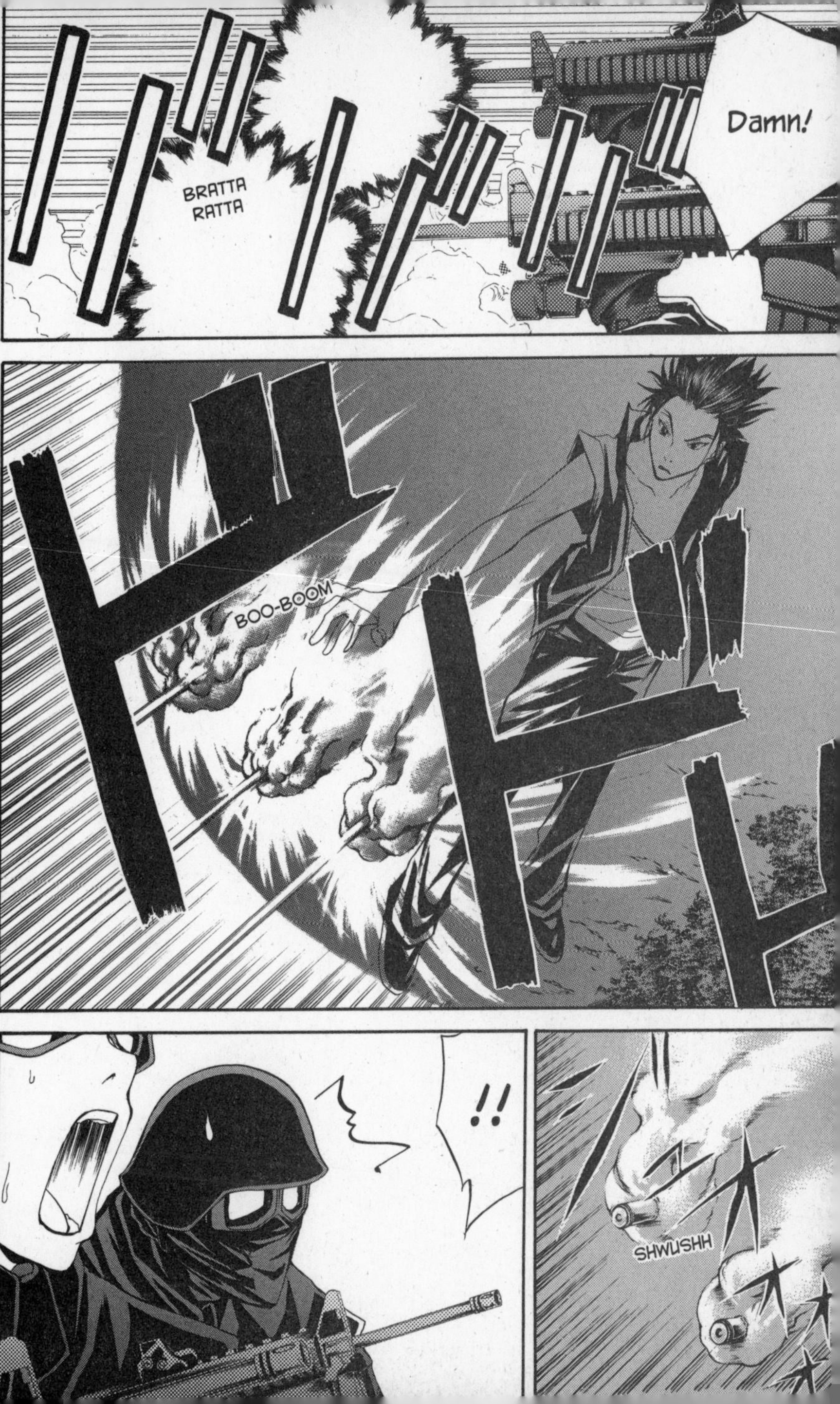
Damn!
BRATTA RATTA
BOO-BOOM
SHWUSHH
!!

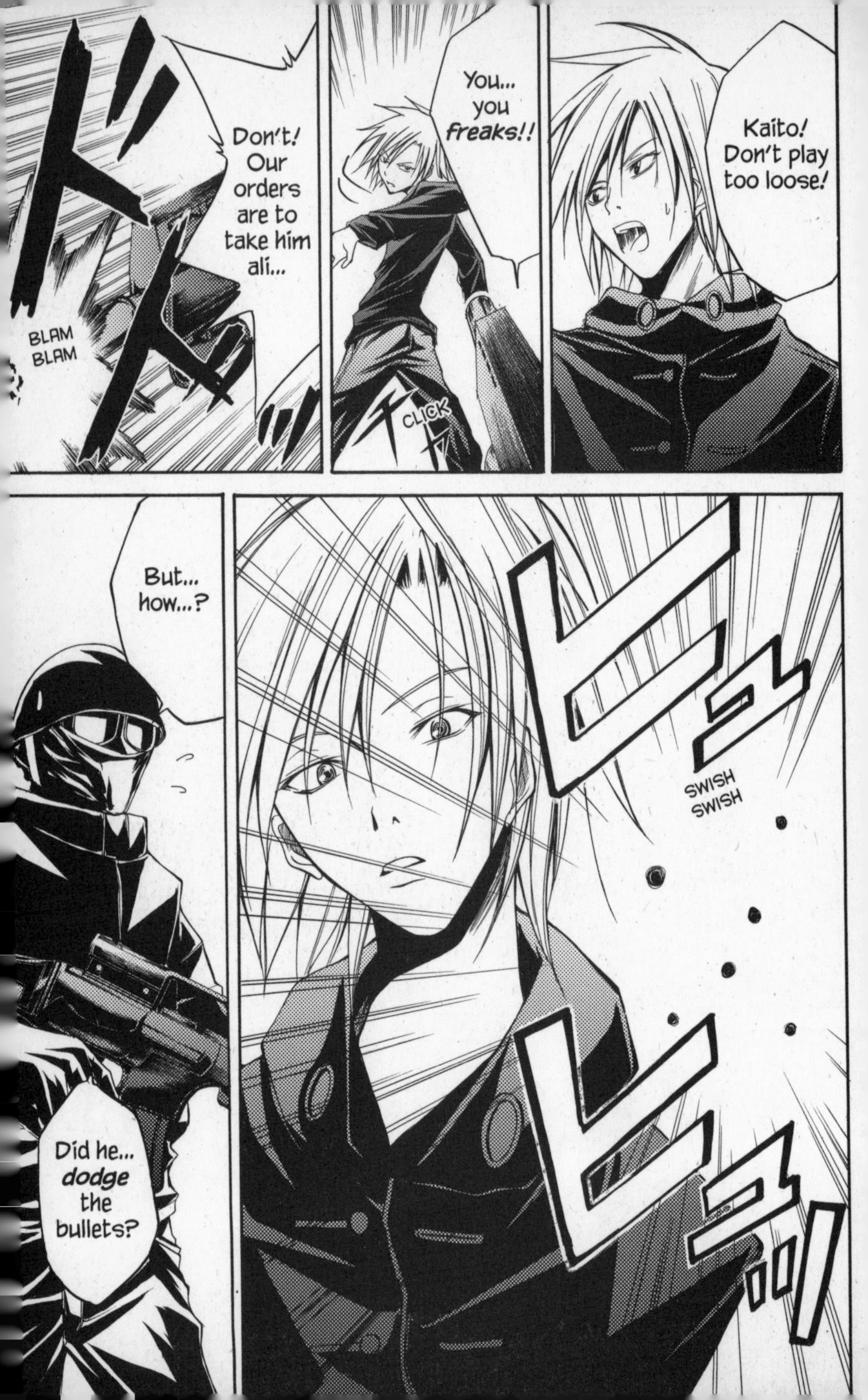
Kaito! Don't play too loose!
You... you *freaks!!*
CLICK
Don't! Our orders are to take him ali...
BLAM BLAM
SWISH SWISH
But... how...?
Did he... *dodge* the bullets?

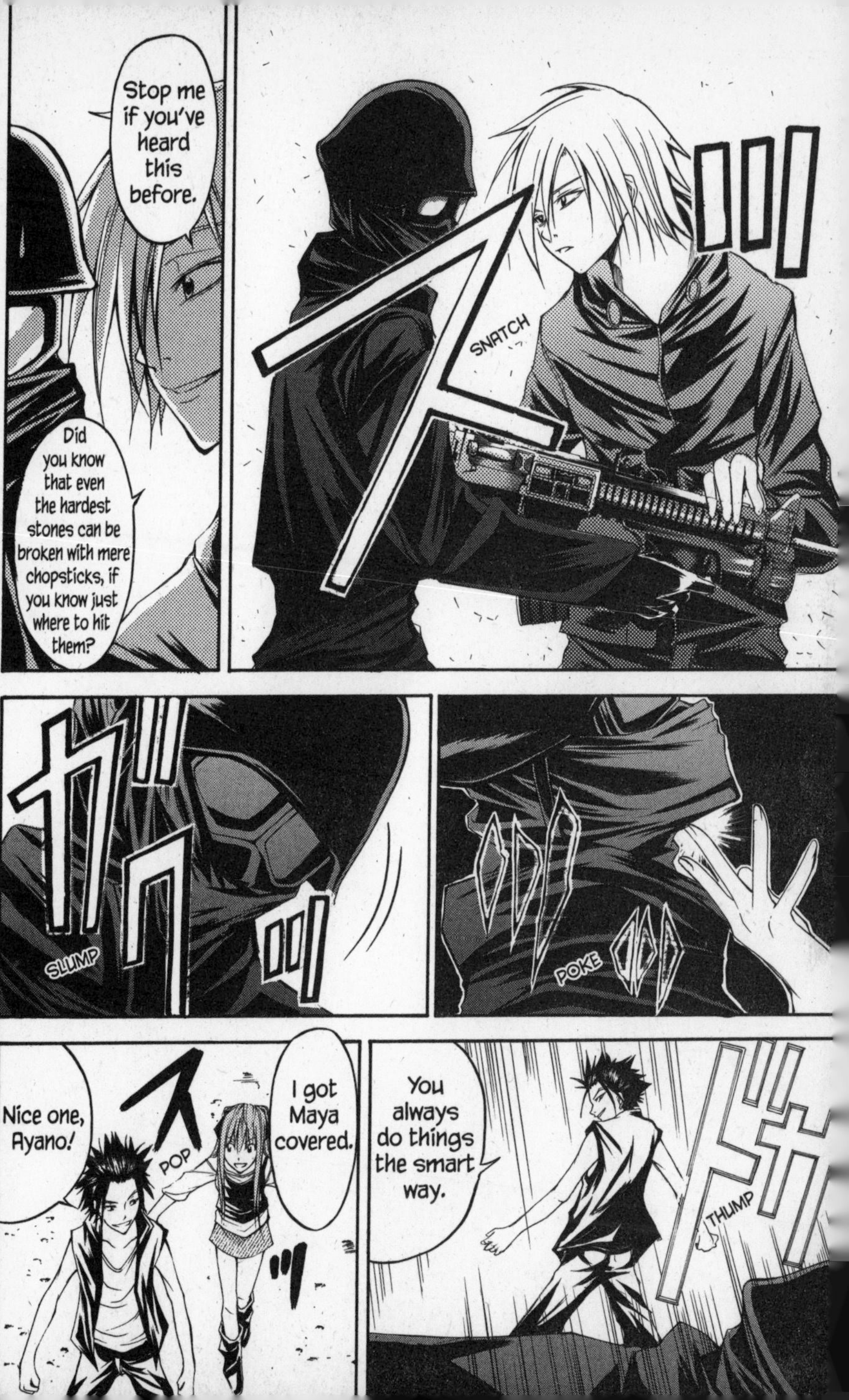
SNATCH
Stop me if you've heard this before.
Did you know that even the hardest stones can be broken with mere chopsticks, if you know just where to hit them?
POKE
SLUMP
You always do things the smart way.
THUMP
I got Maya covered.
POP
Nice one, Ayano!

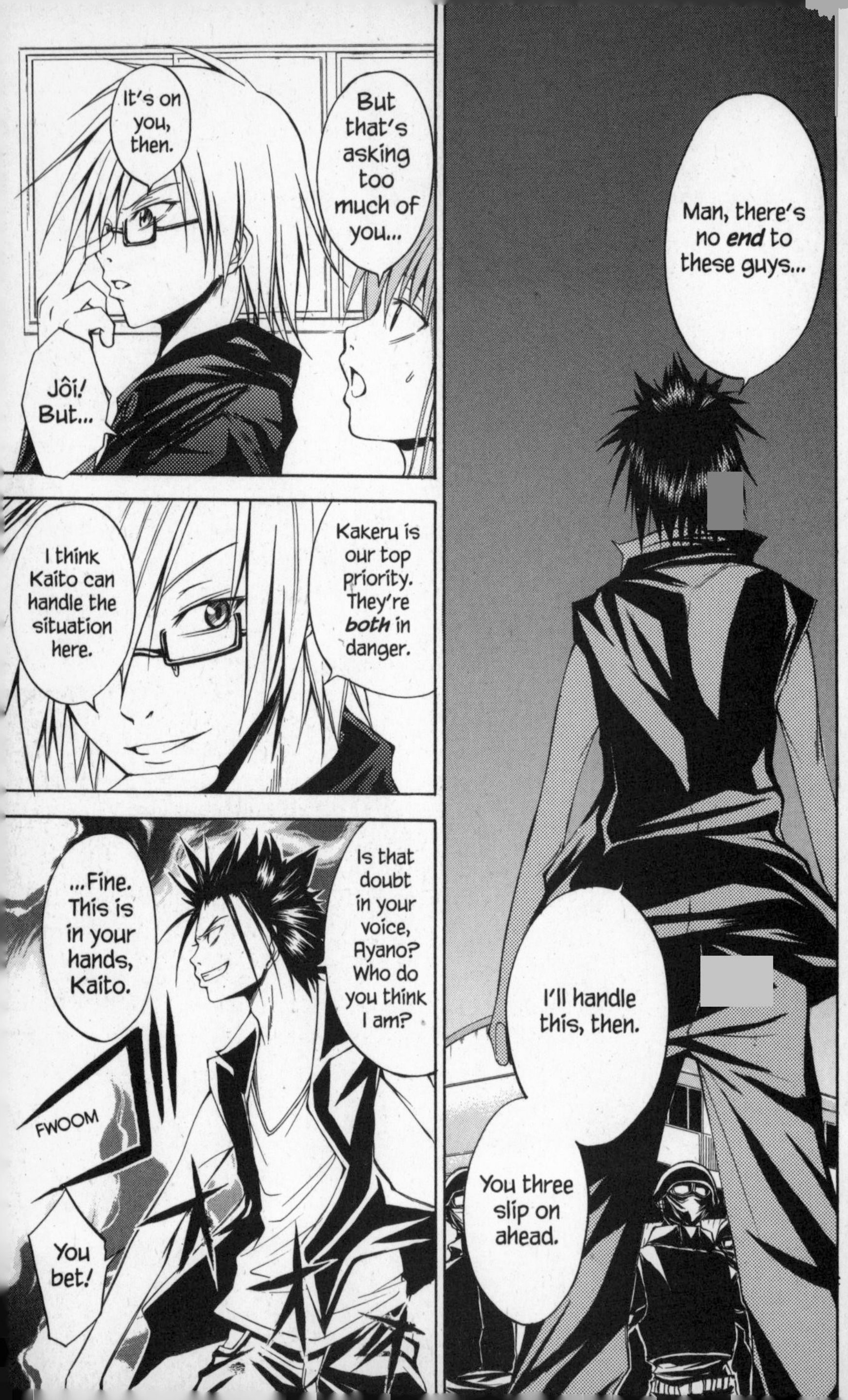

Man, there's no *end* to these guys...
I'll handle this, then.
You three slip on ahead.
But that's asking too much of you...
It's on you, then.
Jôi! But...
Kakeru is our top priority. They're *both* in danger.
I think Kaito can handle the situation here.
Is that doubt in your voice, Ayano? Who do you think I am?
...Fine. This is in your hands, Kaito.
FWOOM
You bet!

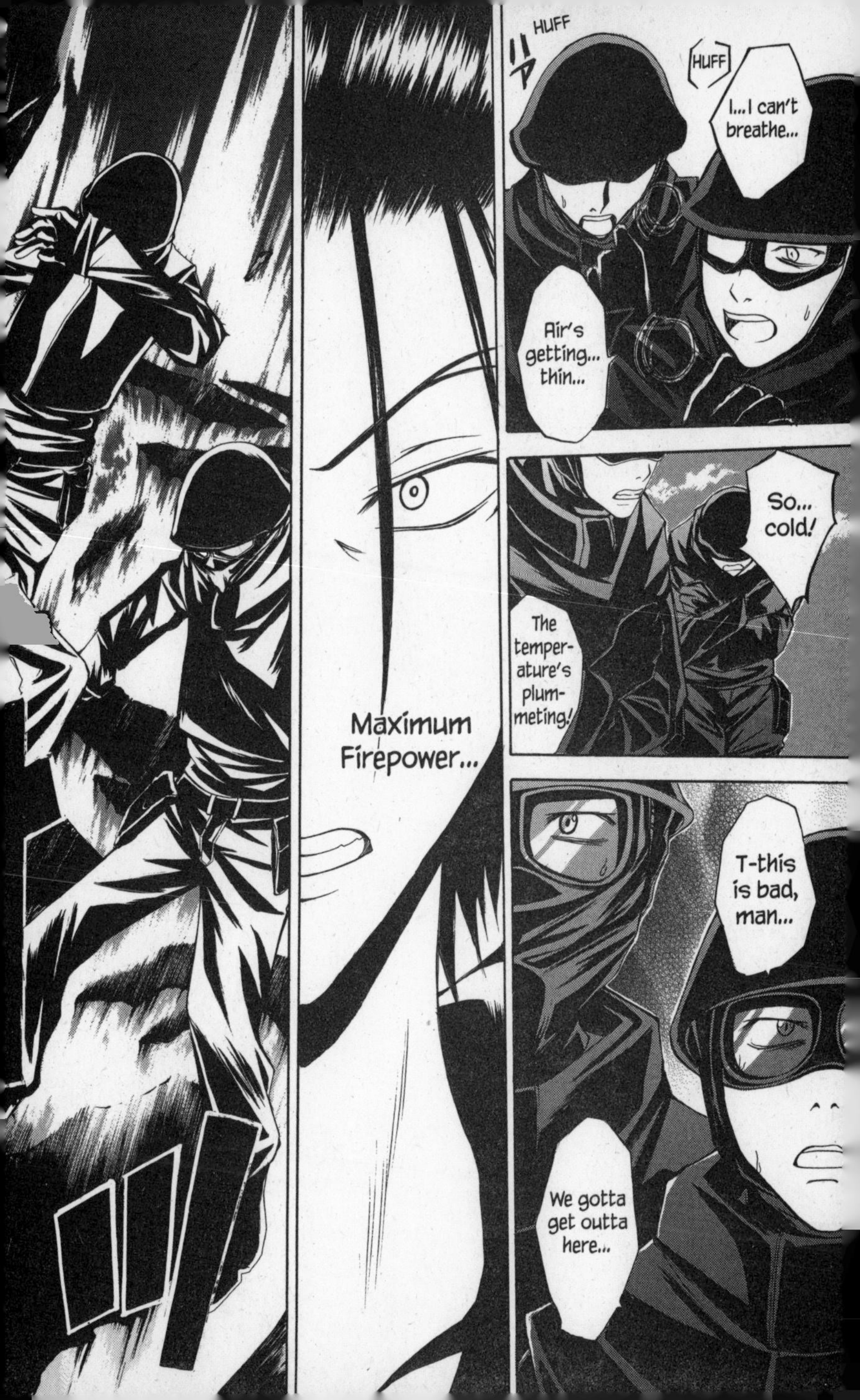
HUFF
ハァ
HUFF
I...I can't breathe...
Air's getting... thin...
So... cold!
The temperature's plummeting!
T-this is bad, man...
We gotta get outta here...
Maximum Firepower...

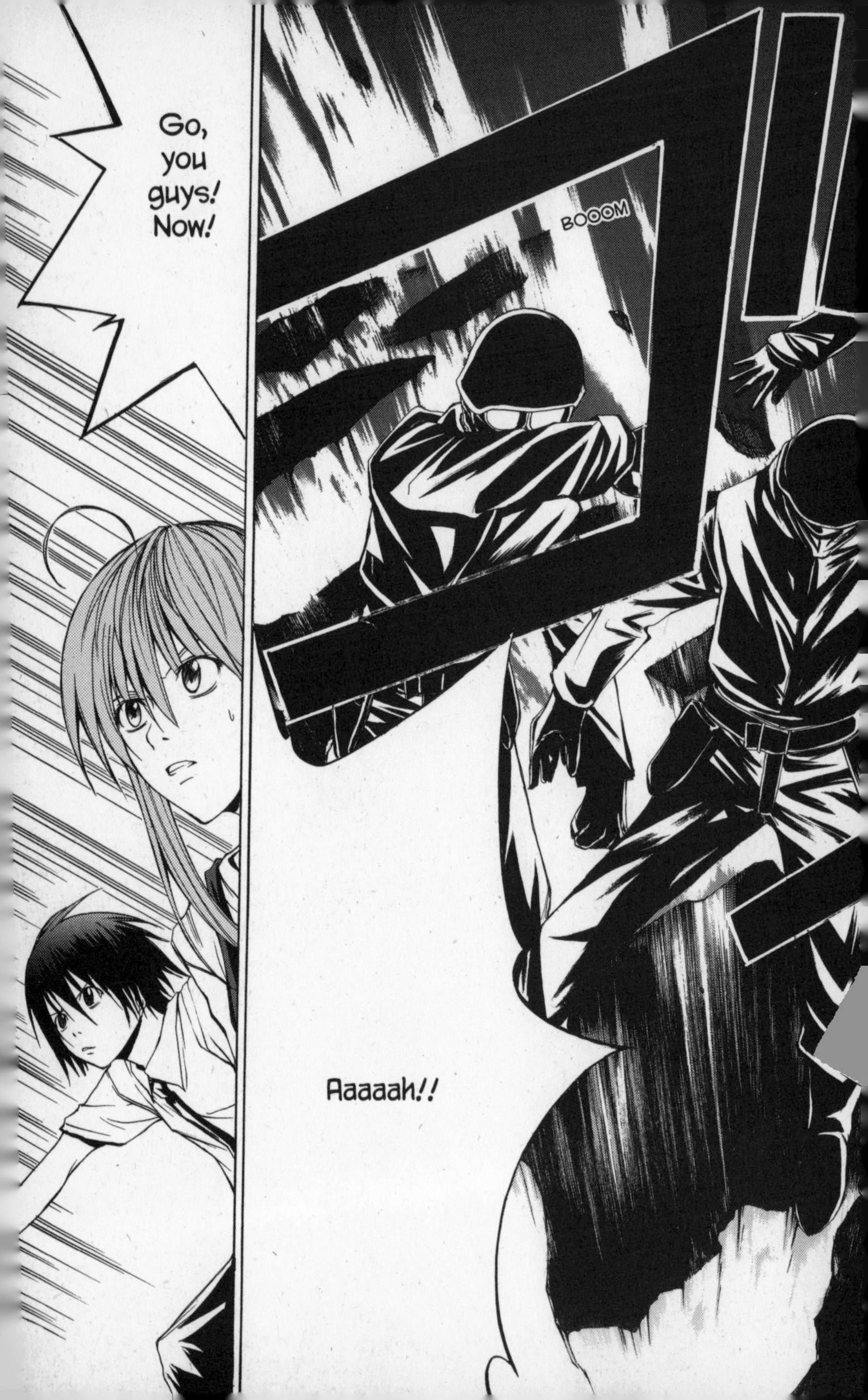
BOOOM
Aaaaah!!
Go, you guys! Now!

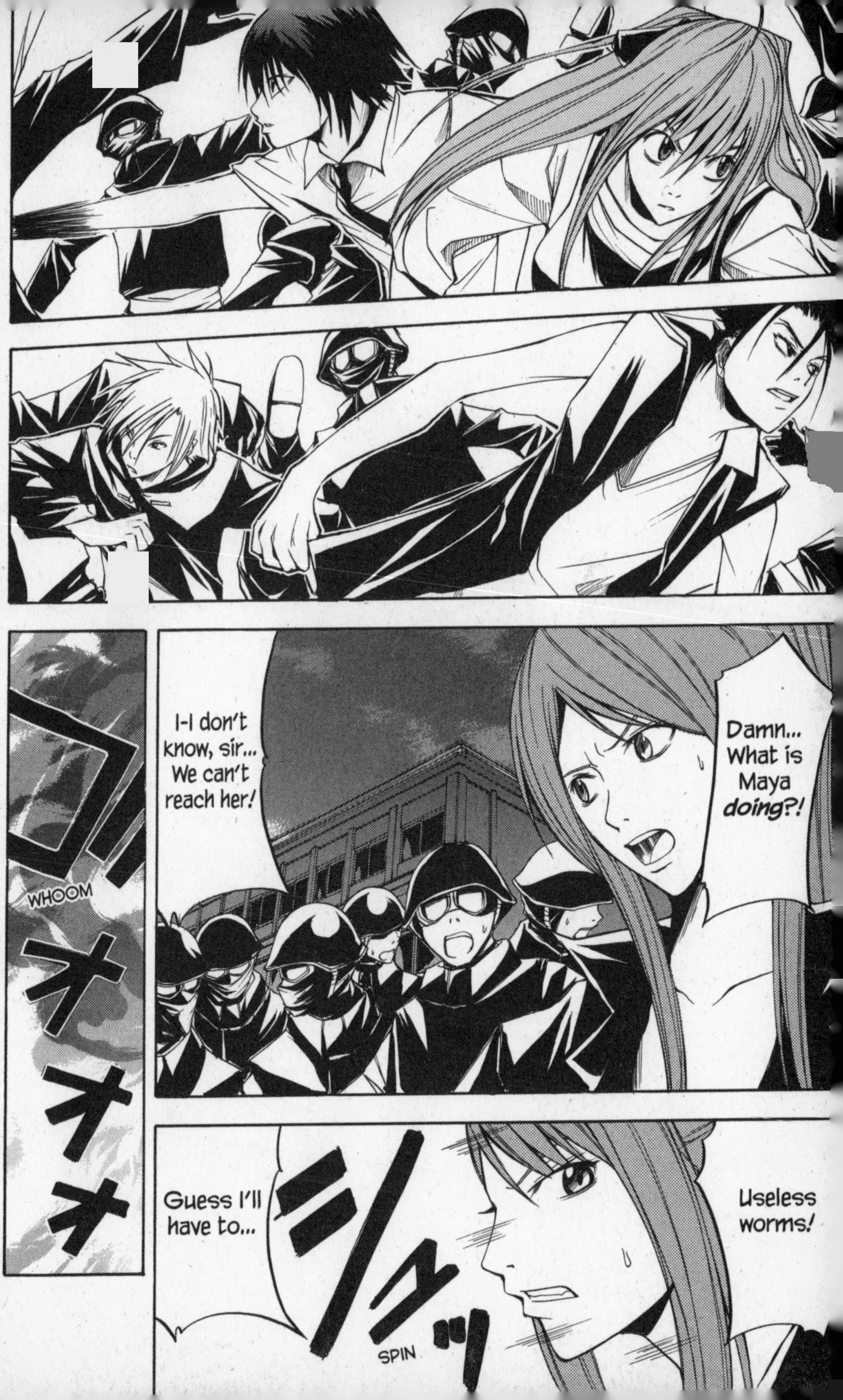
Damn... What is Maya *doing?!*
I-I don't know, sir... We can't reach her!
Useless worms!
Guess I'll have to...
SPIN
WHOOM

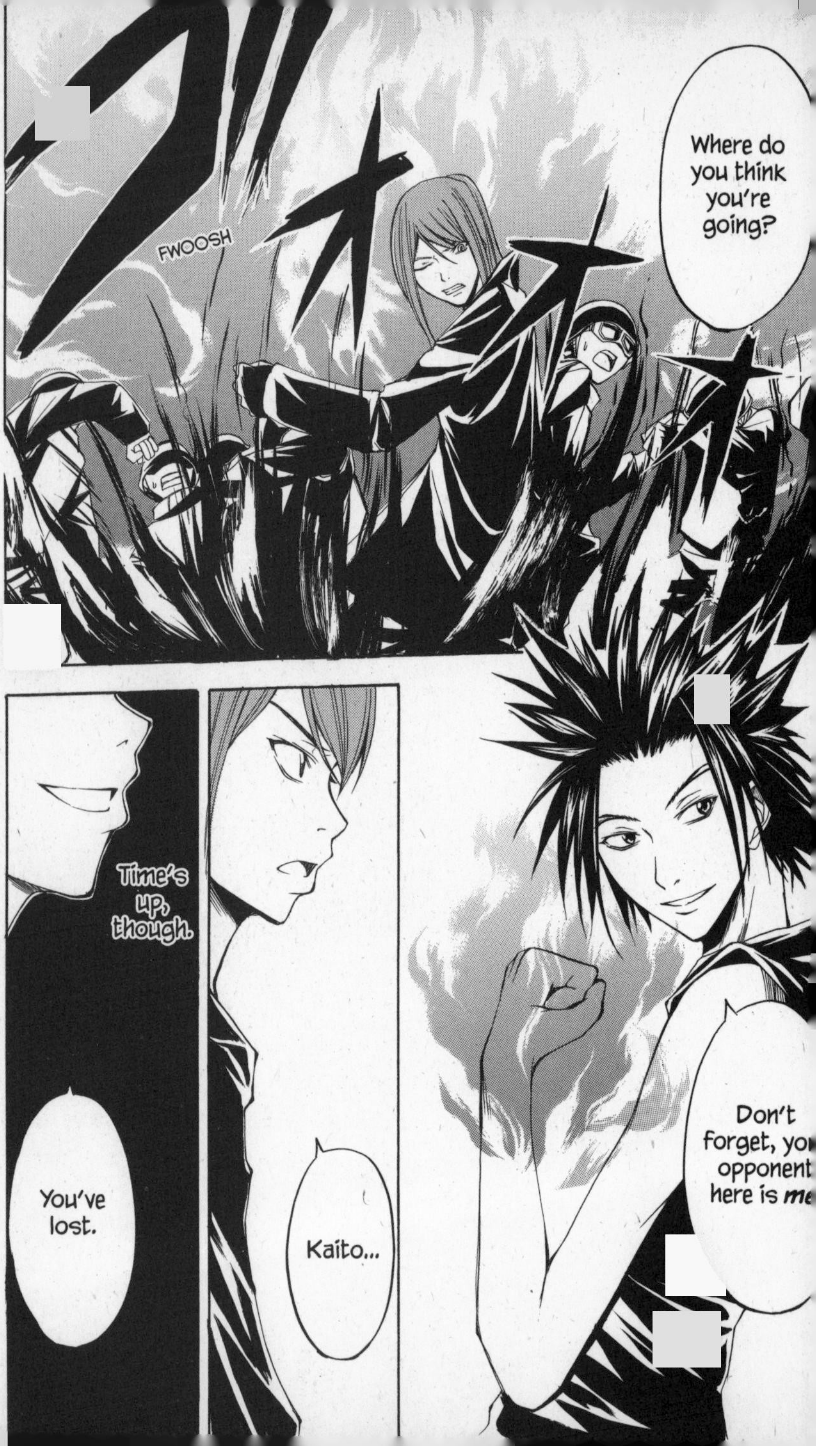
Where do you think you're going?
FWOOSH
Don't forget, yo opponent here is me
Kaito...
Time's up, though.
You've lost.

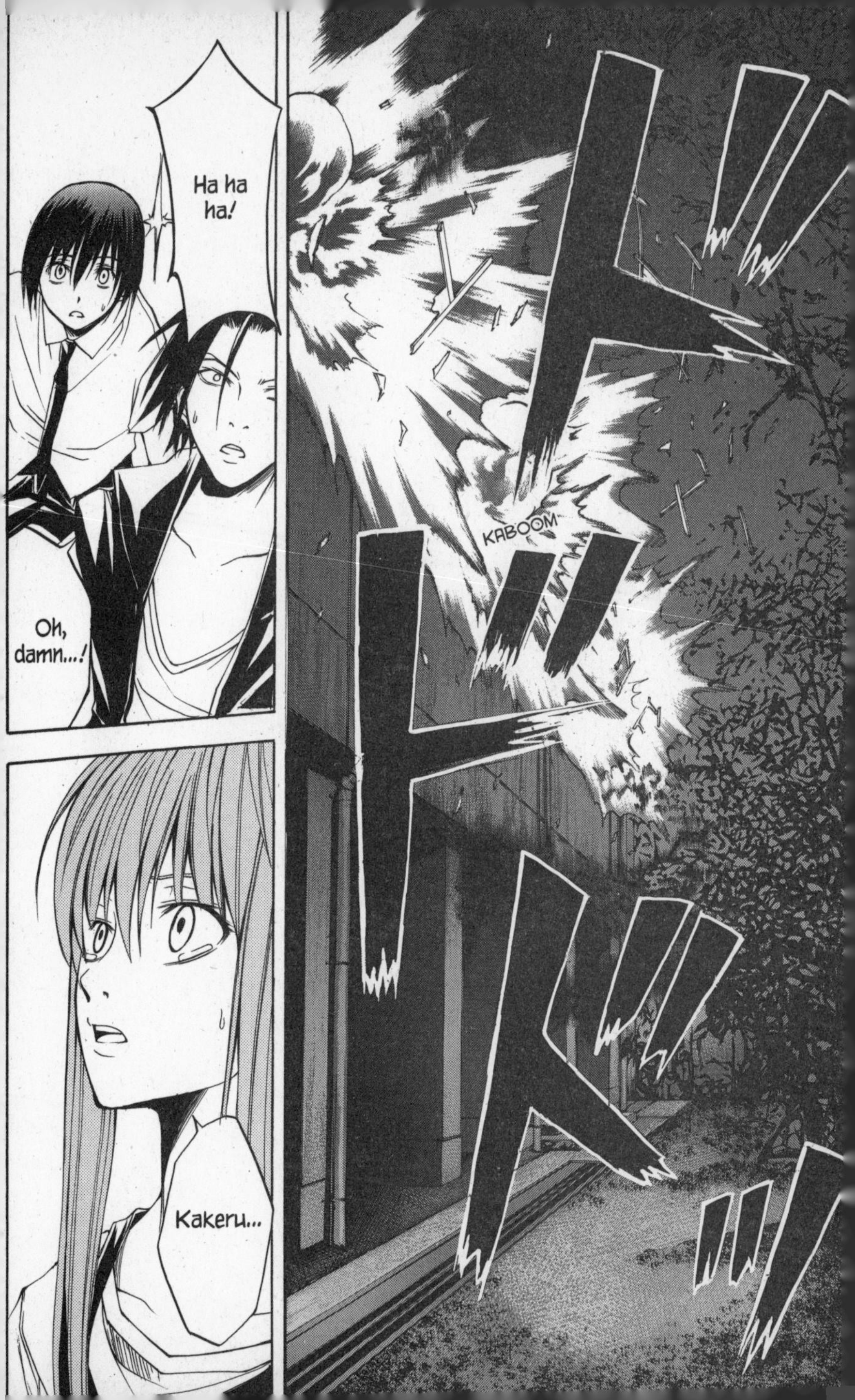
KABOOM
Ha ha ha!
Oh, damn...!
Kakeru...

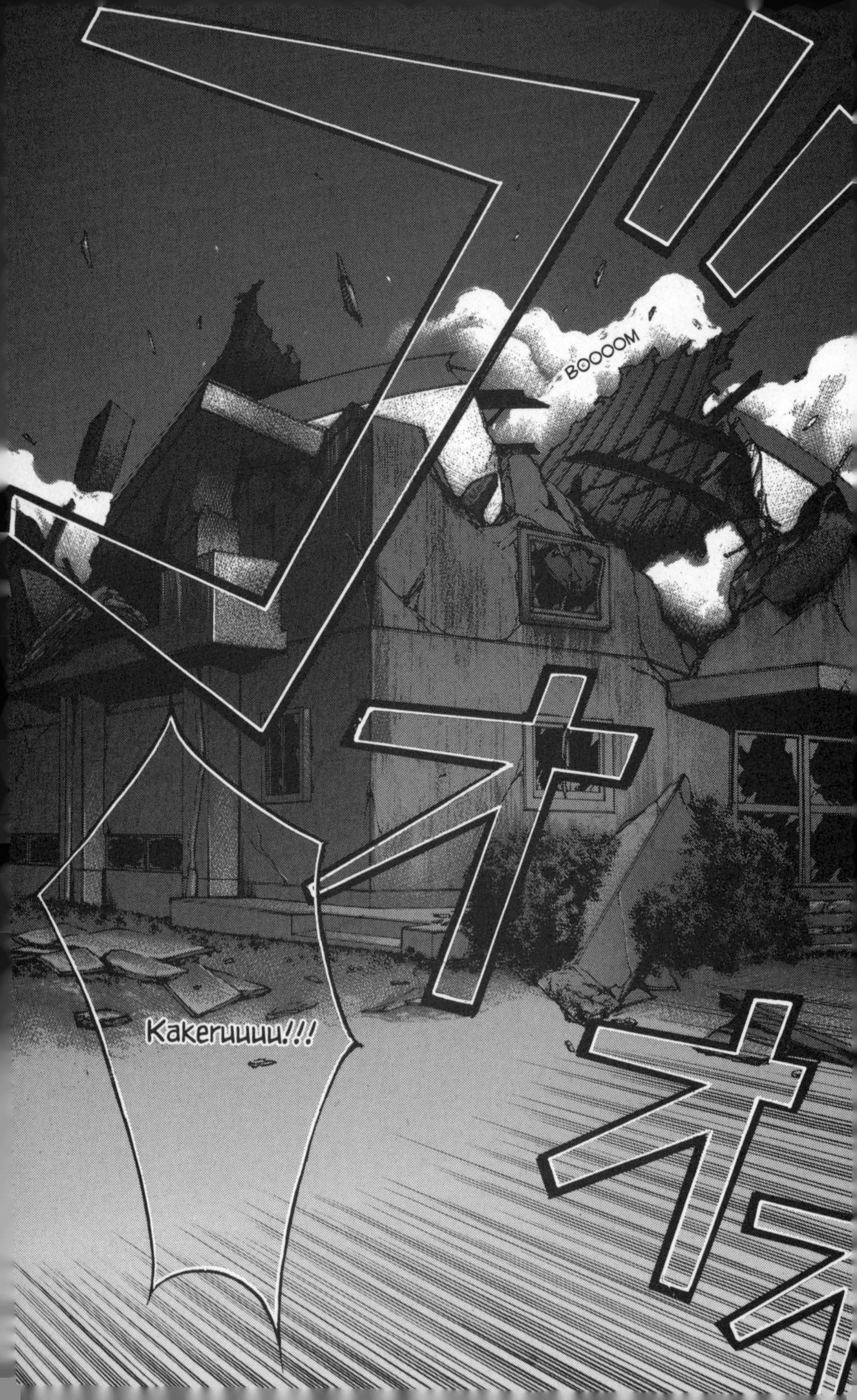
BOOOOM
Kakeruuuu!!!

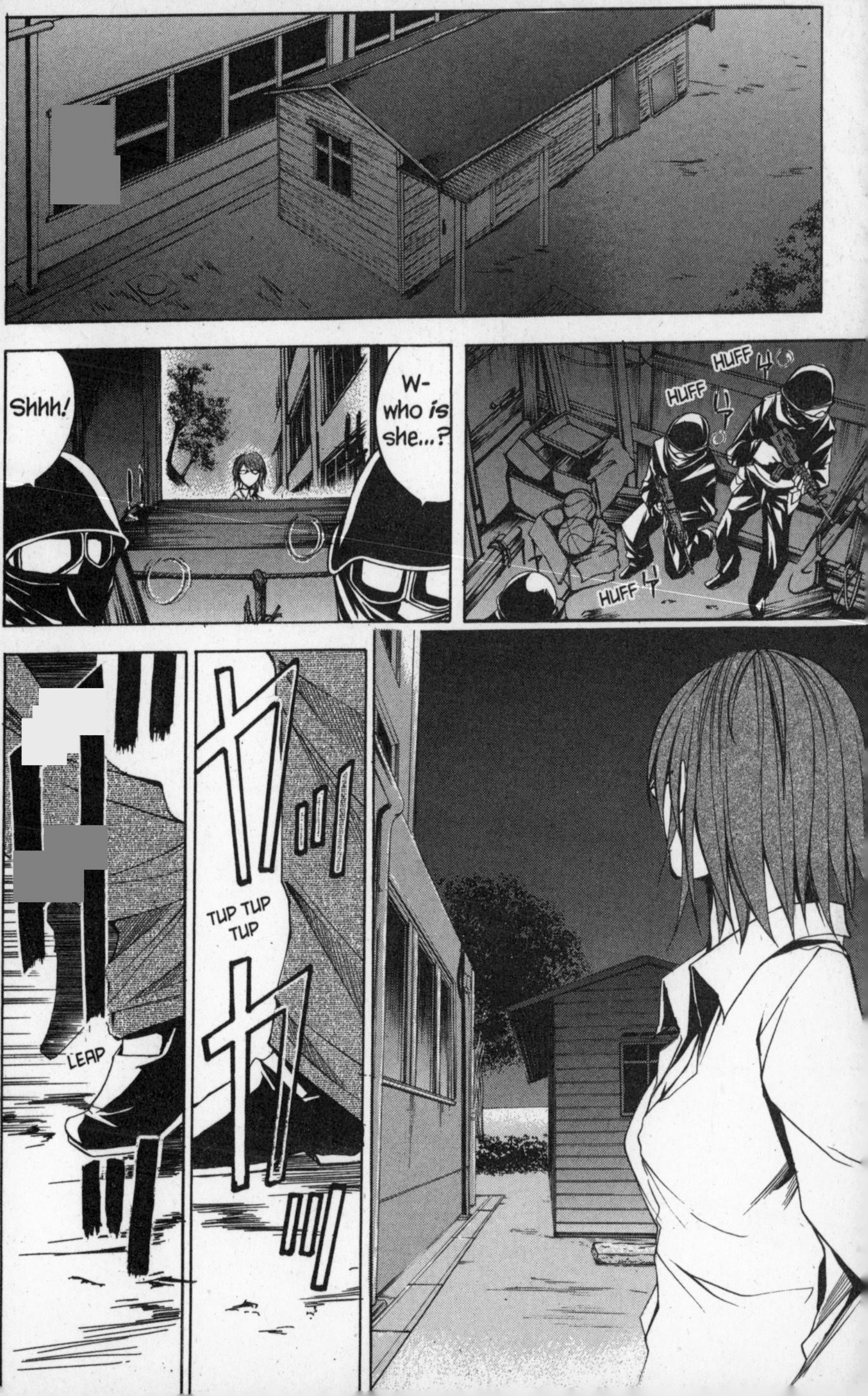
HUFF
HUFF
HUFF
W- who is she...?
Shhh!
TUP TUP TUP
LEAP

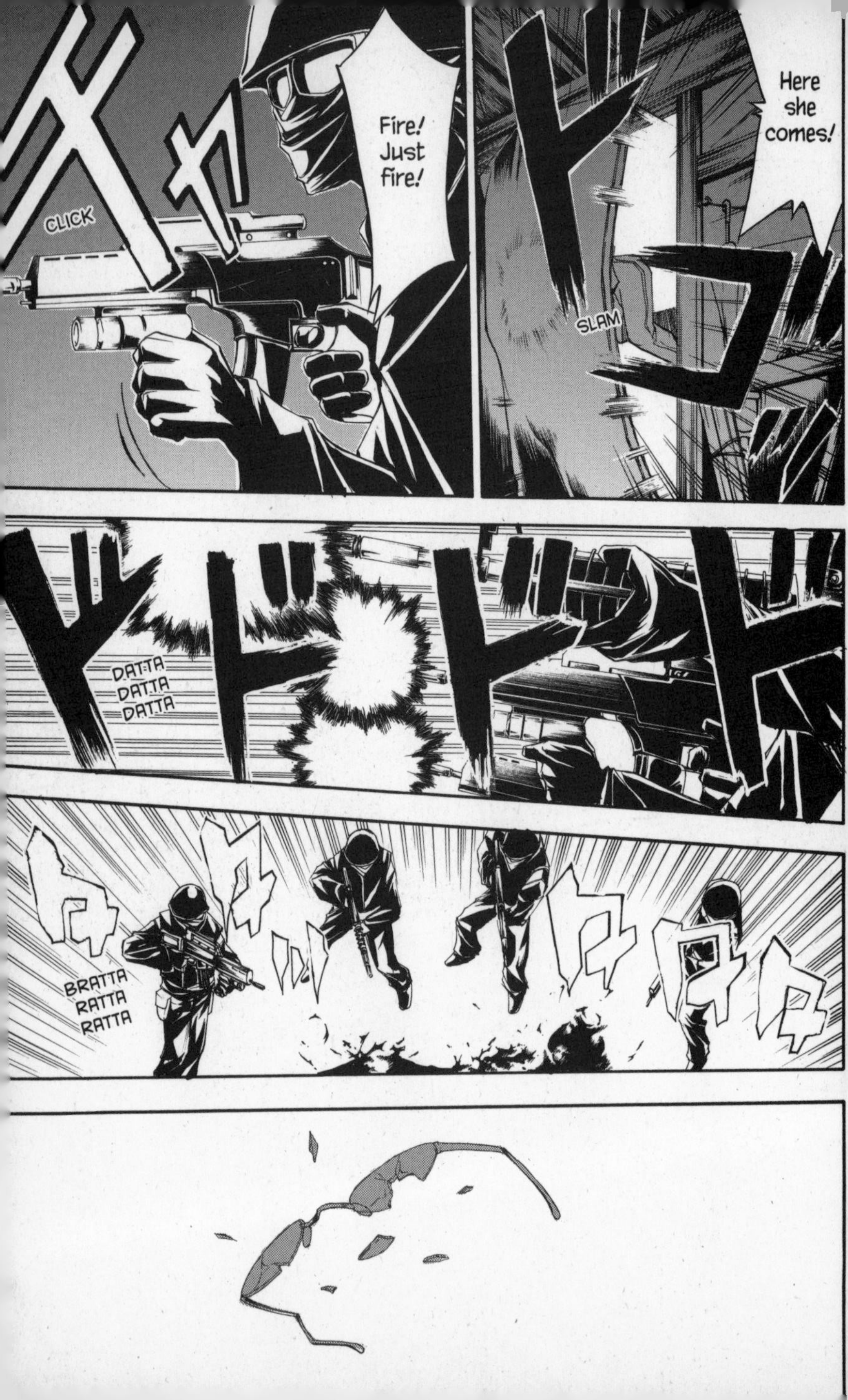
Here she comes!
SLAM
Fire! Just fire!
CLICK
DATTA DATTA DATTA
BRATTA RATTA RATTA

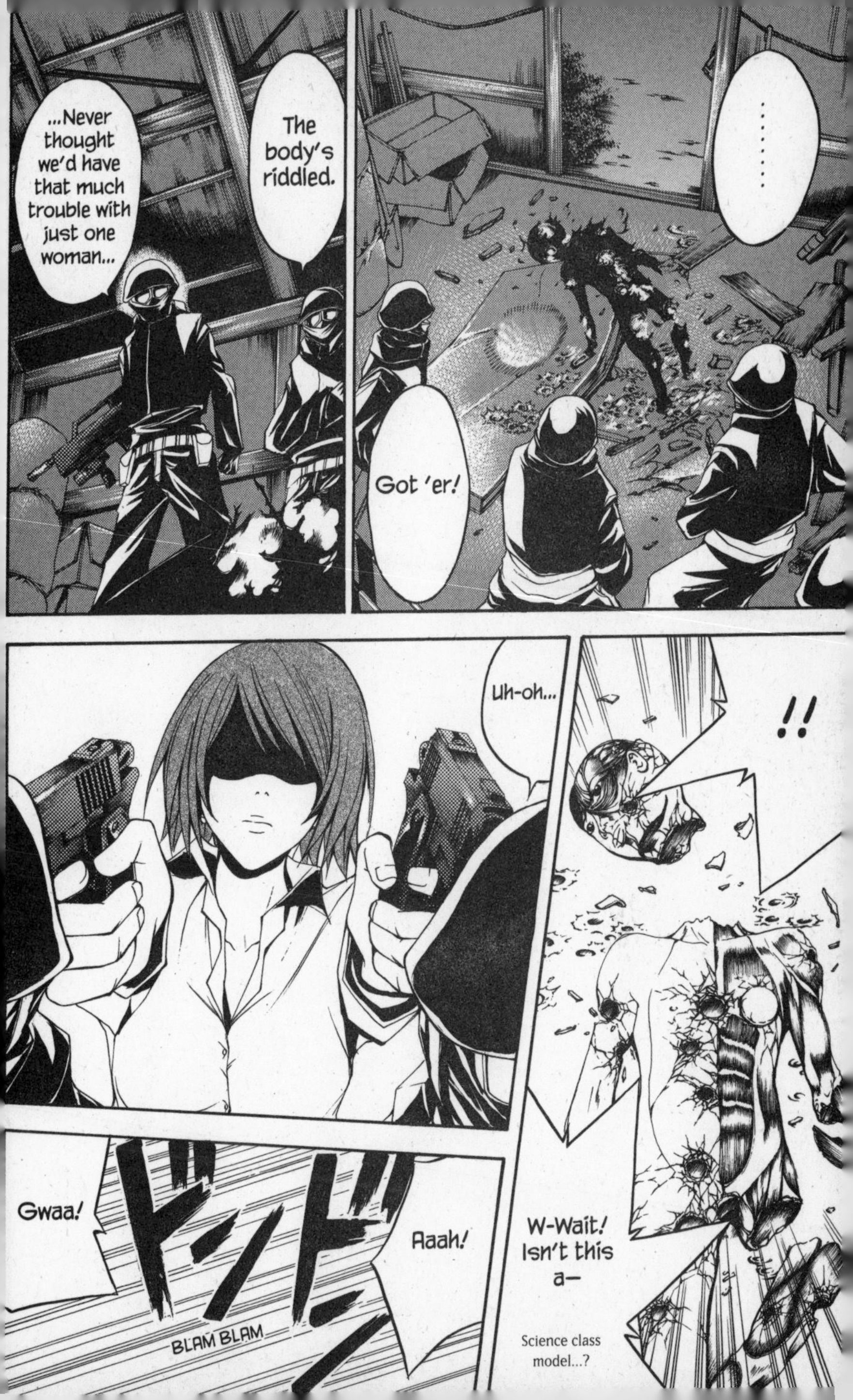

......
Got 'er!
The body's riddled.
...Never thought we'd have that much trouble with just one woman...
!!
W-Wait! Isn't this a—
Science class model...?
Uh-oh...
Aaah!
Gwaa!
BLAM BLAM

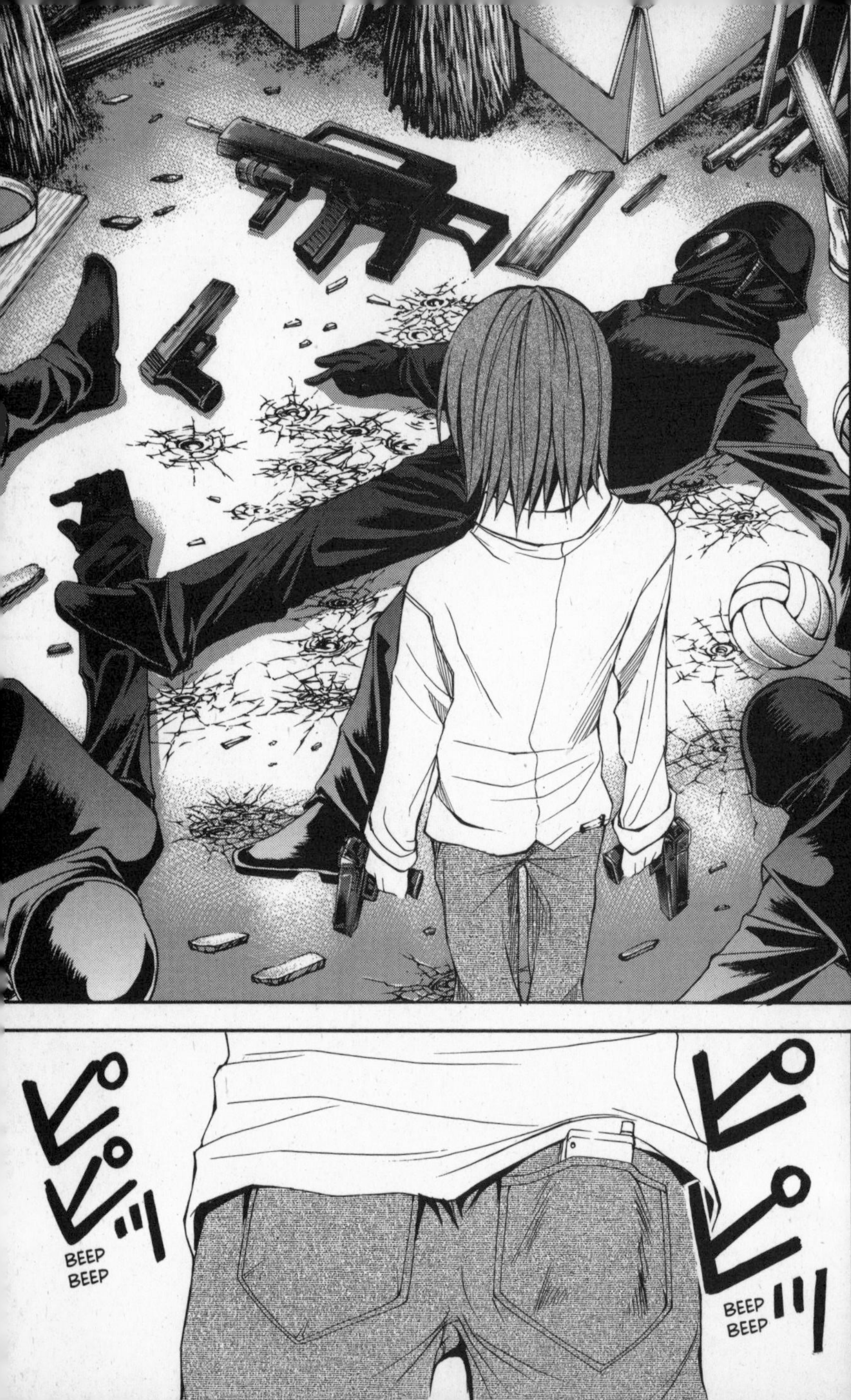
ピピッ
BEEP BEEP
ピピッ
BEEP BEEP

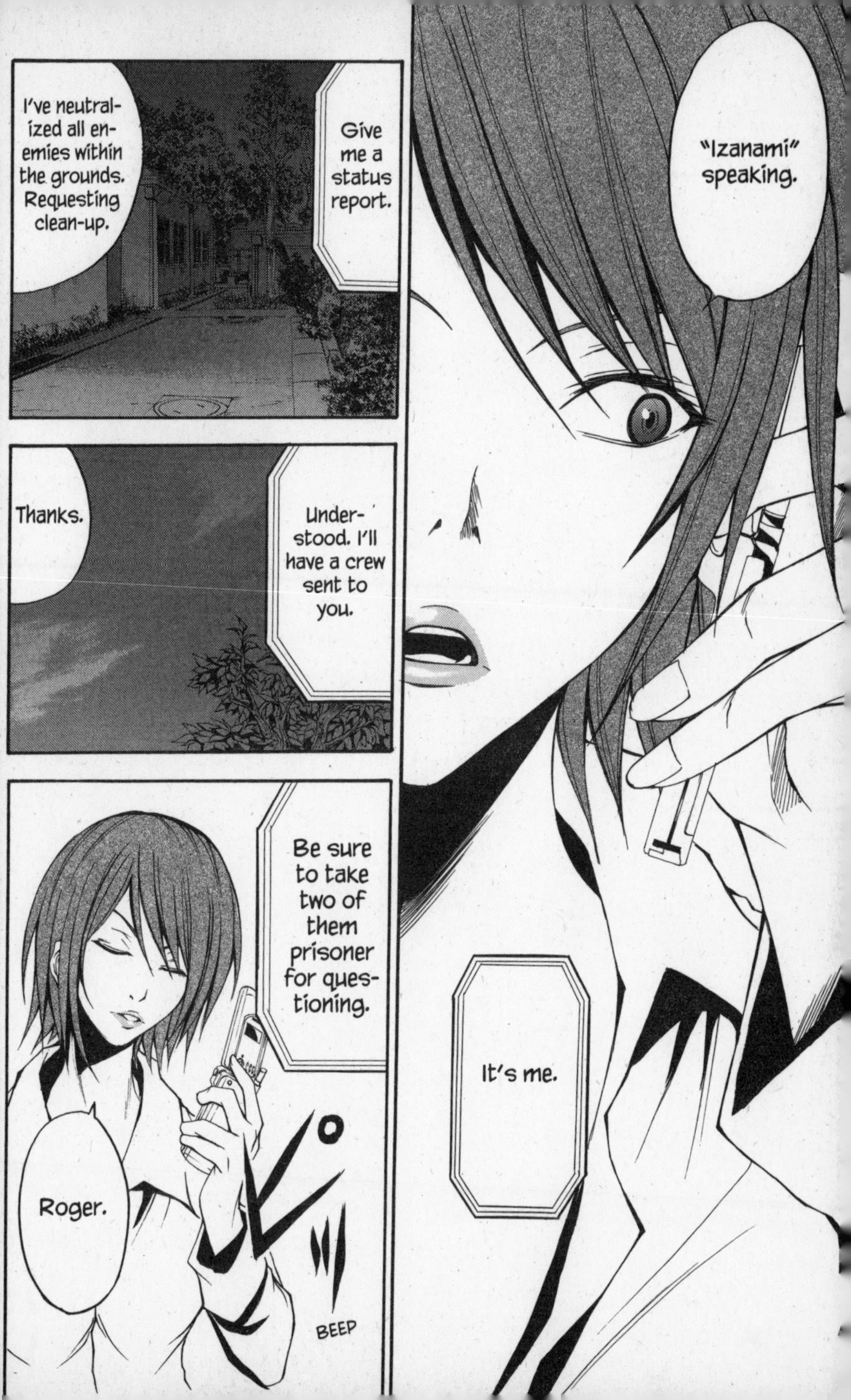
"Izanami" speaking.
It's me.
Give me a status report.
I've neutralized all enemies within the grounds. Requesting clean-up.
Understood. I'll have a crew sent to you.
Thanks.
Be sure to take two of them prisoner for questioning.
Roger.
BEEP

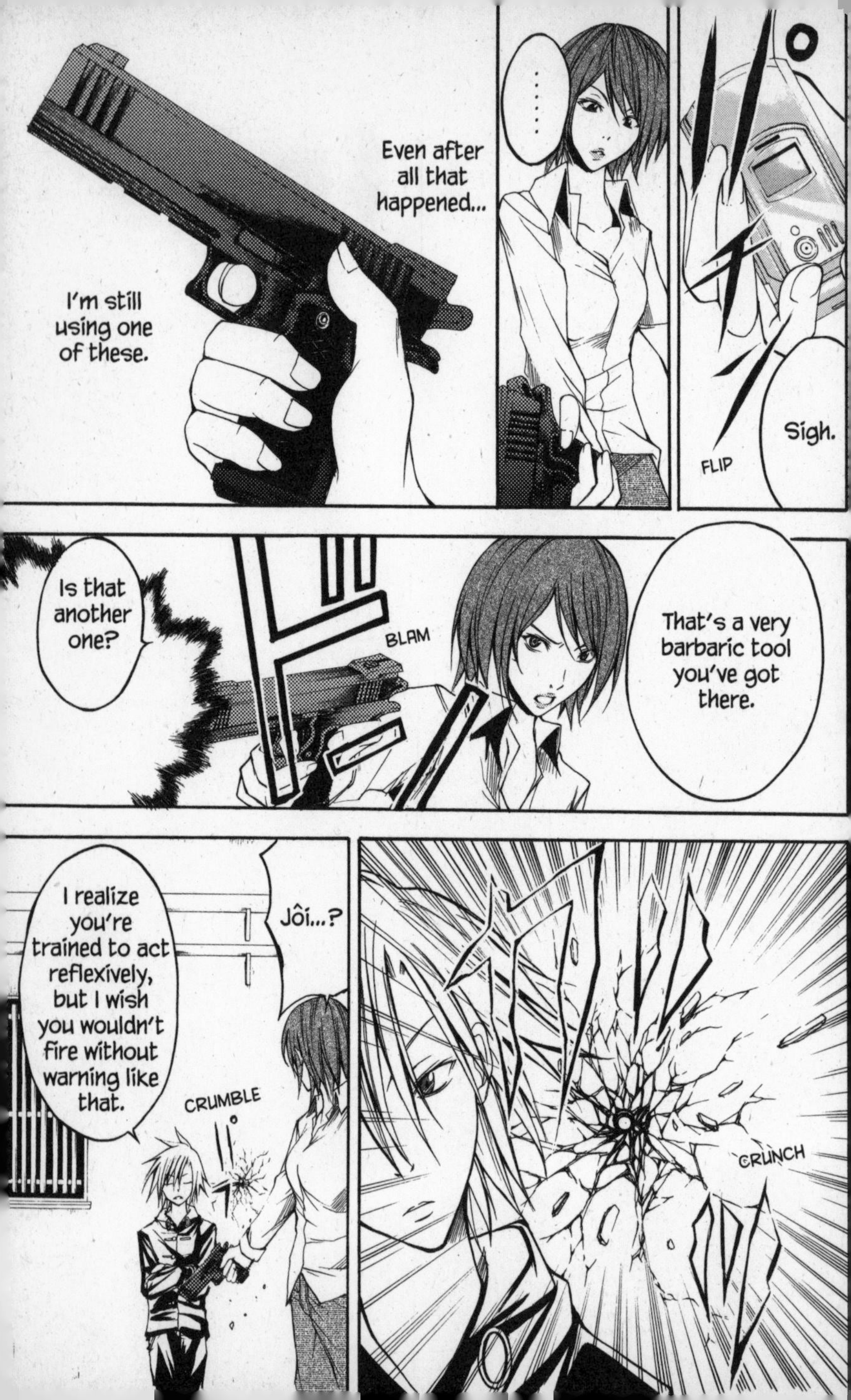
Sigh.
FLIP
......
Even after all that happened...
I'm still using one of these.
That's a very barbaric tool you've got there.
BLAM
Is that another one?
CRUNCH
Jôi...?
CRUMBLE
I realize you're trained to act reflexively, but I wish you wouldn't fire without warning like that.

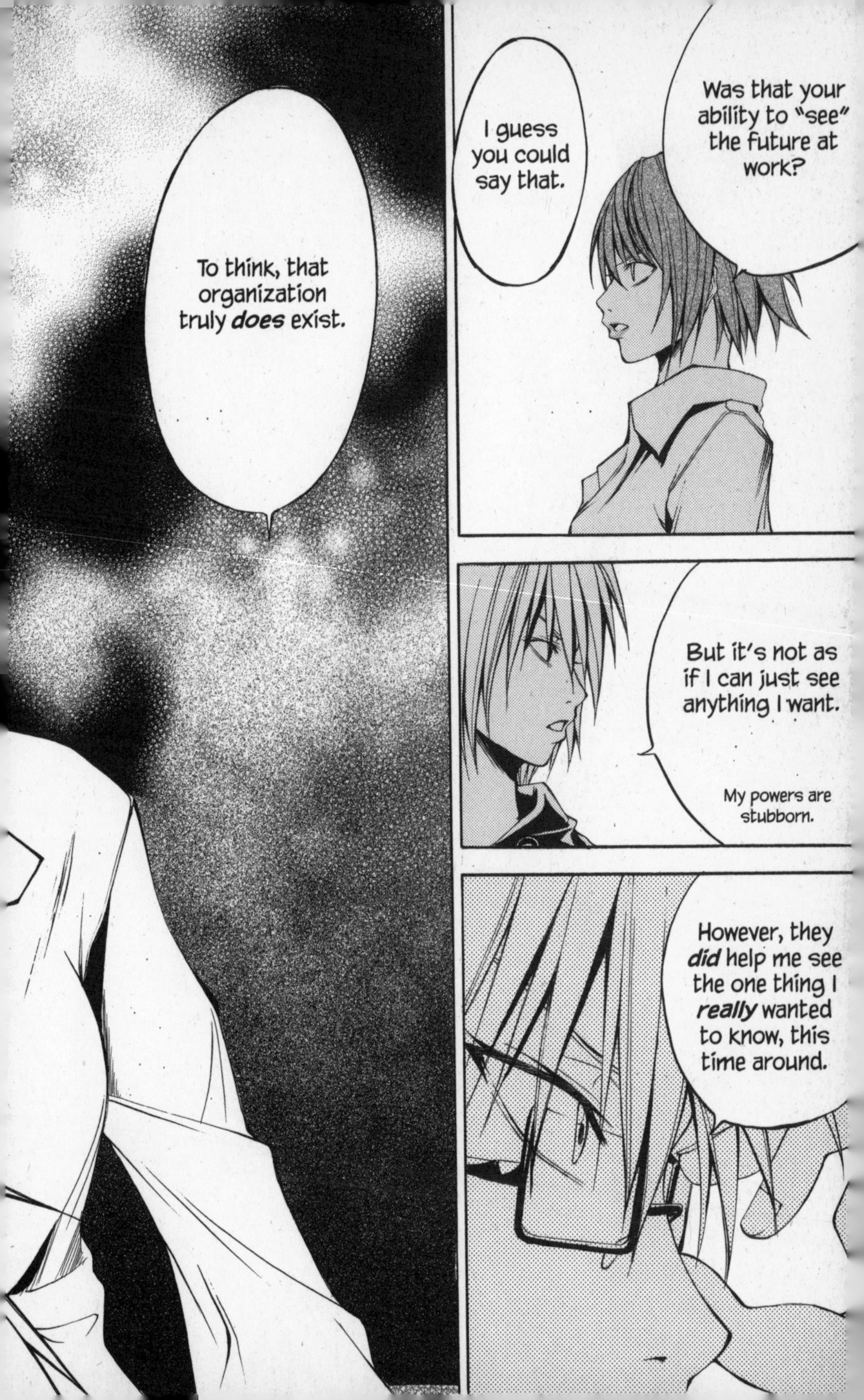
Was that your ability to "see" the future at work?
I guess you could say that.
But it's not as if I can just see anything I want.
My powers are stubborn.
However, they *did* help me see the one thing I *really* wanted to know, this time around.
To think, that organization truly *does* exist.

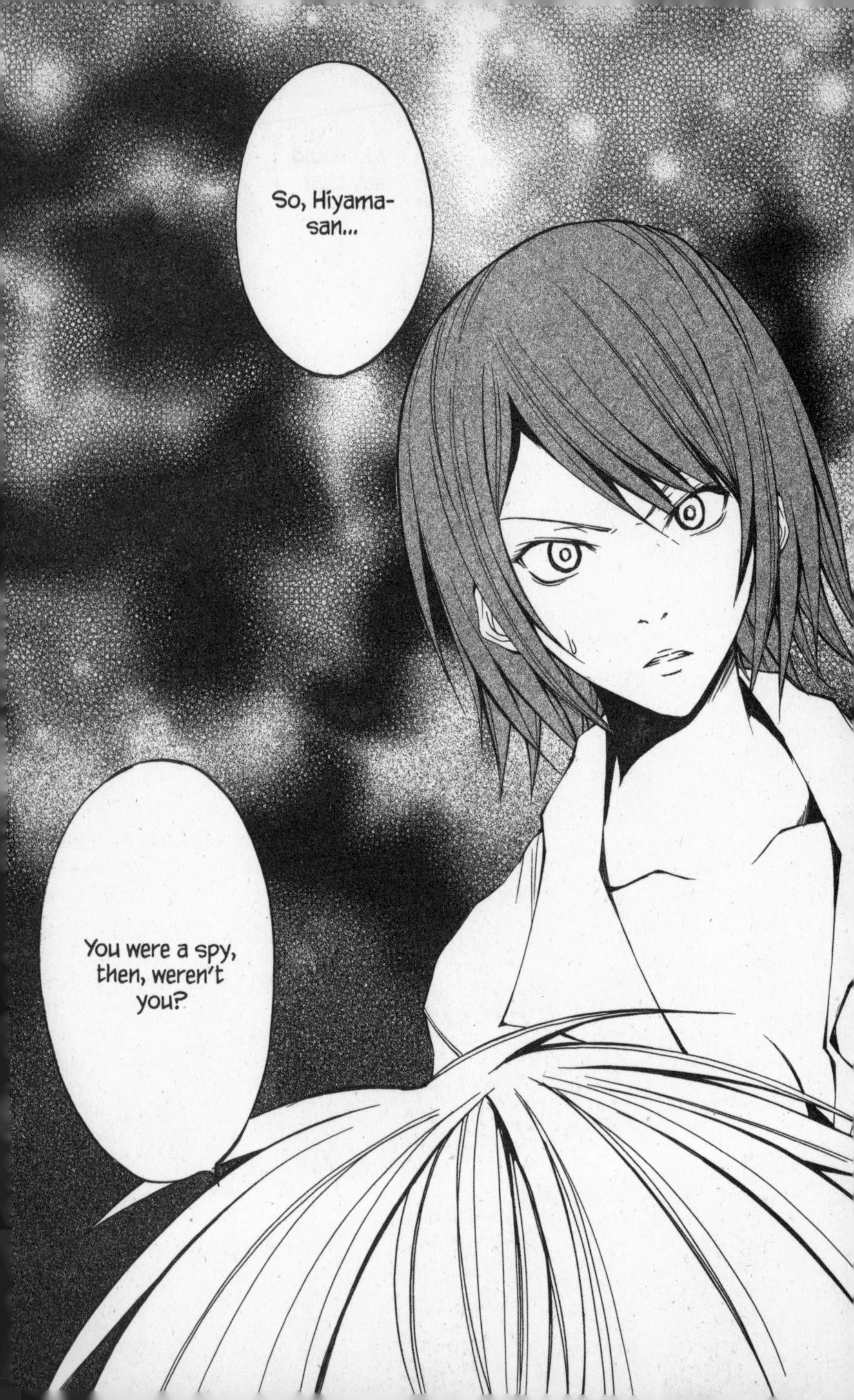
So, Hiyama-san...
You were a spy, then, weren't you?

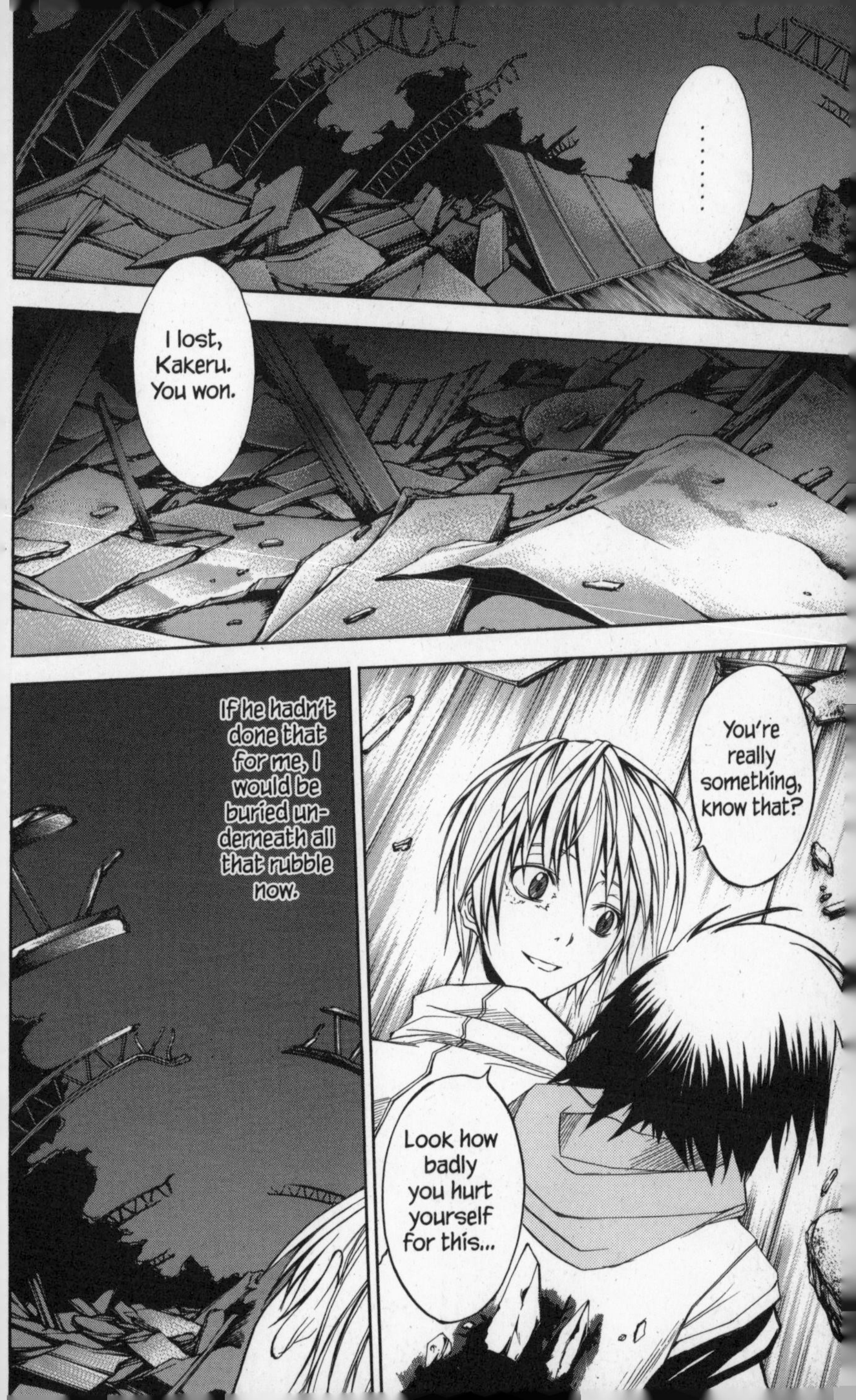
......
I lost, Kakeru. You won.
You're really something, know that?
Look how badly you hurt yourself for this...
If he hadn't done that for me, I would be buried underneath all that rubble now.

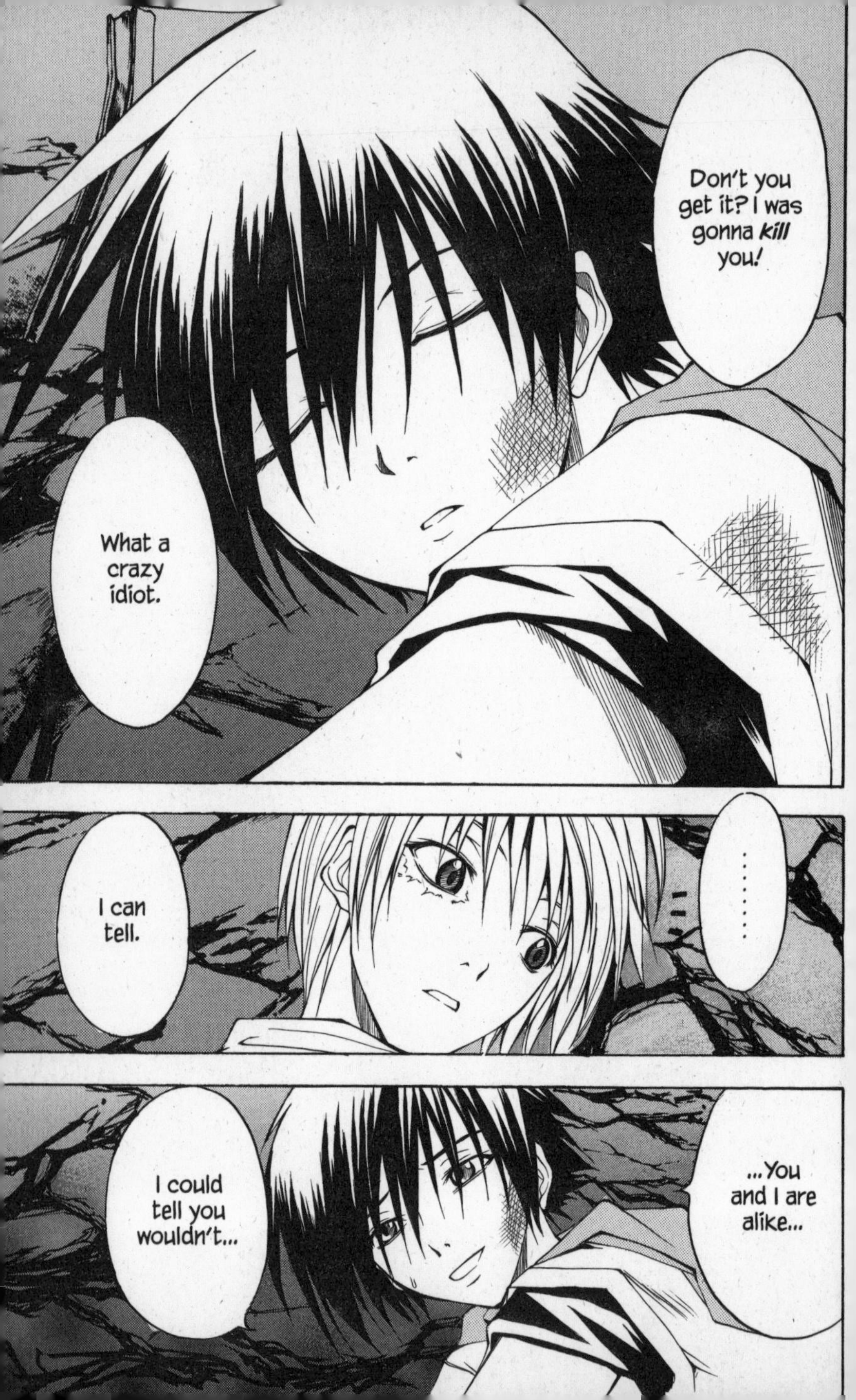
Don't you get it? I was gonna *kill* you!
What a crazy idiot.
........
I can tell.
...You and I are alike...
I could tell you wouldn't...

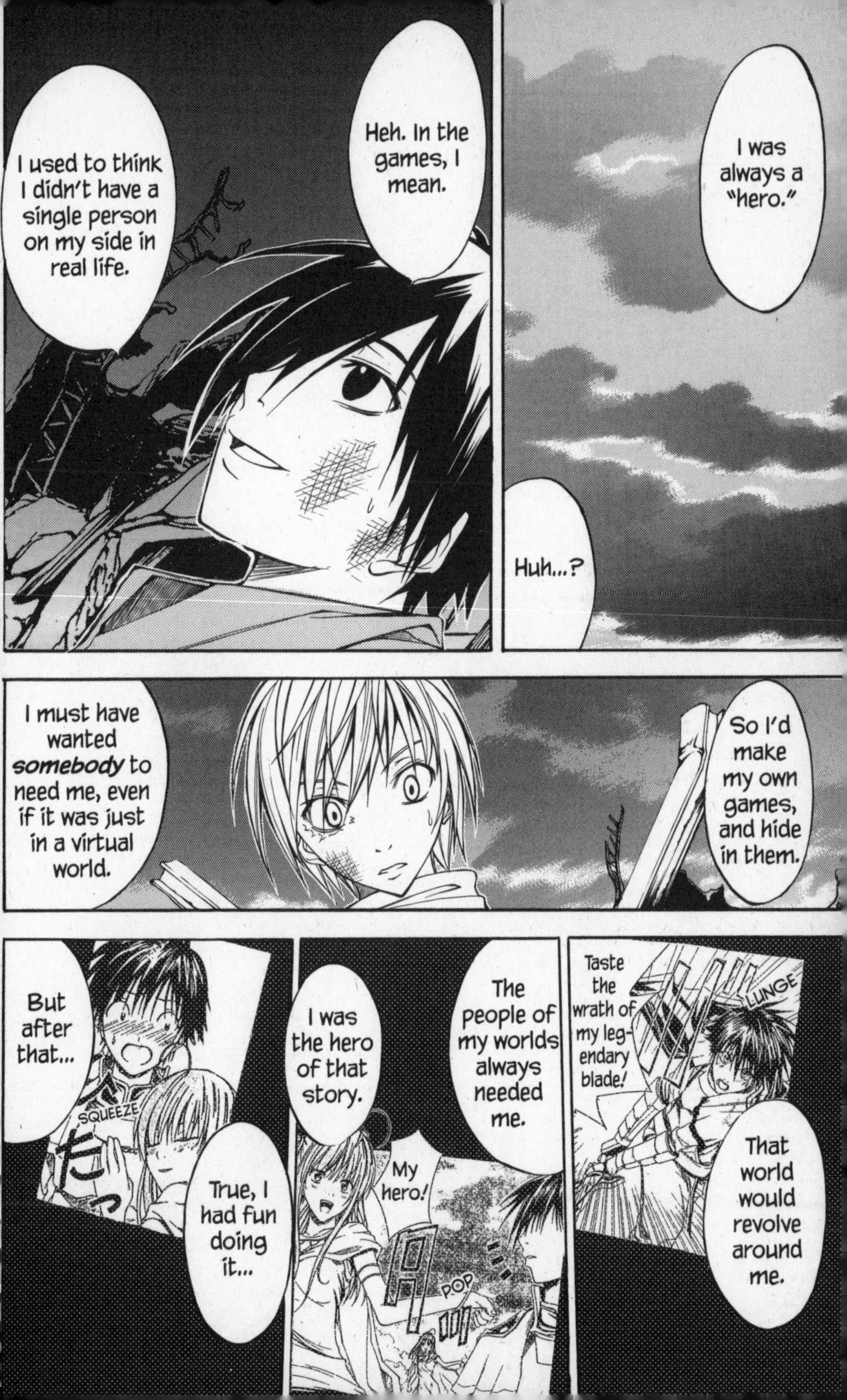
I was always a "hero."
Huh...?
Heh. In the games, I mean.
I used to think I didn't have a single person on my side in real life.
So I'd make my own games, and hide in them.
I must have wanted *somebody* to need me, even if it was just in a virtual world.
Taste the wrath of my legendary blade!
LUNGE
That world would revolve around me.
The people of my worlds always needed me.
I was the hero of that story.
My hero!
POP
True, I had fun doing it...
But after that...
SQUEEZE

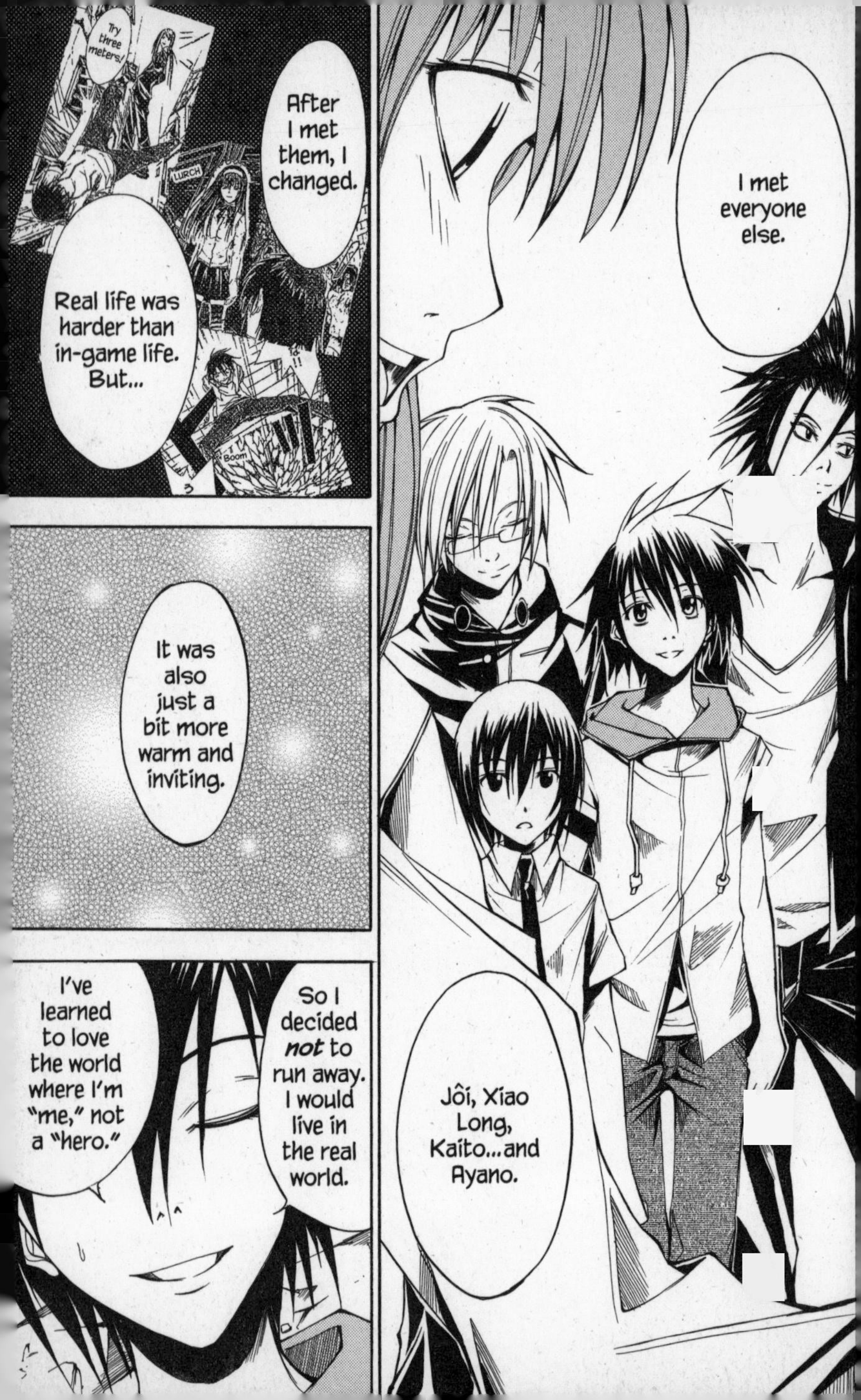

I met everyone else.
Jôi, Xiao Long, Kaito...and Ayano.
After I met them, I changed.
Try three meters!
LURCH
Real life was harder than in-game life. But...
Boom
It was also just a bit more warm and inviting.
So I decided *not* to run away. I would live in the real world.
I've learned to love the world where I'm "me," not a "hero."

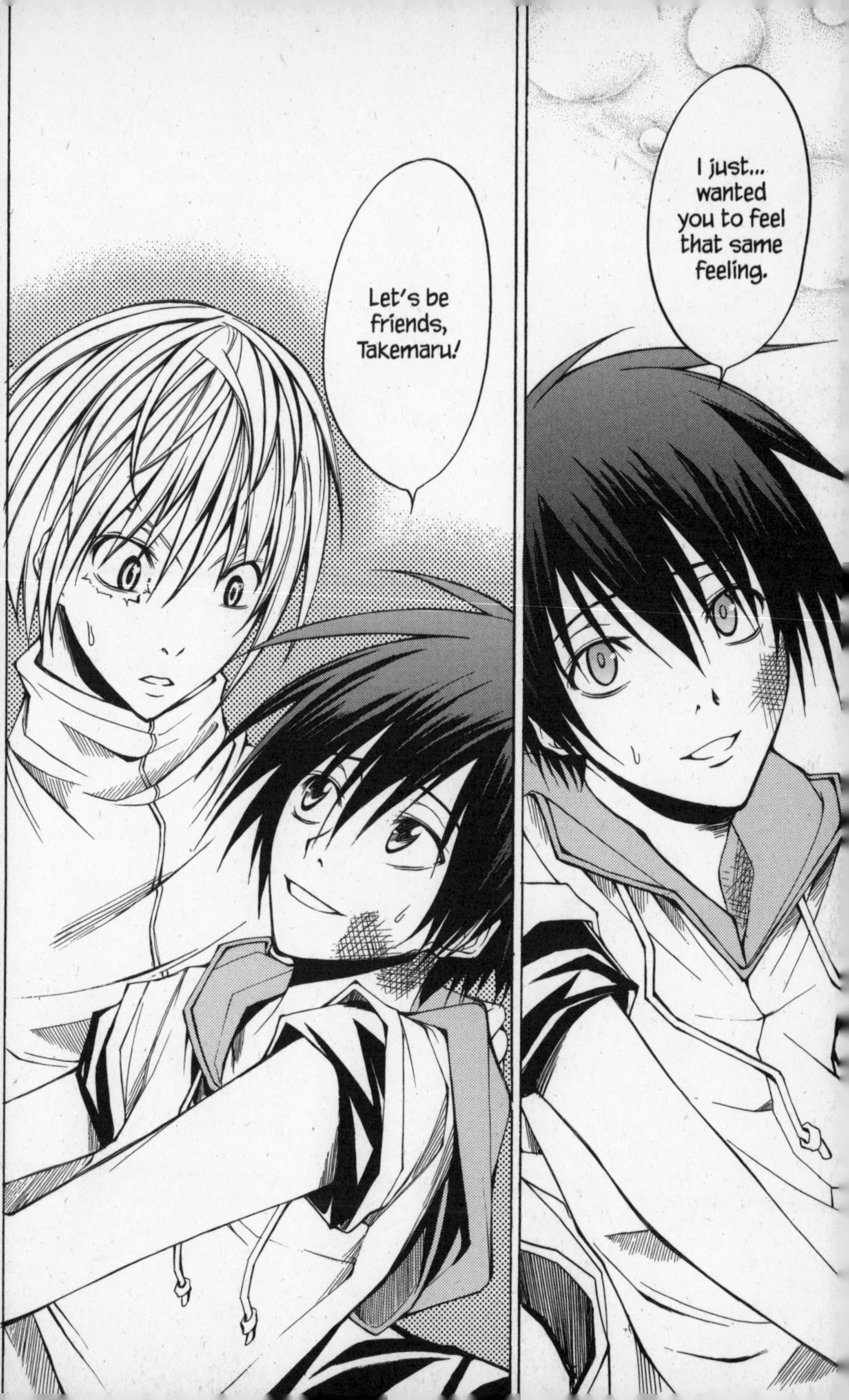
I just... wanted you to feel that same feeling.
Let's be friends, Takemaru!

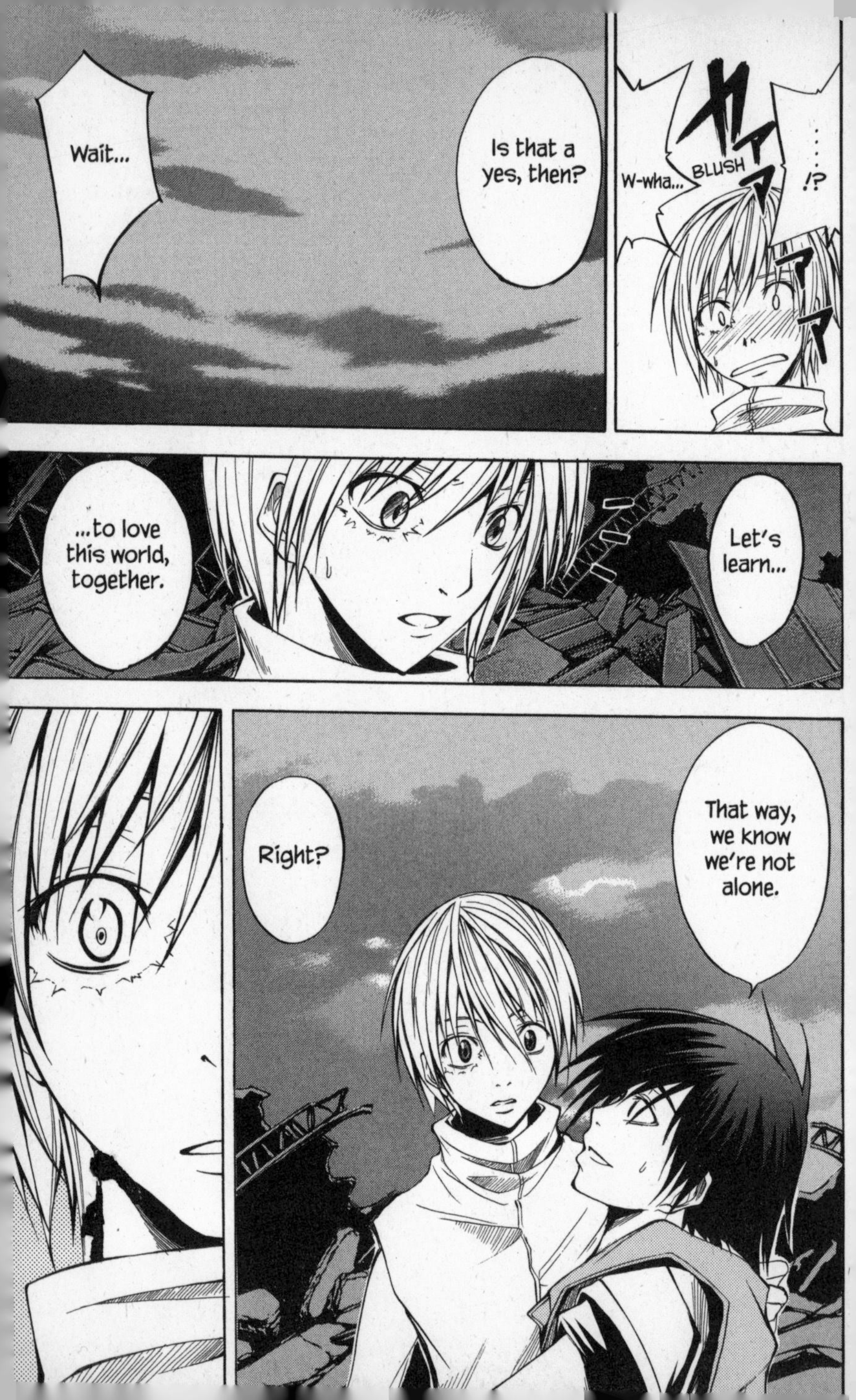

...!?
W-wha...
BLUSH
Is that a yes, then?
Wait...
Let's learn...
...to love this world, together.
That way, we know we're not alone.
Right?

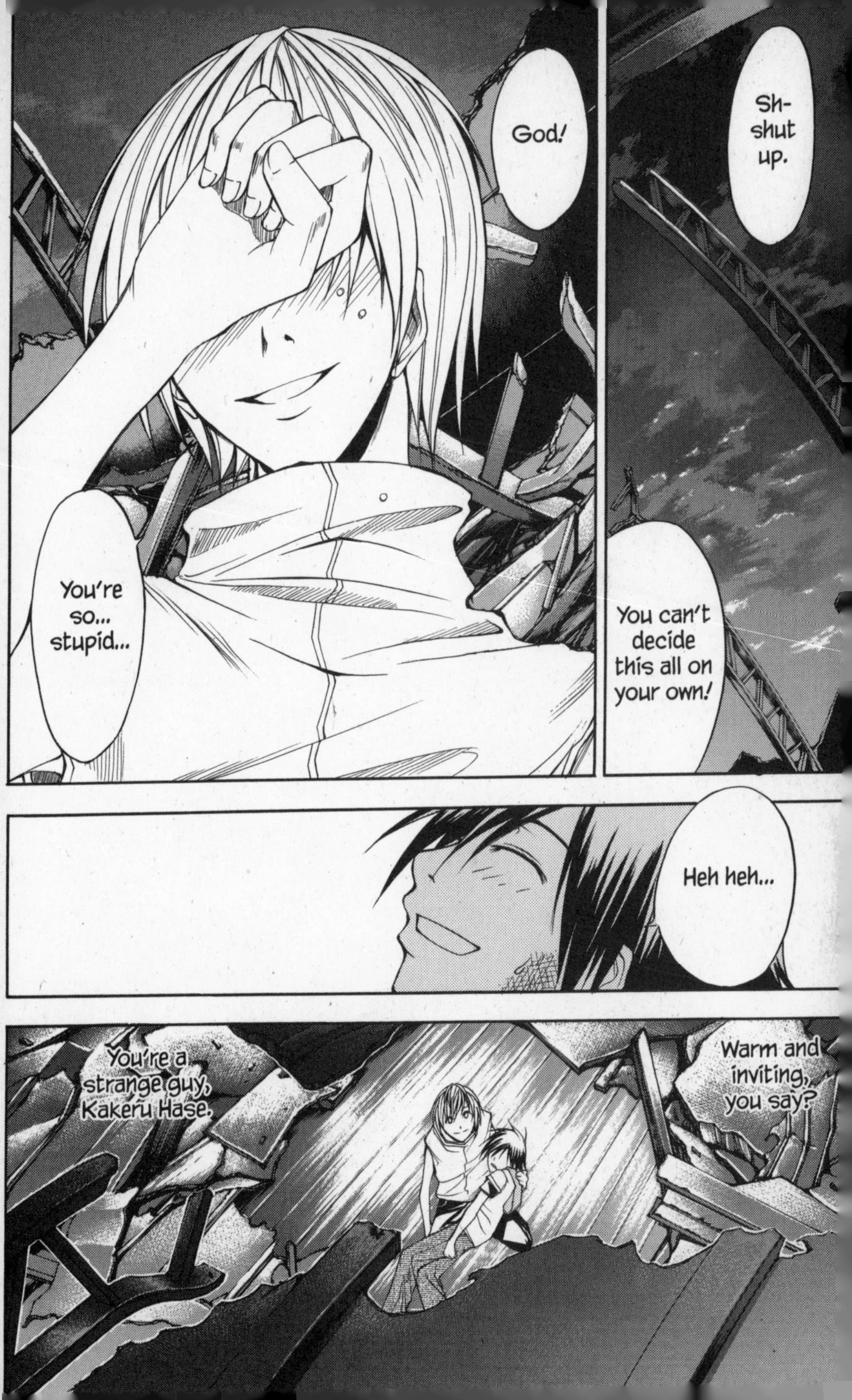
Sh-shut up.
You can't decide this all on your own!
God!
You're so... stupid...
Heh heh...
Warm and inviting, you say?
You're a strange guy, Kakeru Hase.

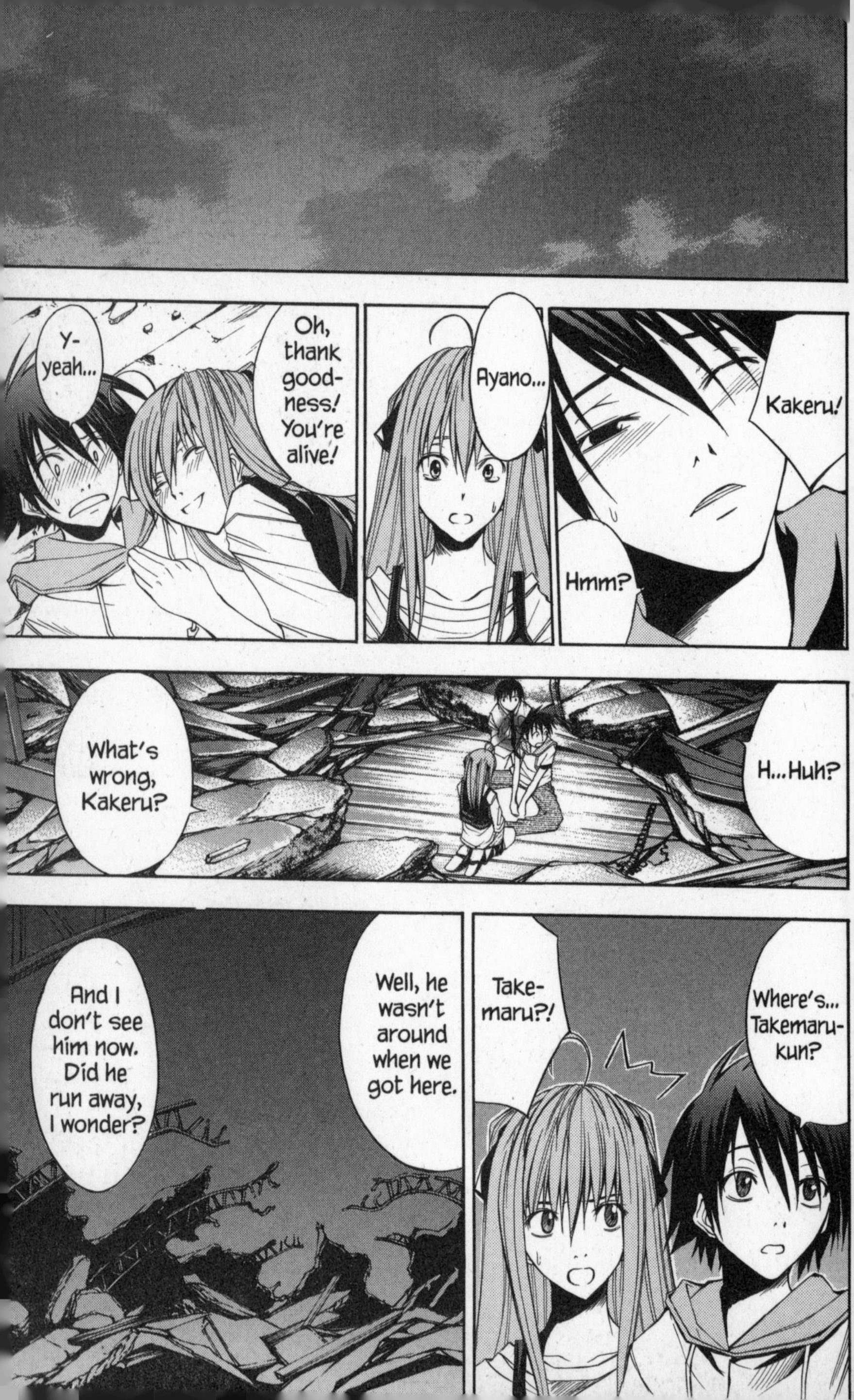
Kakeru!
Hmm?
Ayano...
Oh, thank goodness! You're alive!
Y-yeah...
H...Huh?
What's wrong, Kakeru?
Where's... Takemaru-kun?
Take-maru?!
Well, he wasn't around when we got here.
And I don't see him now. Did he run away, I wonder?

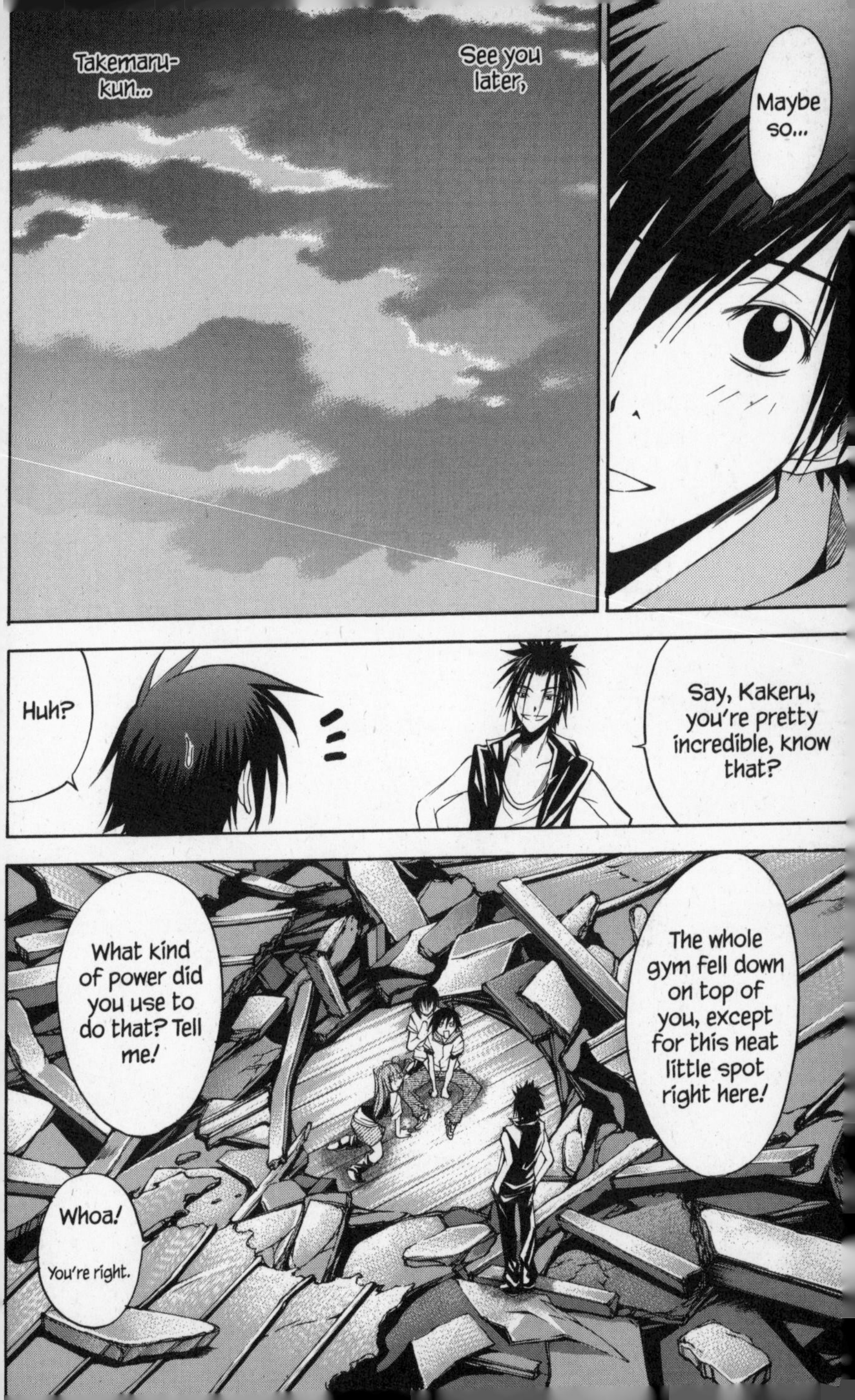
Maybe so...
See you later,
Takemaru-kun...
Say, Kakeru, you're pretty incredible, know that?
Huh?
The whole gym fell down on top of you, except for this neat little spot right here!
What kind of power did you use to do that? Tell me!
Whoa!
You're right.

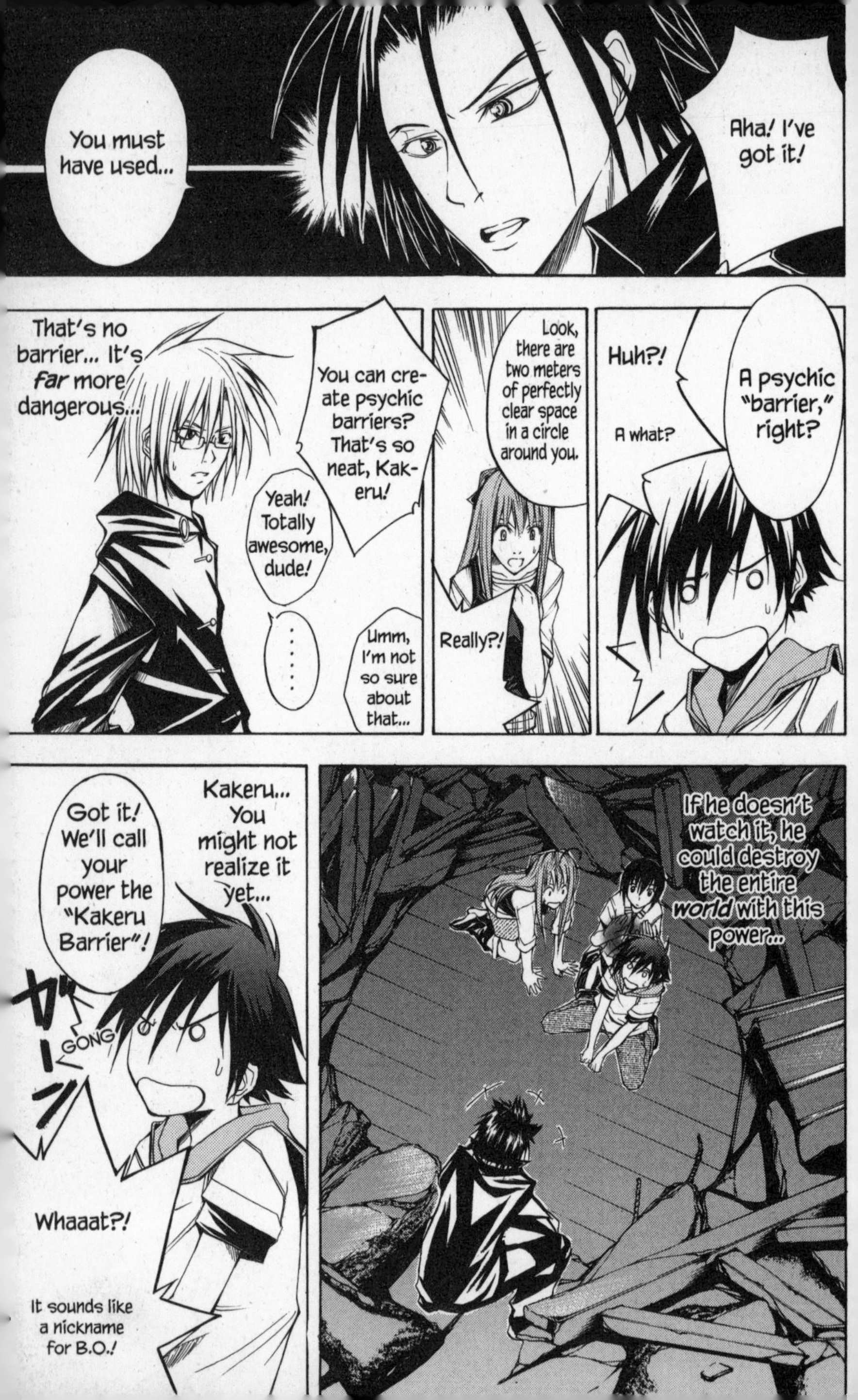

Aha! I've got it!
You must have used...
A psychic "barrier," right?
Huh?!
A what?
Look, there are two meters of perfectly clear space in a circle around you.
Really?!
You can cre-ate psychic barriers? That's so neat, Kak-eru!
Yeah! Totally awesome, dude!
Umm, I'm not so sure about that...
......
That's no barrier... It's *far* more dangerous...
If he doesn't watch it, he could destroy the entire *world* with this power...
Kakeru... You might not realize it yet...
Got it! We'll call your power the "Kakeru Barrier"!
GONG
Whaaat?!
It sounds like a nickname for B.O.!

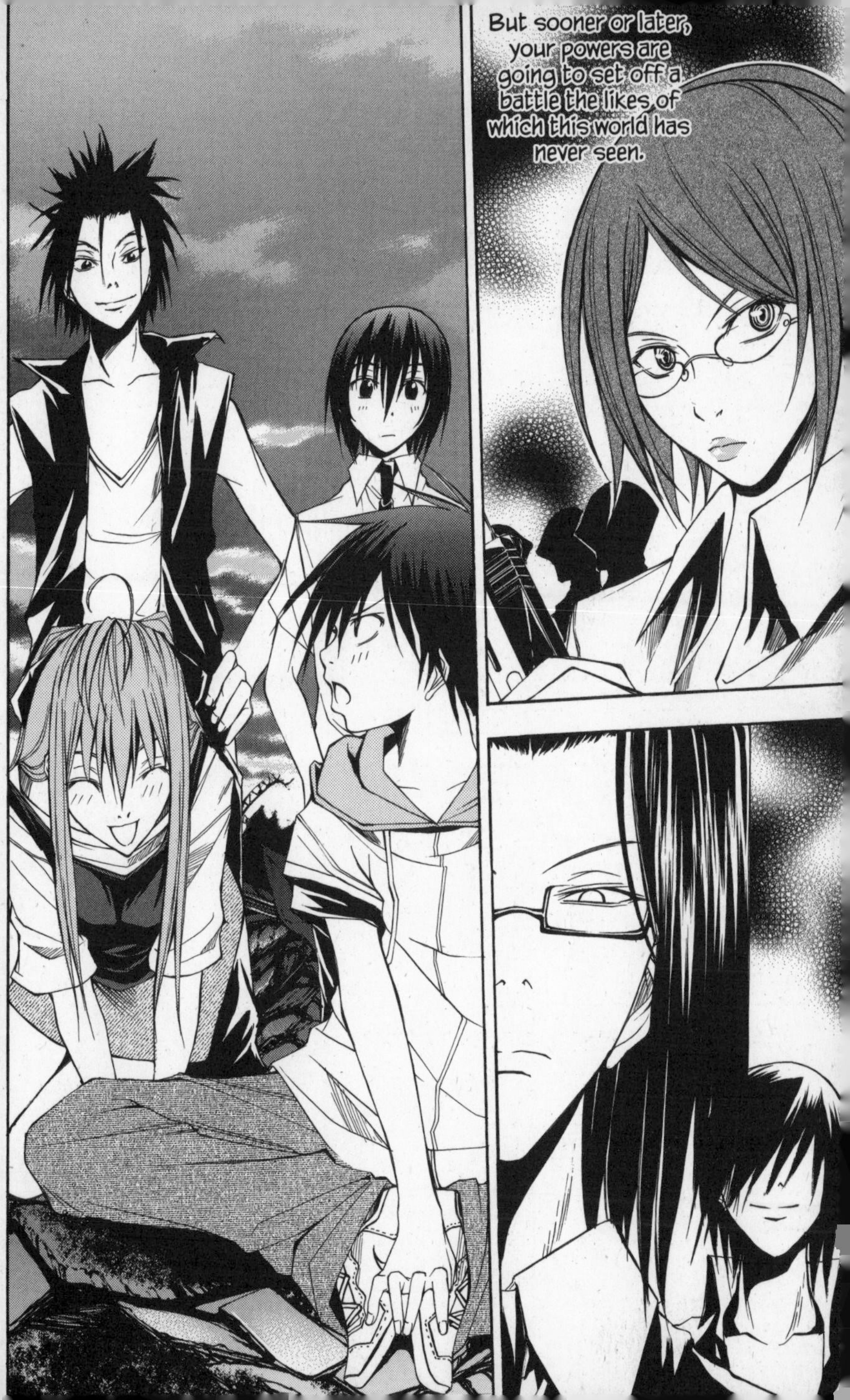
But sooner or later, your powers are going to set off a battle the likes of which this world has never seen.

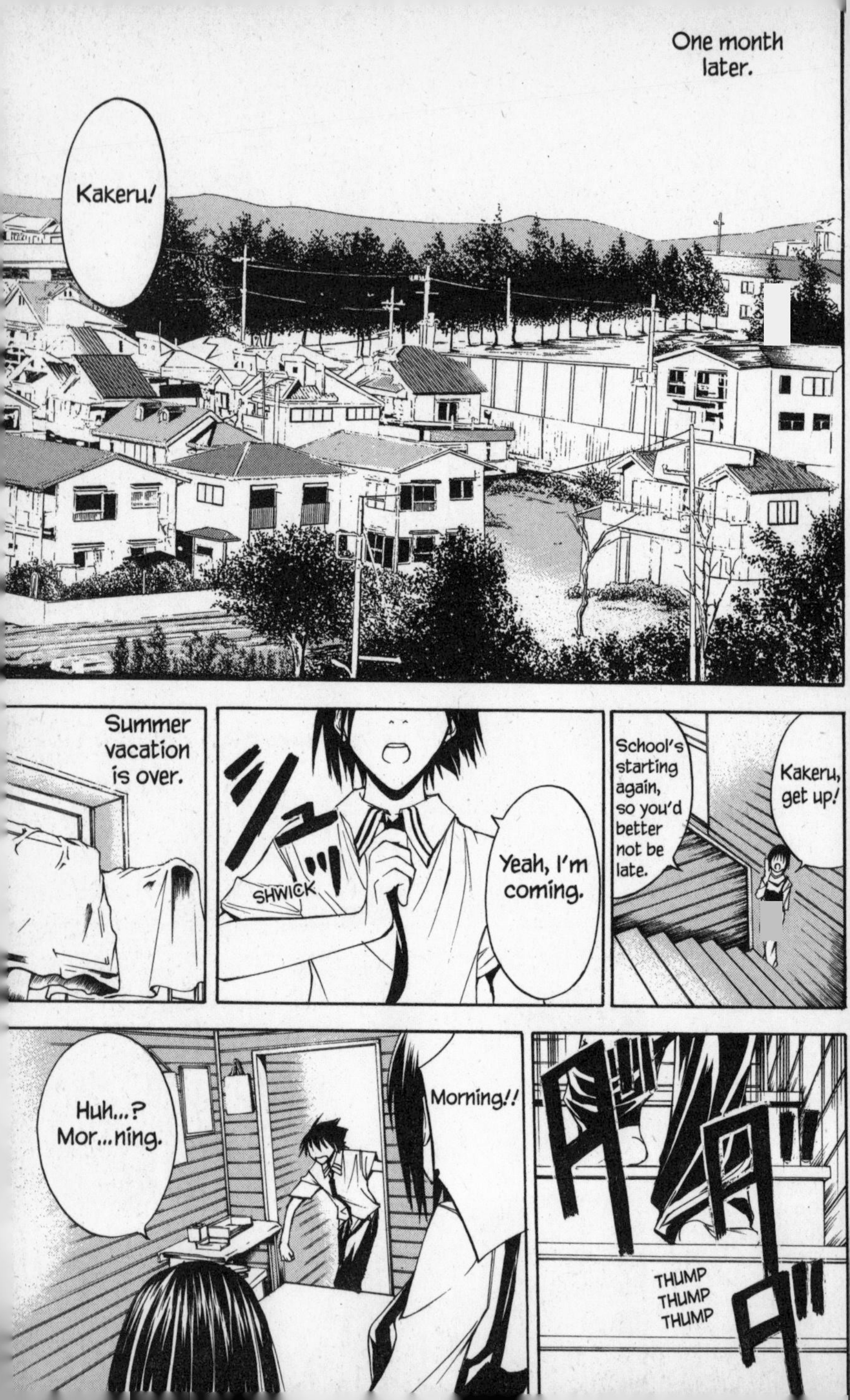
One month later.
Kakeru!
Kakeru, get up!
School's starting again, so you'd better not be late.
Yeah, I'm coming.
SHWICK
Summer vacation is over.
THUMP THUMP THUMP
Morning!!
Huh...? Mor...ning.

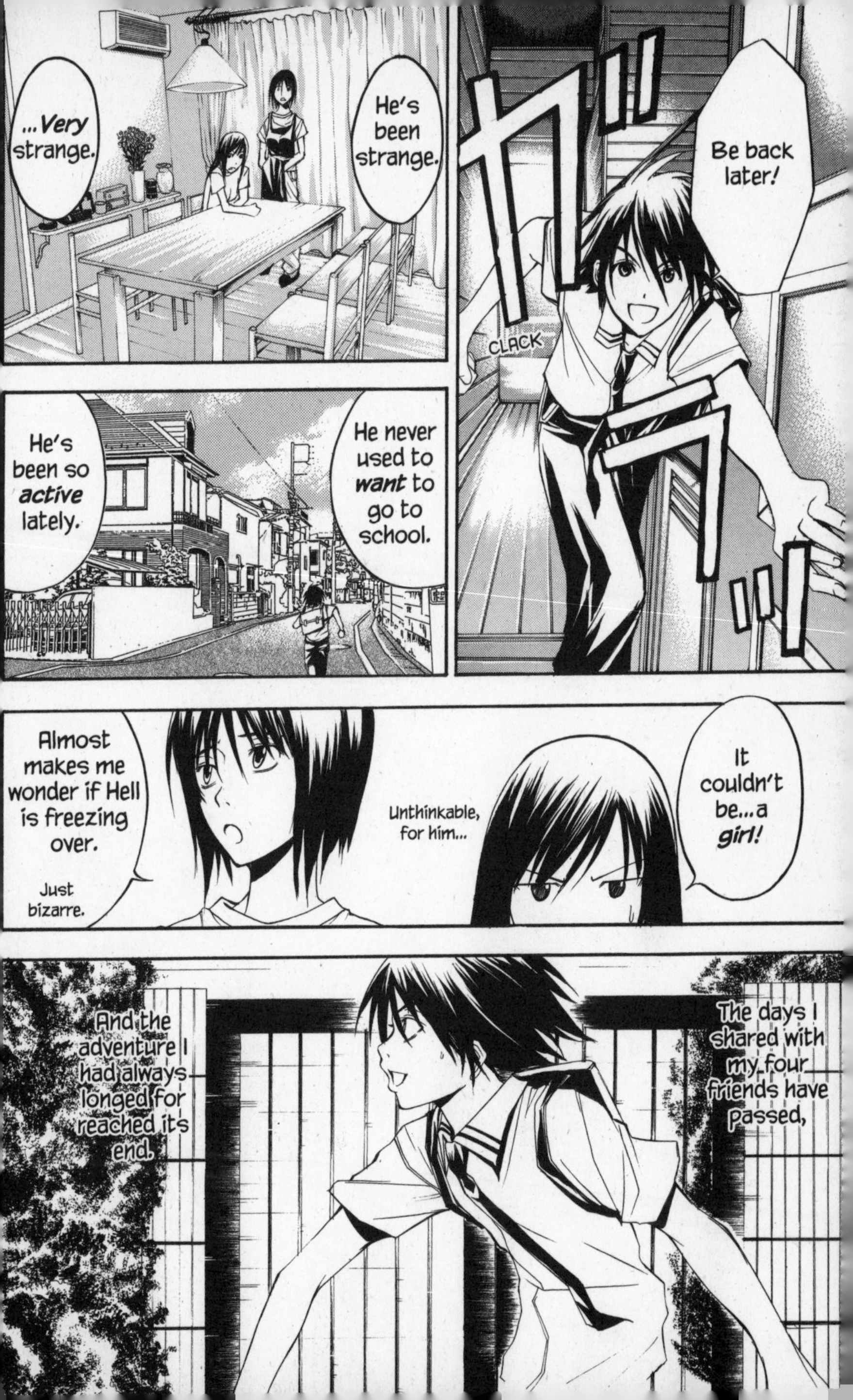
Be back later!
CLACK
He's been strange.
...Very strange.
He never used to want to go to school.
He's been so active lately.
It couldn't be...a girl!
Unthinkable, for him...
Almost makes me wonder if Hell is freezing over.
Just bizarre.
The days I shared with my four friends have passed,
And the adventure I had always longed for reached its end.

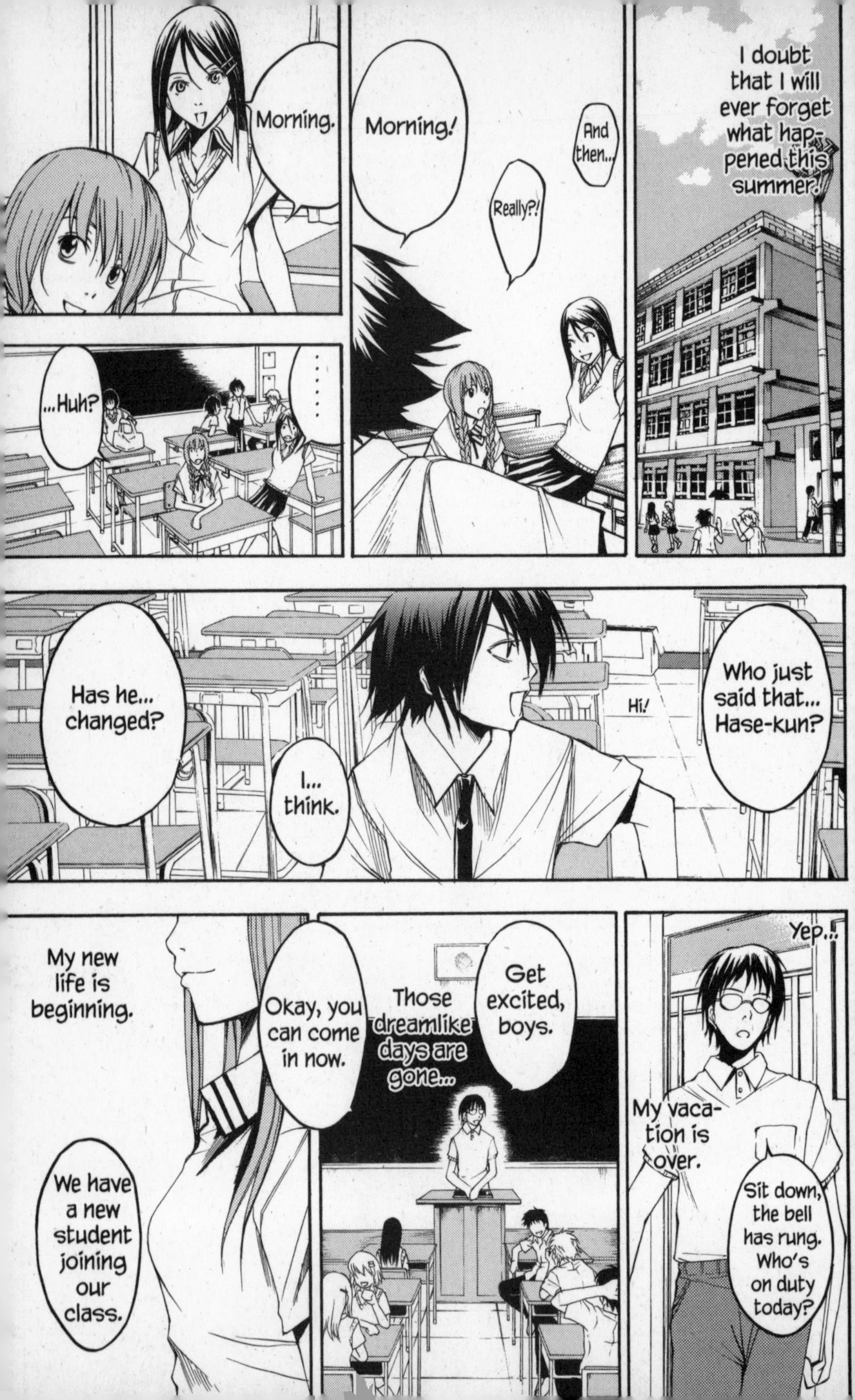
I doubt that I will ever forget what happened this summer.
And then...
Morning!
Really?!
Morning.
......
...Huh?
Who just said that... Hase-kun?
Hi!
I... think.
Has he... changed?
Yep...
My vacation is over.
Sit down, the bell has rung. Who's on duty today?
Get excited, boys.
Those dreamlike days are gone...
Okay, you can come in now.
My new life is beginning.
We have a new student joining our class.

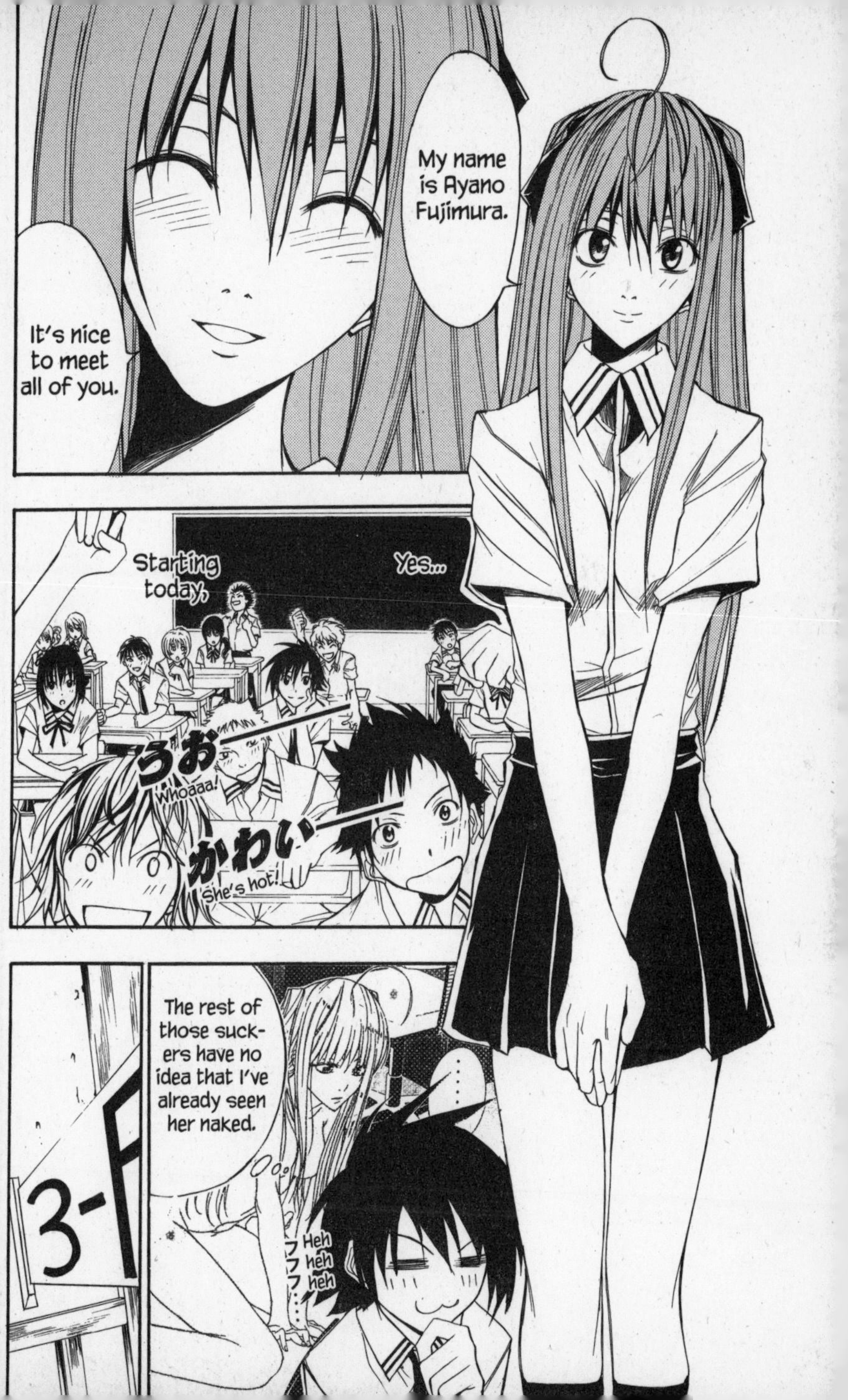
My name is Ayano Fujimura.
It's nice to meet all of you.
Yes...
Starting today,
うお
Whoaaa!
かわい
She's hot!
The rest of those suckers have no idea that I've already seen her naked.
...
3-F
フフフ...
Heh heh heh

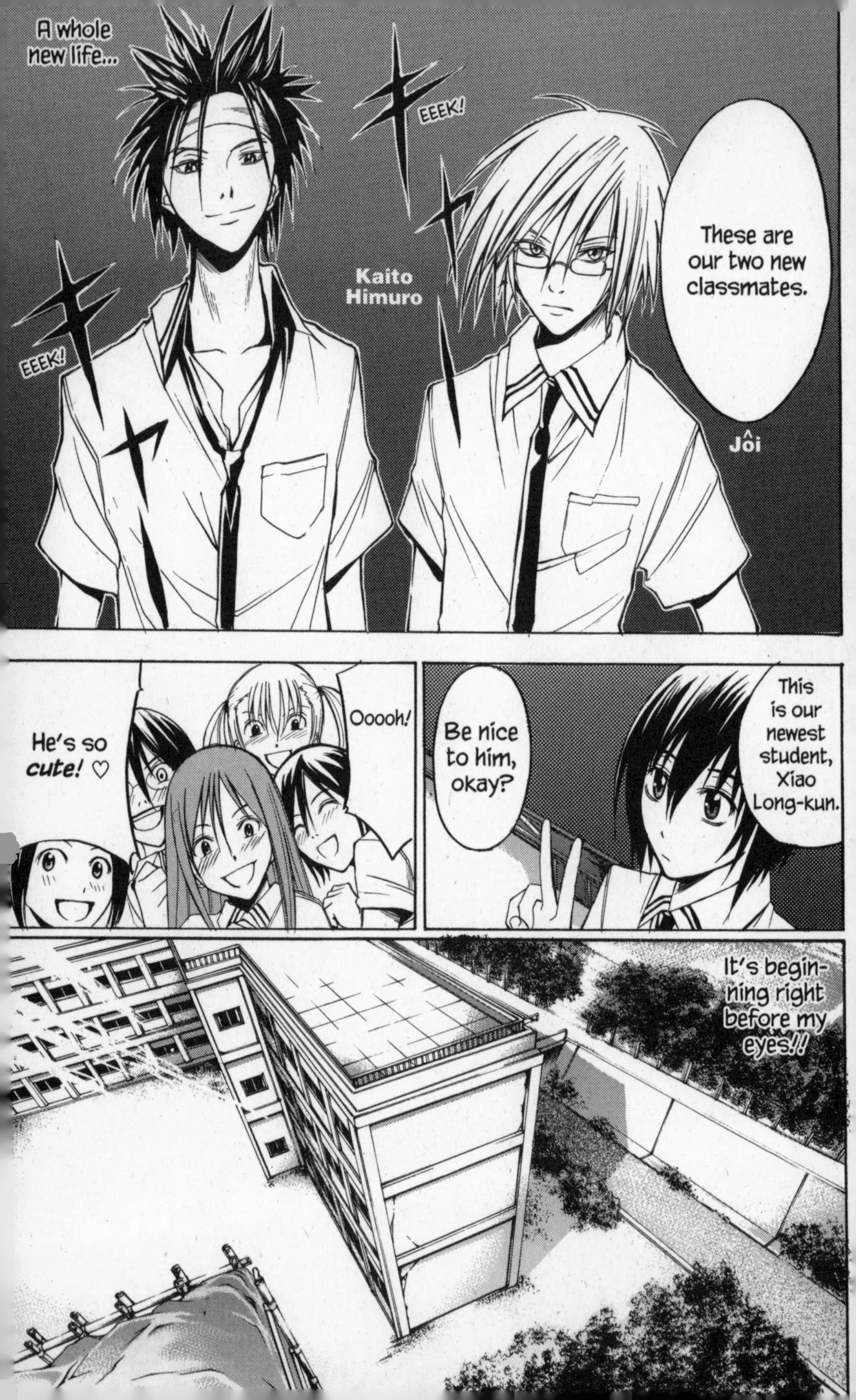
These are our two new classmates.
Jôi
EEEK!
Kaito Himuro
A whole new life...
EEEK!
This is our newest student, Xiao Long-kun.
Be nice to him, okay?
Ooooh!
He's so *cute!* ♡
It's begin-ning right before my eyes!!

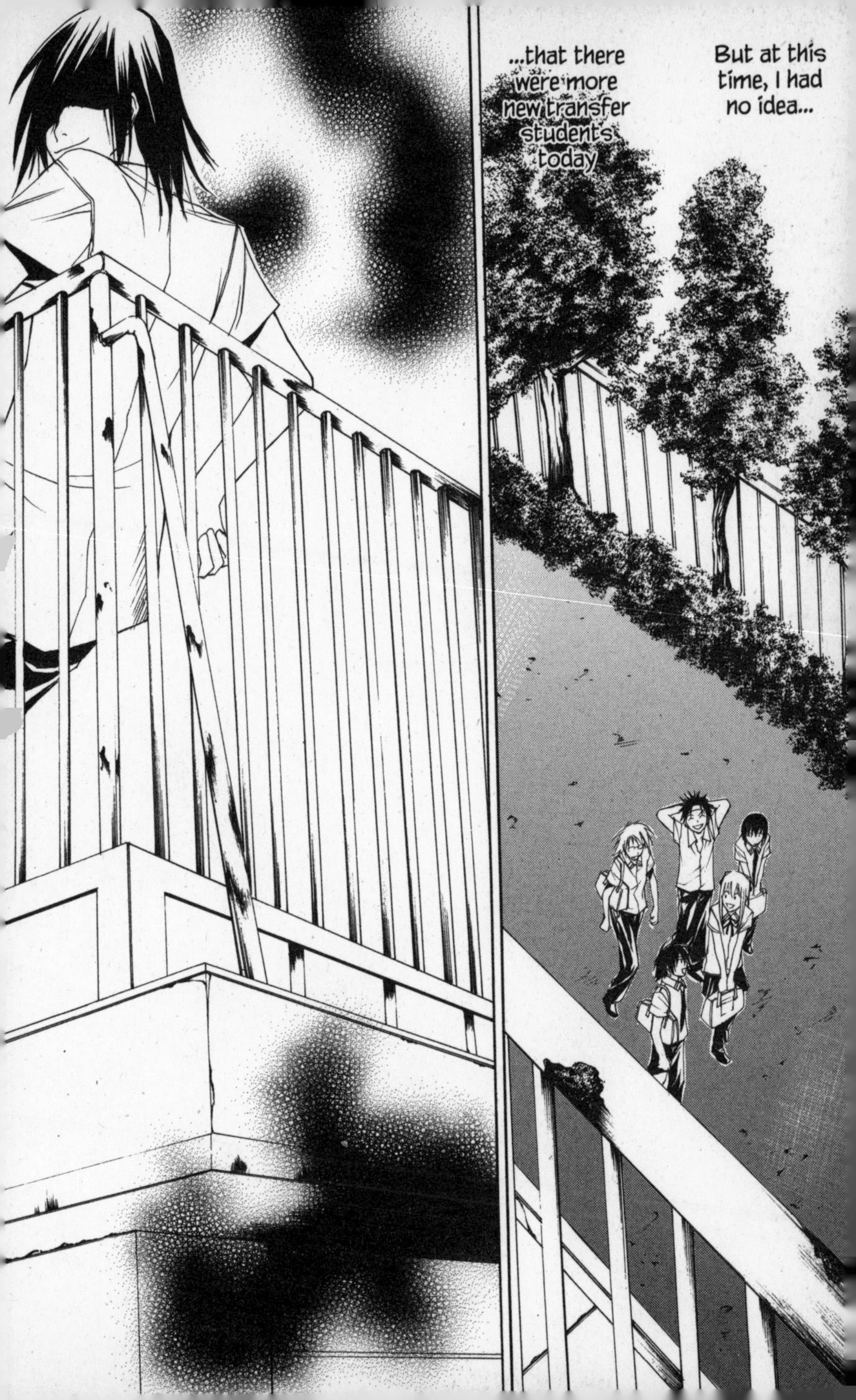
But at this time, I had no idea...
...that there were more new transfer students today

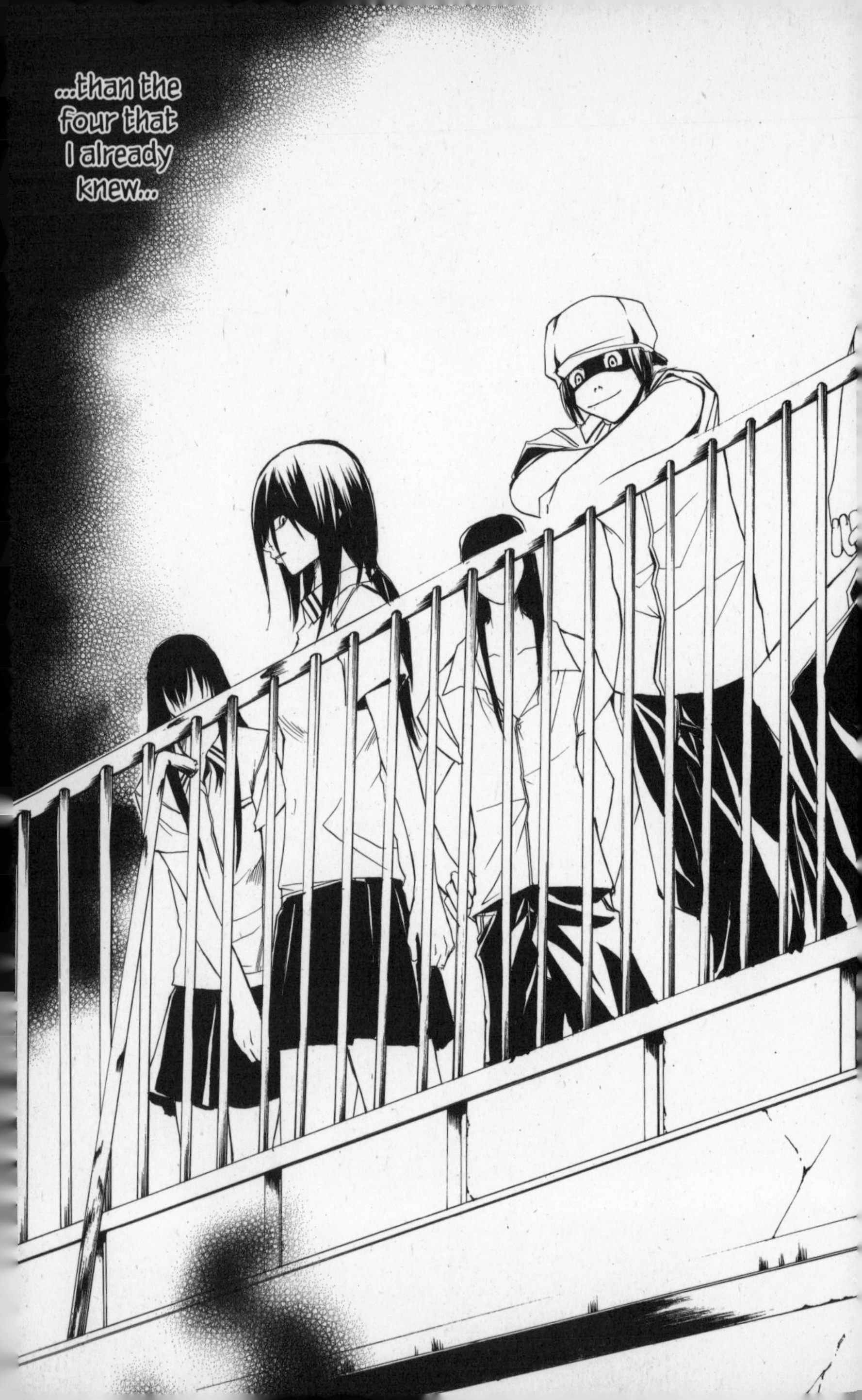
...than the four that I already knew...

**Psycho Busters**

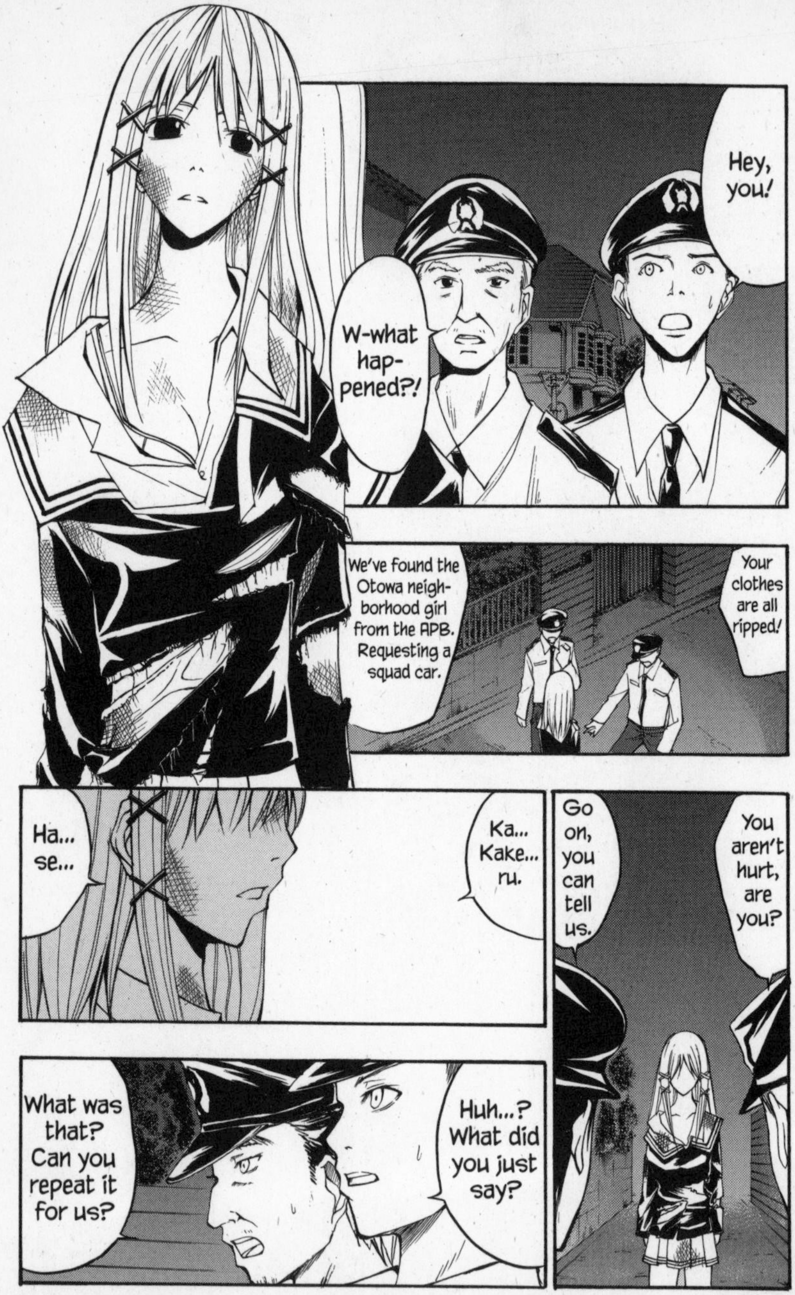
Hey, you!
W-what hap-pened?!
Your clothes are all ripped!
We've found the Otowa neigh-borhood girl from the APB. Requesting a squad car.
You aren't hurt, are you?
Go on, you can tell us.
Ka... Kake... ru.
Ha... se...
Huh...? What did you just say?
What was that? Can you repeat it for us?

# CASE 10 – Disappearance

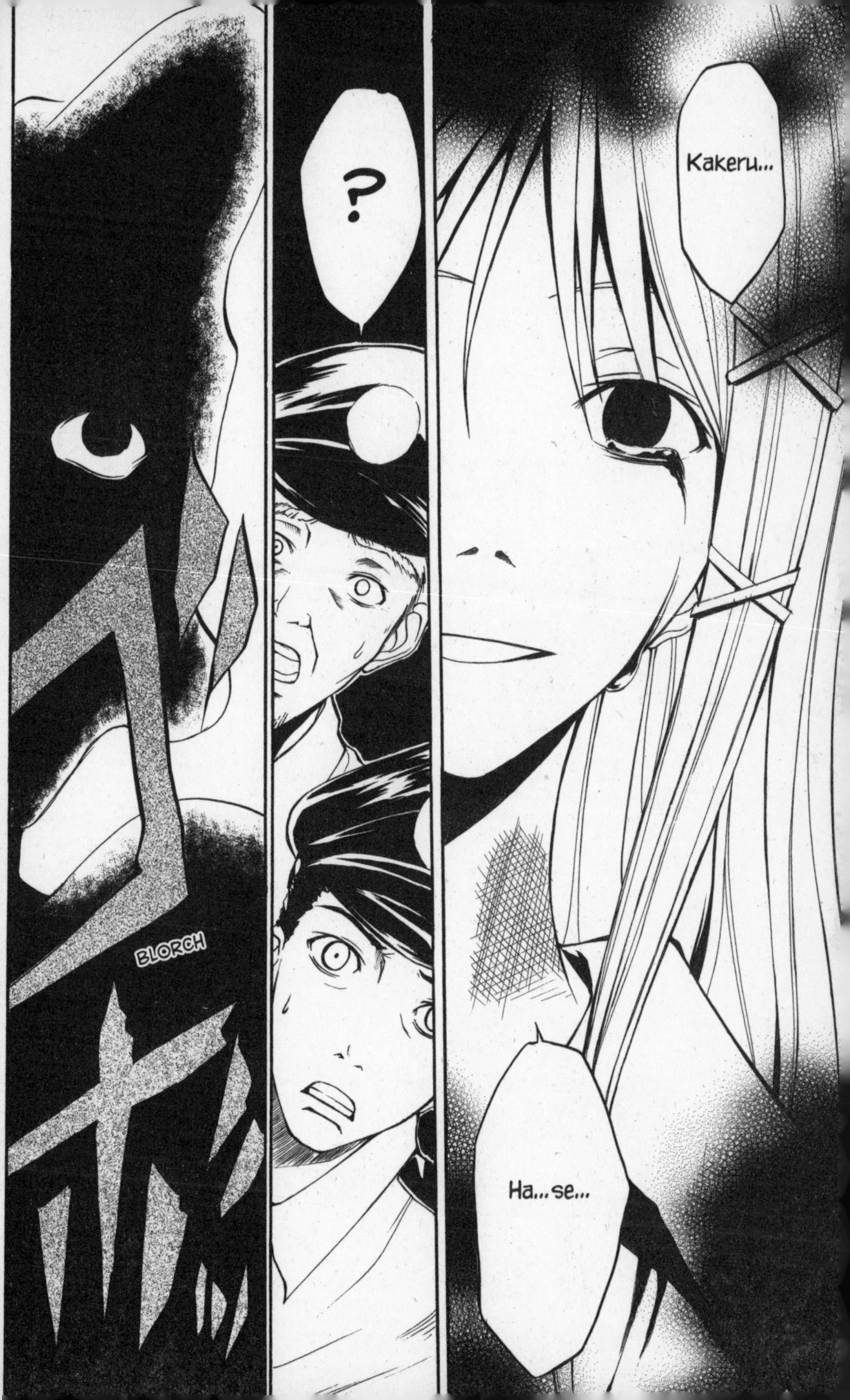
Kakeru...
Ha...se...
?
BLORCH

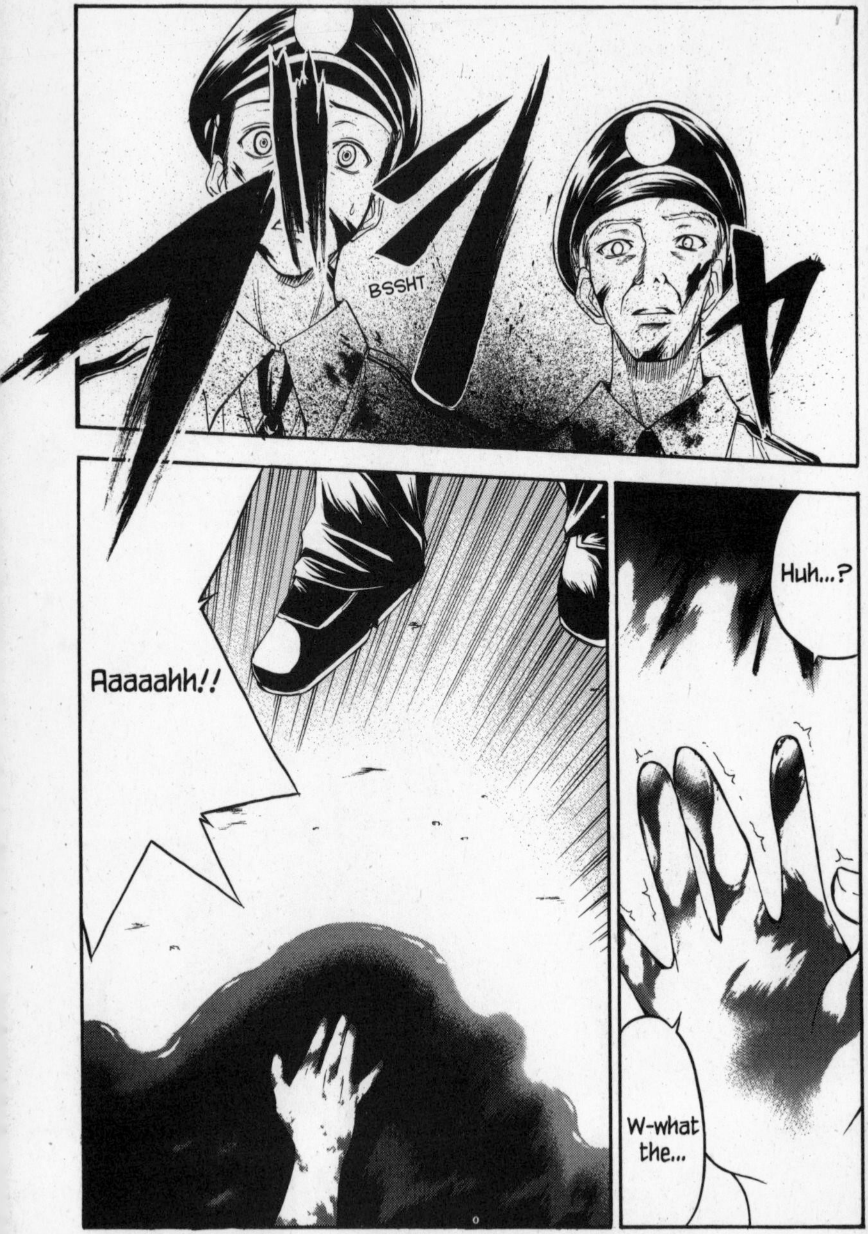
BSSHT
Huh...?
W-what the...
Aaaaahh!!

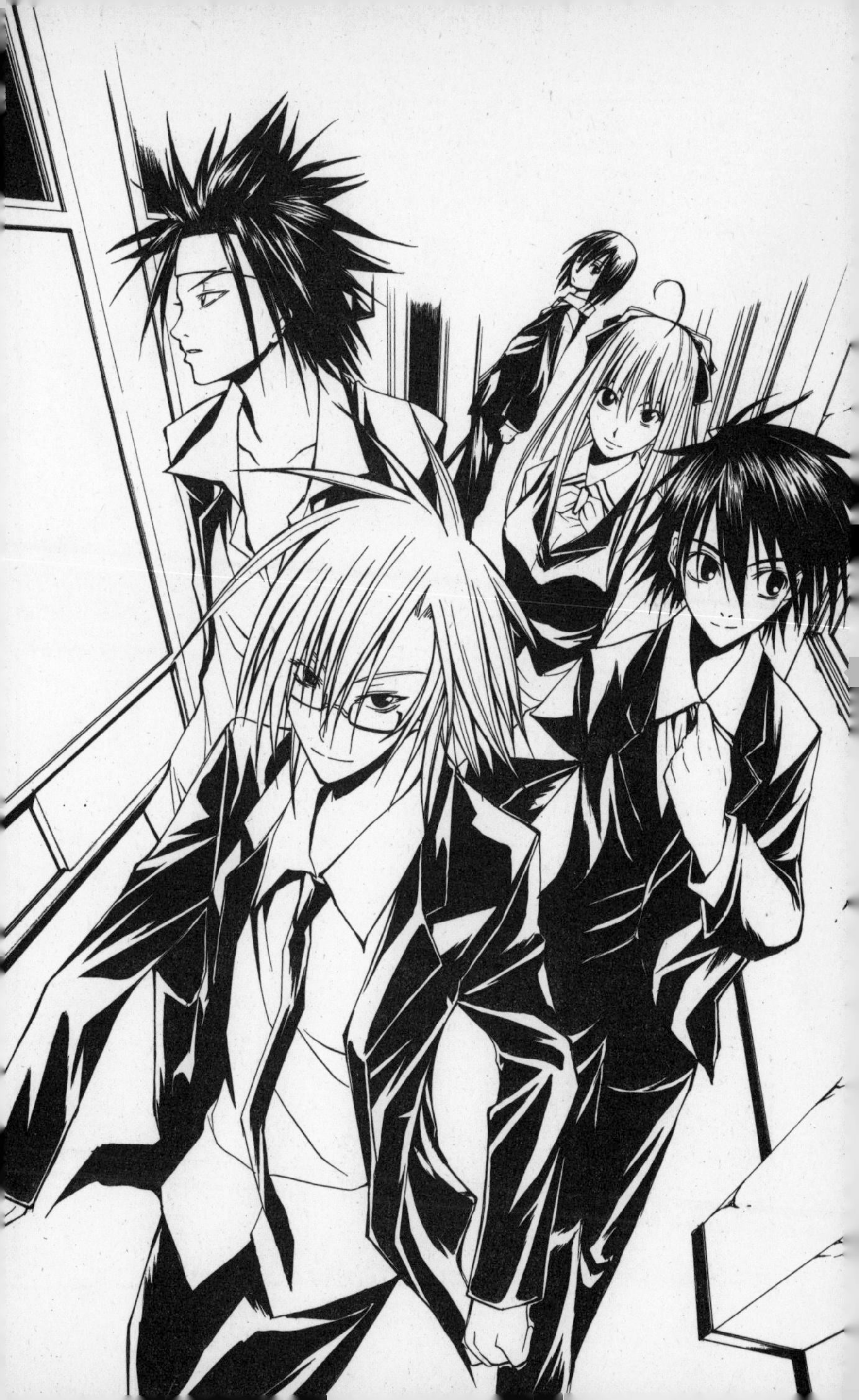

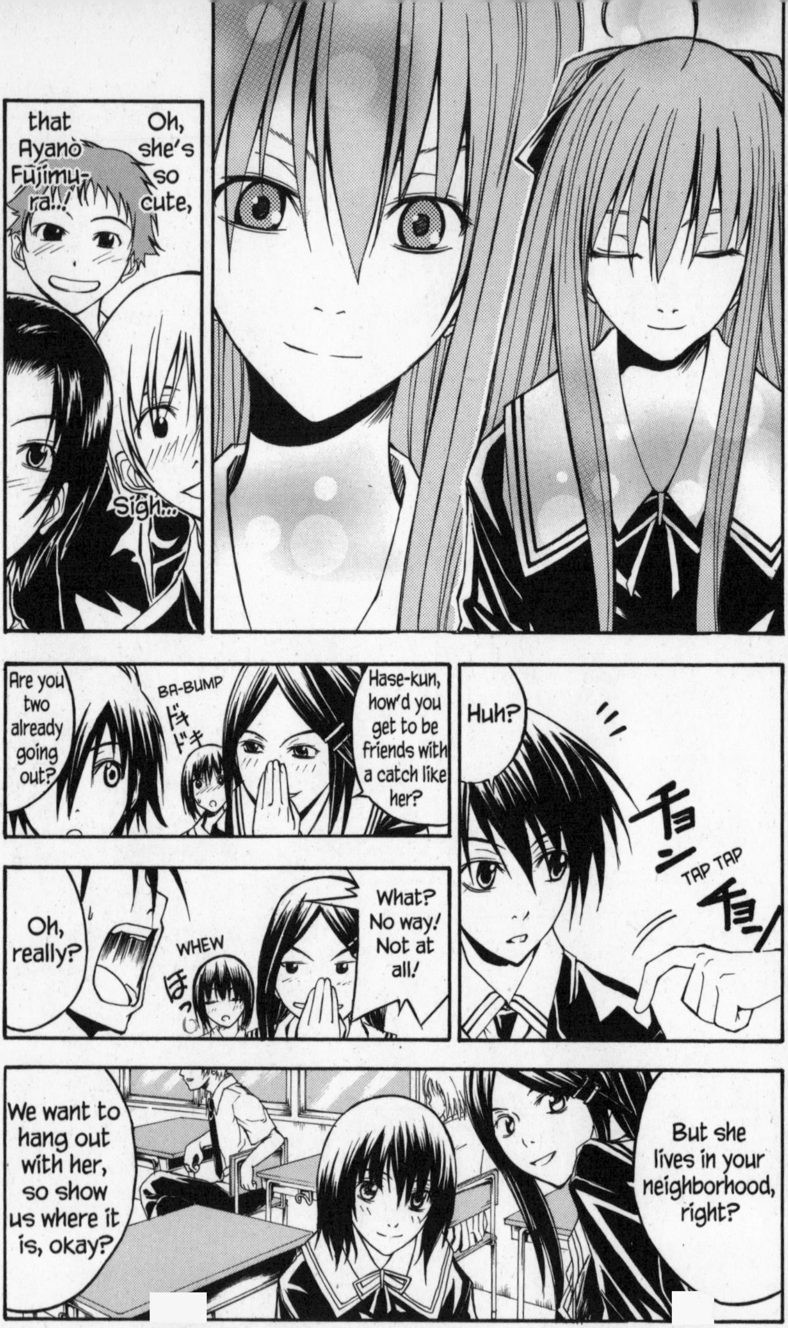
Oh, she's so cute, that Ayano Fujimura!!
Sigh...
Huh?
TAP TAP
チョン チョン
Hase-kun, how'd you get to be friends with a catch like her?
BA-BUMP
ドキドキ
Are you two already going out?
What? No way! Not at all!
WHEW
ほっ
Oh, really?
But she lives in your neighborhood, right?
We want to hang out with her, so show us where it is, okay?

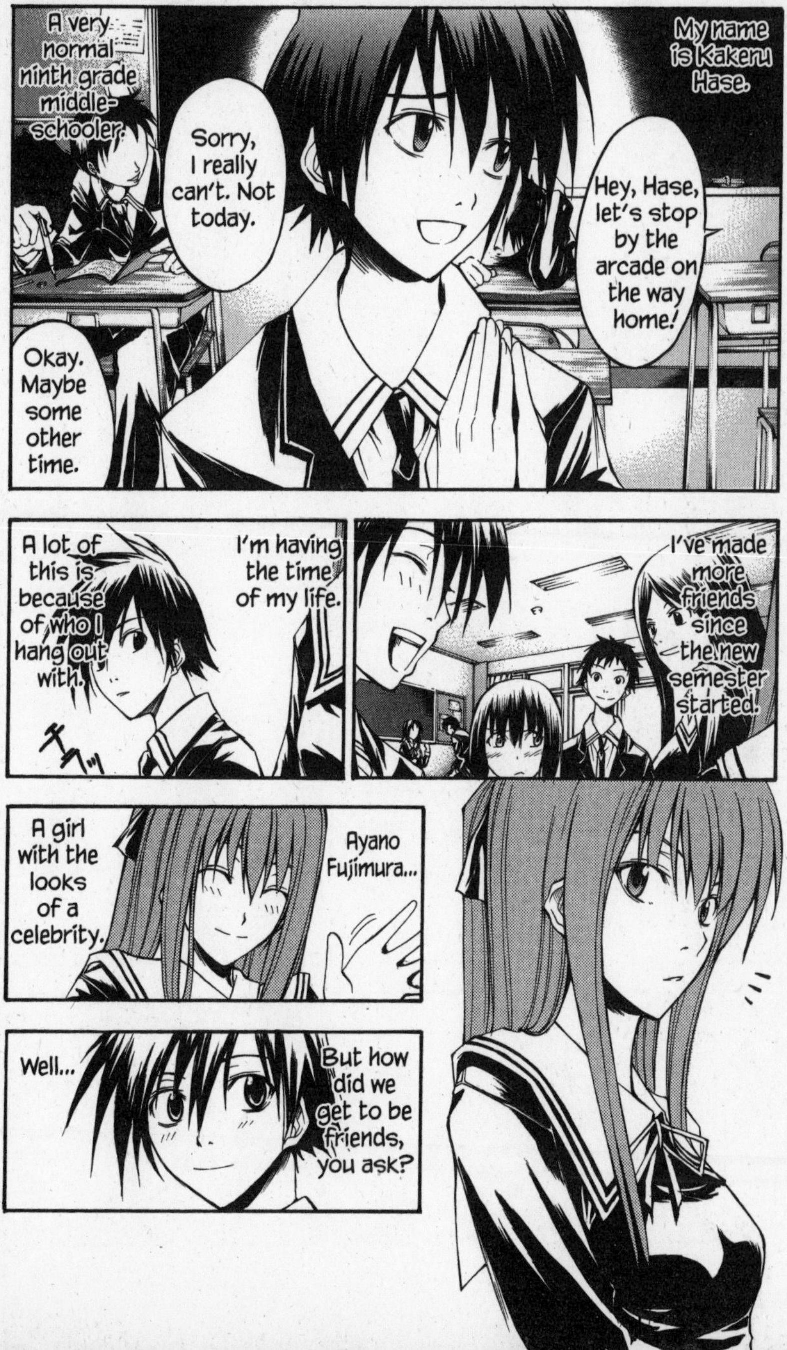
My name is Kakeru Hase.
Hey, Hase, let's stop by the arcade on the way home!
Sorry, I really can't. Not today.
A very normal ninth grade middle-schooler.
Okay. Maybe some other time.
I've made more friends since the new semester started!
I'm having the time of my life.
A lot of this is because of who I hang out with.
Ayano Fujimura...
A girl with the looks of a celebrity.
But how did we get to be friends, you ask?
Well...

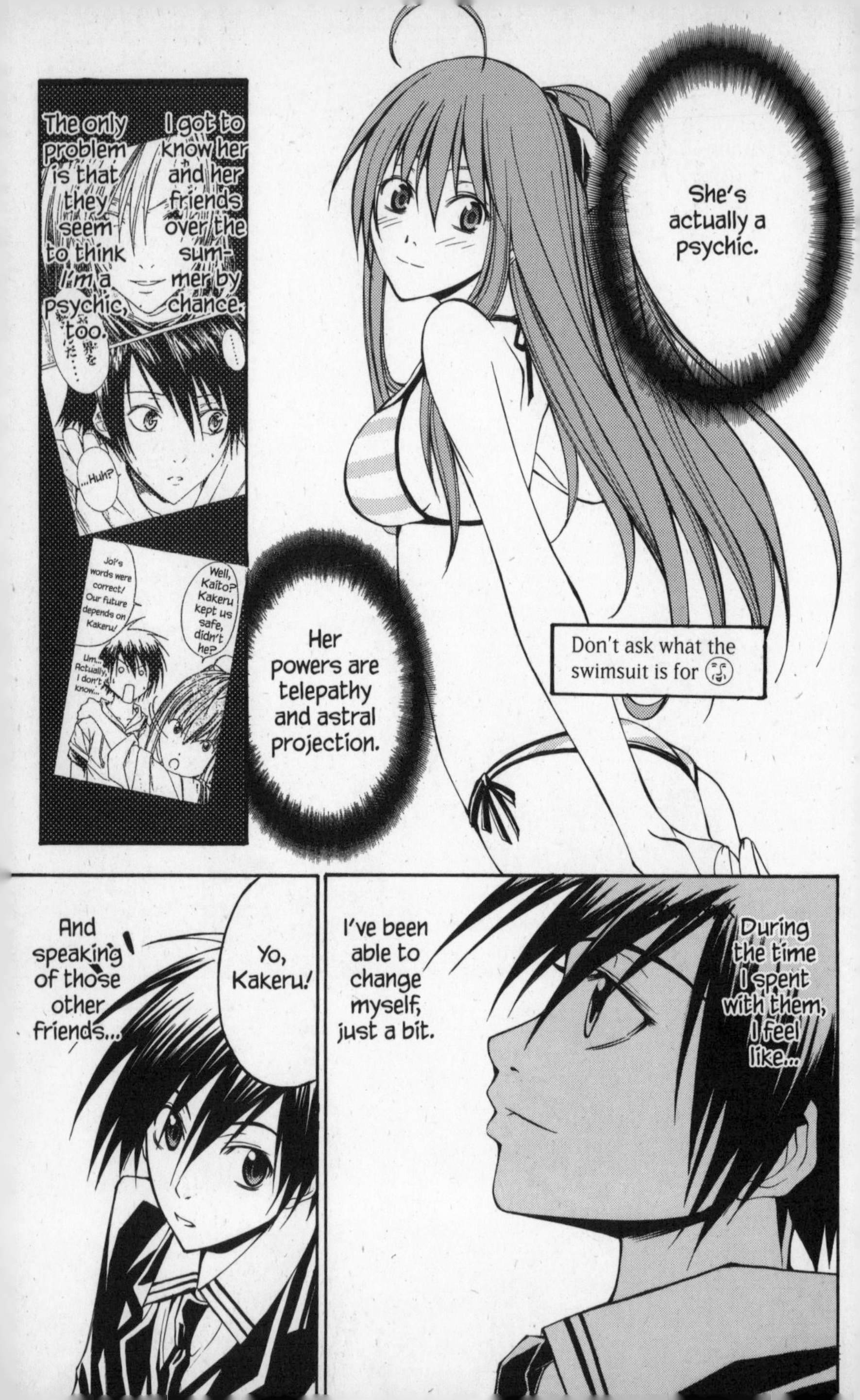
She's actually a psychic.
Her powers are telepathy and astral projection.
Don't ask what the swimsuit is for
I got to know her and her friends over the summer by chance.
The only problem is that they seem to think I'm a psychic, too.
...Huh?
Well, Kaito? Kakeru kept us safe, didn't he?
Joi's words were correct! Our future depends on Kakeru!
Um... Actually, I don't know...
During the time I spent with them, I feel like...
I've been able to change myself, just a bit.
Yo, Kakeru!
And speaking of those other friends...

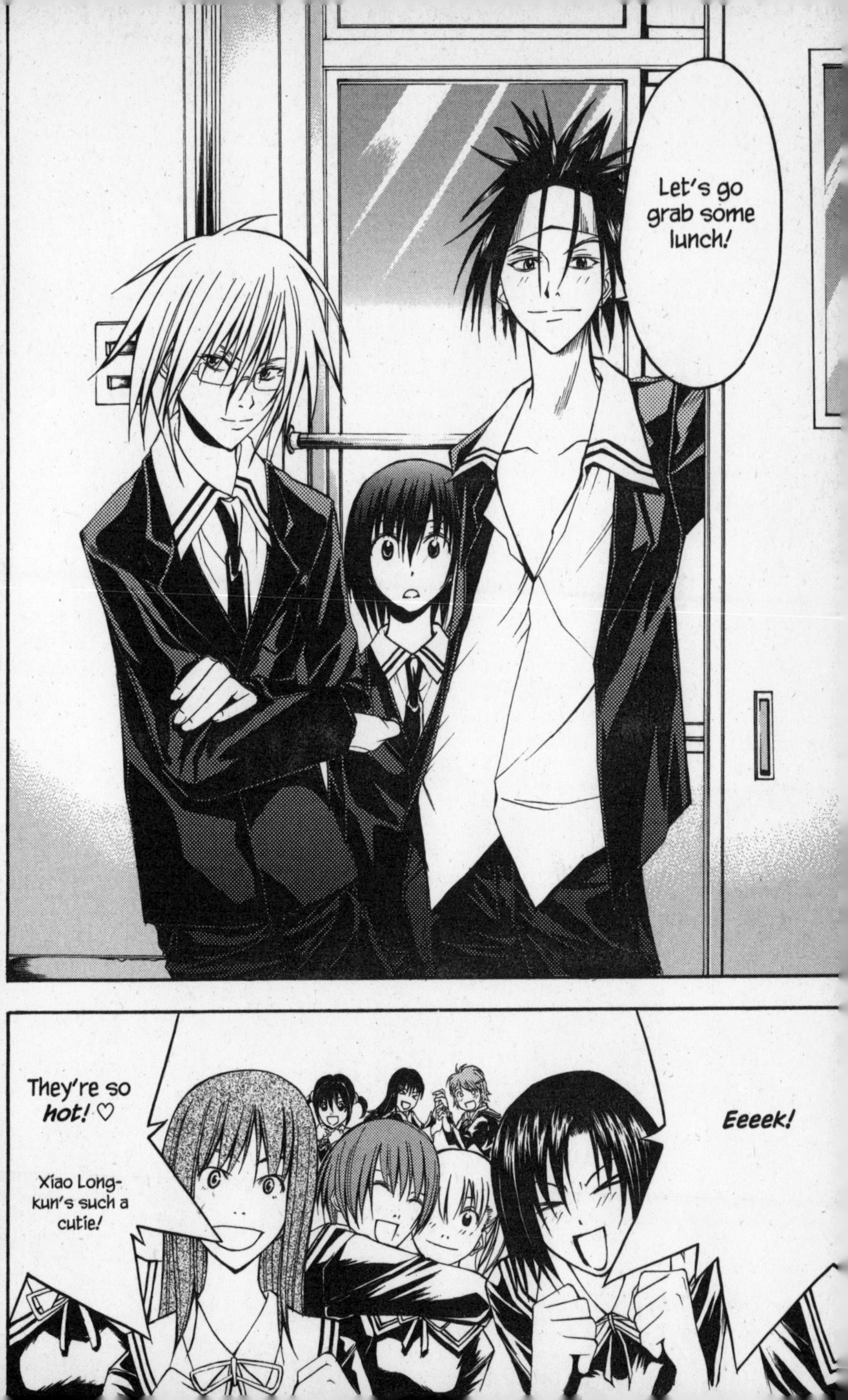
Let's go grab some lunch!
Eeeek!
They're so hot! ♡
Xiao Long-kun's such a cutie!

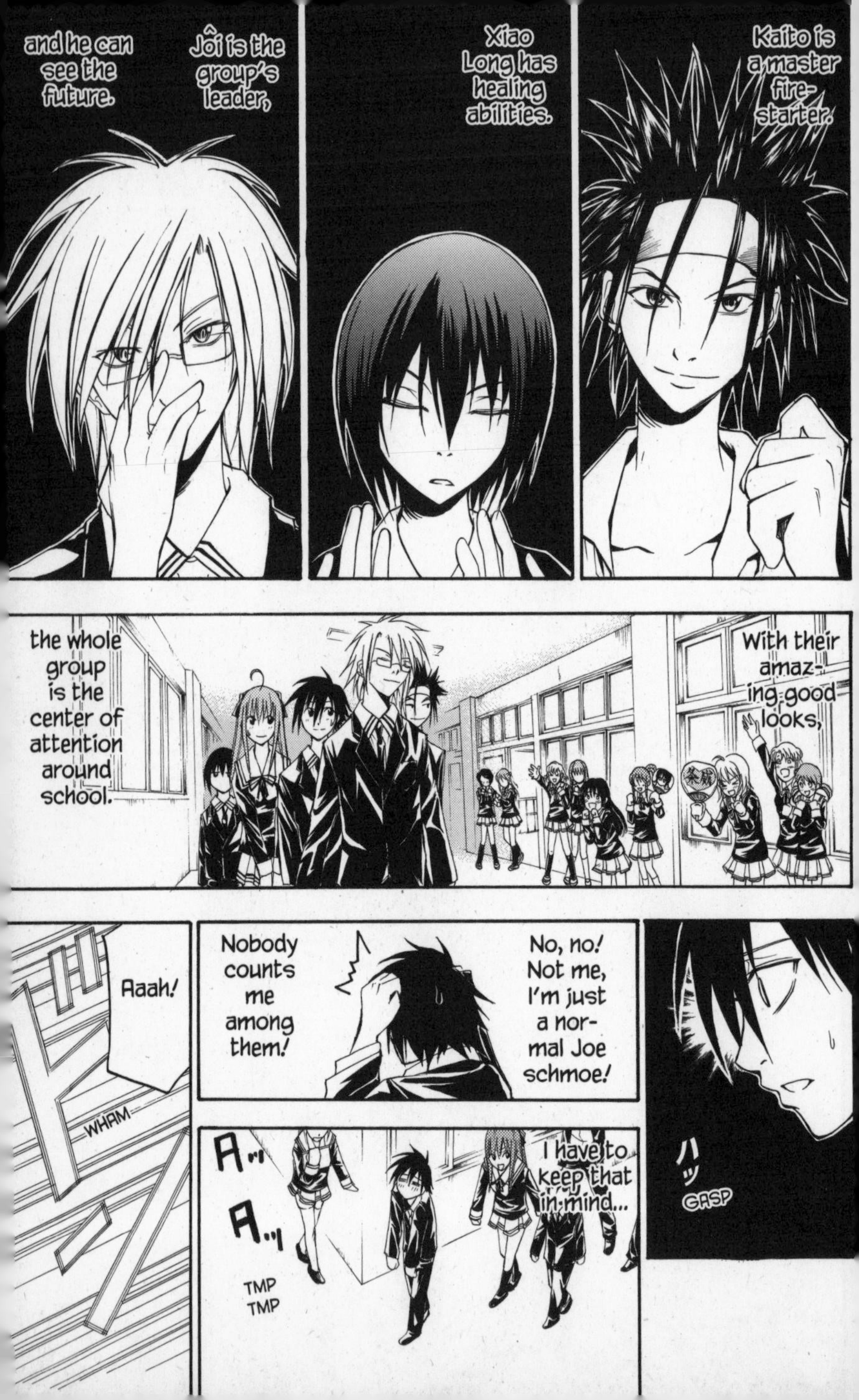
Kaito is a master fire-starter.
Xiao Long has healing abilities.
Jôi is the group's leader,
and he can see the future.
With their amazing good looks,
the whole group is the center of attention around school.
ハッ
GASP
No, no! Not me, I'm just a normal Joe schmoe!
Nobody counts me among them!
I have to keep that in mind...
A..
A..
TMP
TMP
Aaah!
WHAM

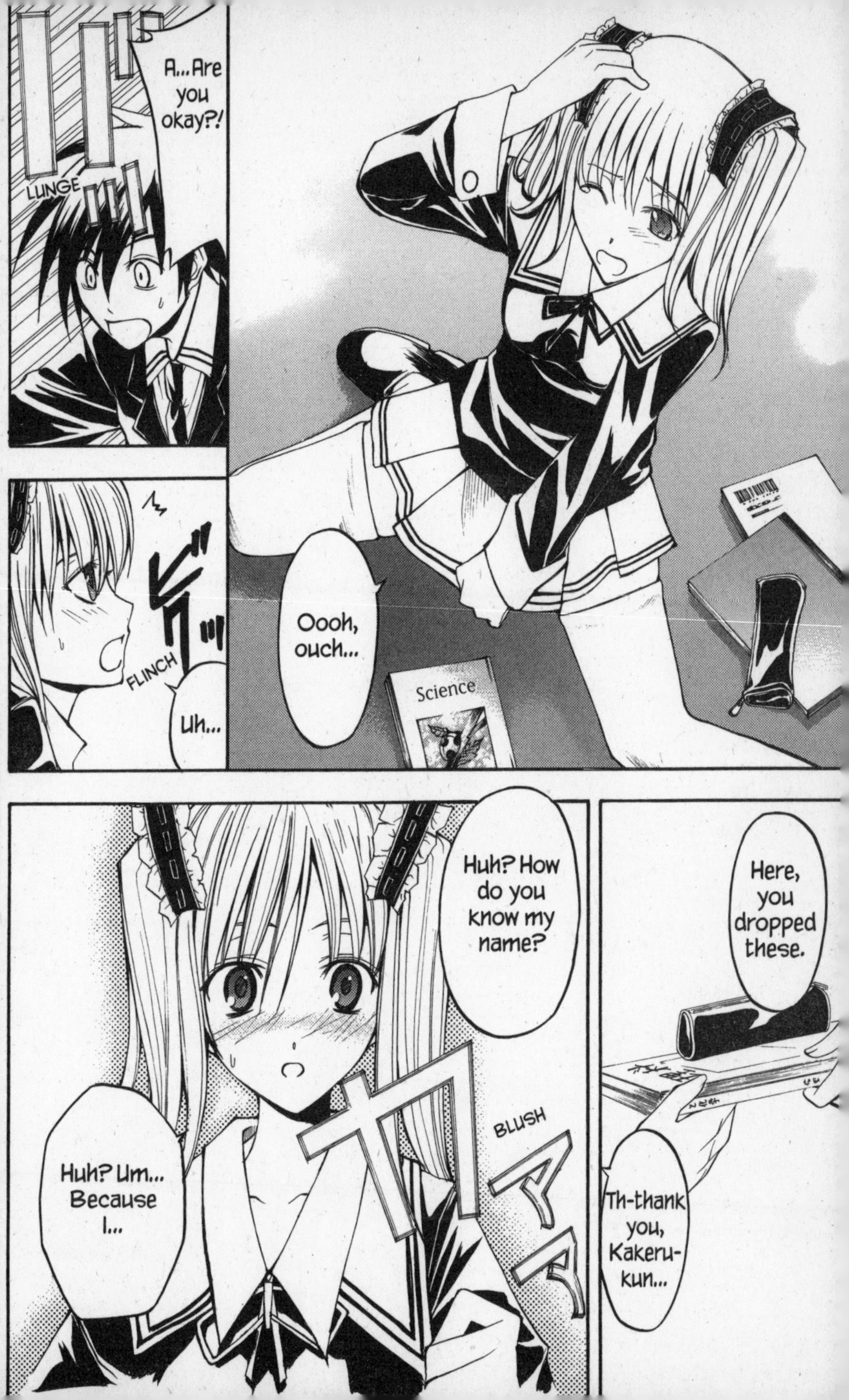
Oooh, ouch...
Science
A...Are you okay?!
LUNGE
FLINCH
Uh...
Here, you dropped these.
Th-thank you, Kakeru-kun...
Huh? How do you know my name?
BLUSH
Huh? Um... Because I...

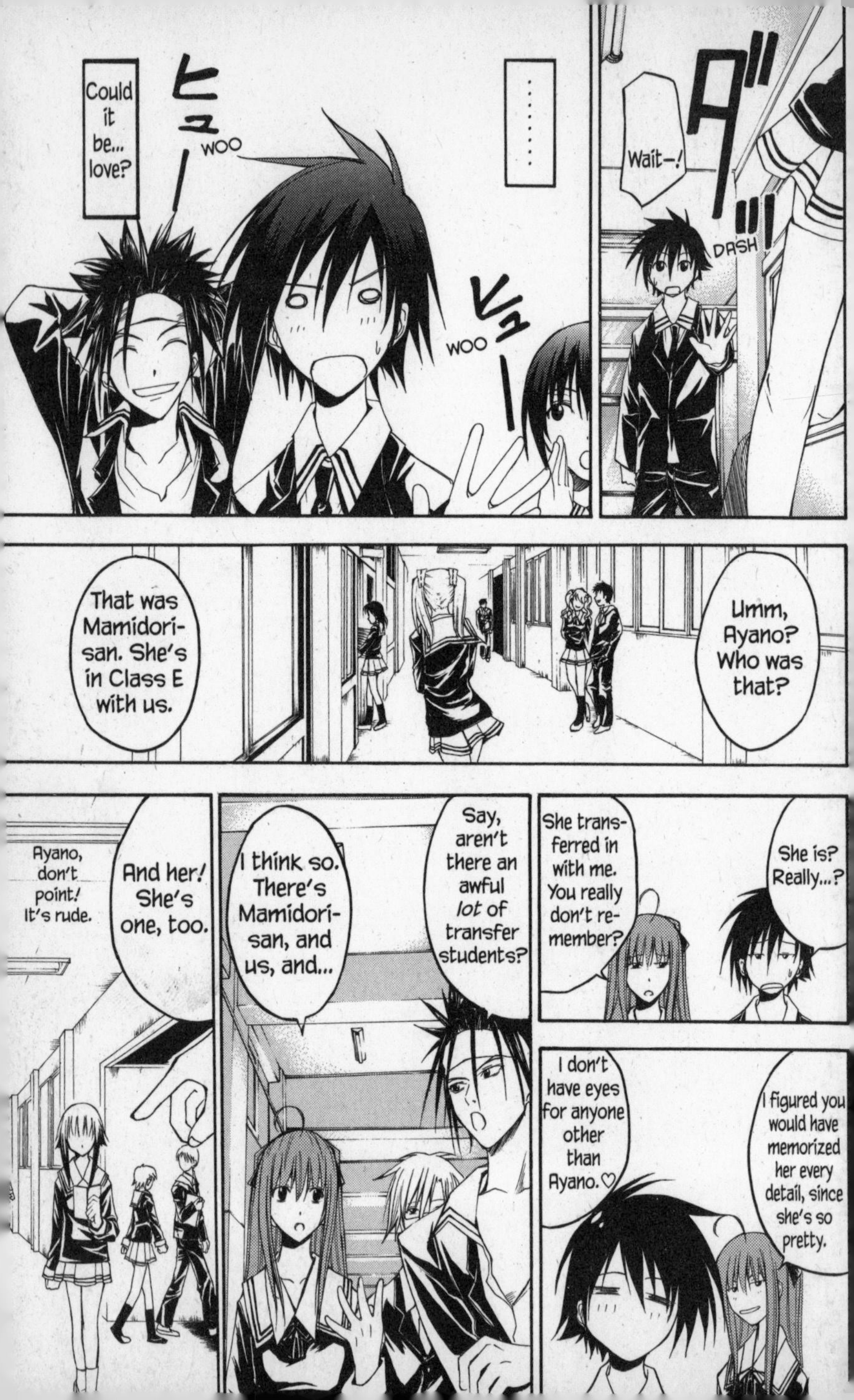
Wait—!
ダッ
DASH
……
ヒュー
WOO
Could it be... love?
ヒュー
WOO
Umm, Ayano? Who was that?
That was Mamidori-san. She's in Class E with us.
She is? Really...?
She transferred in with me. You really don't remember?
I figured you would have memorized her every detail, since she's so pretty.
I don't have eyes for anyone other than Ayano.♡
Say, aren't there an awful *lot* of transfer students?
I think so. There's Mamidori-san, and us, and...
And her! She's one, too.
Ayano, don't point! It's rude.

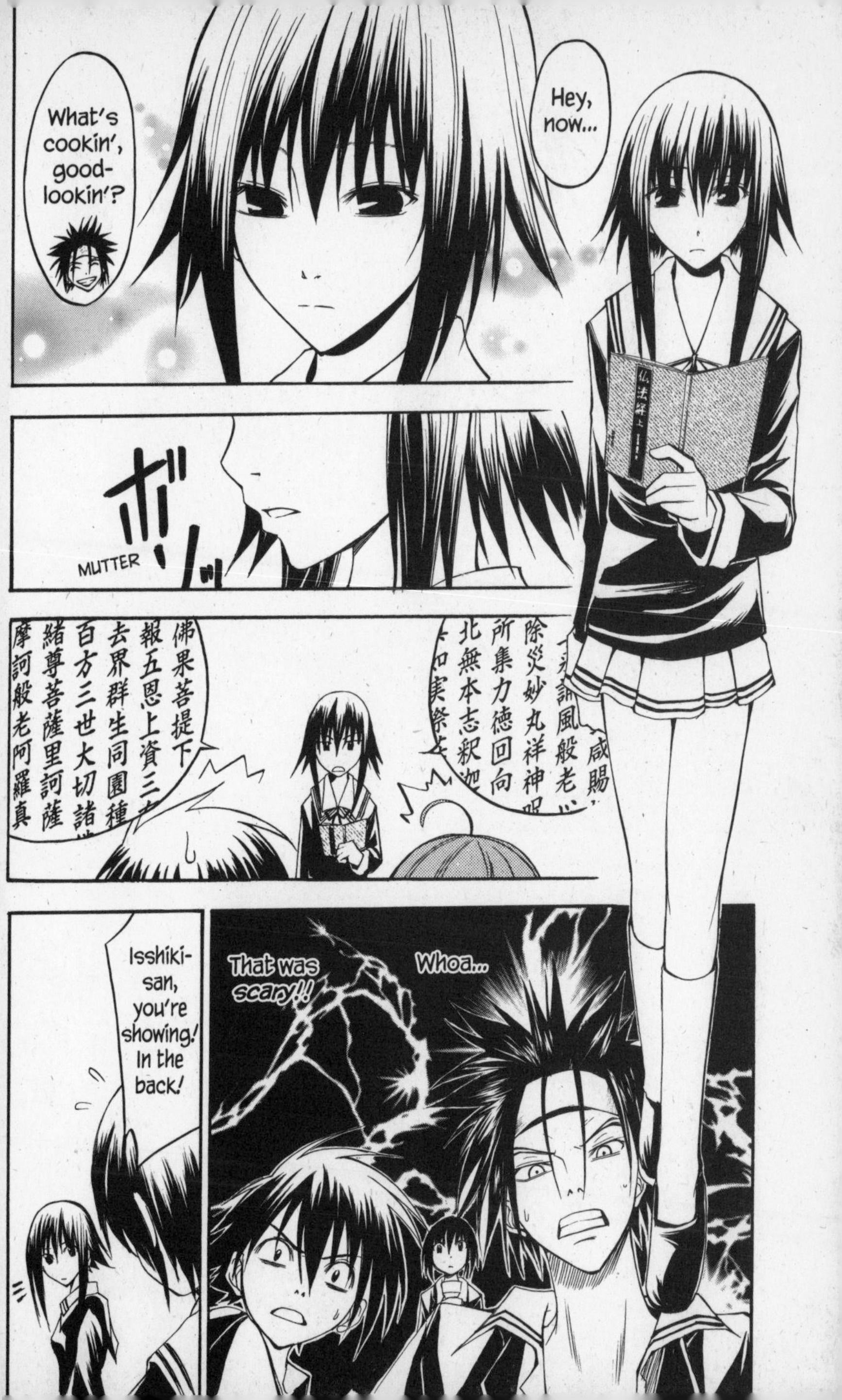
Hey, now...
What's cookin', good-lookin'?
MUTTER
咸賜
風般老
除災妙丸祥神
所集力徳回向
北無本志釈迦
佛果菩提下
報五恩上資三
去界群生同園種
百方三世大切諸
緒尊菩薩里訶薩
摩訶般老阿羅真
Whoa...
That was scary!!
Isshiki-san, you're showing! In the back!

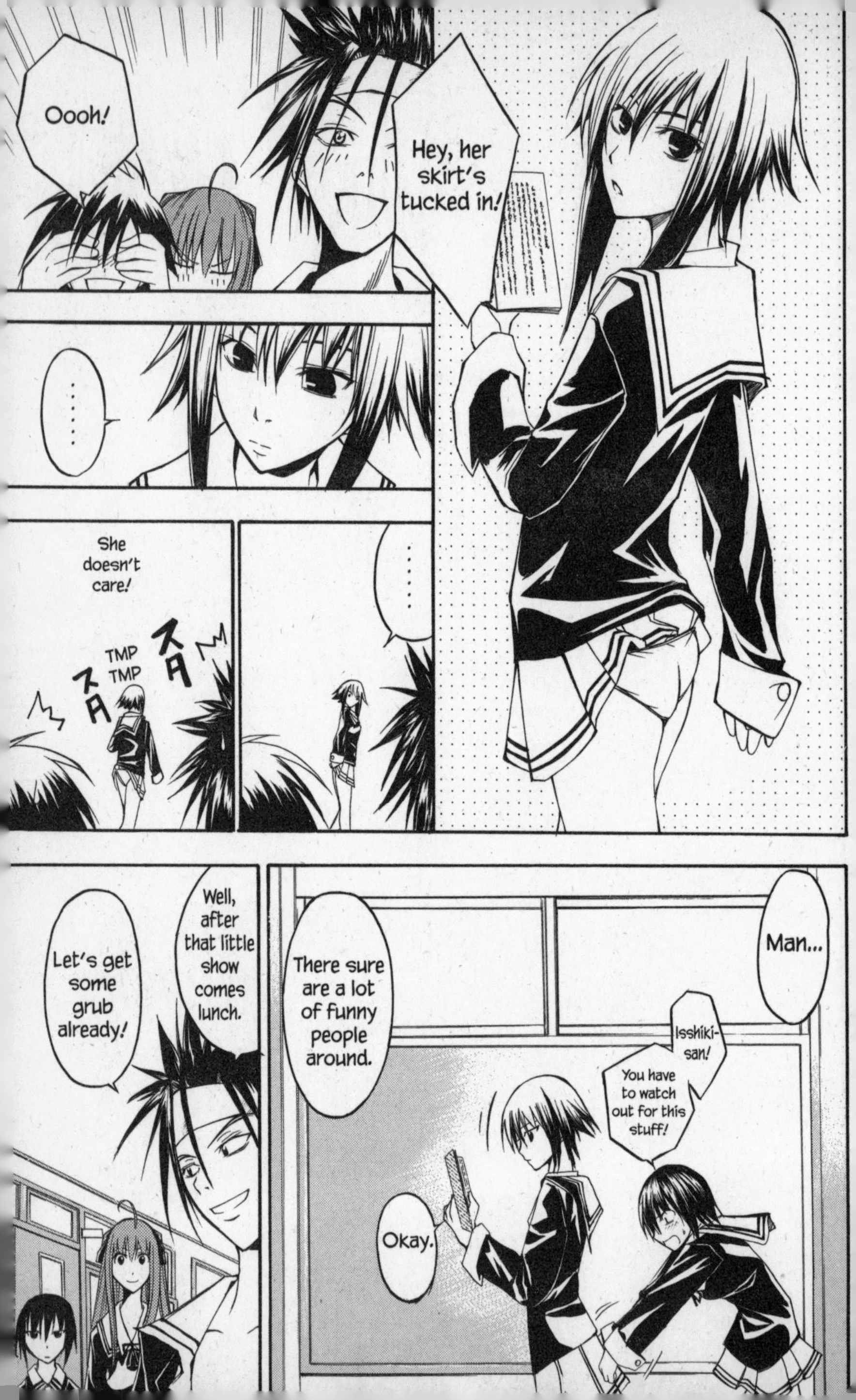
Hey, her skirt's tucked in!
Oooh!
......
......
She doesn't care!
TMP TMP
Man...
Isshiki-san!
You have to watch out for this stuff!
Okay.
There sure are a lot of funny people around.
Well, after that little show comes lunch.
Let's get some grub already!

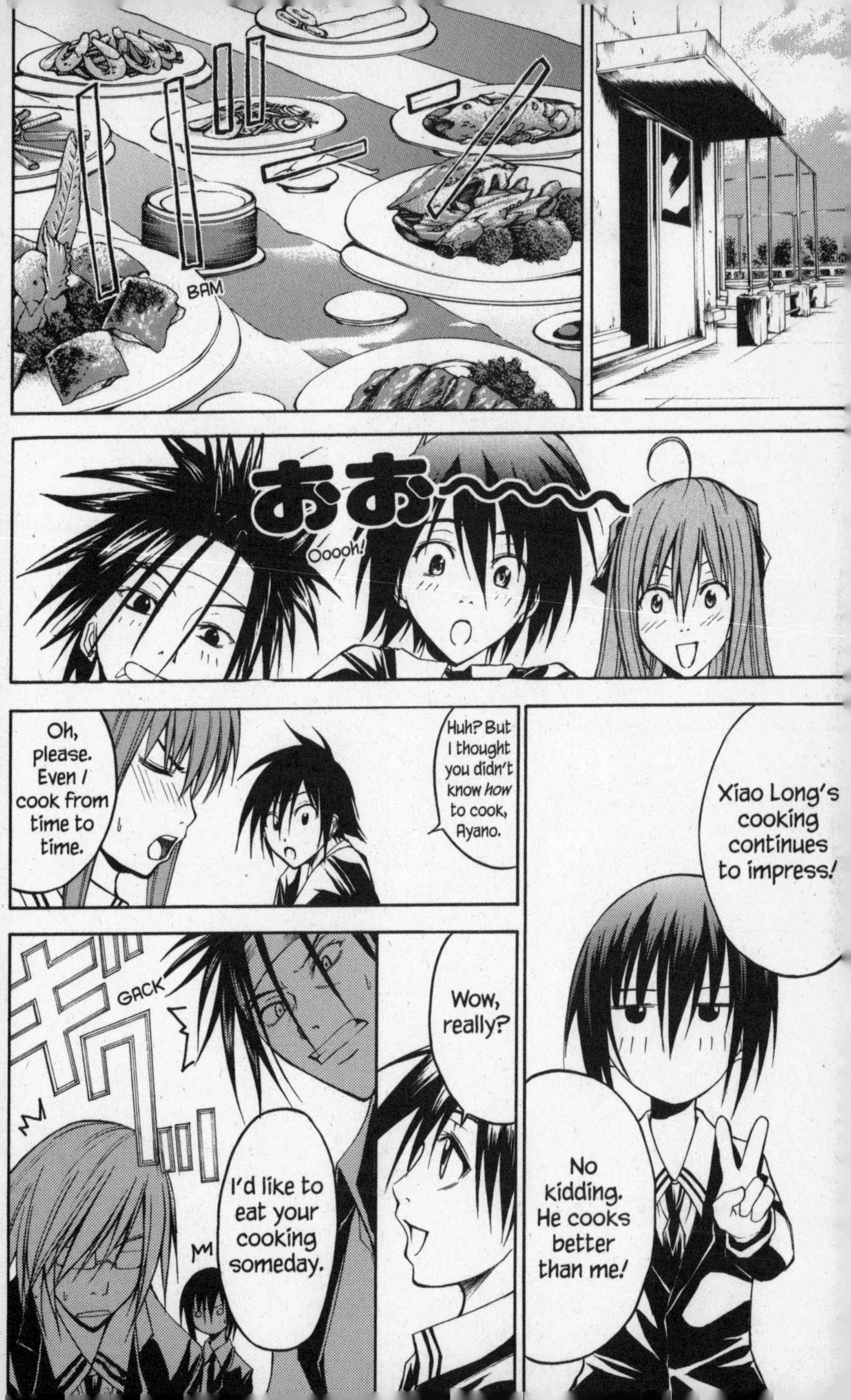
BAM
おお〜〜〜
Ooooh!
Xiao Long's cooking continues to impress!
No kidding. He cooks better than me!
Huh? But I thought you didn't know *how* to cook, Ayano.
Oh, please. Even *I* cook from time to time.
Wow, really?
I'd like to eat your cooking someday.
GACK

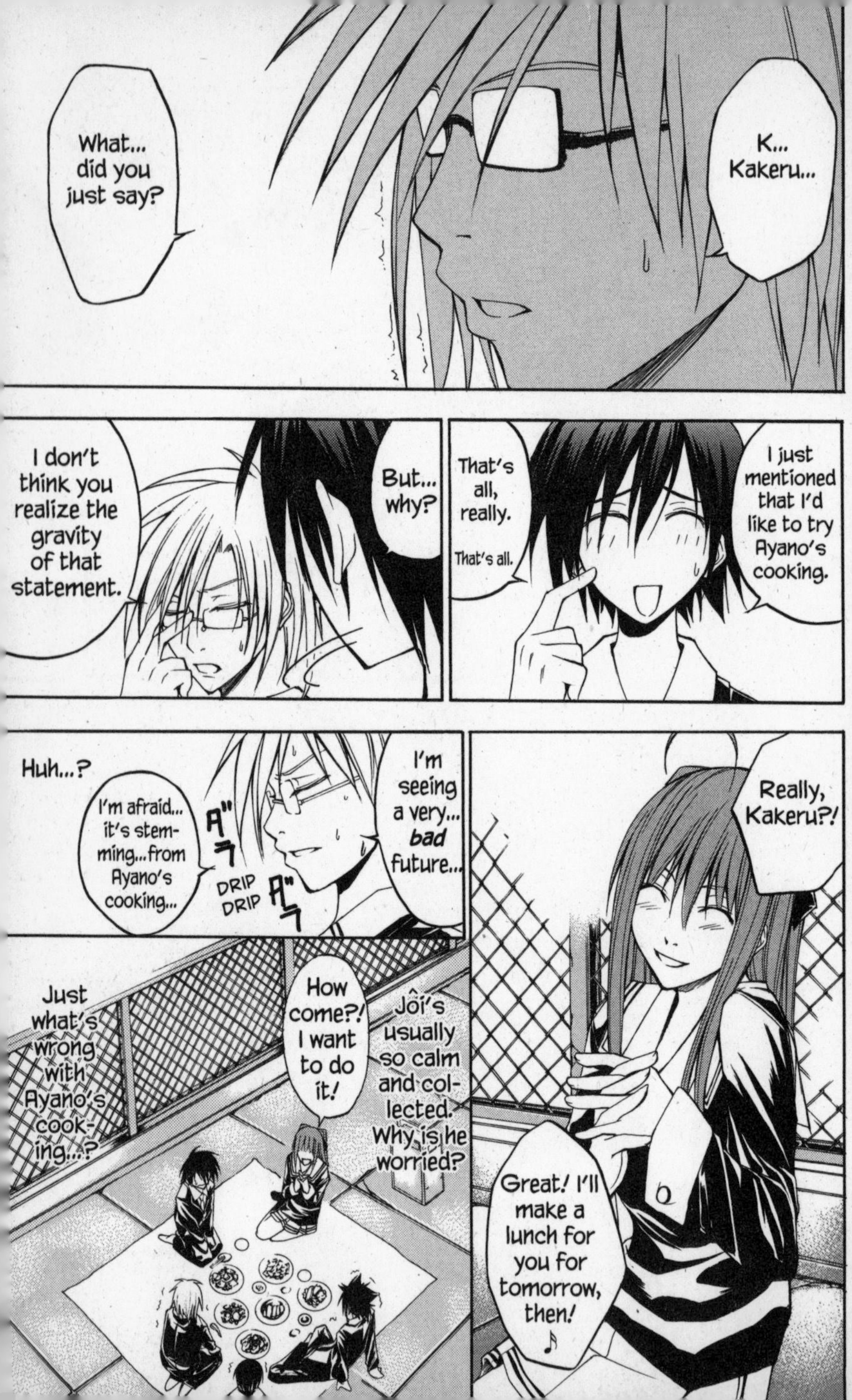
K... Kakeru...
What... did you just say?
I just mentioned that I'd like to try Ayano's cooking.
That's all, really.
That's all.
But... why?
I don't think you realize the gravity of that statement.
Really, Kakeru?!
Great! I'll make a lunch for you for tomorrow, then! ♪
I'm seeing a very... *bad* future...
DRIP DRIP
I'm afraid... it's stem-ming...from Ayano's cooking...
Huh...?
How come?! I want to do it!
Jôi's usually so calm and col-lected. Why is he worried?
Just what's wrong with Ayano's cook-ing...?

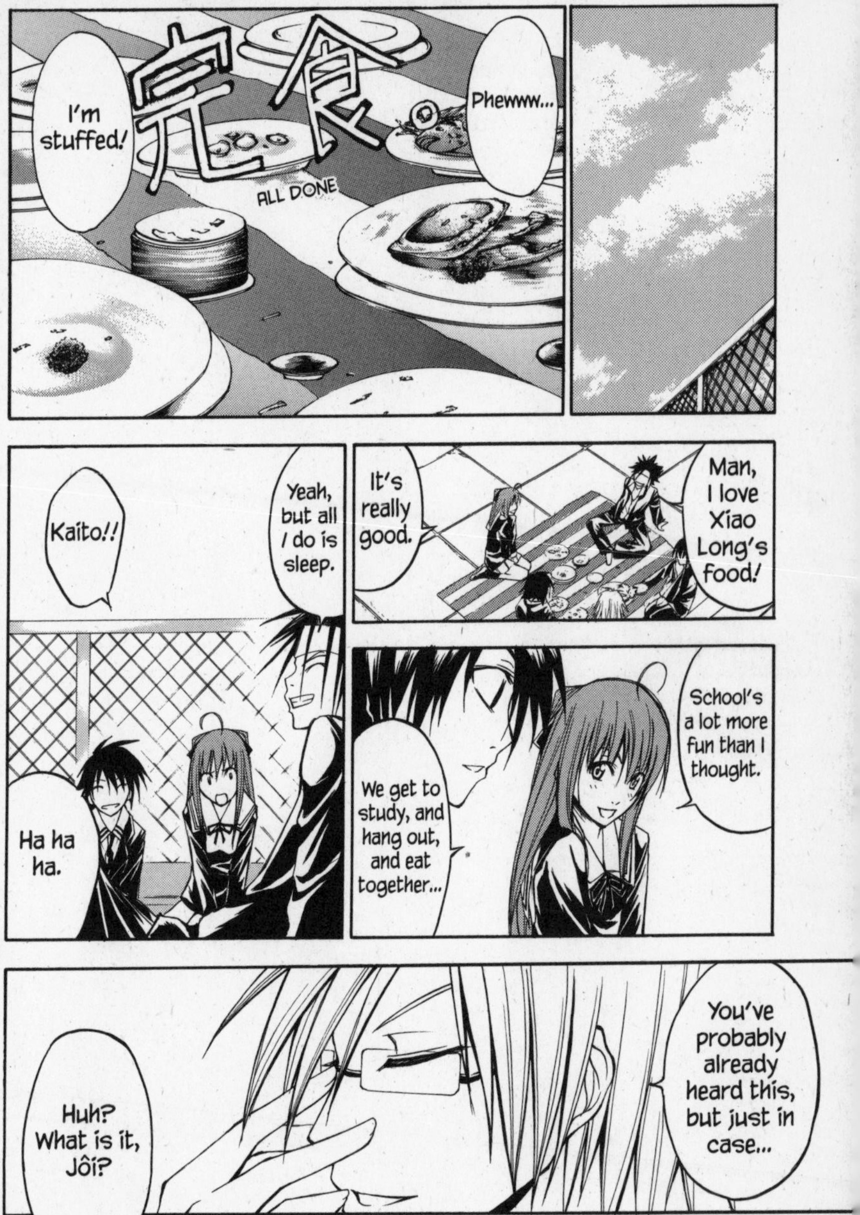
Phewww...
完食。
ALL DONE
I'm stuffed!
Man, I love Xiao Long's food!
It's really good.
Yeah, but all I do is sleep.
Kaito!!
School's a lot more fun than I thought.
We get to study, and hang out, and eat together...
Ha ha ha.
You've probably already heard this, but just in case...
Huh? What is it, Jôi?

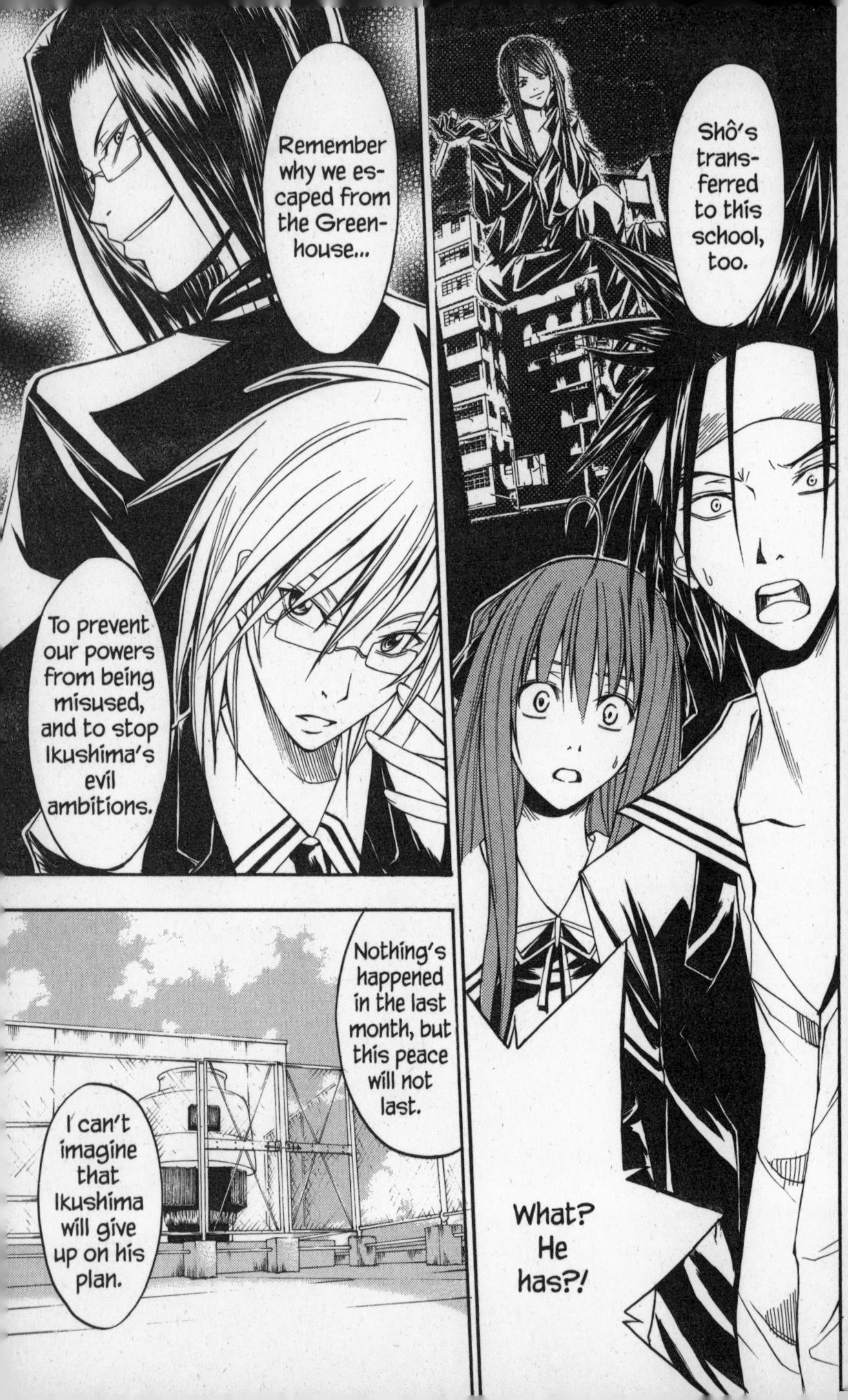
Shô's trans-ferred to this school, too.
What? He has?!
Remember why we es-caped from the Green-house...
To prevent our powers from being misused, and to stop Ikushima's evil ambitions.
Nothing's happened in the last month, but this peace will not last.
I can't imagine that Ikushima will give up on his plan.

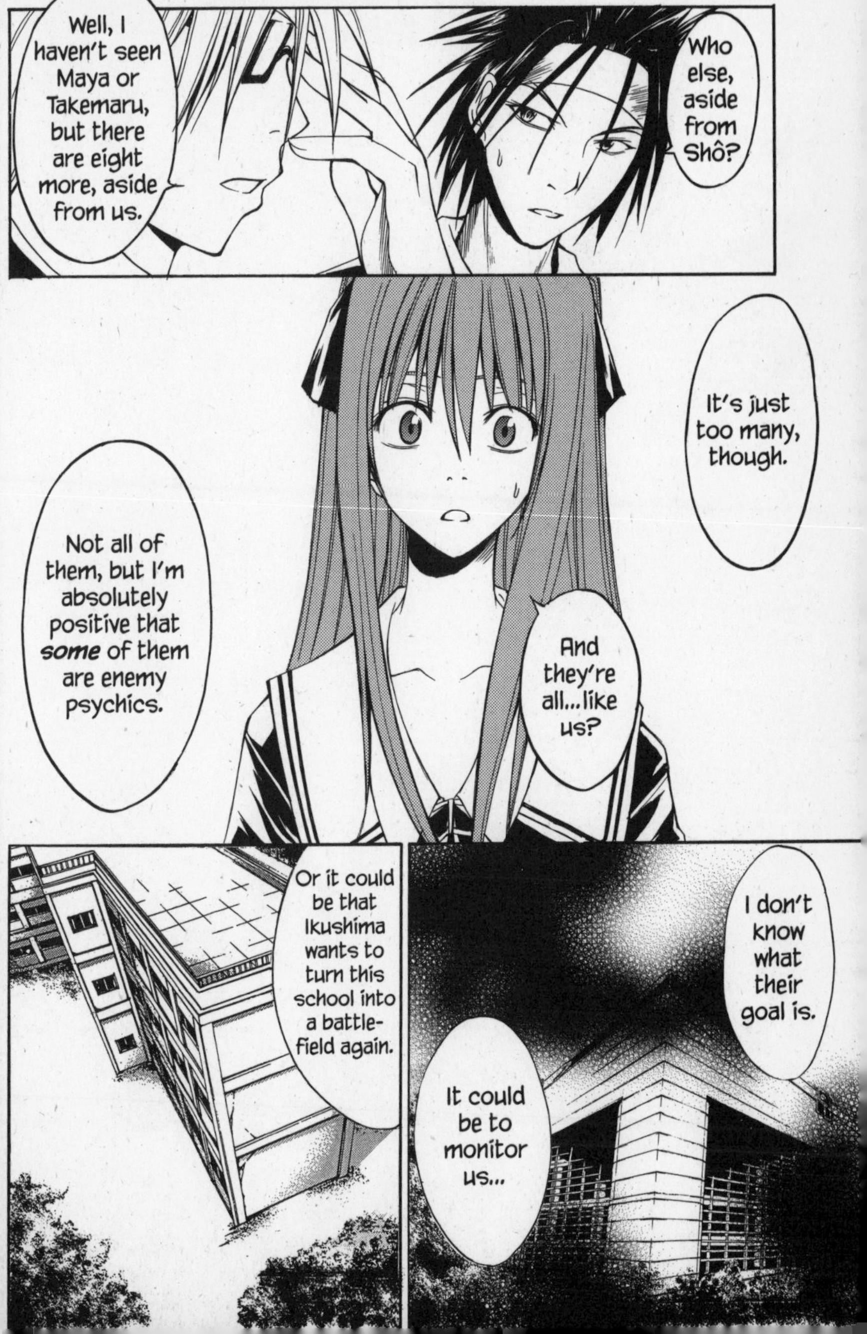
Who else, aside from Shô?
Well, I haven't seen Maya or Takemaru, but there are eight more, aside from us.
It's just too many, though.
And they're all...like us?
Not all of them, but I'm absolutely positive that *some* of them are enemy psychics.
I don't know what their goal is.
It could be to monitor us...
Or it could be that Ikushima wants to turn this school into a battle-field again.

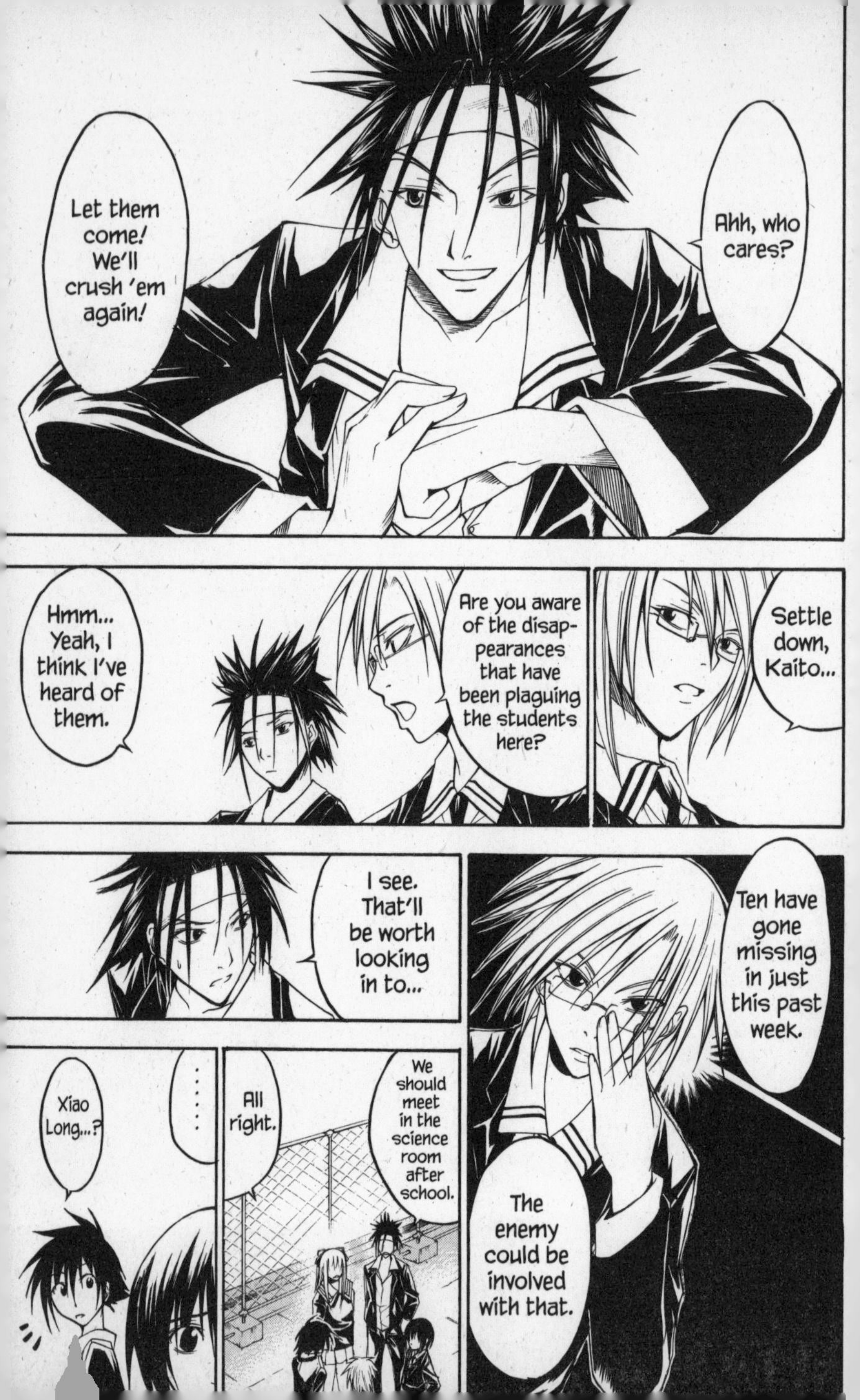
Ahh, who cares?
Let them come! We'll crush 'em again!
Settle down, Kaito...
Are you aware of the disappearances that have been plaguing the students here?
Hmm... Yeah, I think I've heard of them.
Ten have gone missing in just this past week.
The enemy could be involved with that.
I see. That'll be worth looking in to...
We should meet in the science room after school.
All right.
......
Xiao Long...?

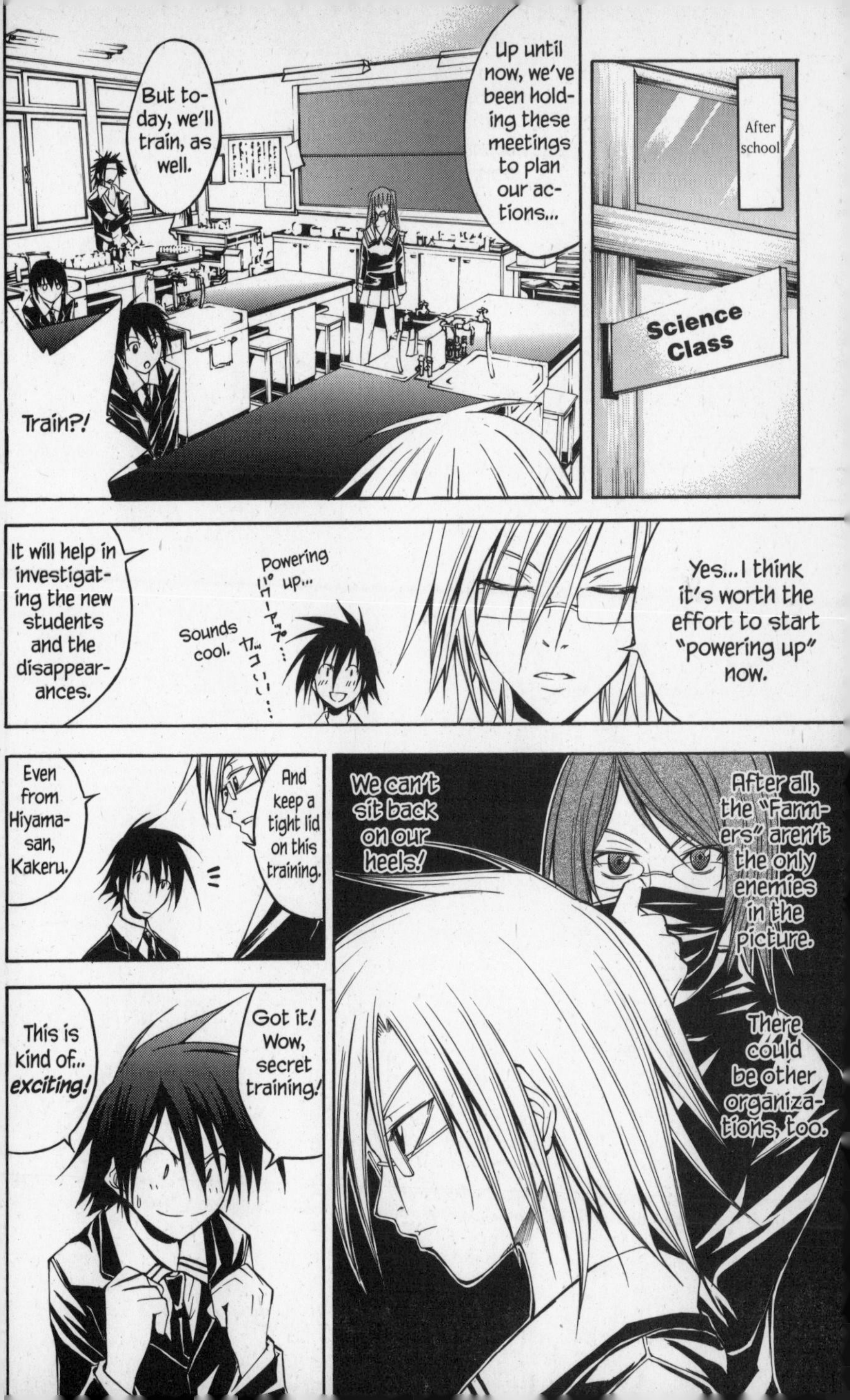
After school
Science Class
Up until now, we've been holding these meetings to plan our actions...
But today, we'll train, as well.
Train?!
Yes...I think it's worth the effort to start "powering up" now.
Powering up...
パワーアップ…
Sounds cool.
カッコいい…
It will help in investigating the new students and the disappearances.
After all, the "Farmers" aren't the only enemies in the picture.
We can't sit back on our heels!
There could be other organizations, too.
And keep a tight lid on this training.
Even from Hiyama-san, Kakeru.
Got it! Wow, secret training!
This is kind of... *exciting!*

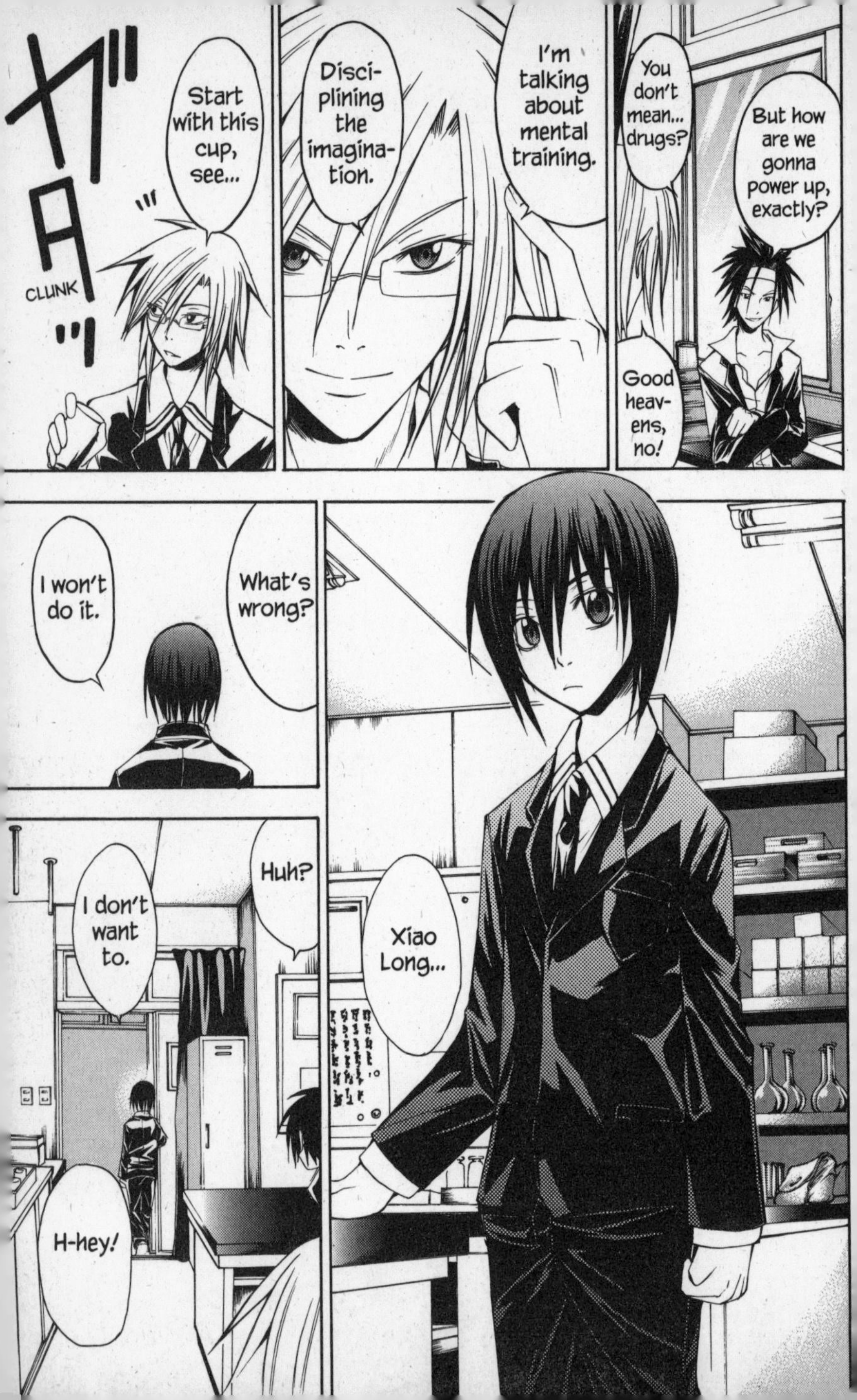
But how are we gonna power up, exactly?
You don't mean... drugs?
Good heavens, no!
I'm talking about mental training.
Disciplining the imagination.
Start with this cup, see...
CLUNK
Xiao Long...
What's wrong?
I won't do it.
Huh?
I don't want to.
H-hey!

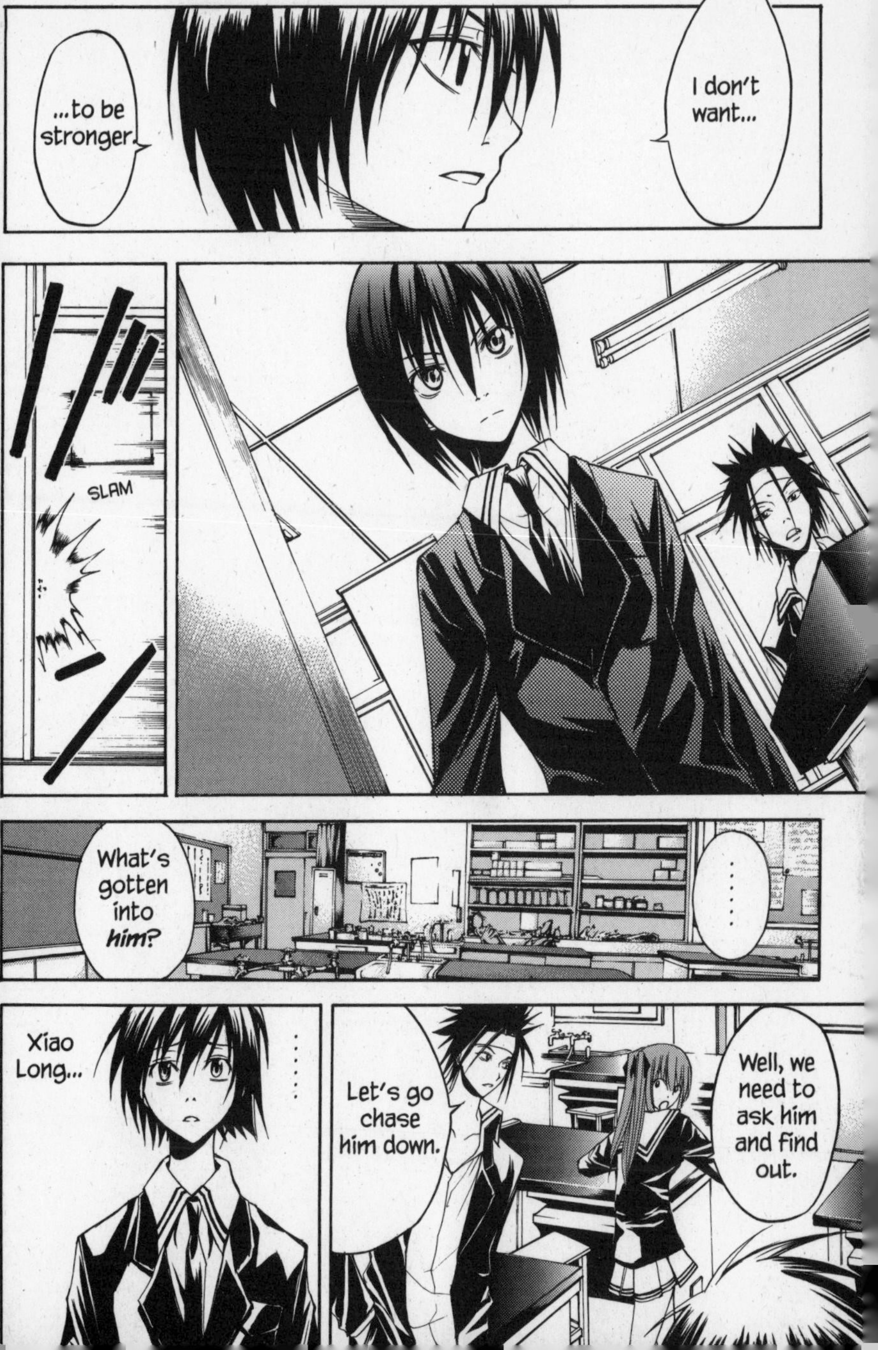
I don't want...
...to be stronger.
SLAM
What's gotten into *him*?
......
Well, we need to ask him and find out.
Let's go chase him down.
......
Xiao Long...

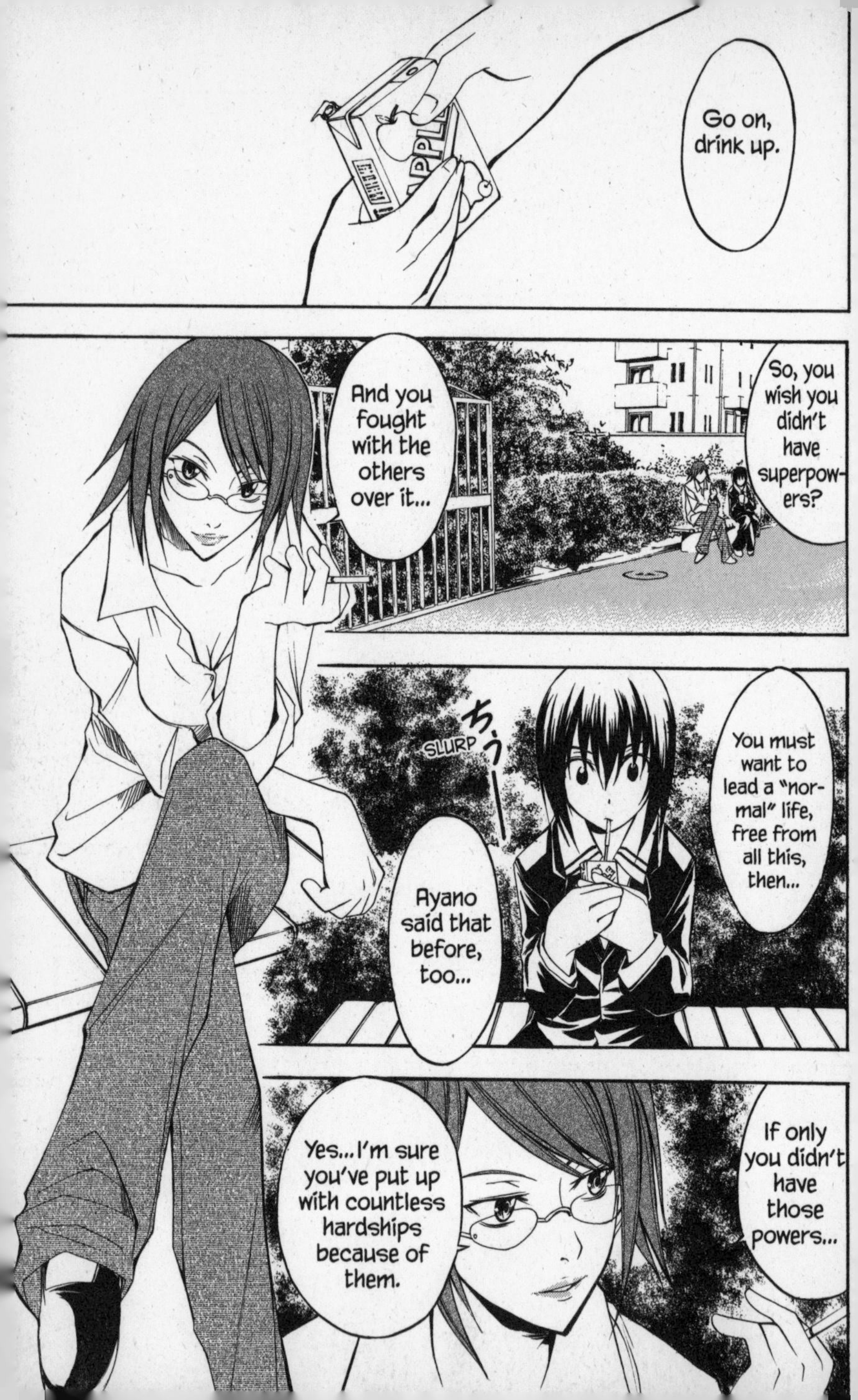
Go on, drink up.
So, you wish you didn't have superpowers?
And you fought with the others over it...
You must want to lead a "normal" life, free from all this, then...
ちうー
SLURP
Ayano said that before, too...
If only you didn't have those powers...
Yes...I'm sure you've put up with countless hardships because of them.

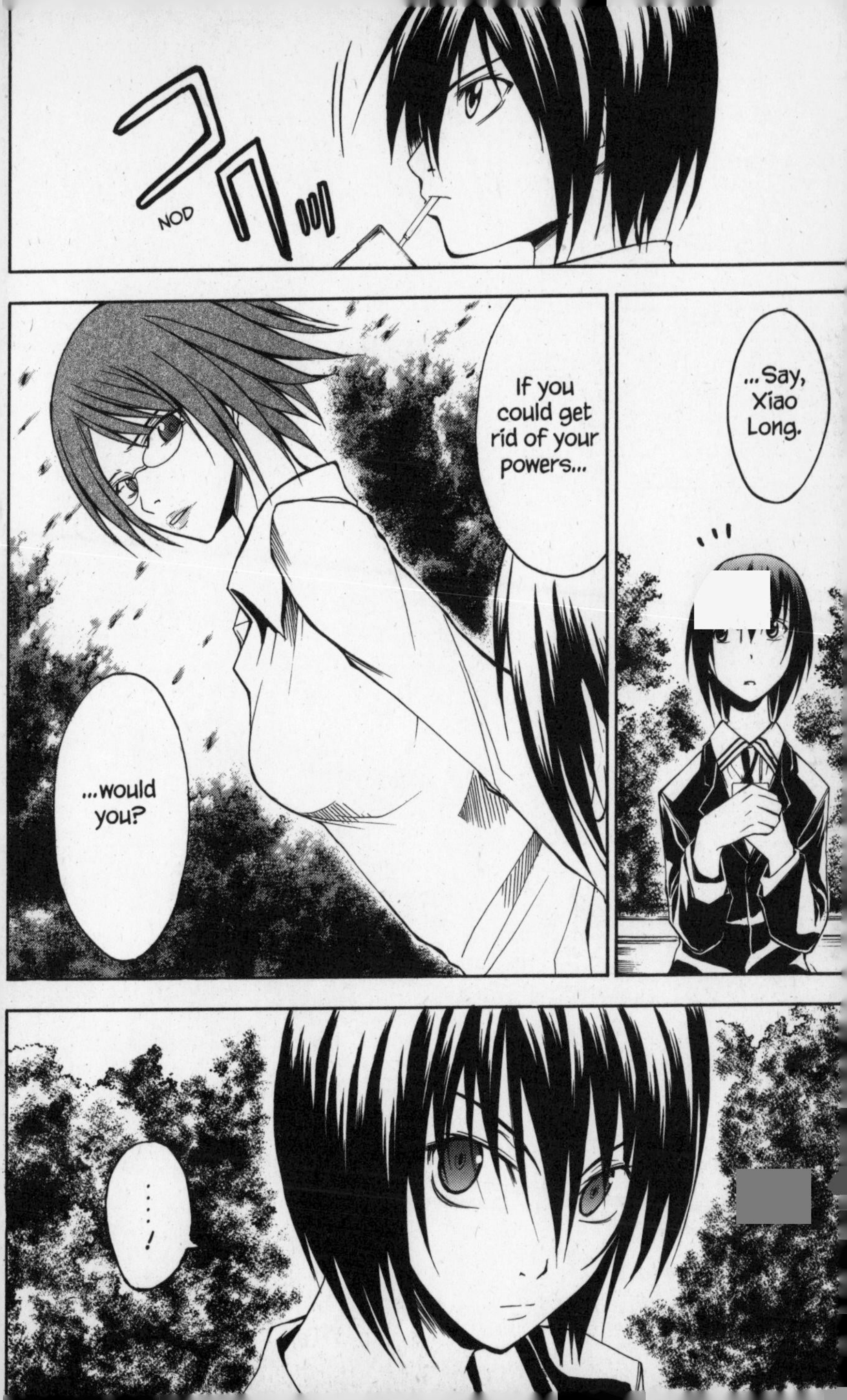
NOD
...Say, Xiao Long.
If you could get rid of your powers...
...would you?
...!

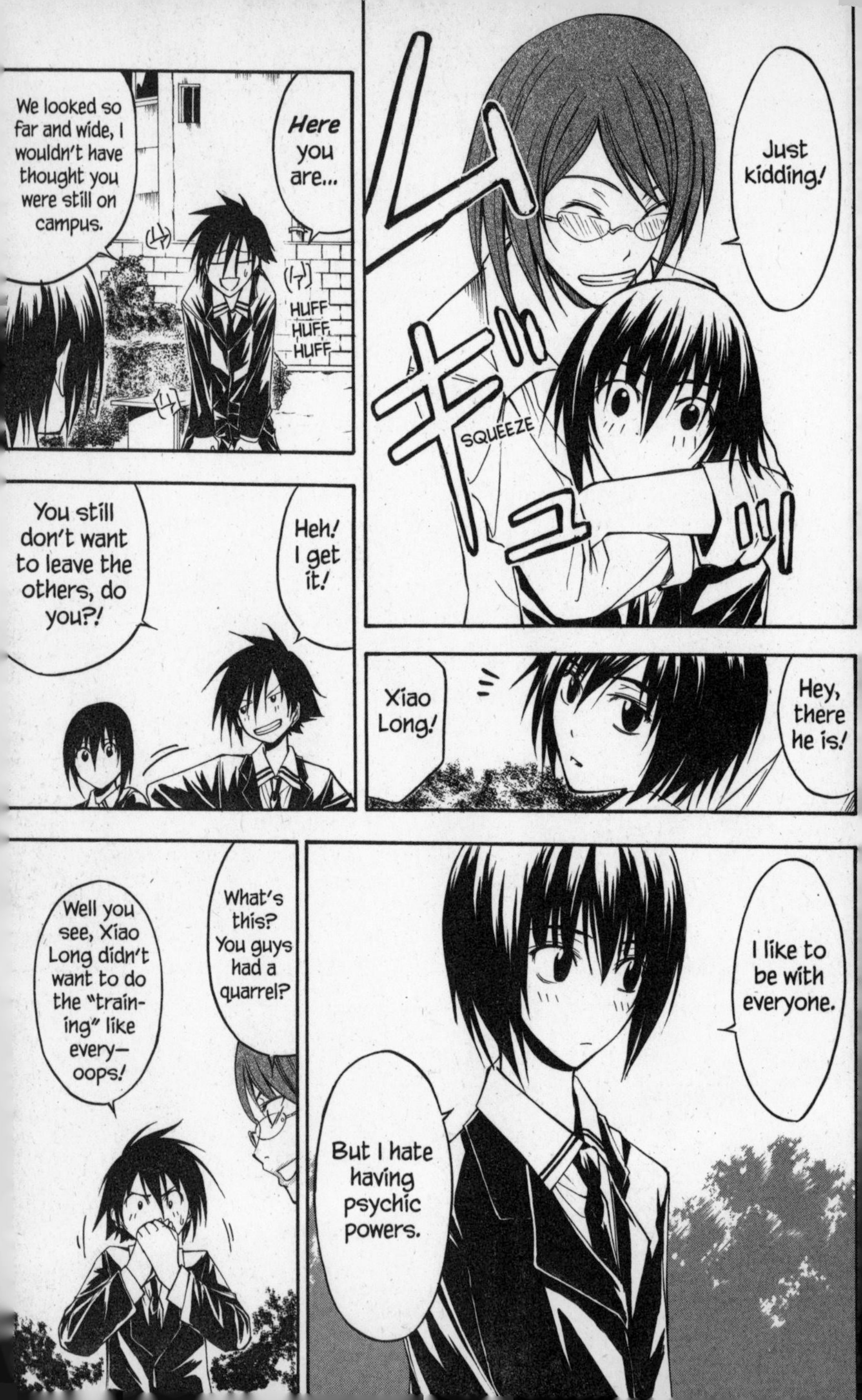

Just kidding!
SQUEEZE
Hey, there he is!
Xiao Long!
Here you are...
We looked so far and wide, I wouldn't have thought you were still on campus.
HUFF HUFF HUFF
Heh! I get it!
You still don't want to leave the others, do you?!
I like to be with everyone.
But I hate having psychic powers.
What's this? You guys had a quarrel?
Well you see, Xiao Long didn't want to do the "train-ing" like every— oops!

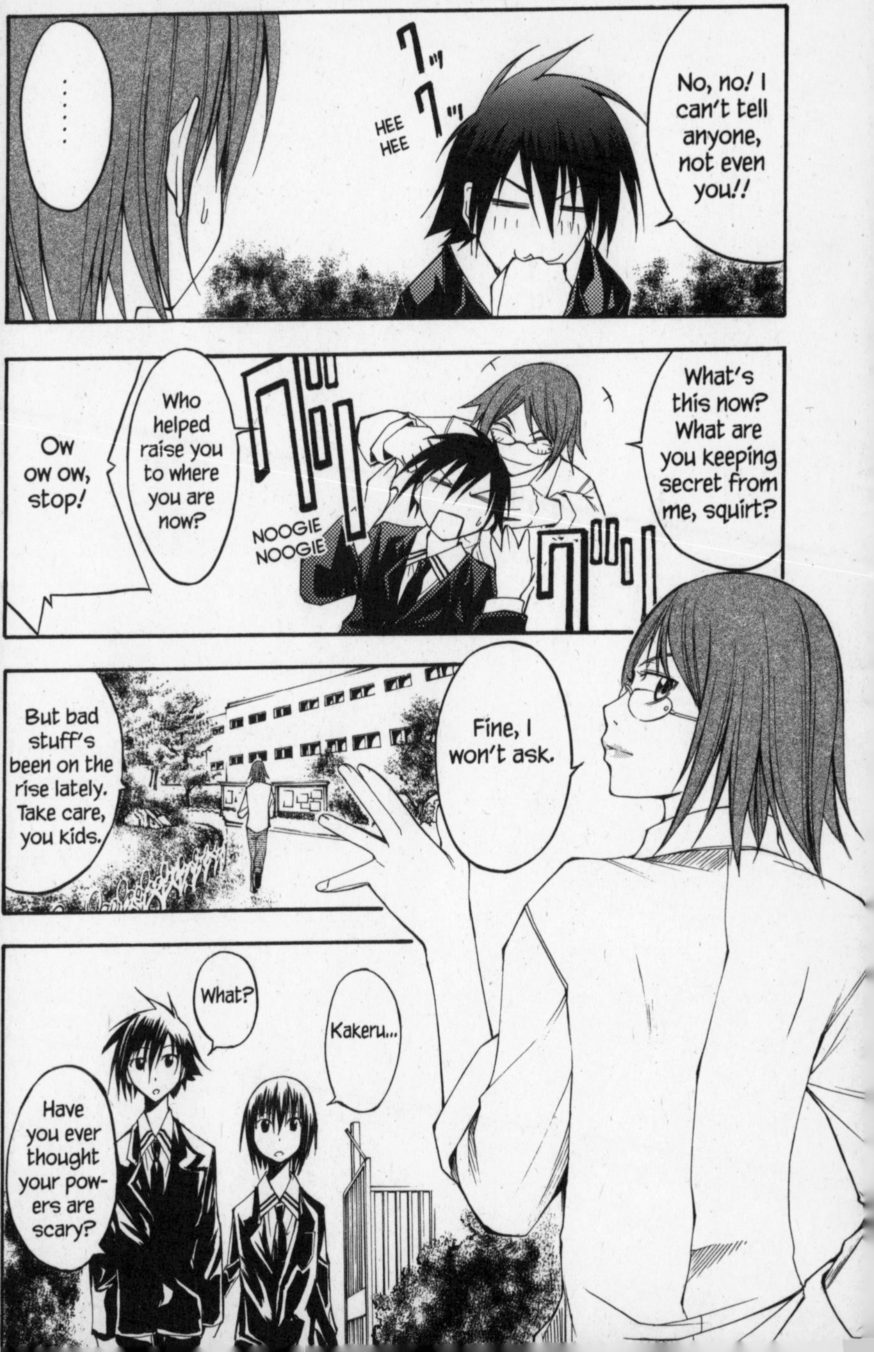
No, no! I can't tell anyone, not even you!!
HEE HEE
......
What's this now? What are you keeping secret from me, squirt?
NOOGIE NOOGIE
Who helped raise you to where you are now?
Ow ow ow, stop!
Fine, I won't ask.
But bad stuff's been on the rise lately. Take care, you kids.
Kakeru...
What?
Have you ever thought your powers are scary?

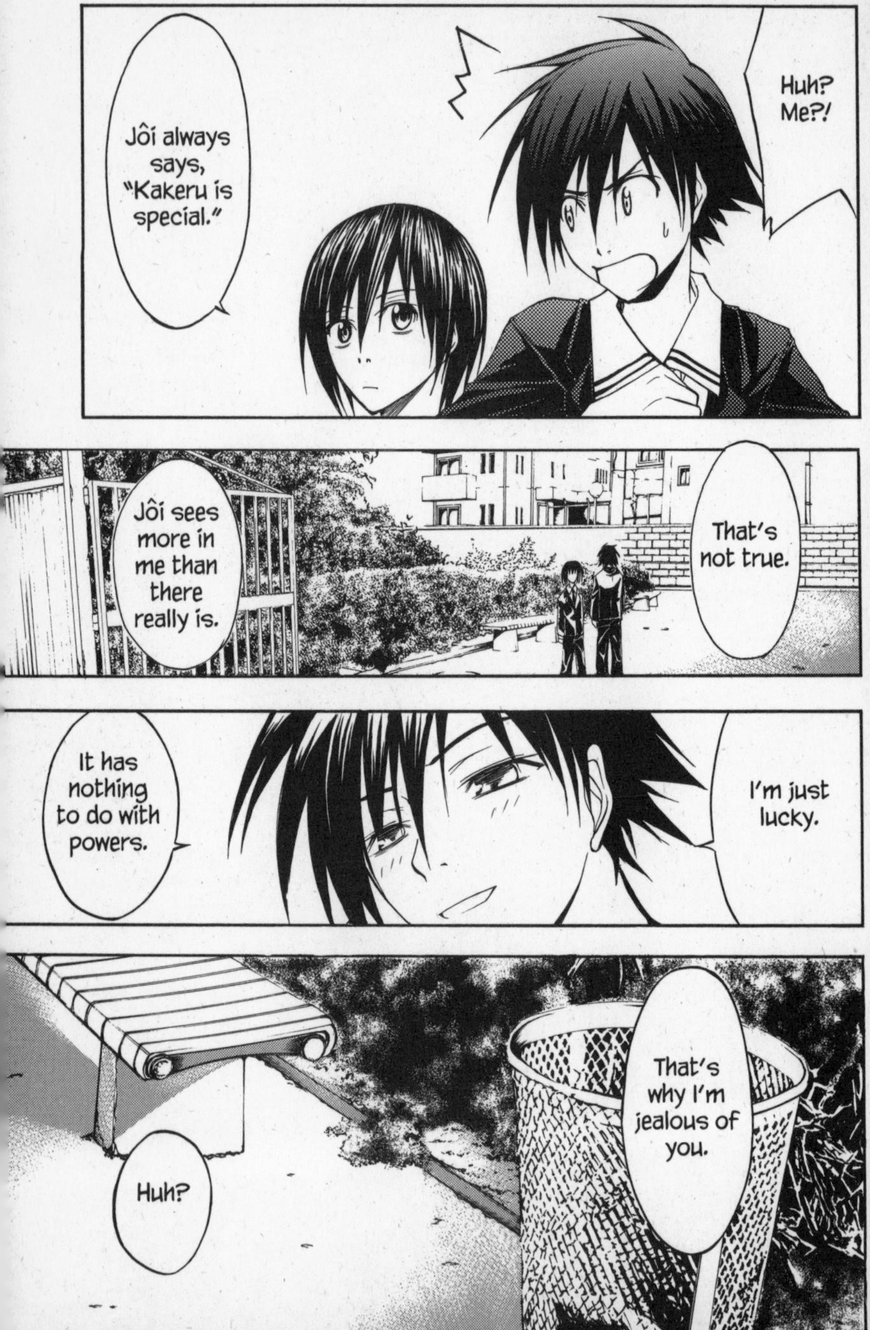
Huh? Me?!
Jôi always says, "Kakeru is special."
That's not true.
Jôi sees more in me than there really is.
I'm just lucky.
It has nothing to do with powers.
That's why I'm jealous of you.
Huh?

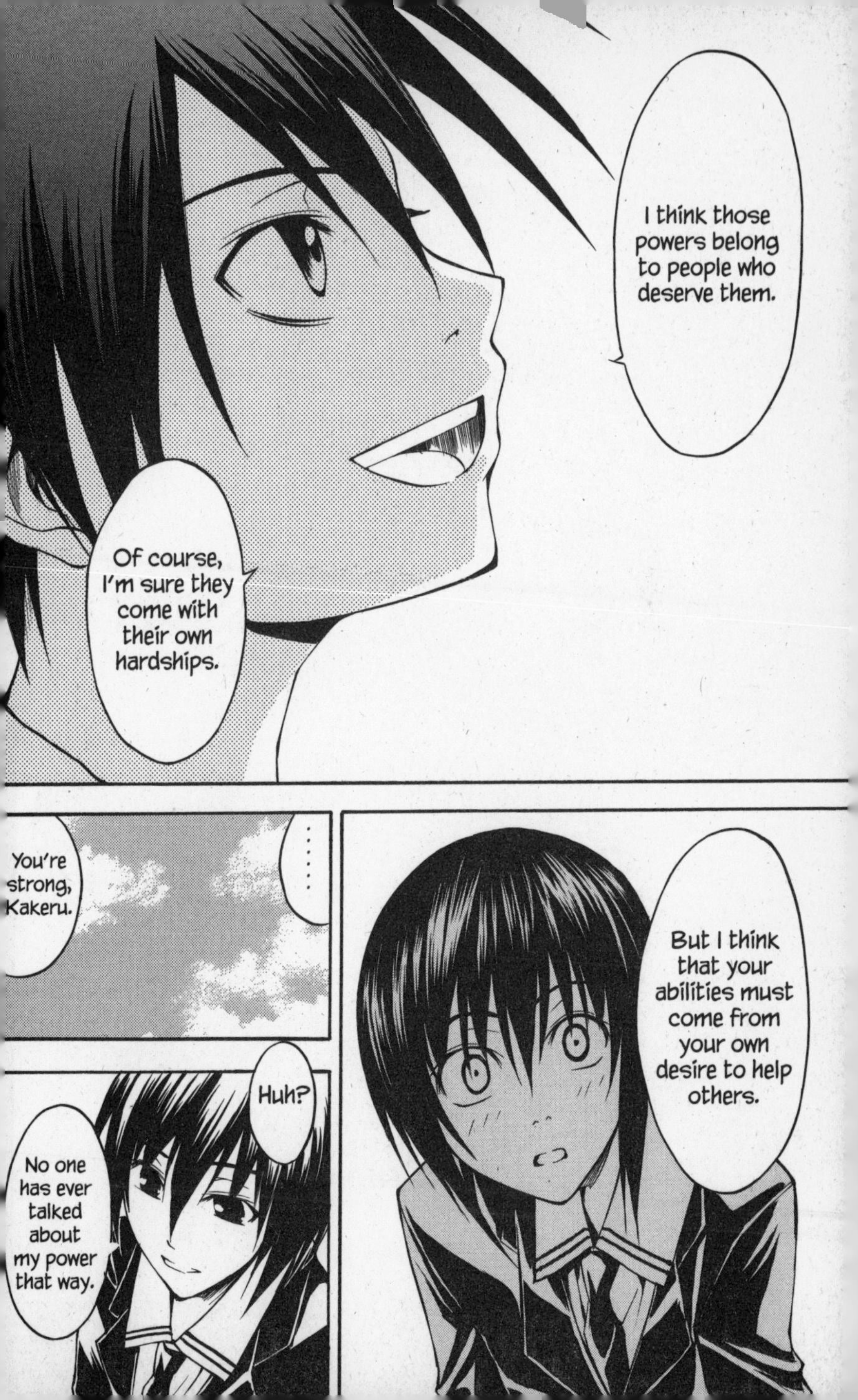
I think those powers belong to people who deserve them.
Of course, I'm sure they come with their own hardships.
But I think that your abilities must come from your own desire to help others.
......
You're strong, Kakeru.
Huh?
No one has ever talked about my power that way.

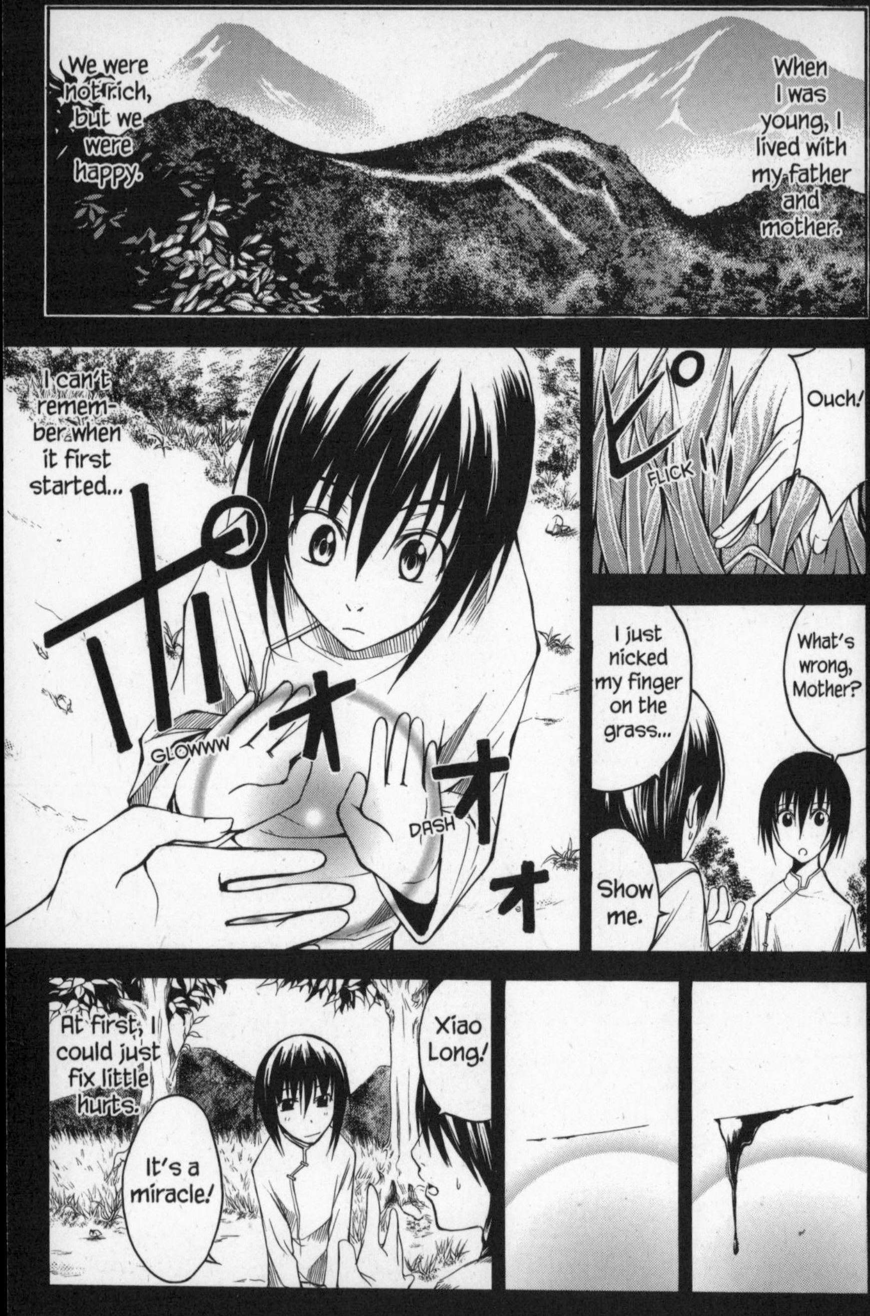
When I was young, I lived with my father and mother.
We were not rich, but we were happy.
Ouch!
FLICK
What's wrong, Mother?
I just nicked my finger on the grass...
Show me.
I can't remember when it first started...
GLOWWW
DASH
Xiao Long!
At first, I could just fix little hurts.
It's a miracle!

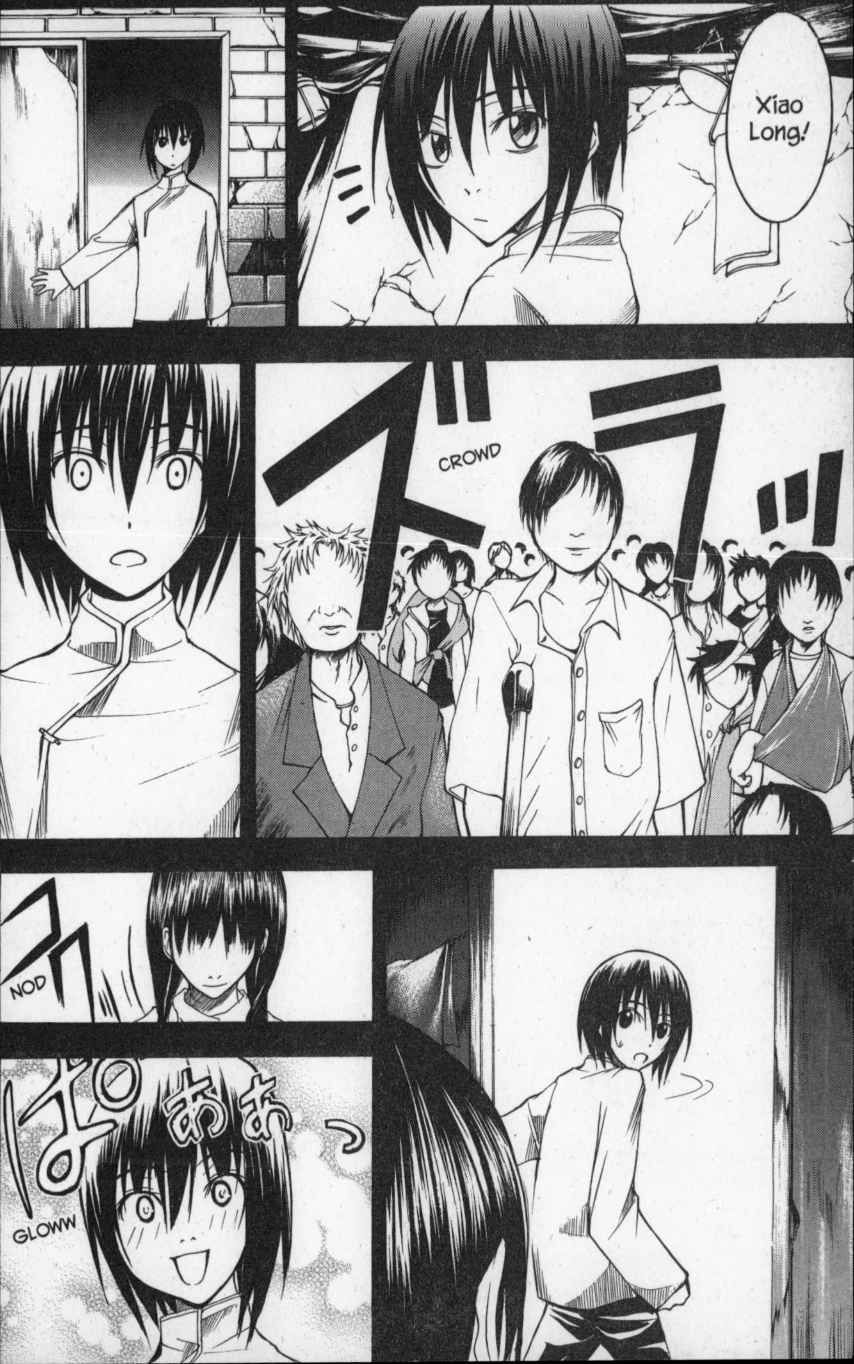
Xiao Long!
CROWD
NOD
GLOWW

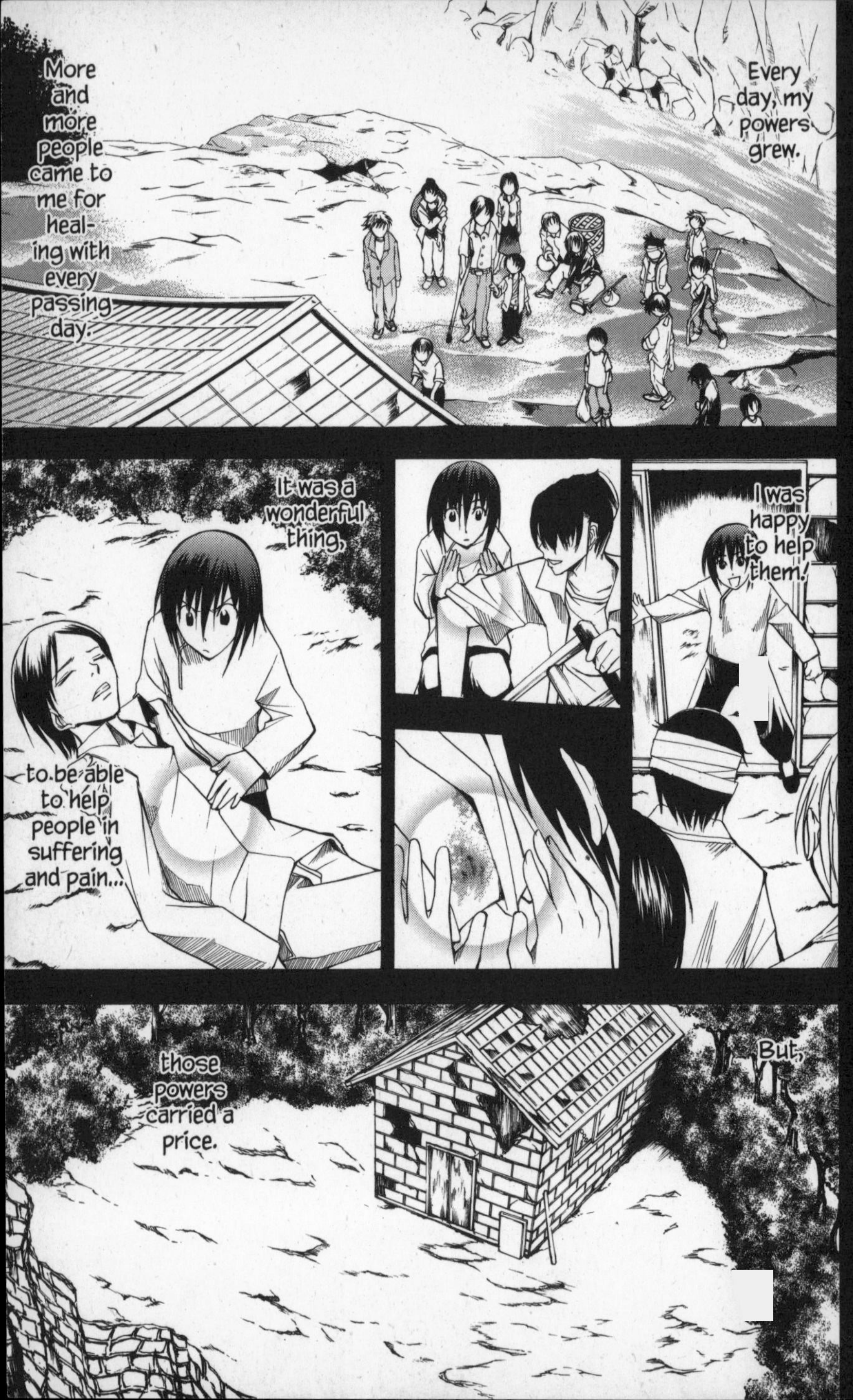
Every day, my powers grew.
More and more people came to me for heal-ing with every passing day.
I was happy to help them!
It was a wonderful thing,
to be able to help people in suffering and pain...
But,
those powers carried a price.

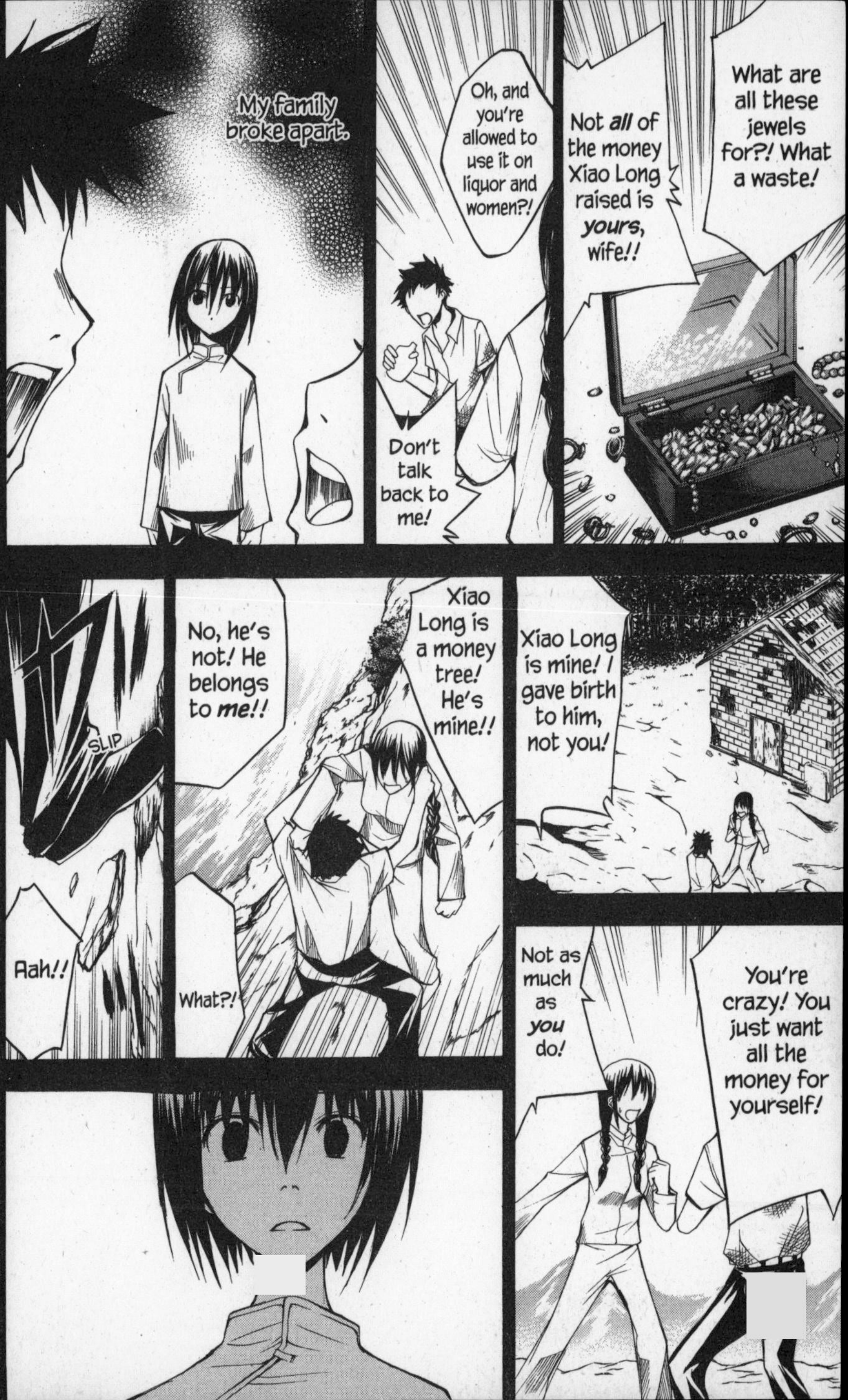
What are all these jewels for?! What a waste!
Not *all* of the money Xiao Long raised is *yours*, wife!!
Oh, and you're allowed to use it on liquor and women?!
Don't talk back to me!
My family broke apart.
Xiao Long is mine! I gave birth to him, not you!
You're crazy! You just want all the money for yourself!
Not as much as *you* do!
Xiao Long is a money tree! He's mine!!
No, he's not! He belongs to *me*!!
What?!
SLIP
Aah!!

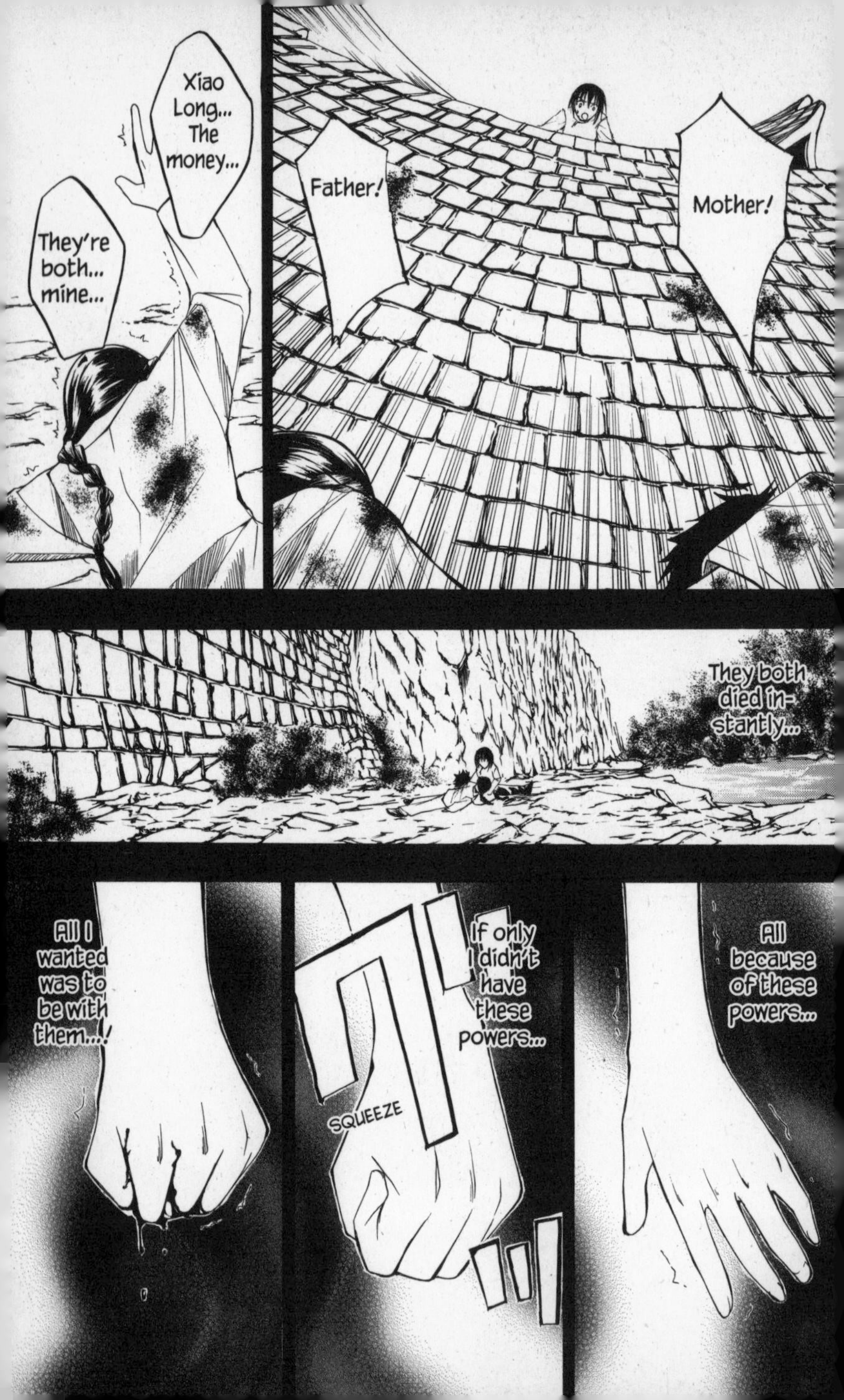
Mother!
Father!
Xiao Long... The money...
They're both... mine...
They both died instantly...
All because of these powers...
If only I didn't have these powers...
SQUEEZE
All I wanted was to be with them...!

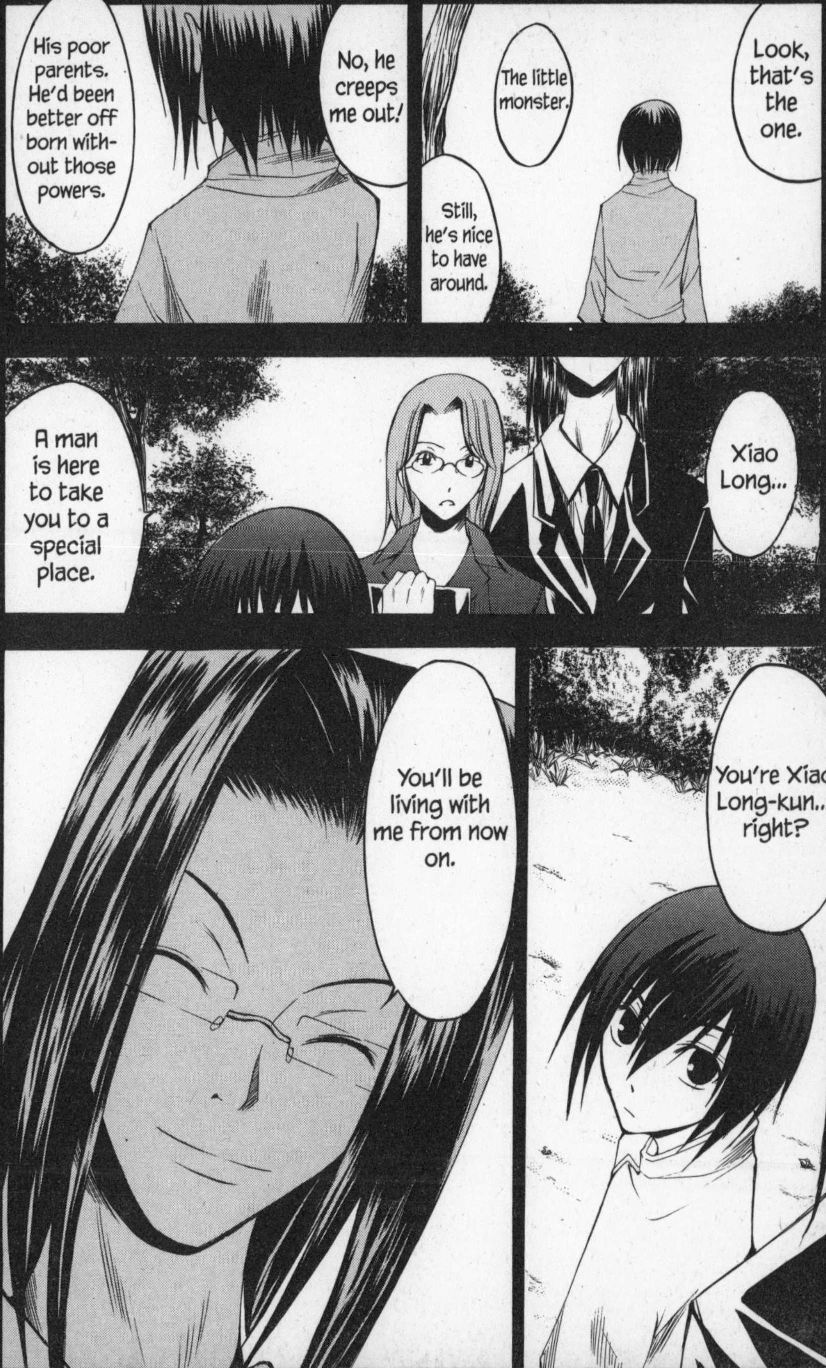
Look, that's the one.
The little monster.
Still, he's nice to have around.
No, he creeps me out!
His poor parents. He'd been better off born without those powers.
Xiao Long...
A man is here to take you to a special place.
You're Xiao Long-kun... right?
You'll be living with me from now on.

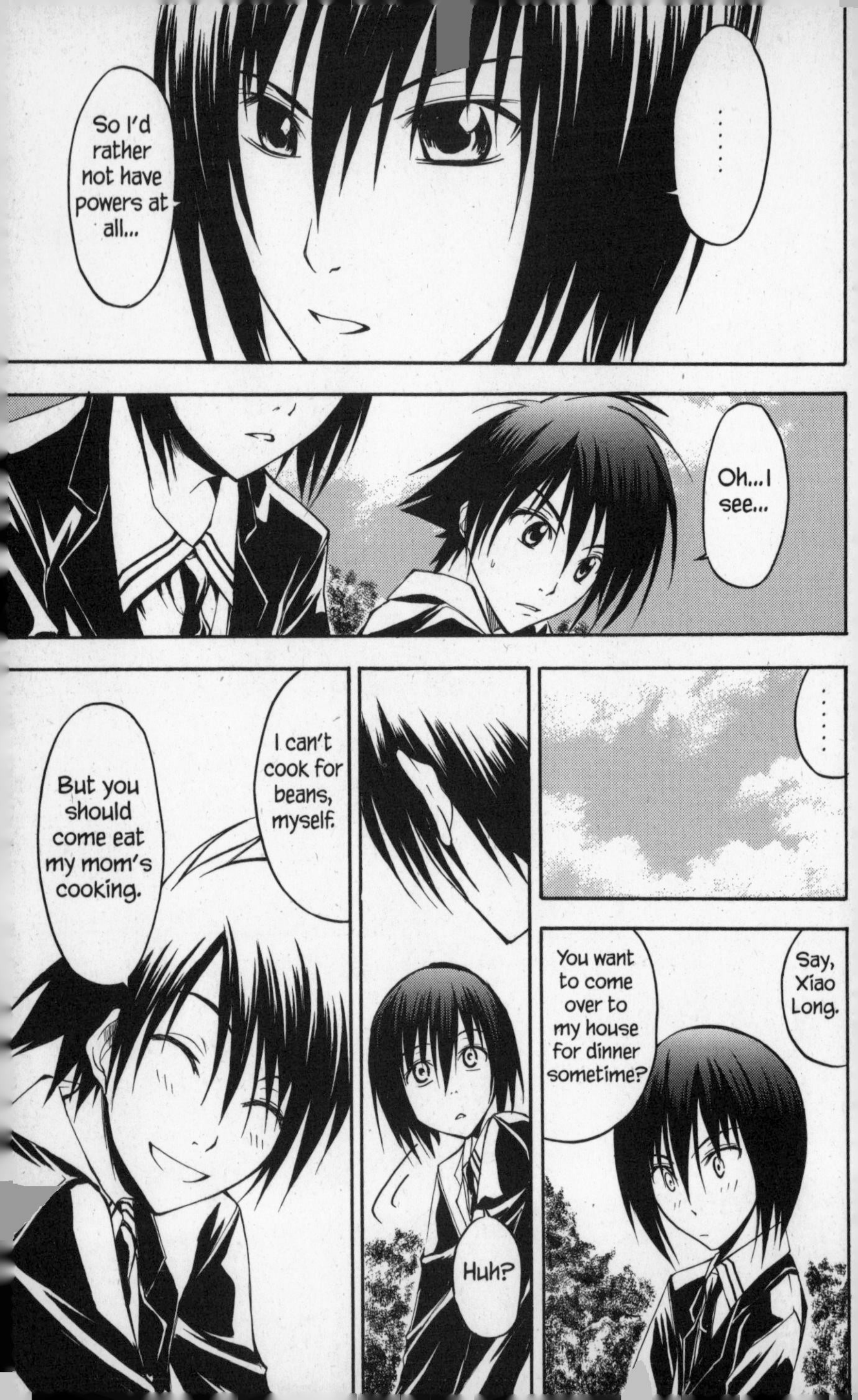
......
So I'd rather not have powers at all...
Oh...I see...
......
Say, Xiao Long.
You want to come over to my house for dinner sometime?
Huh?
I can't cook for beans, myself.
But you should come eat my mom's cooking.

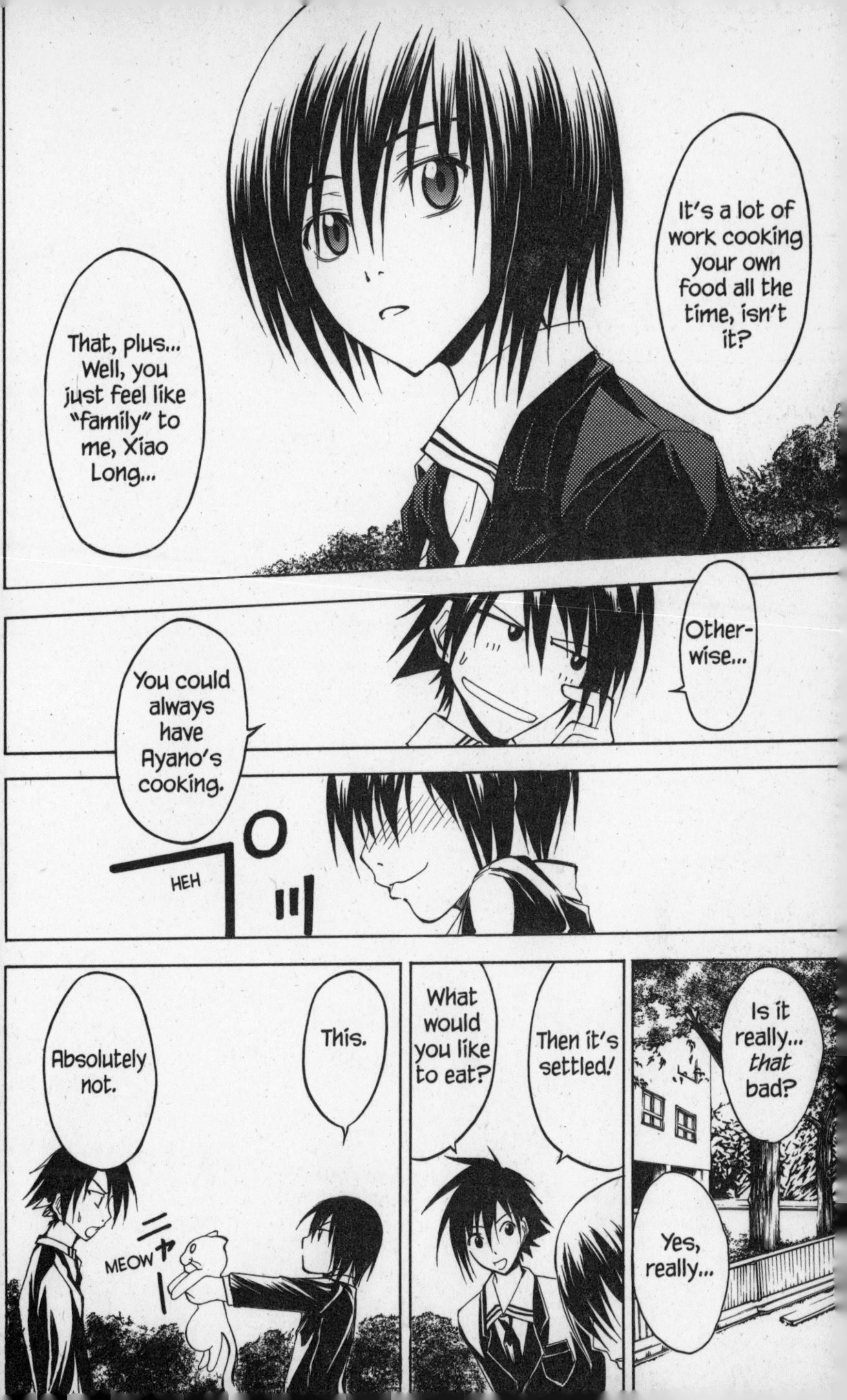
It's a lot of work cooking your own food all the time, isn't it?
That, plus... Well, you just feel like "family" to me, Xiao Long...
Otherwise...
You could always have Ayano's cooking.
HEH
Is it really... *that* bad?
Yes, really...
Then it's settled!
What would you like to eat?
This.
MEOW
Absolutely not.

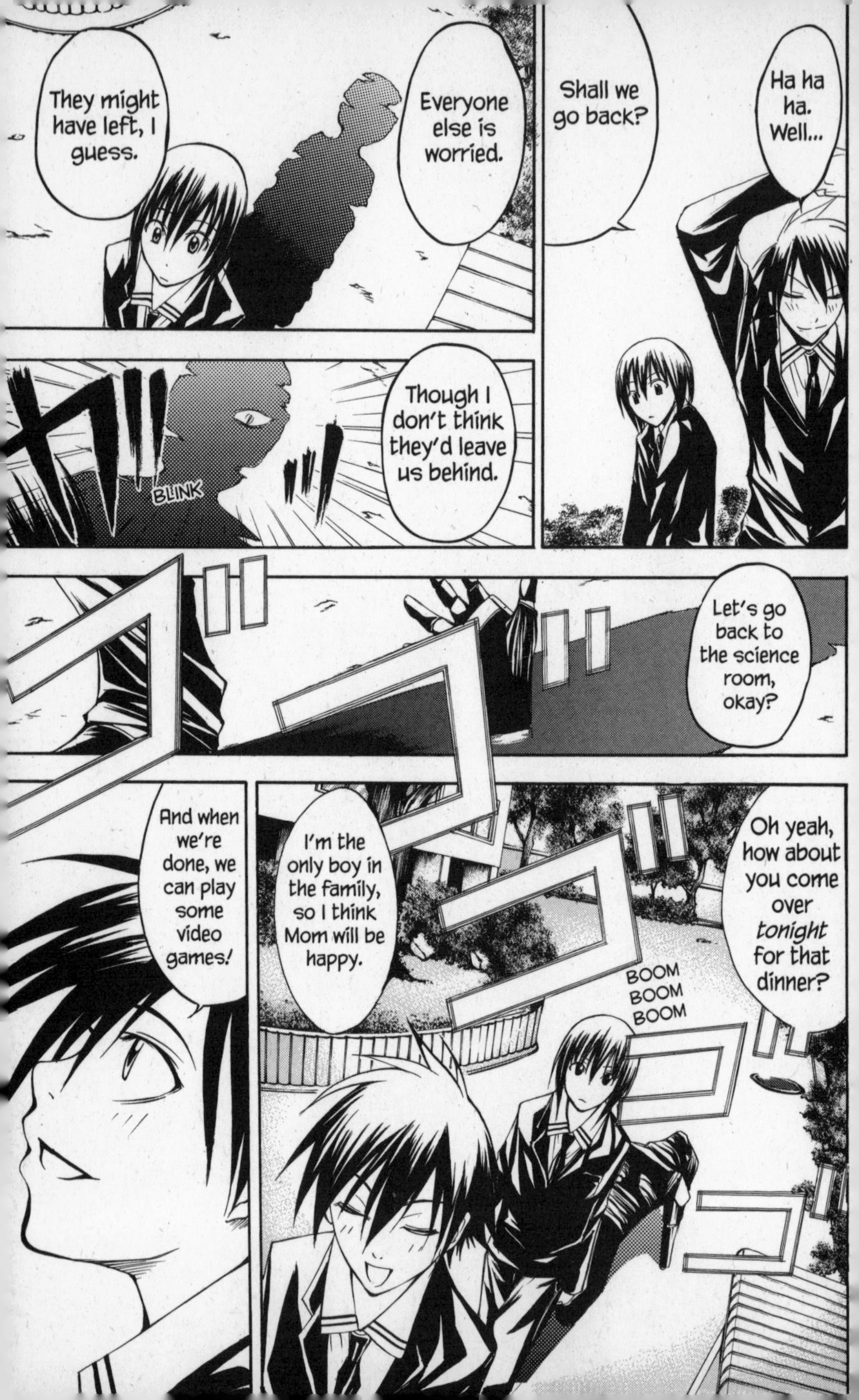
Ha ha ha. Well...
Shall we go back?
Everyone else is worried.
They might have left, I guess.
Though I don't think they'd leave us behind.
BLINK
Let's go back to the science room, okay?
Oh yeah, how about you come over *tonight* for that dinner?
BOOM BOOM BOOM
I'm the only boy in the family, so I think Mom will be happy.
And when we're done, we can play some video games!

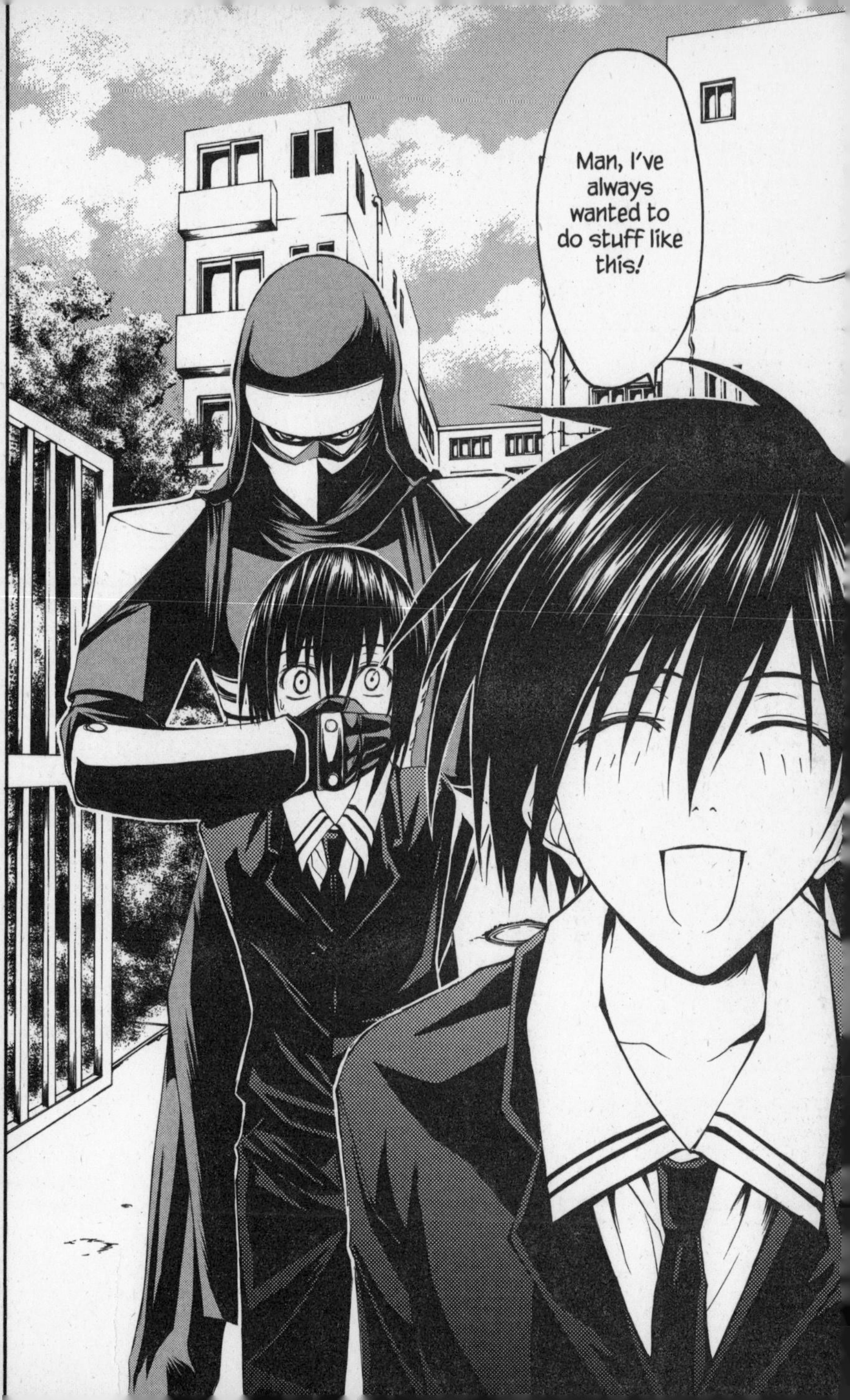
Man, I've always wanted to do stuff like this!

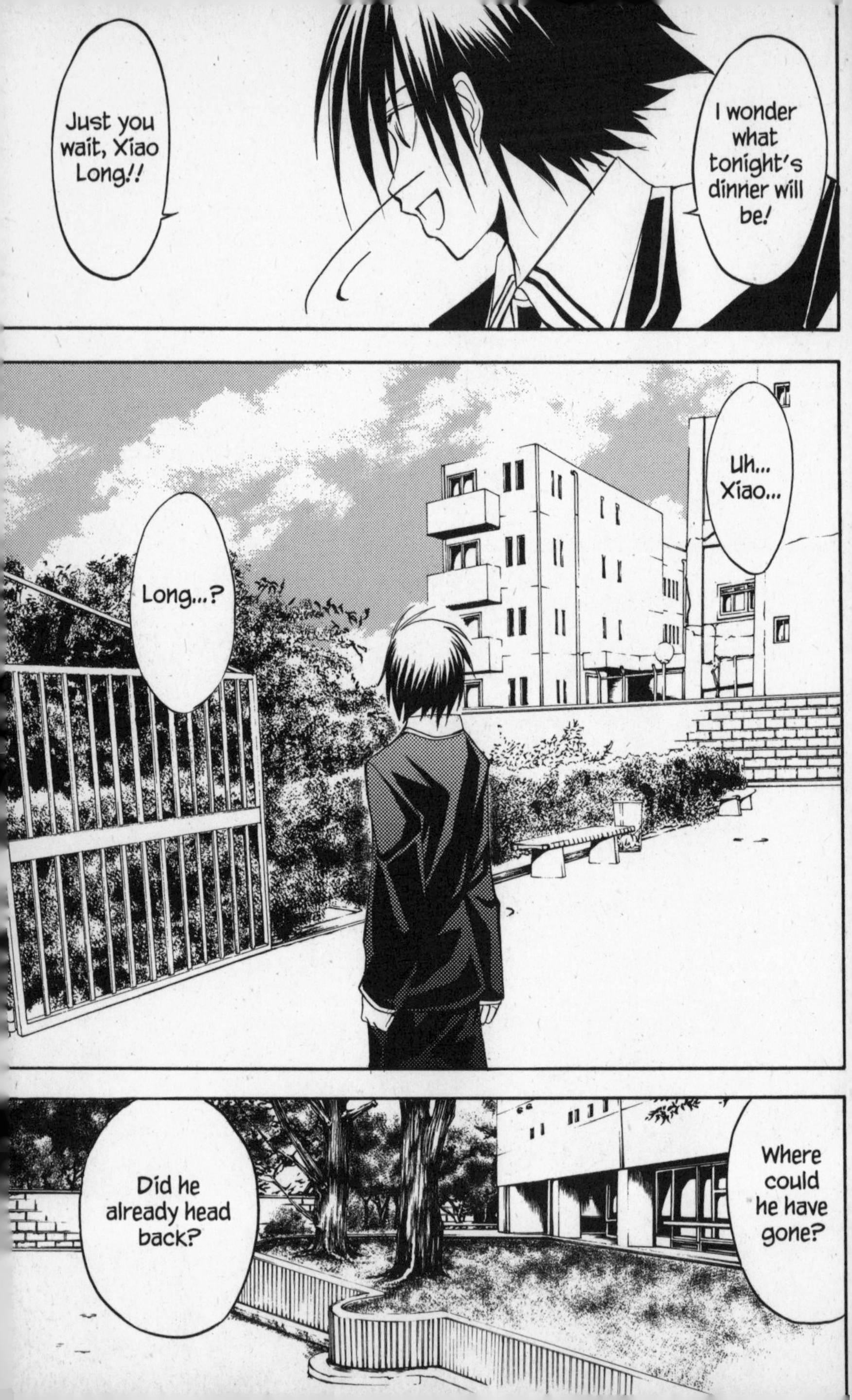
I wonder what tonight's dinner will be!
Just you wait, Xiao Long!!
Uh... Xiao...
Long...?
Where could he have gone?
Did he already head back?

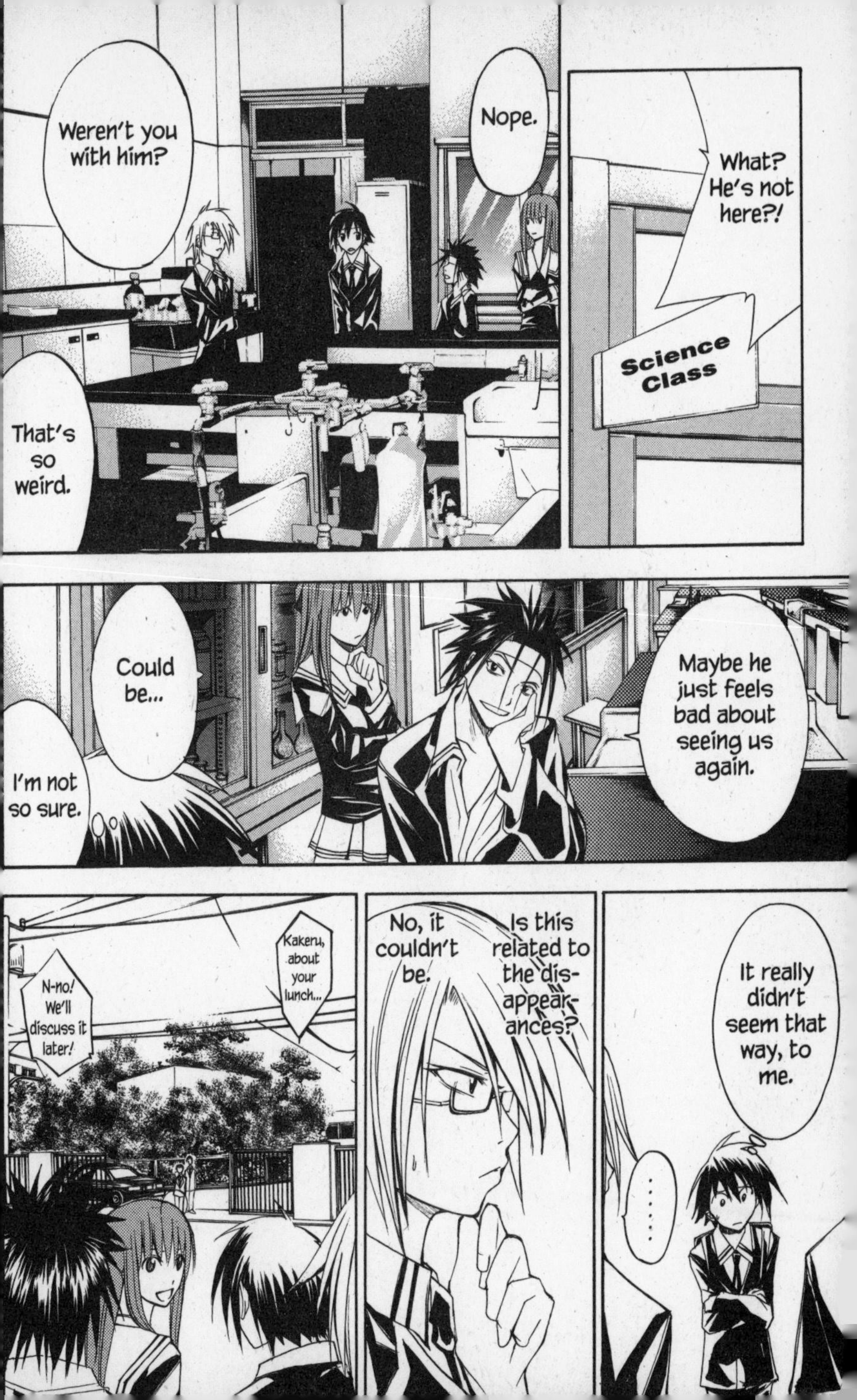
What? He's not here?!
Science Class
Nope.
Weren't you with him?
That's so weird.
Maybe he just feels bad about seeing us again.
Could be...
I'm not so sure.
It really didn't seem that way, to me.
......
Is this related to the disappearances?
No, it couldn't be.
Kakeru, about your lunch...
N-no! We'll discuss it later!

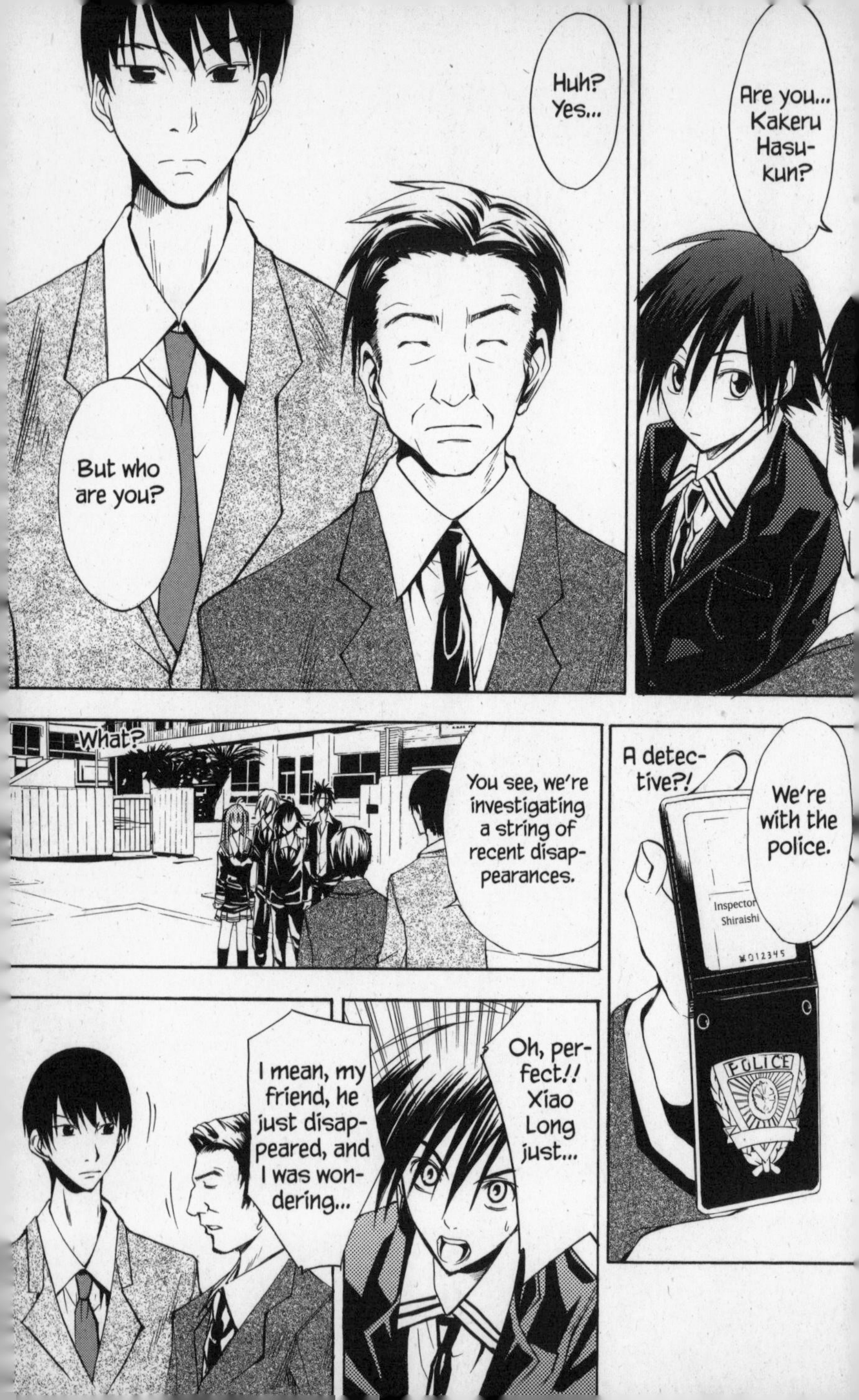
Are you... Kakeru Hasu-kun?
Huh? Yes...
But who are you?
We're with the police.
Inspector Shiraishi
POLICE
A detective?!
You see, we're investigating a string of recent disappearances.
What?
Oh, perfect!! Xiao Long just...
I mean, my friend, he just disappeared, and I was wondering...

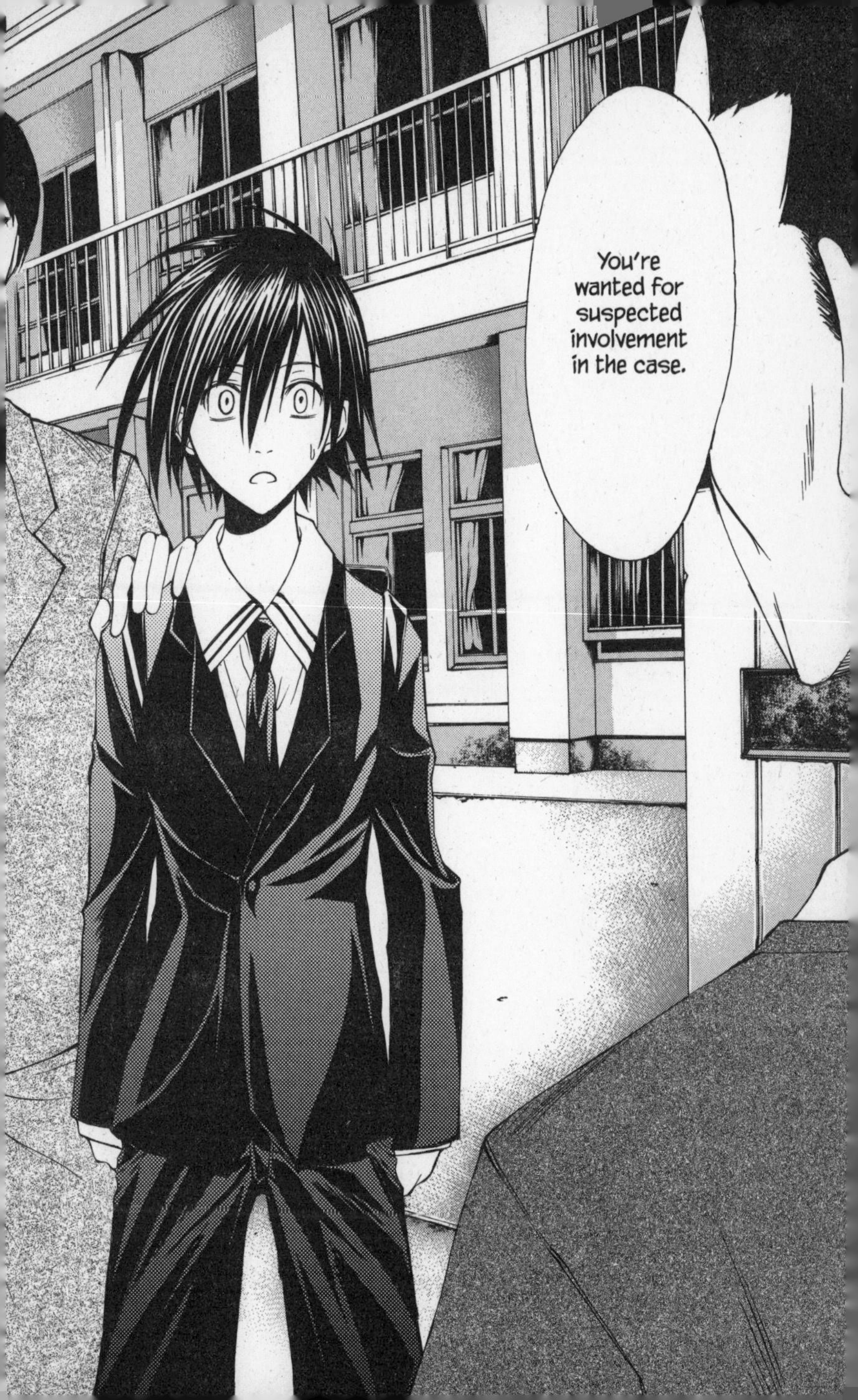
You're wanted for suspected involvement in the case.

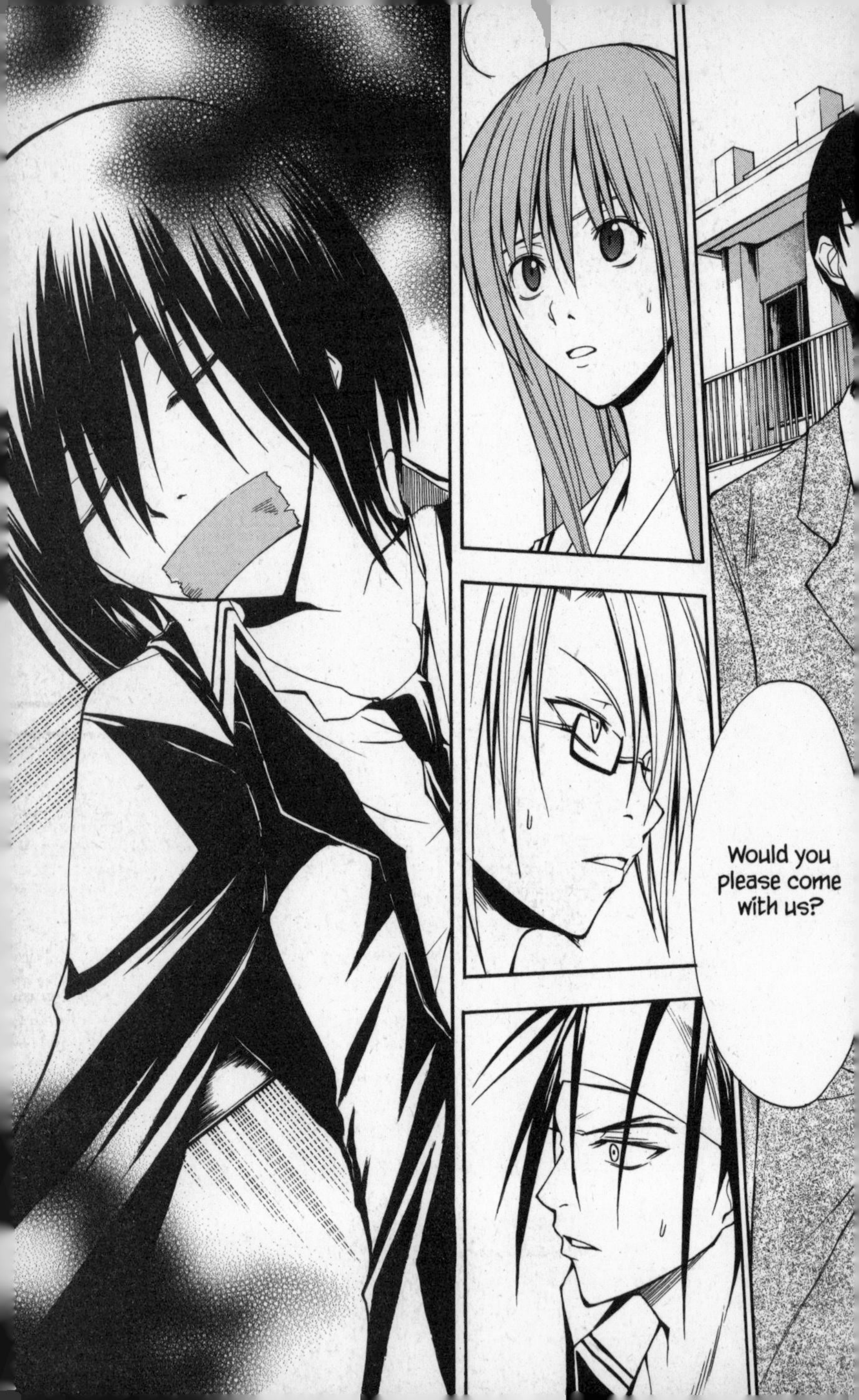
Would you please come with us?

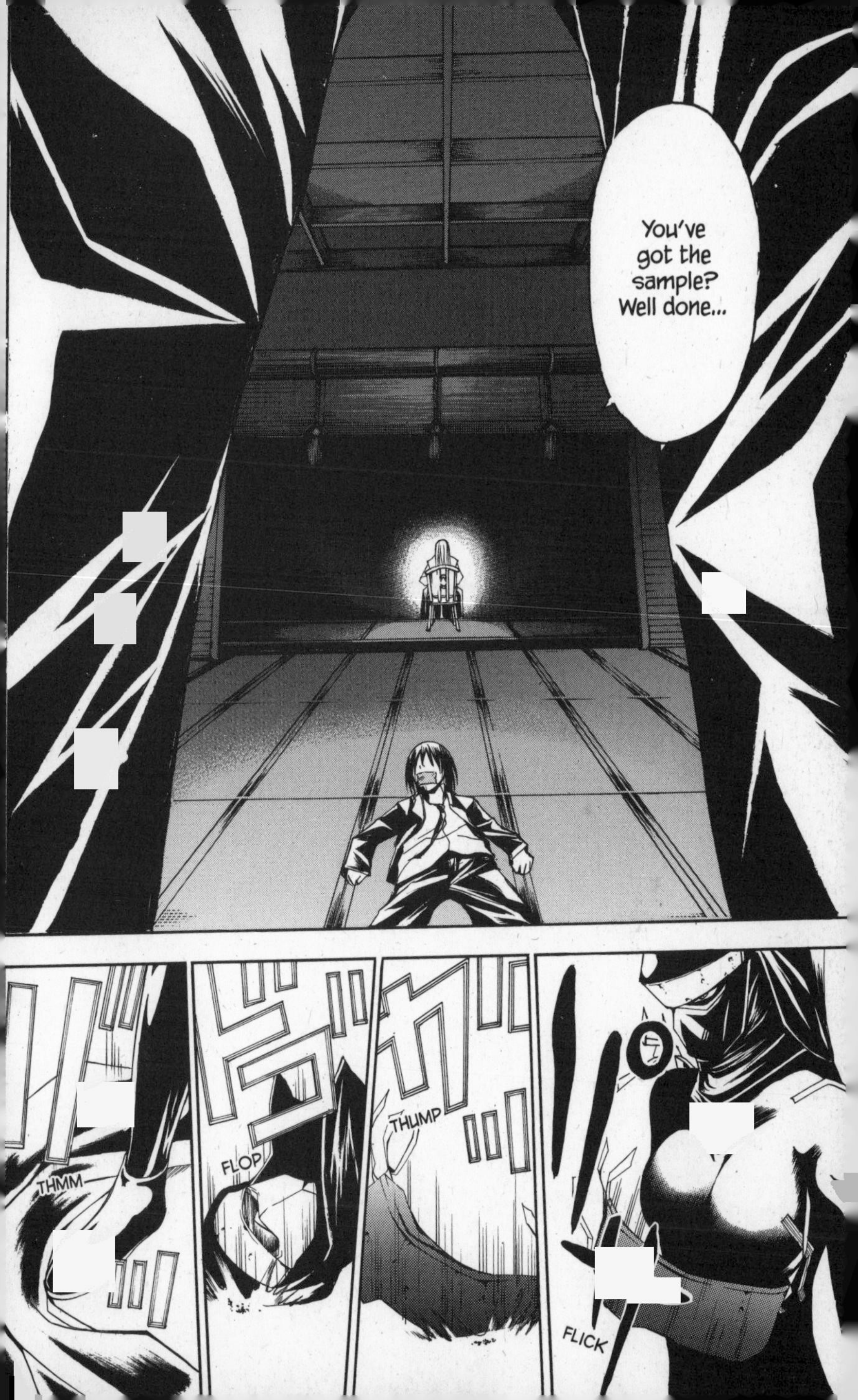
You've got the sample? Well done...
FLICK
THUMP
FLOP
THMM

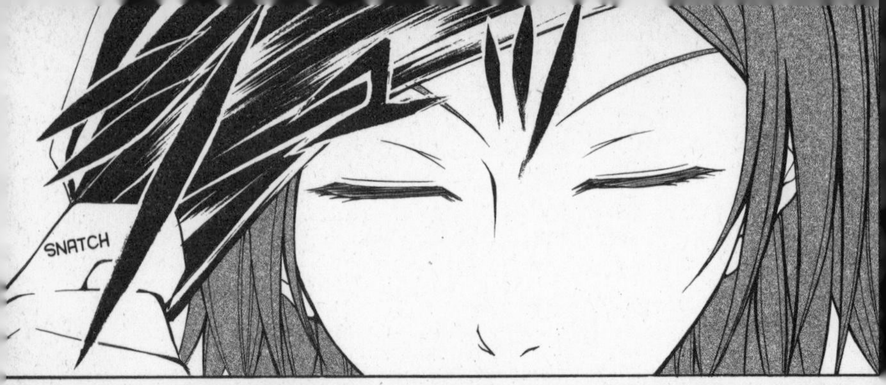
SNATCH
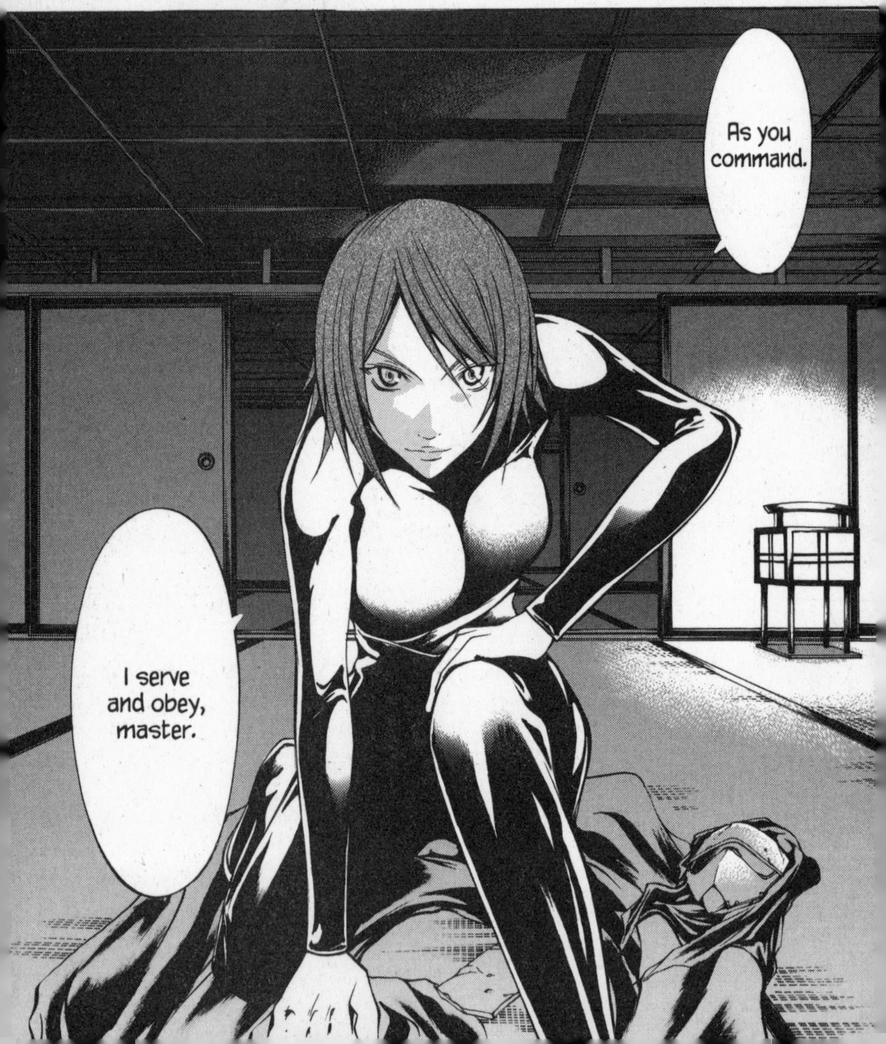
As you command.
I serve and obey, master.

**Psycho Busters**

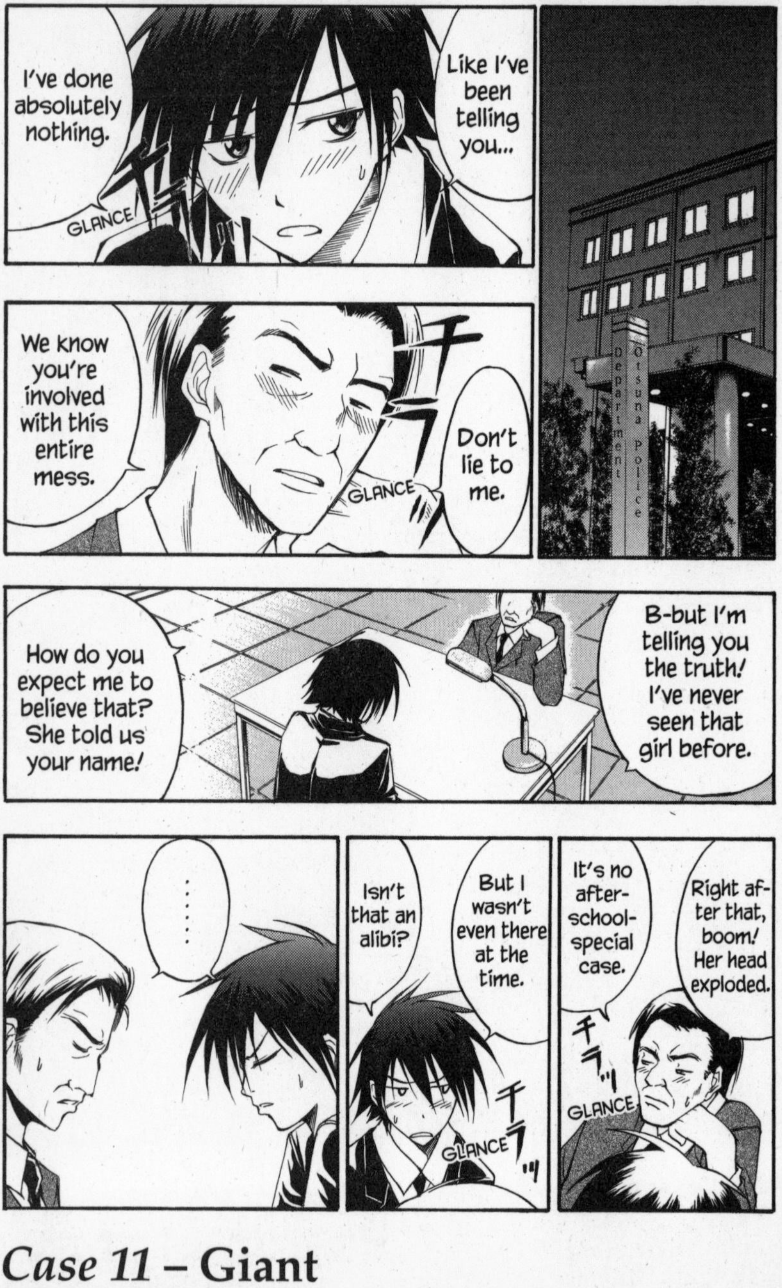
Otsuna Police Department
Like I've been telling you...
I've done absolutely nothing.
GLANCE
Don't lie to me.
We know you're involved with this entire mess.
GLANCE
B-but I'm telling you the truth! I've never seen that girl before.
How do you expect me to believe that? She told us your name!
Right after that, boom! Her head exploded.
It's no after-school-special case.
GLANCE
But I wasn't even there at the time.
Isn't that an alibi?
GLANCE
......

# Case 11 – Giant

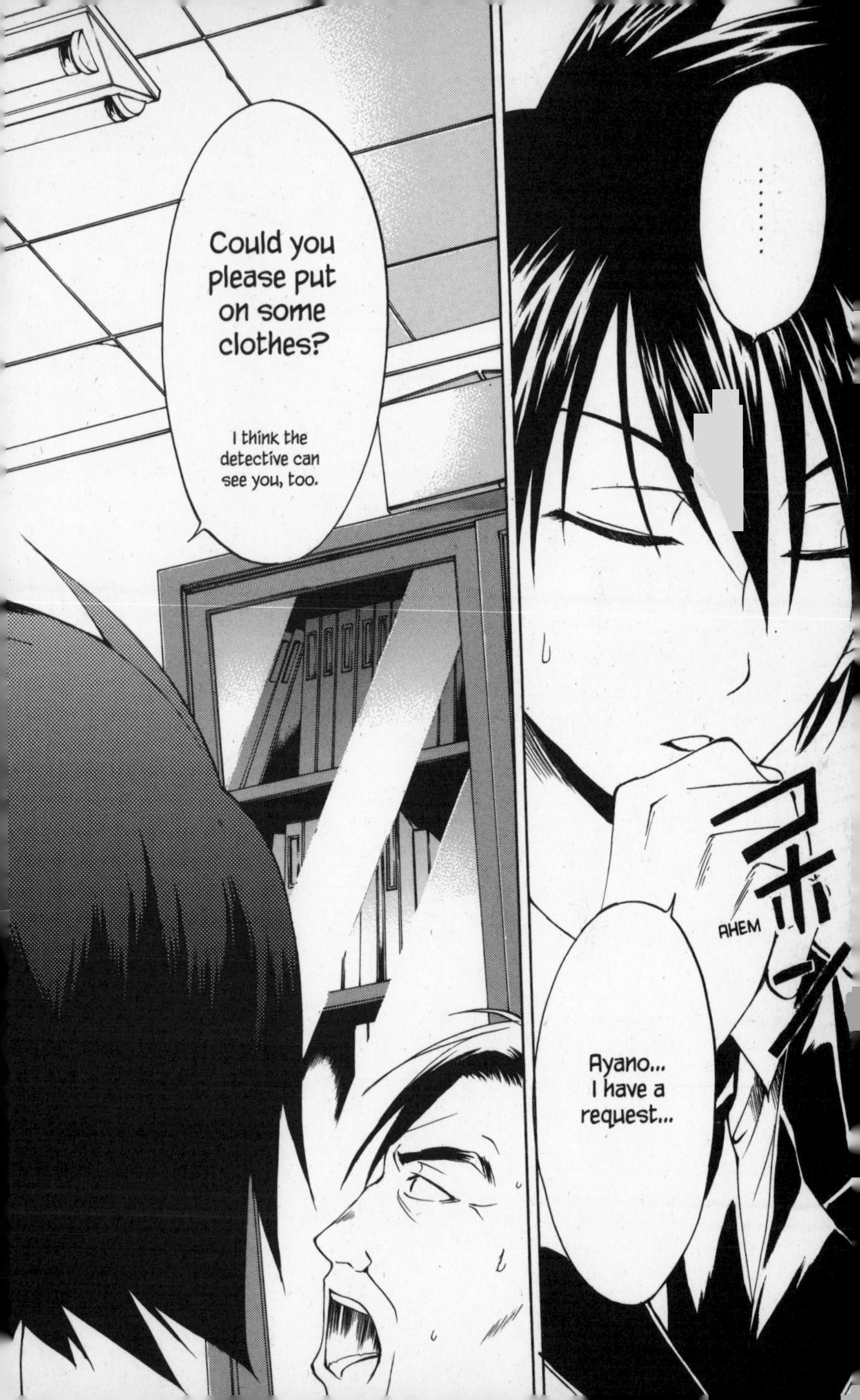
......
AHEM
Ayano... I have a request...
Could you please put on some clothes?
I think the detective can see you, too.

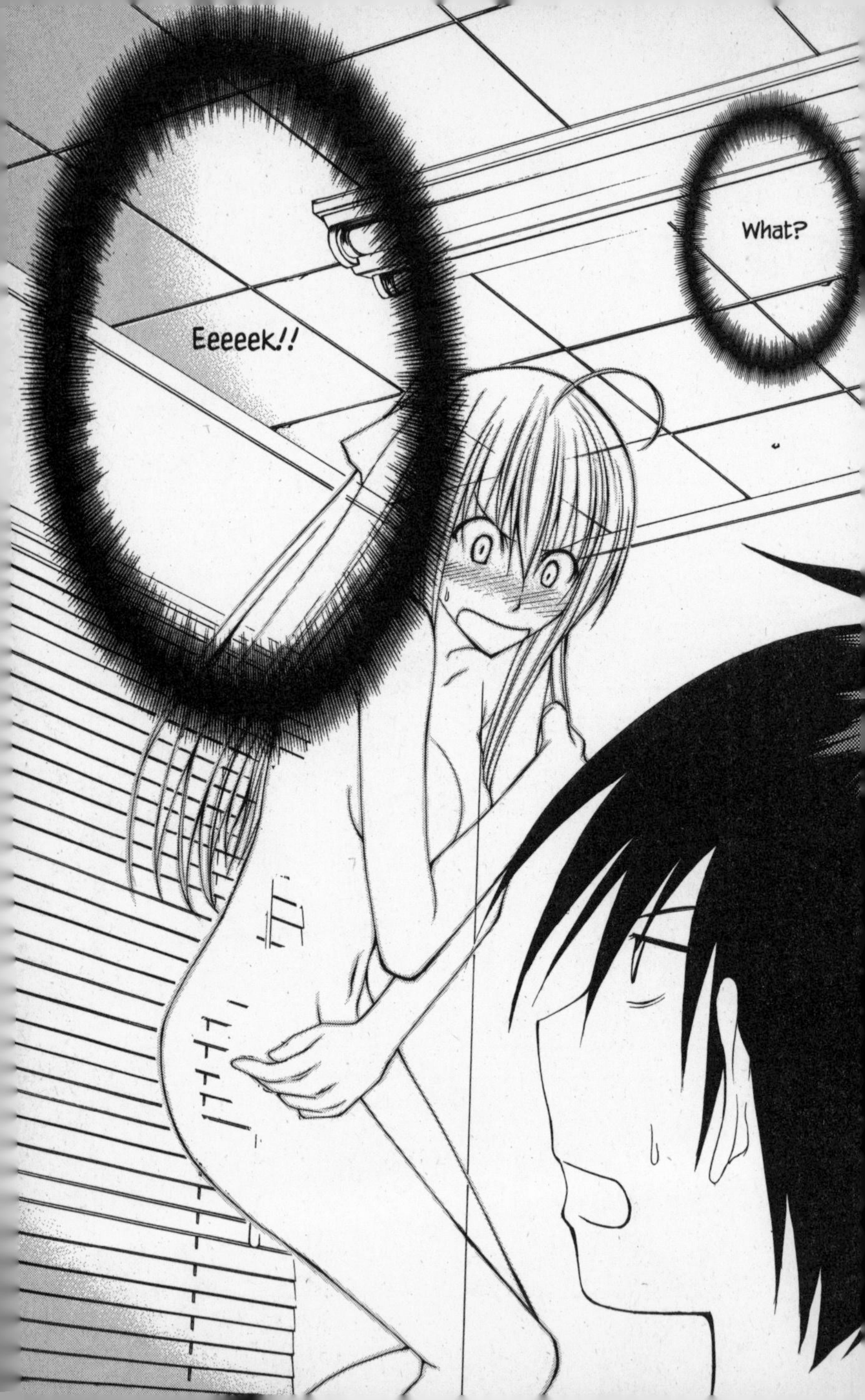
What?
Eeeeek!!

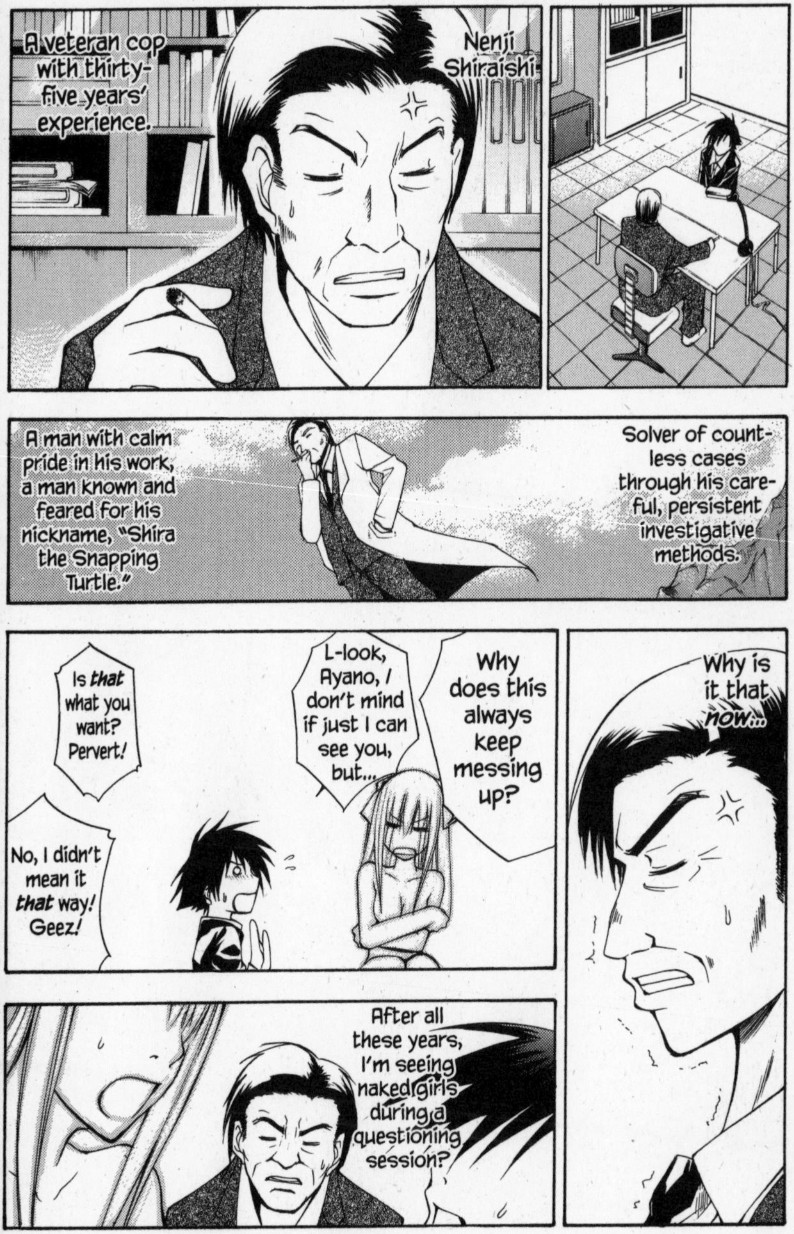
Nenji Shiraishi
A veteran cop with thirty-five years' experience.
Solver of countless cases through his careful, persistent investigative methods.
A man with calm pride in his work, a man known and feared for his nickname, "Shira the Snapping Turtle."
Why is it that *now*...
Why does this always keep messing up?
L-look, Ayano, I don't mind if just I can see you, but...
Is *that* what you want? Pervert!
No, I didn't mean it *that* way! Geez!
After all these years, I'm seeing naked girls during a questioning session?

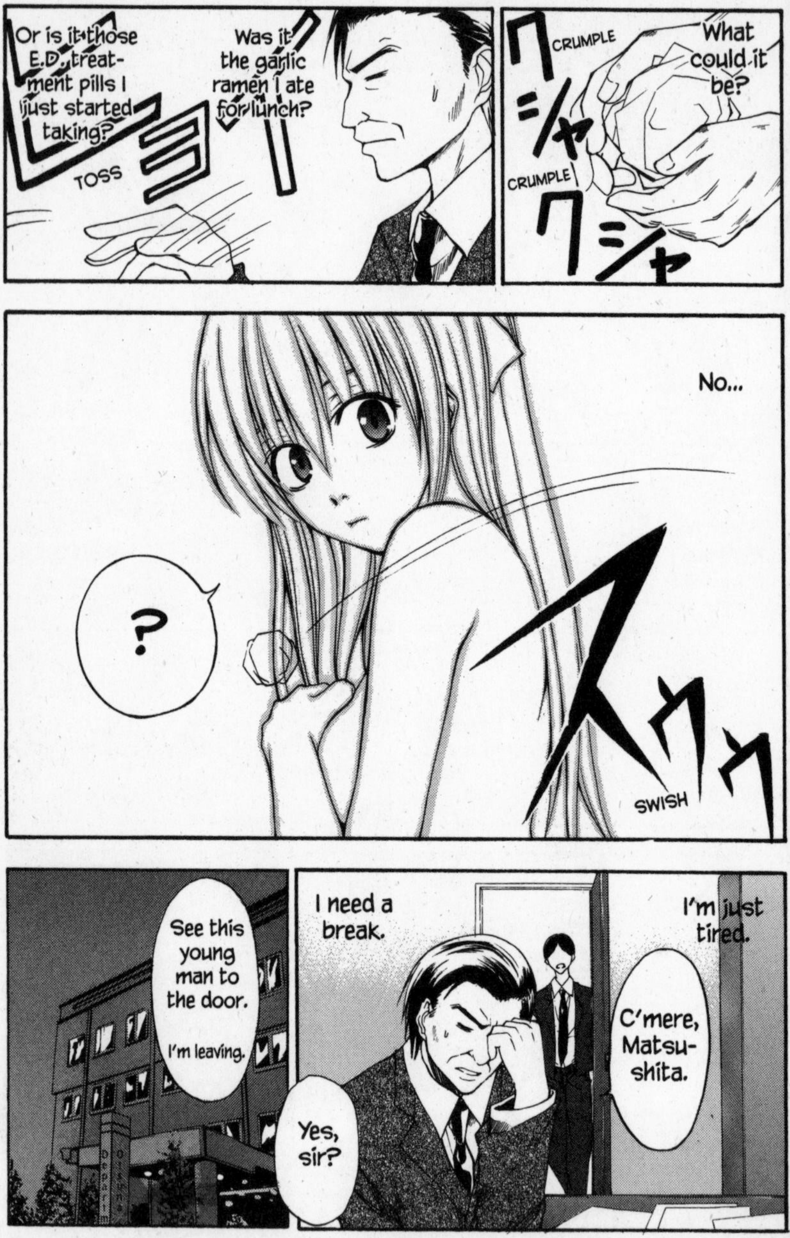
What could it be?
CRUMPLE
CRUMPLE
Was it the garlic ramen I ate for lunch?
Or is it those E.D. treat-ment pills I just started taking?
TOSS
No...
?
SWISH
I'm just tired.
I need a break.
C'mere, Matsu-shita.
Yes, sir?
See this young man to the door.
I'm leaving.

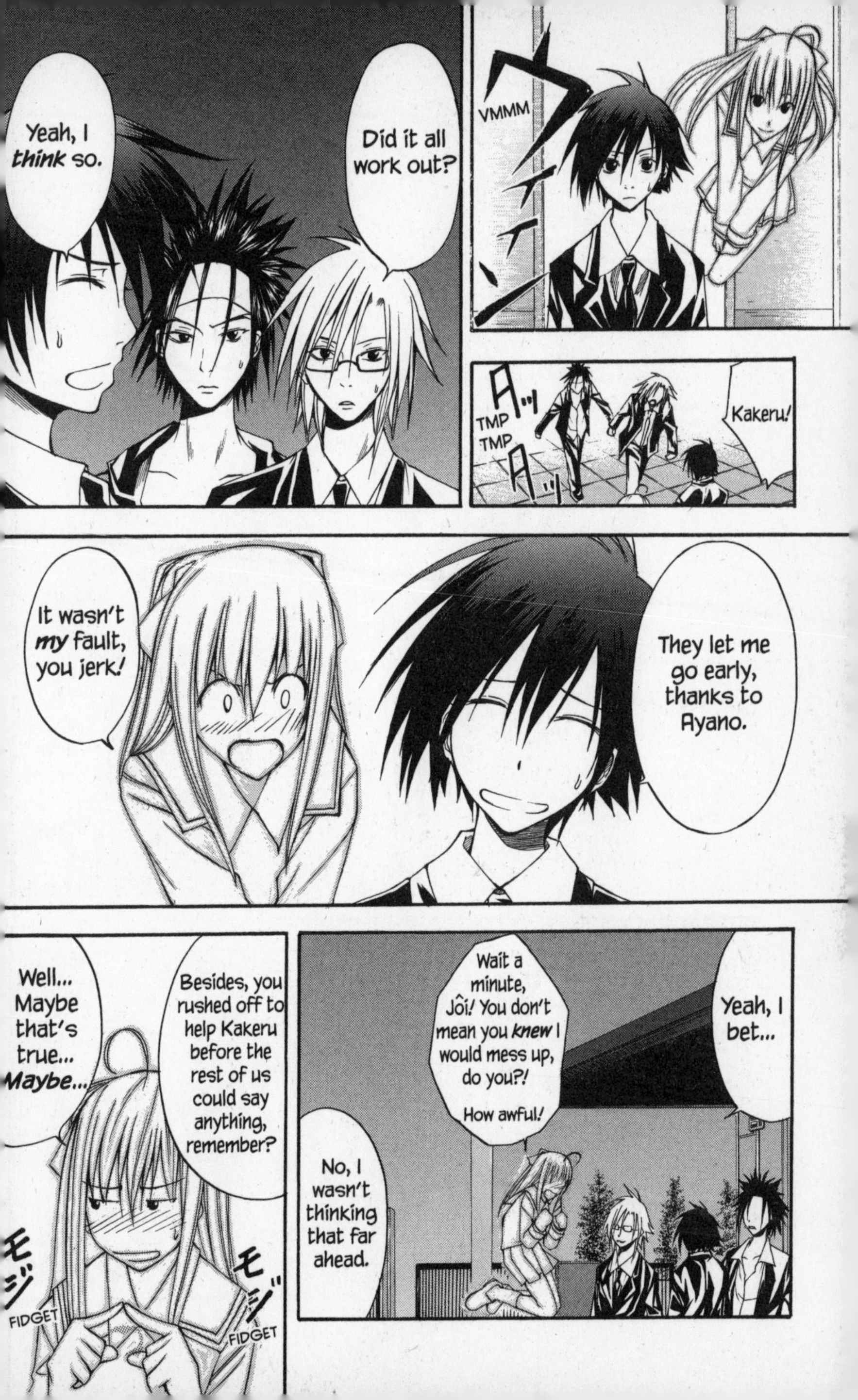
VMMM
Kakeru!
TMP TMP
Did it all work out?
Yeah, I *think* so.
They let me go early, thanks to Ayano.
It wasn't *my* fault, you jerk!
Yeah, I bet...
Wait a minute, Jôi! You don't mean you *knew* I would mess up, do you?!
How awful!
No, I wasn't thinking that far ahead.
Besides, you rushed off to help Kakeru before the rest of us could say anything, remember?
Well... Maybe that's true... *Maybe*...
FIDGET
FIDGET

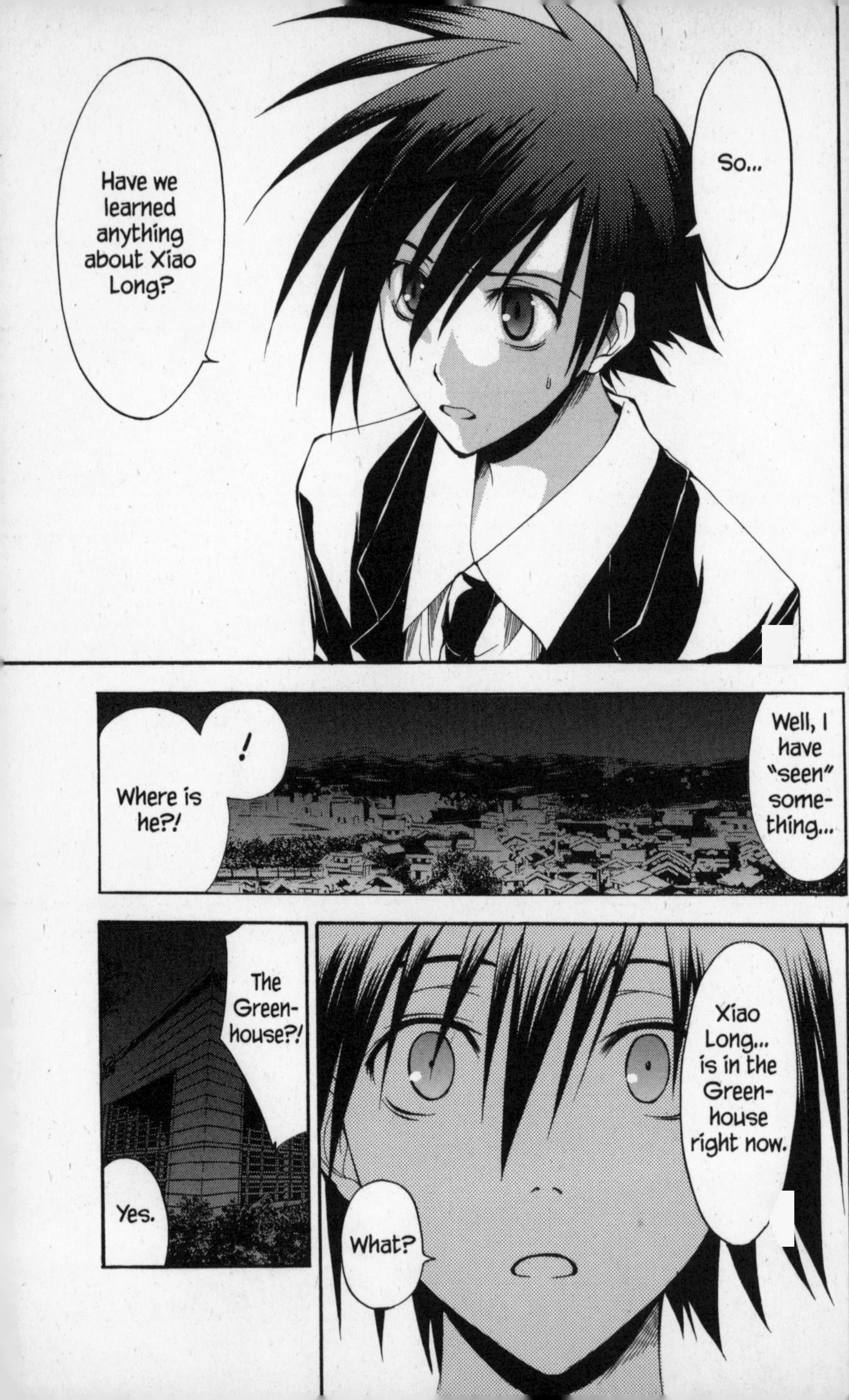
So...
Have we learned anything about Xiao Long?
Well, I have "seen" something...
!
Where is he?!
Xiao Long... is in the Greenhouse right now.
What?
The Greenhouse?!
Yes.

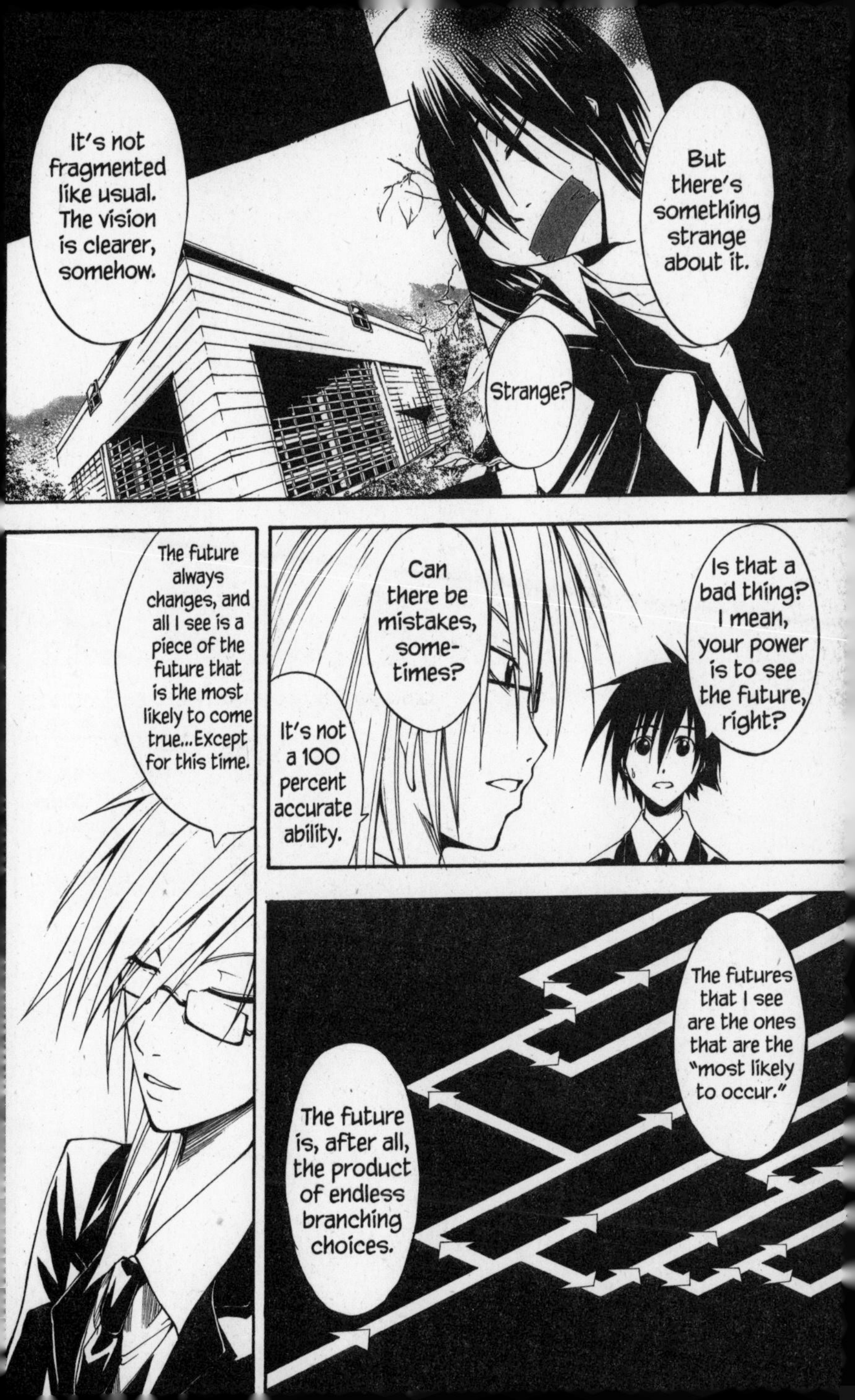
But there's something strange about it.
It's not fragmented like usual. The vision is clearer, somehow.
Strange?
Is that a bad thing? I mean, your power is to see the future, right?
Can there be mistakes, some-times?
It's not a 100 percent accurate ability.
The futures that I see are the ones that are the "most likely to occur."
The future is, after all, the product of endless branching choices.
The future always changes, and all I see is a piece of the future that is the most likely to come true...Except for this time.

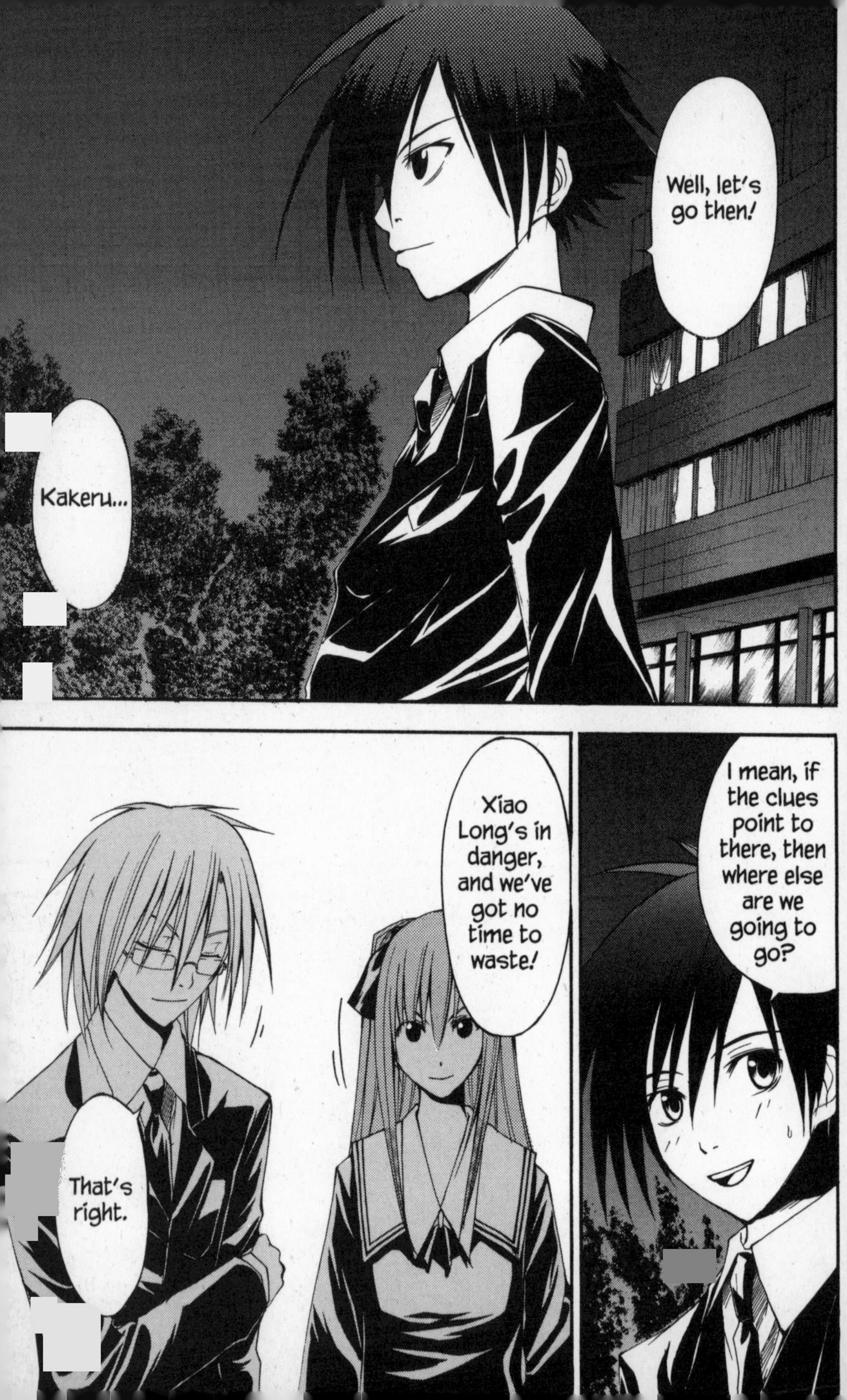
Well, let's go then!
Kakeru...
I mean, if the clues point to there, then where else are we going to go?
Xiao Long's in danger, and we've got no time to waste!
That's right.

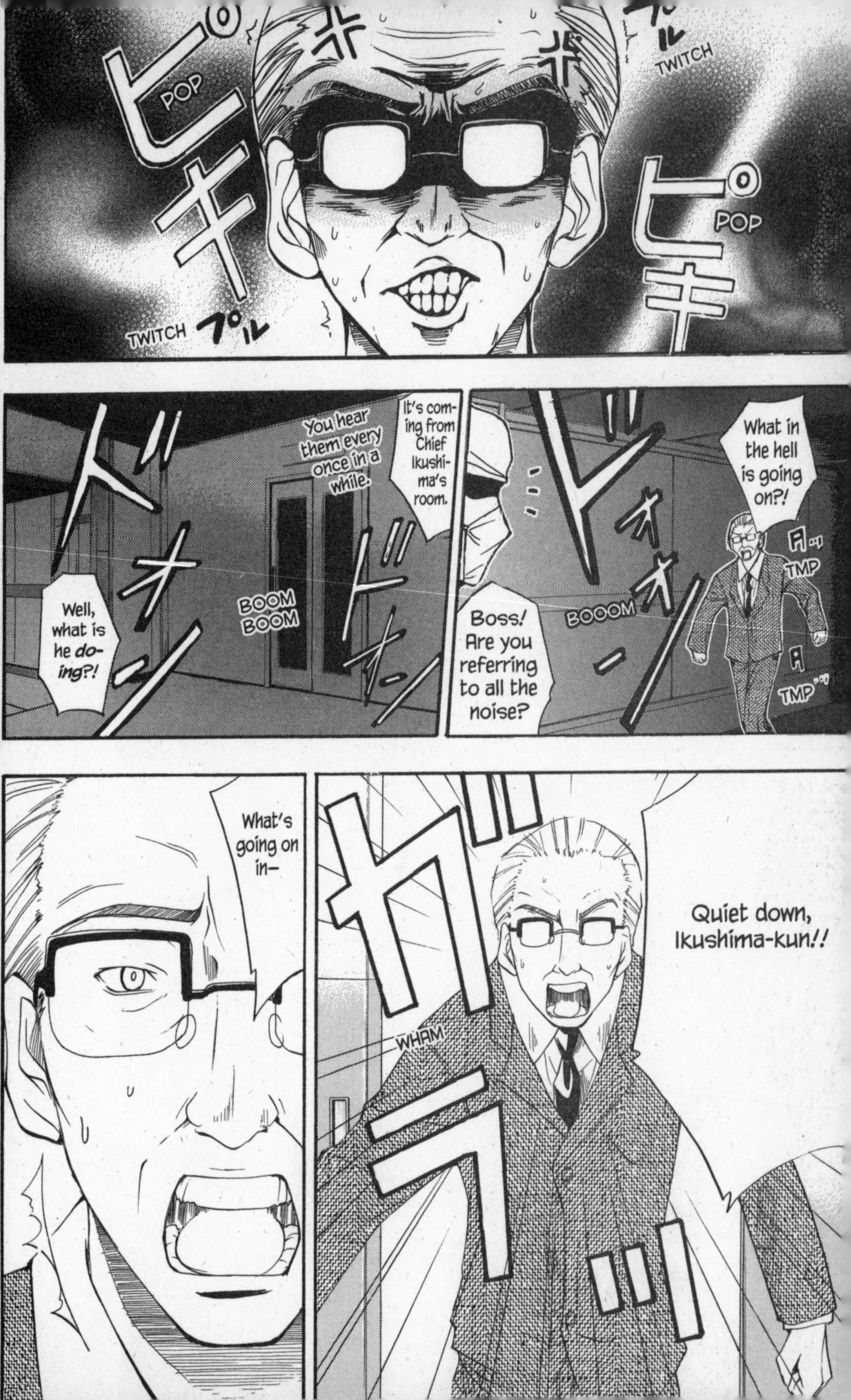
TWITCH
POP
POP
TWITCH
What in the hell is going on?!
TMP
TMP
BOOOM
Boss! Are you referring to all the noise?
It's coming from Chief Ikushima's room.
You hear them every once in a while.
BOOM BOOM
Well, what is he doing?!
Quiet down, Ikushima-kun!!
WHAM
What's going on in–

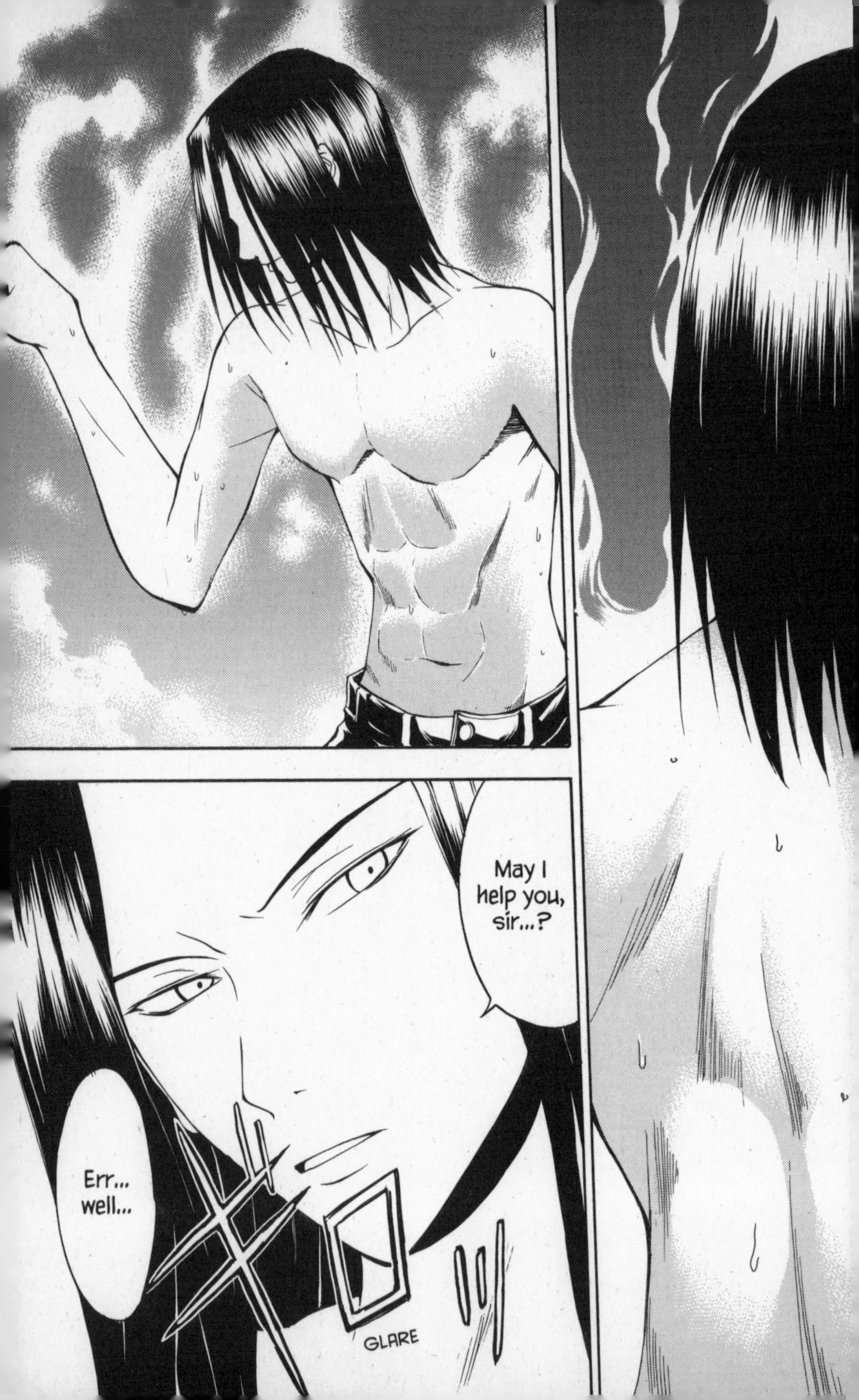
May I help you, sir...?
Err... well...
GLARE

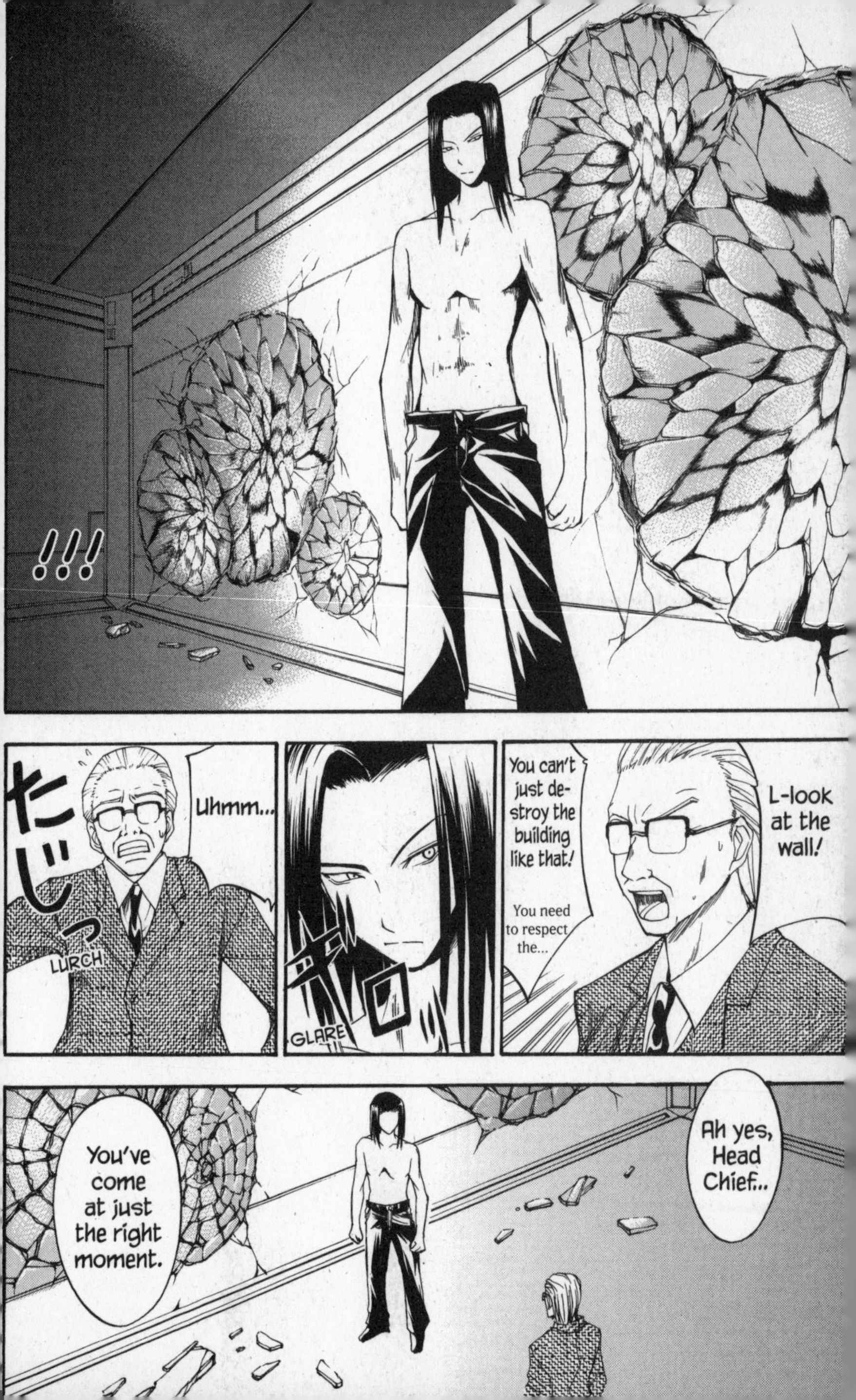
!!!
L-look at the wall!
You can't just destroy the building like that!
You need to respect the...
GLARE
Uhmm...
たじっ
LURCH
Ah yes, Head Chief...
You've come at just the right moment.

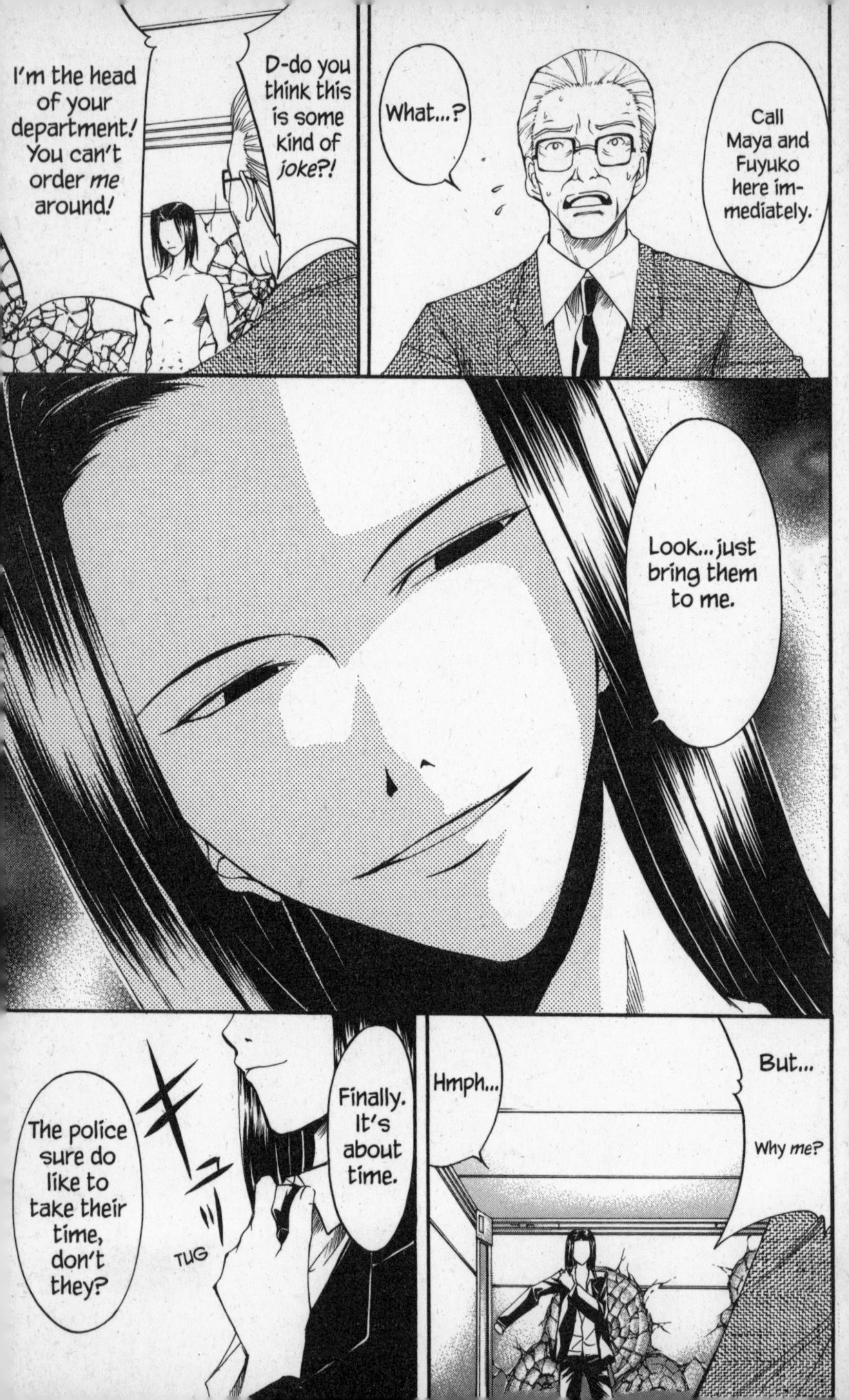
Call Maya and Fuyuko here im-mediately.
What...?
D-do you think this is some kind of *joke*?!
I'm the head of your department! You can't order *me* around!
Look... just bring them to me.
But...
Why *me*?
Hmph...
Finally. It's about time.
The police sure do like to take their time, don't they?
TUG

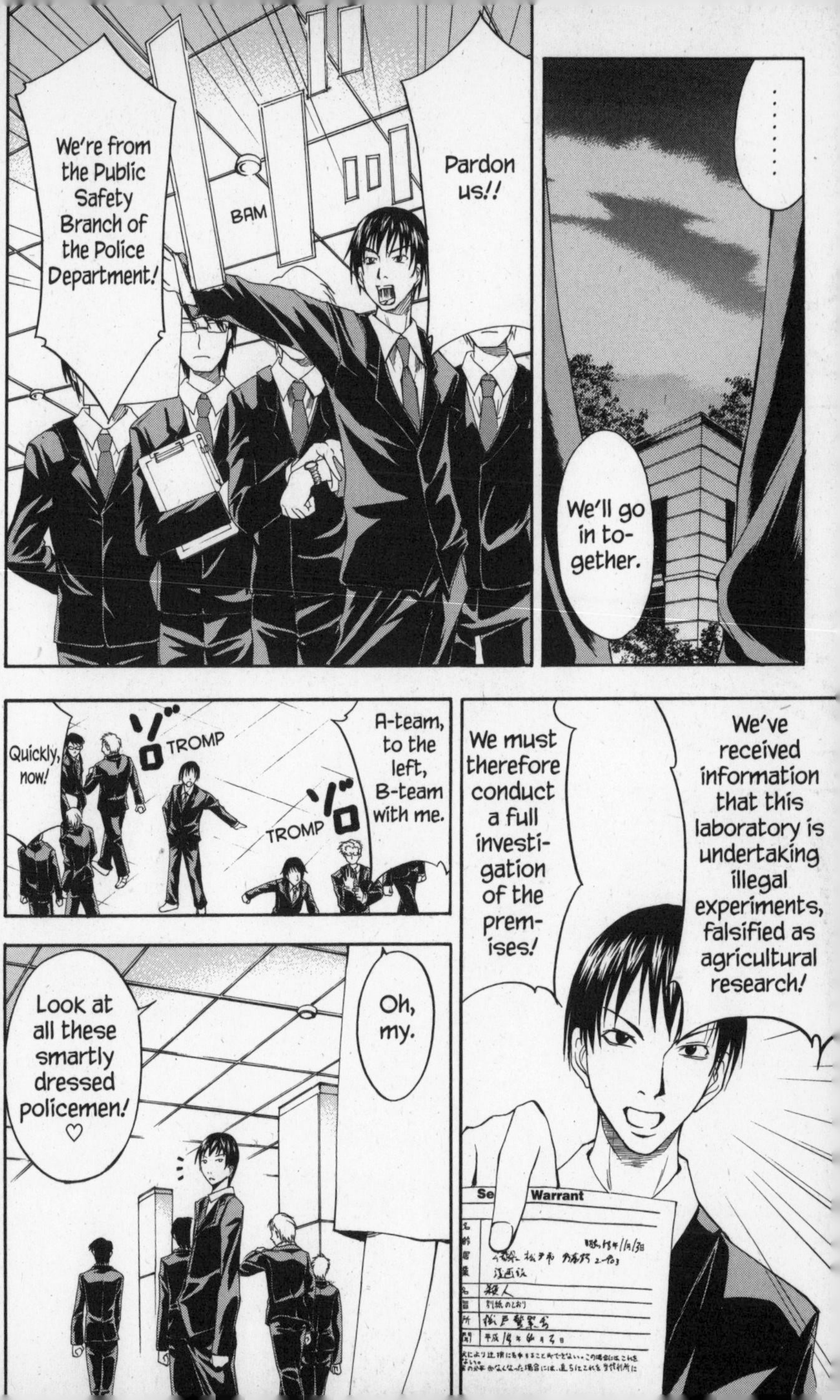
......
We'll go in together.
Pardon us!!
BAM
We're from the Public Safety Branch of the Police Department!
We've received information that this laboratory is undertaking illegal experiments, falsified as agricultural research!
We must therefore conduct a full investigation of the premises!
Warrant
A-team, to the left, B-team with me.
ゾロ
TROMP
ゾロ
TROMP
Quickly, now!
Oh, my.
Look at all these smartly dressed policemen! ♡

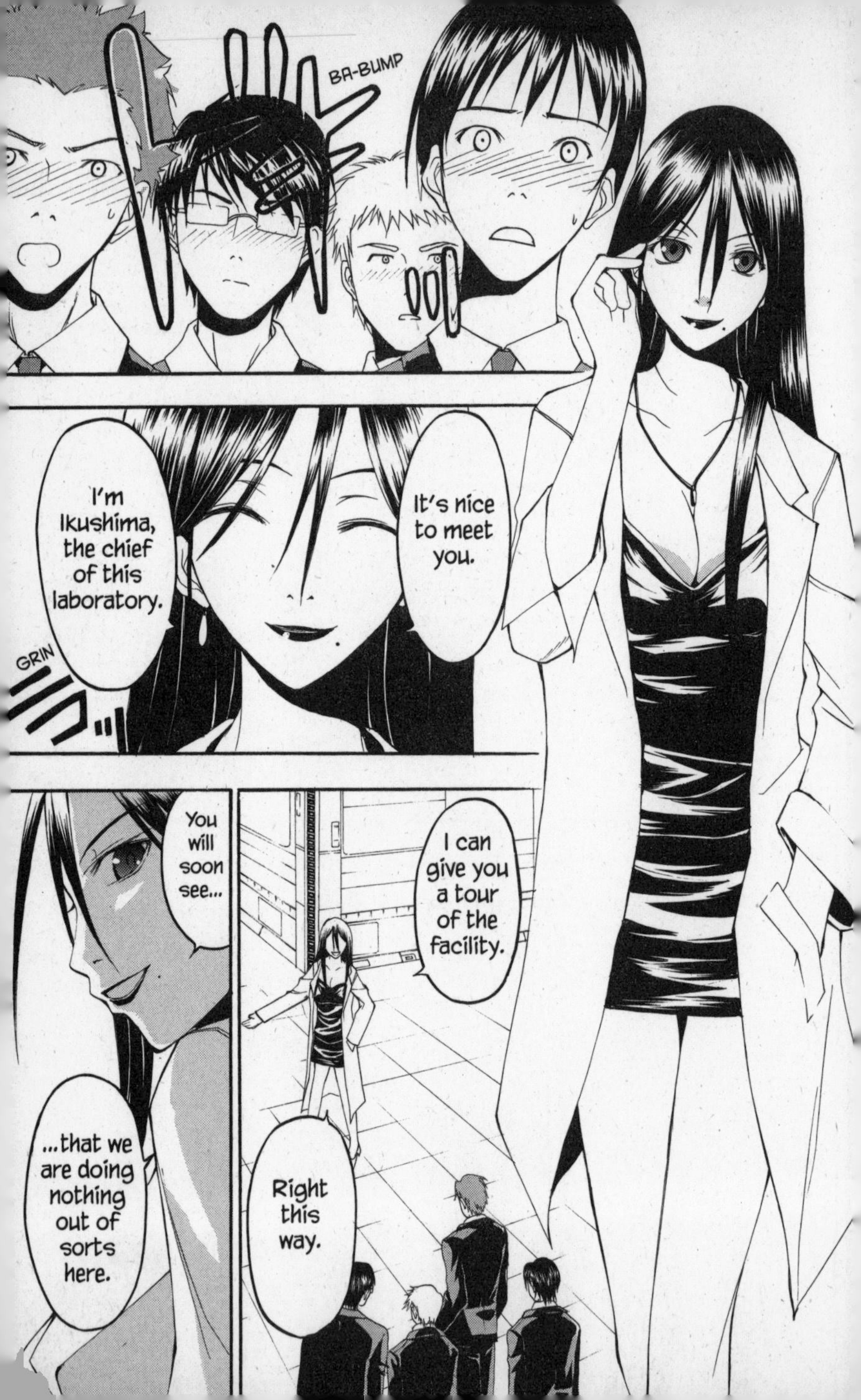
BA-BUMP
It's nice to meet you.
I'm Ikushima, the chief of this laboratory.
GRIN
I can give you a tour of the facility.
Right this way.
You will soon see...
...that we are doing nothing out of sorts here.

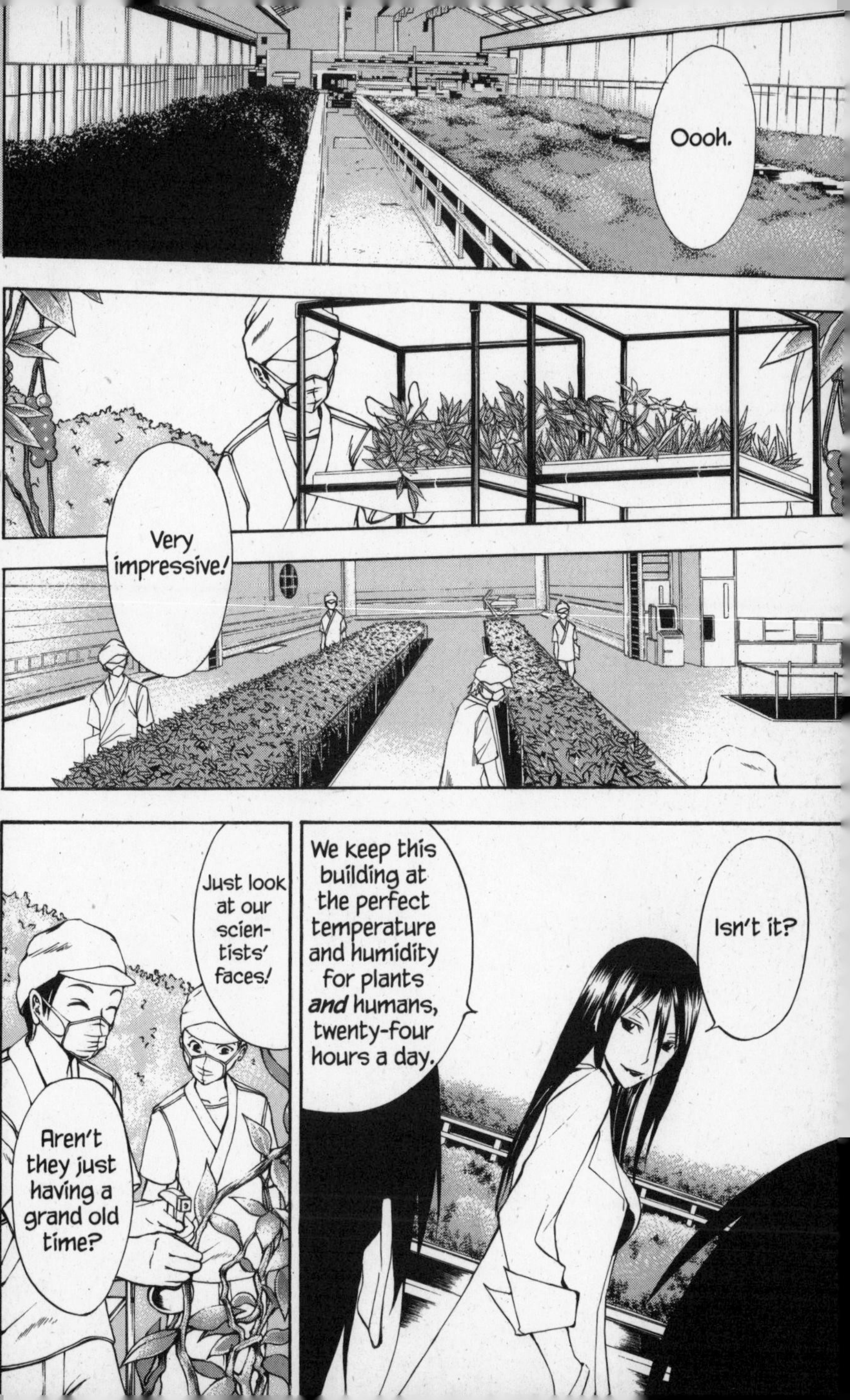
Oooh.
Very impressive!
Isn't it?
We keep this building at the perfect temperature and humidity for plants *and* humans, twenty-four hours a day.
Just look at our scien-tists' faces!
Aren't they just having a grand old time?

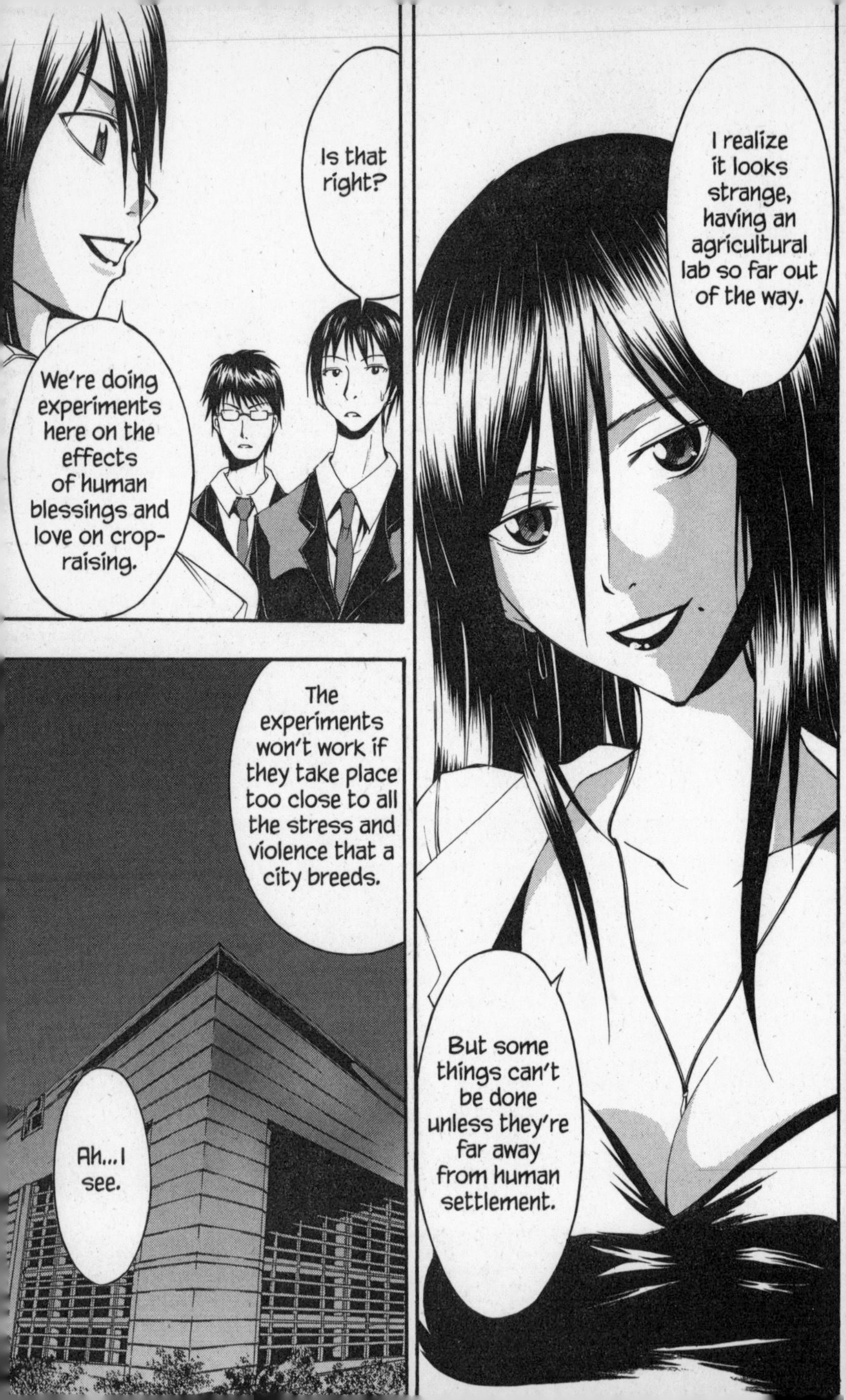
I realize it looks strange, having an agricultural lab so far out of the way.
But some things can't be done unless they're far away from human settlement.
Is that right?
We're doing experiments here on the effects of human blessings and love on crop-raising.
The experiments won't work if they take place too close to all the stress and violence that a city breeds.
Ah...I see.

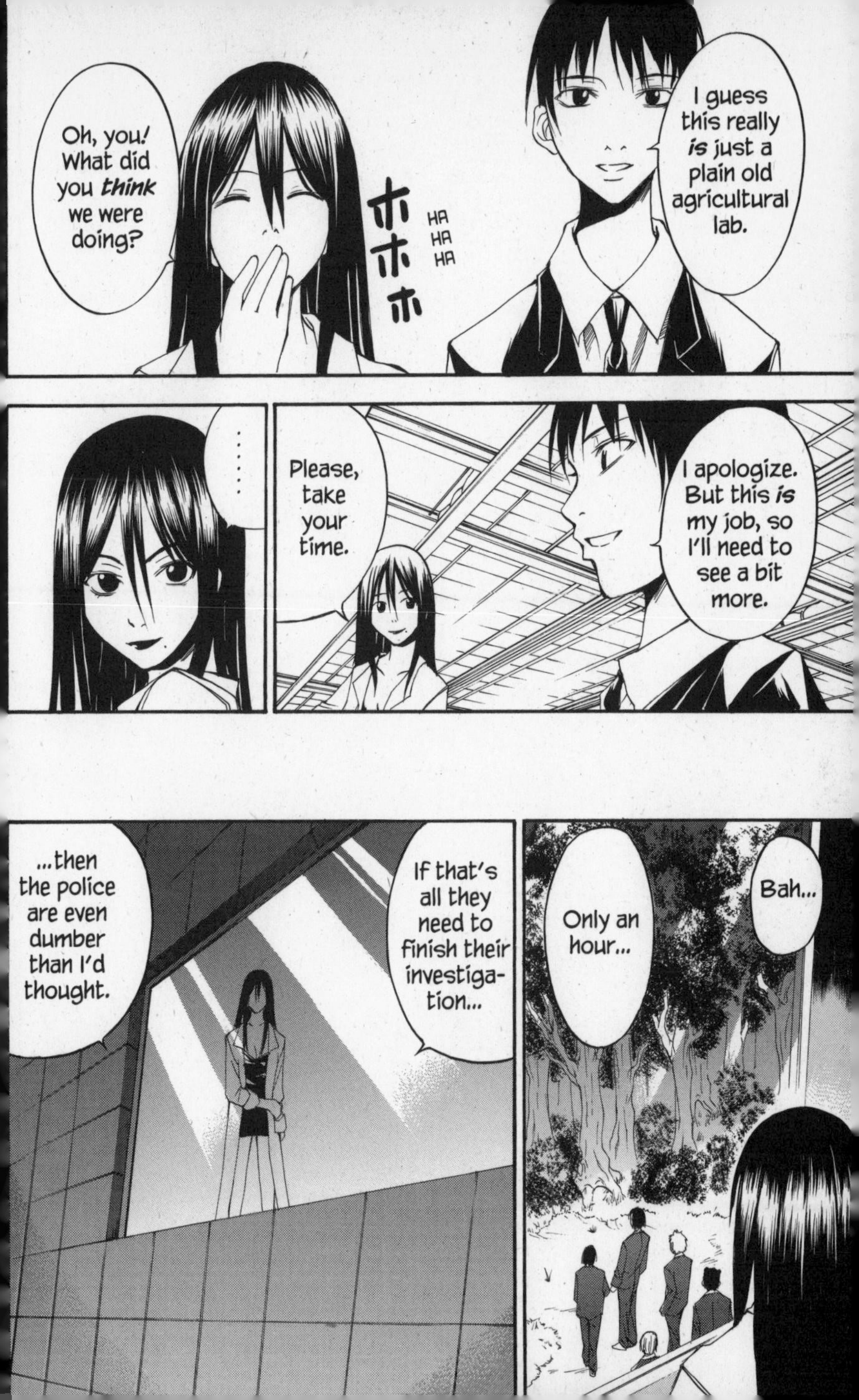

I guess this really *is* just a plain old agricultural lab.
ホホホ
HA HA HA
Oh, you! What did you *think* we were doing?
I apologize. But this *is* my job, so I'll need to see a bit more.
Please, take your time.
......
Bah...
Only an hour...
If that's all they need to finish their investiga-tion...
...then the police are even dumber than I'd thought.

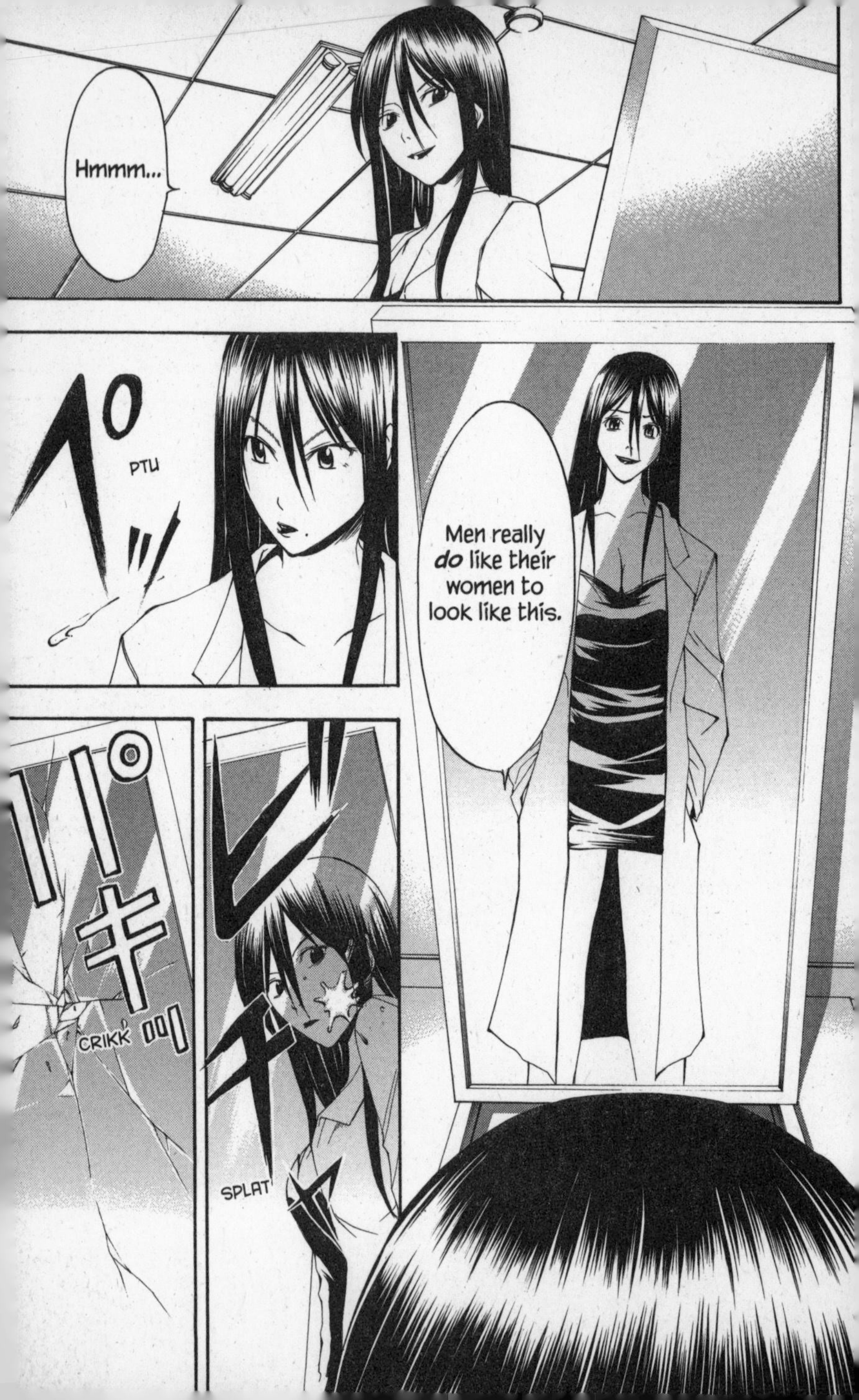
Hmmm...
Men really *do* like their women to look like this.
PTU
SPLAT
CRIKK

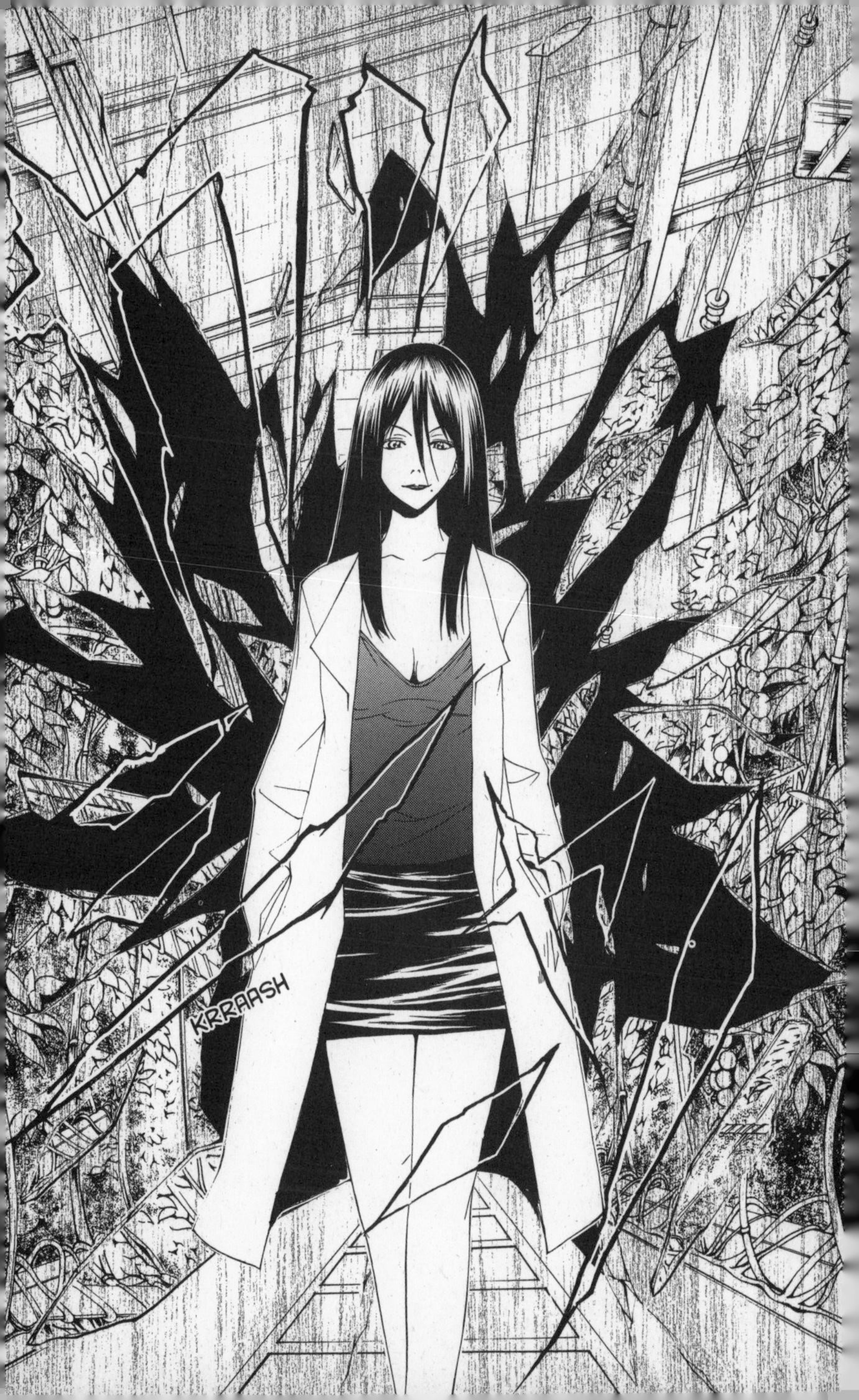
KRRAASH

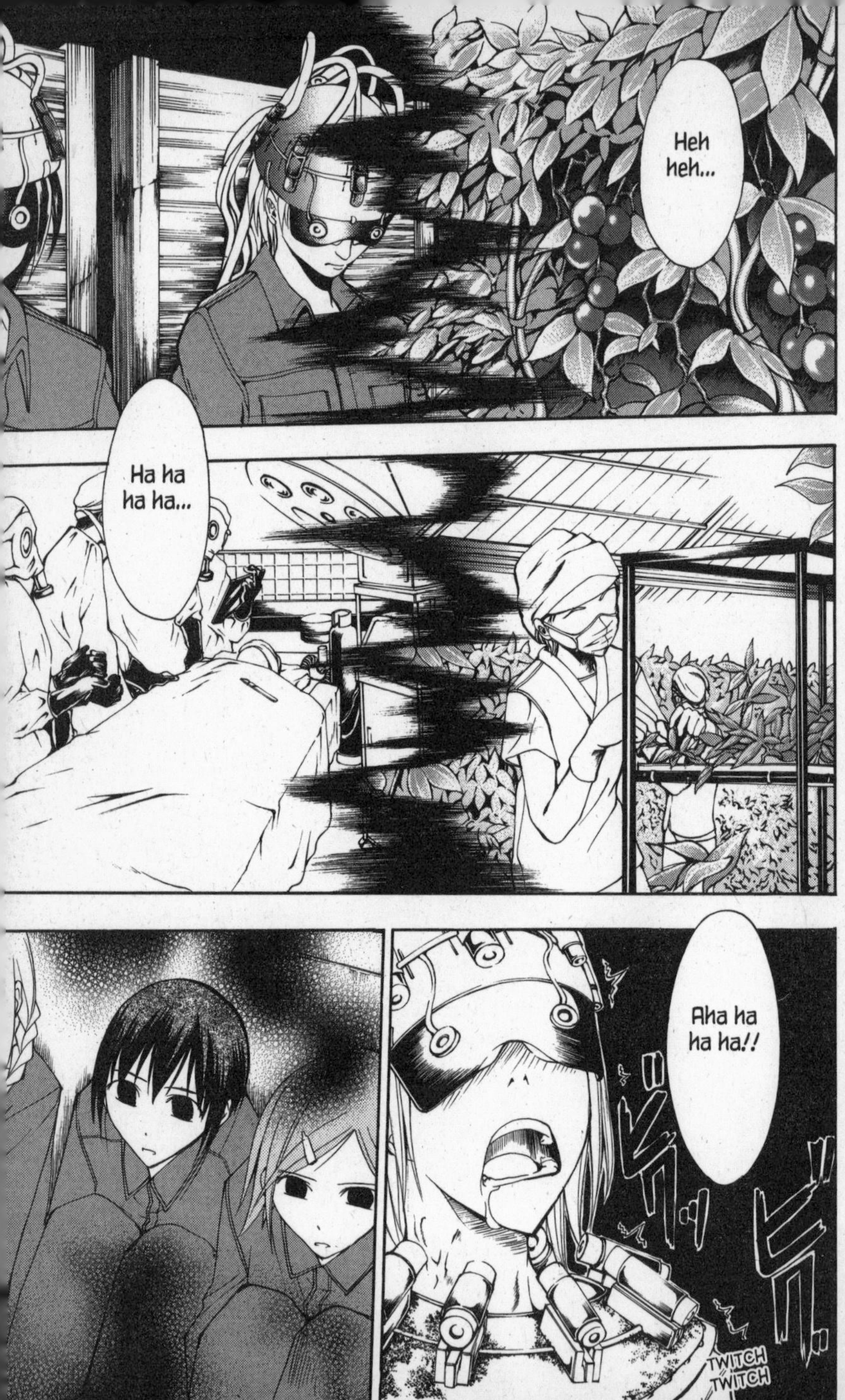
Heh heh...
Ha ha ha ha...
Aha ha ha ha!!
TWITCH TWITCH

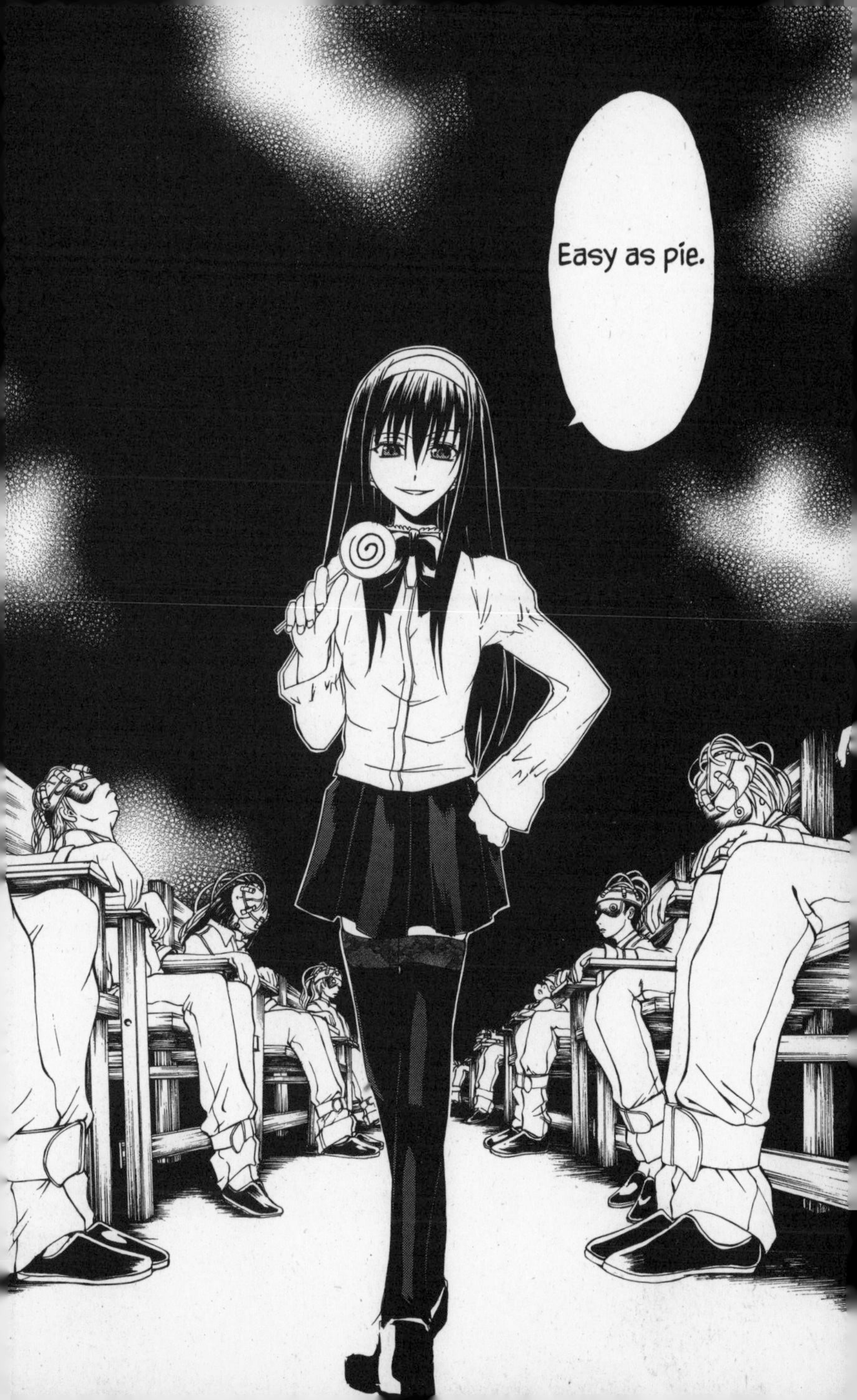
Easy as pie.

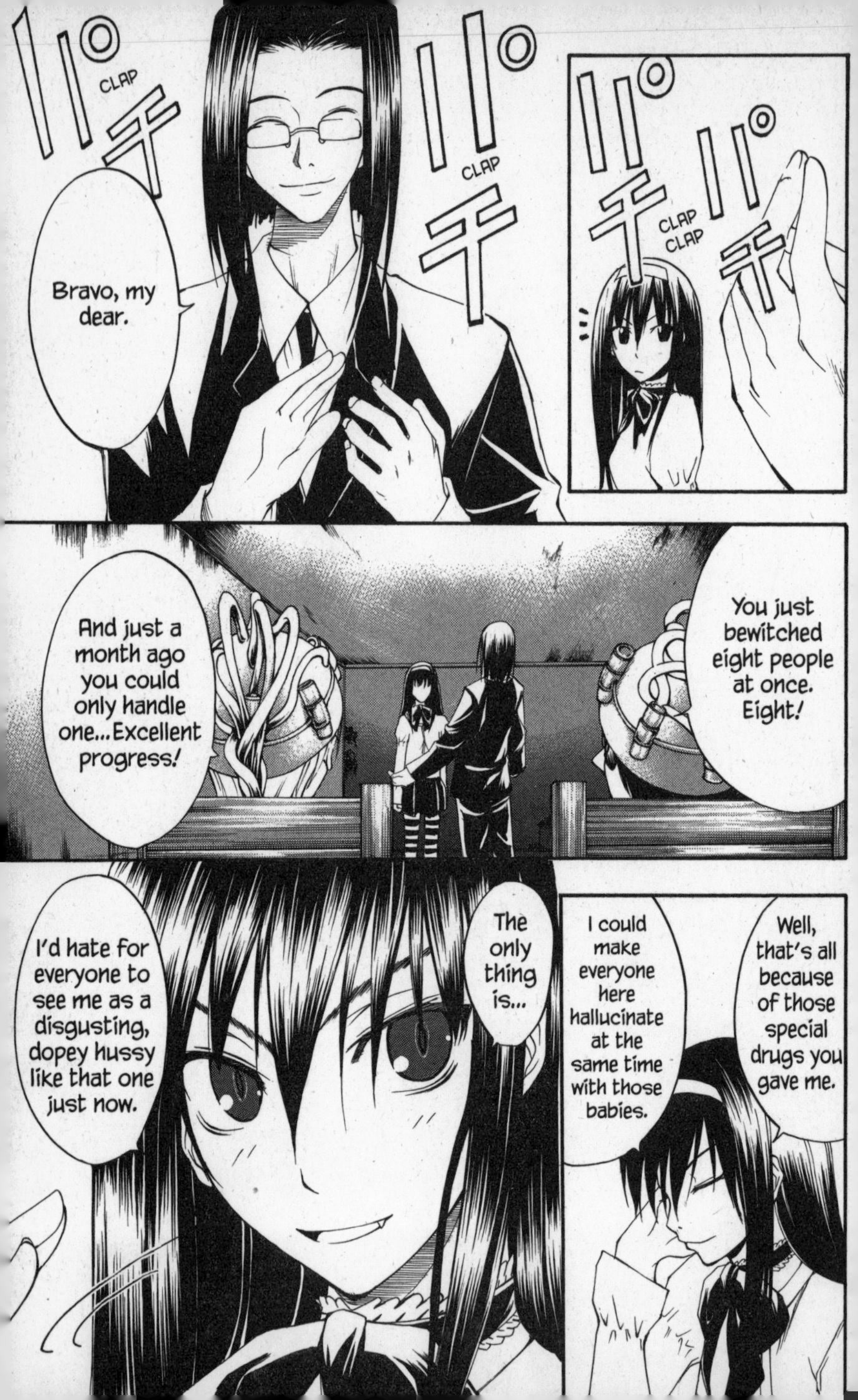
パチ パチ
CLAP CLAP
パチ
CLAP
パチ
CLAP
Bravo, my dear.
You just bewitched eight people at once. Eight!
And just a month ago you could only handle one...Excellent progress!
Well, that's all because of those special drugs you gave me.
I could make everyone here hallucinate at the same time with those babies.
The only thing is...
I'd hate for everyone to see me as a disgusting, dopey hussy like that one just now.

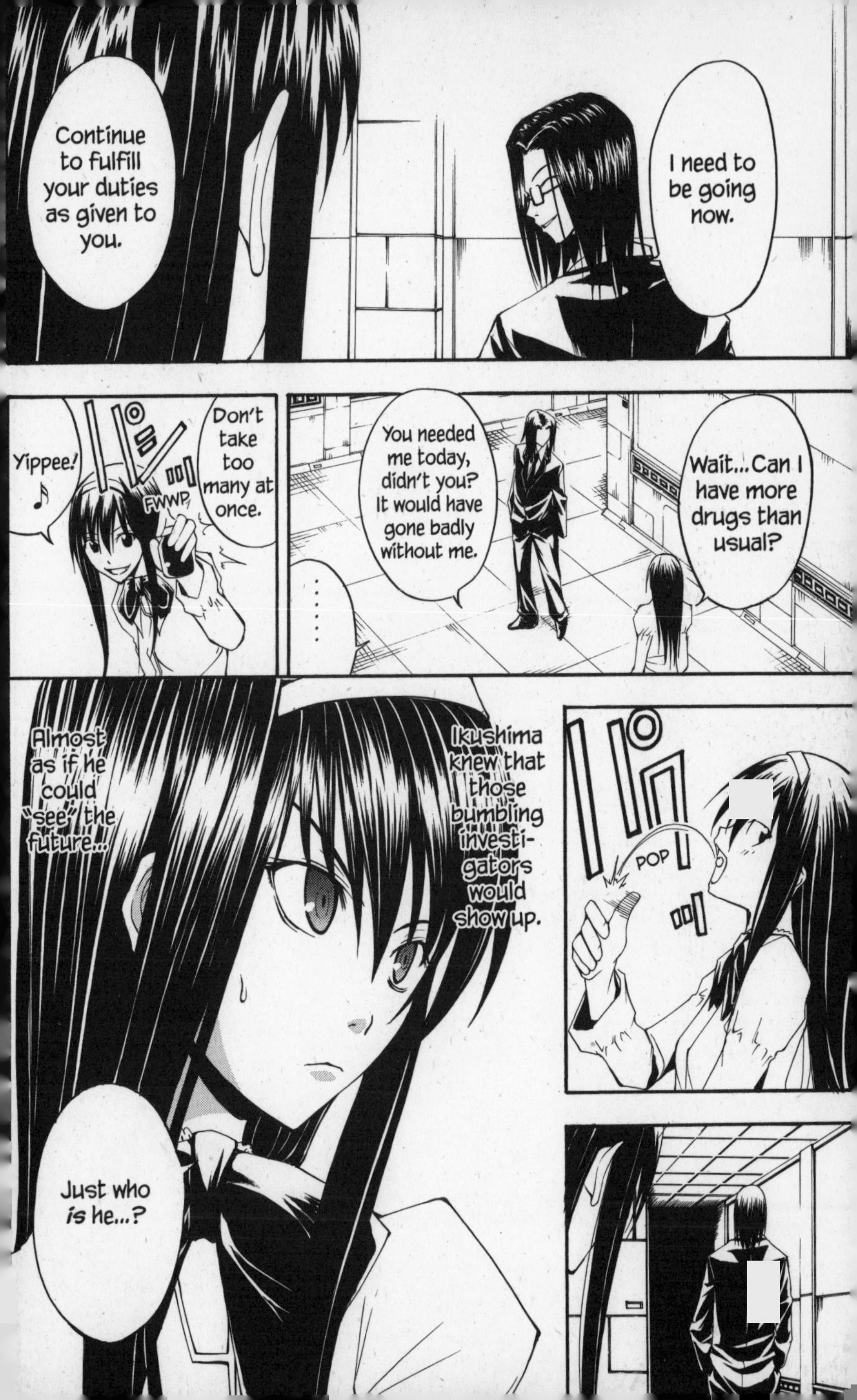
I need to be going now.
Continue to fulfill your duties as given to you.
Wait...Can I have more drugs than usual?
You needed me today, didn't you? It would have gone badly without me.
......
Don't take too many at once.
FWWP
Yippee! ♪
POP
Ikushima knew that those bumbling investigators would show up.
Almost as if he could "see" the future...
Just who *is* he...?

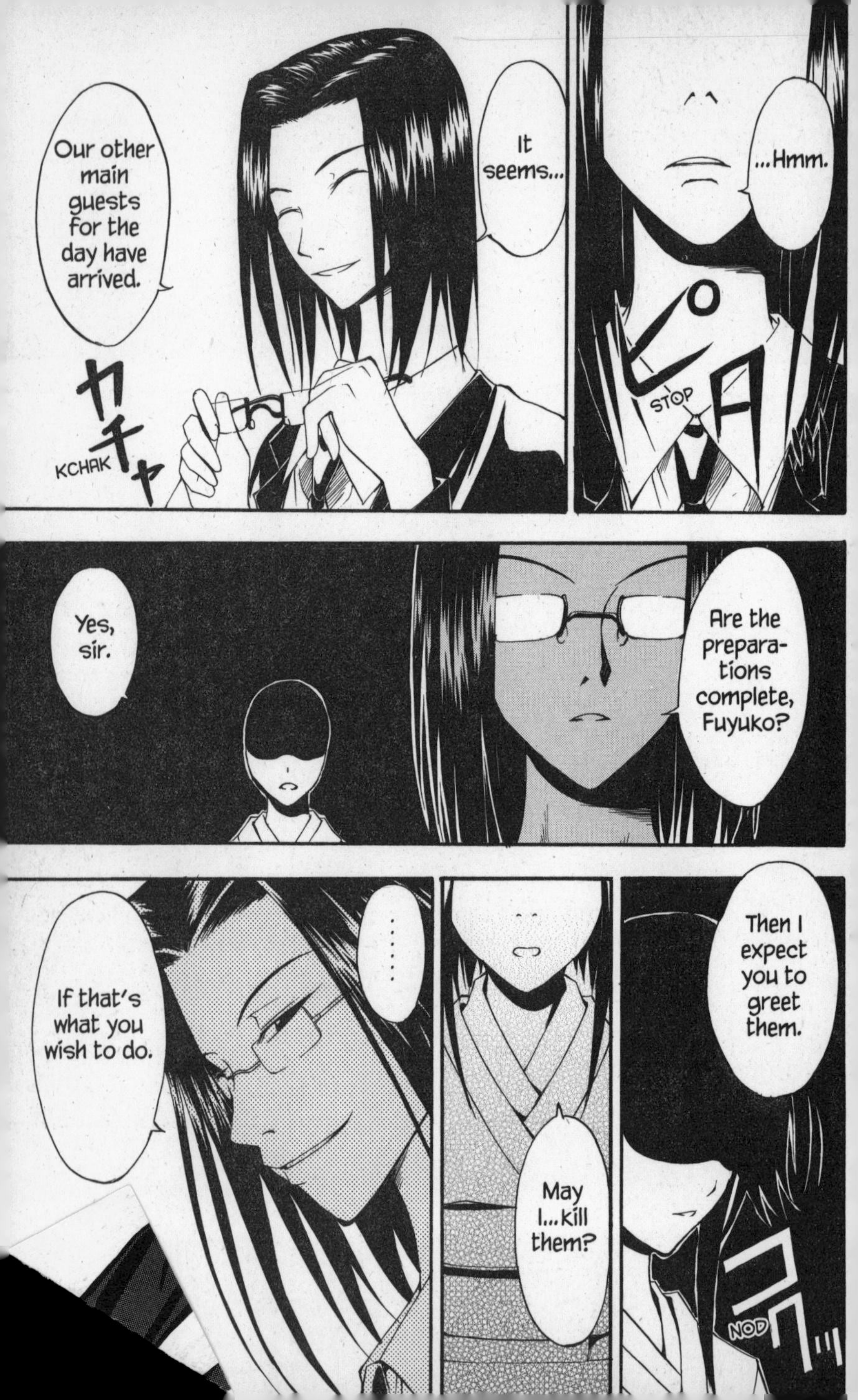
...Hmm.
ピタ
STOP
It seems...
Our other main guests for the day have arrived.
カチャ
KCHAK
Are the preparations complete, Fuyuko?
Yes, sir.
Then I expect you to greet them.
コクッ
NOD
May I...kill them?
......
If that's what you wish to do.

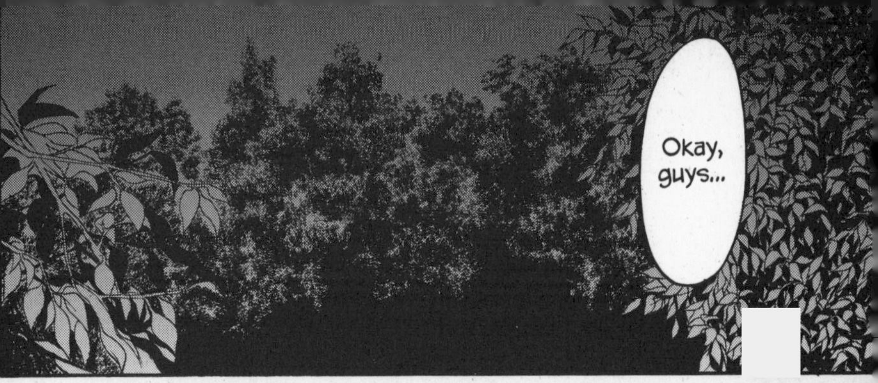
Okay, guys...
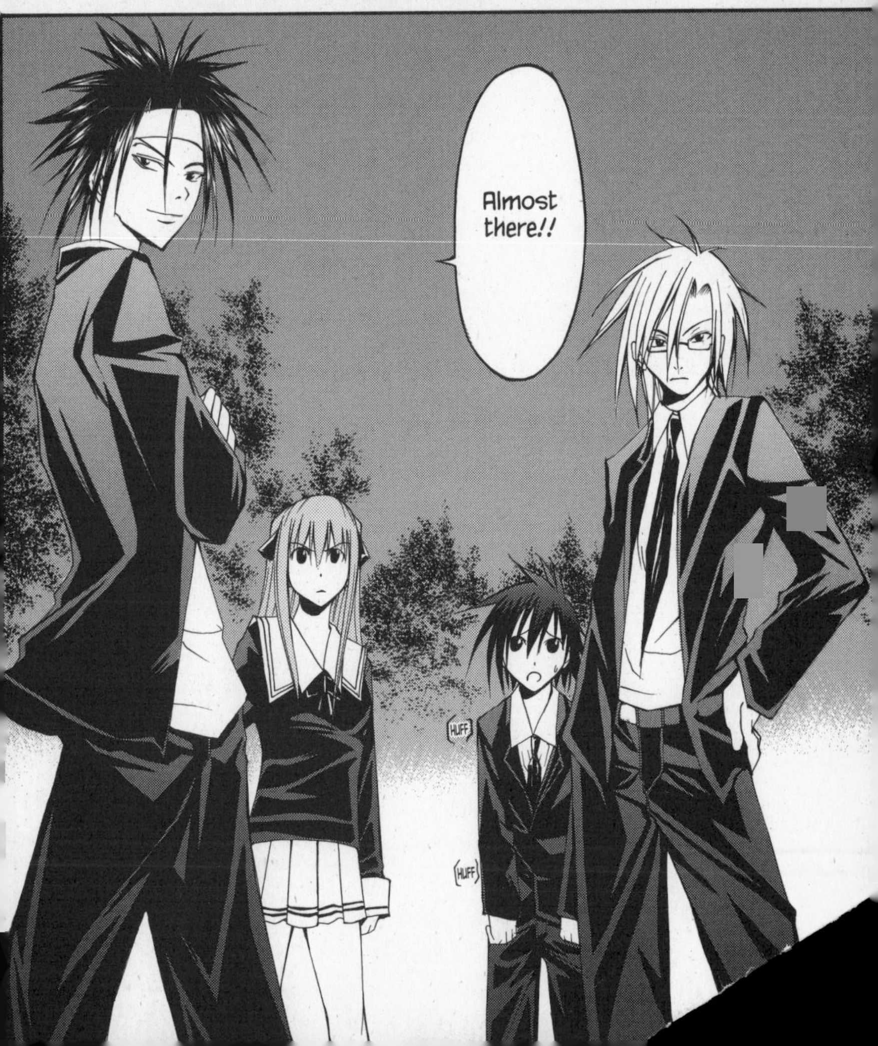
Almost there!!
HUFF
HUFF

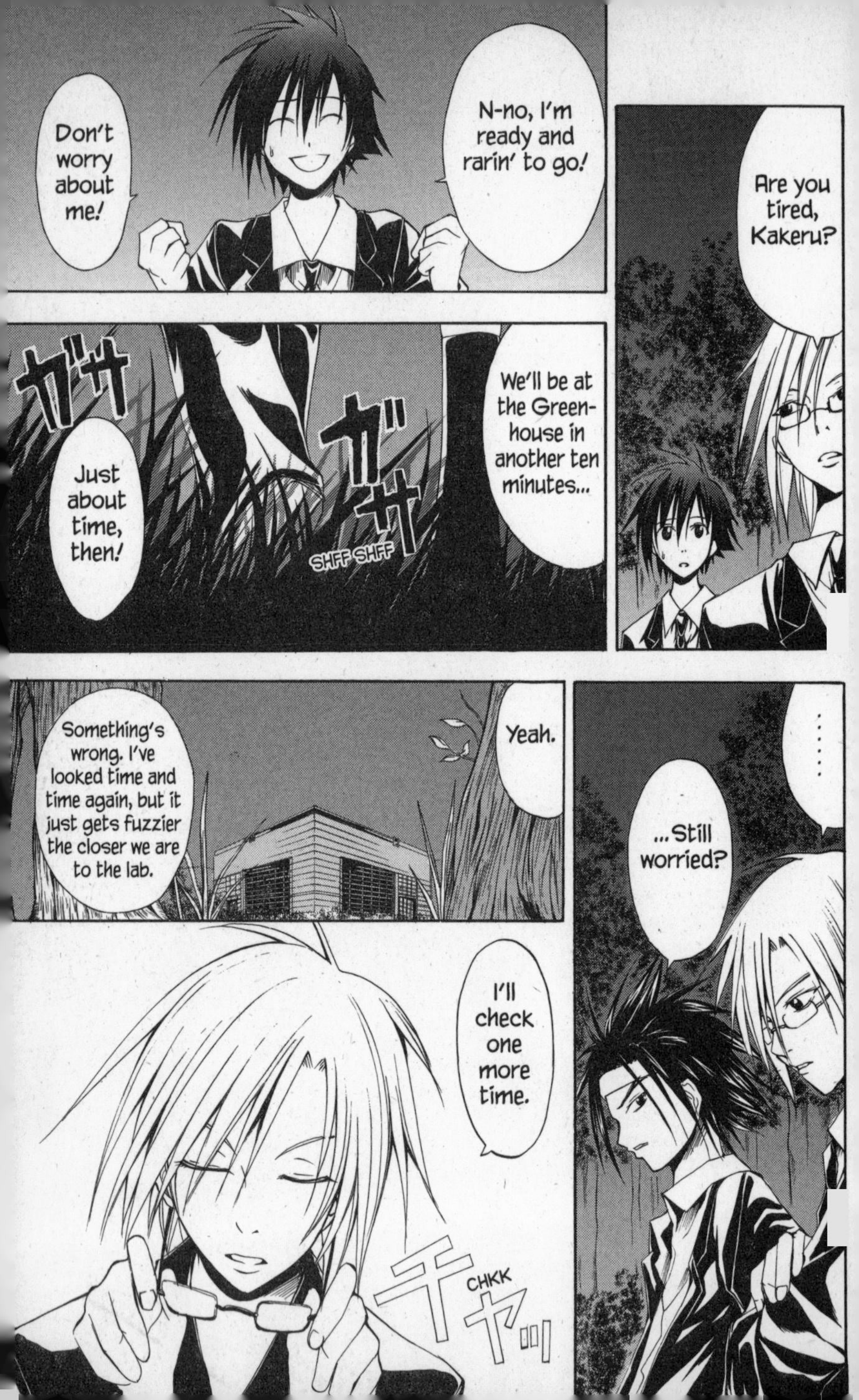
Are you tired, Kakeru?
N-no, I'm ready and rarin' to go!
Don't worry about me!
We'll be at the Green-house in another ten minutes...
Just about time, then!
ガサ
ガサ
SHFF SHFF
......
...Still worried?
Yeah.
Something's wrong. I've looked time and time again, but it just gets fuzzier the closer we are to the lab.
I'll check one more time.
チャッ
CHKK

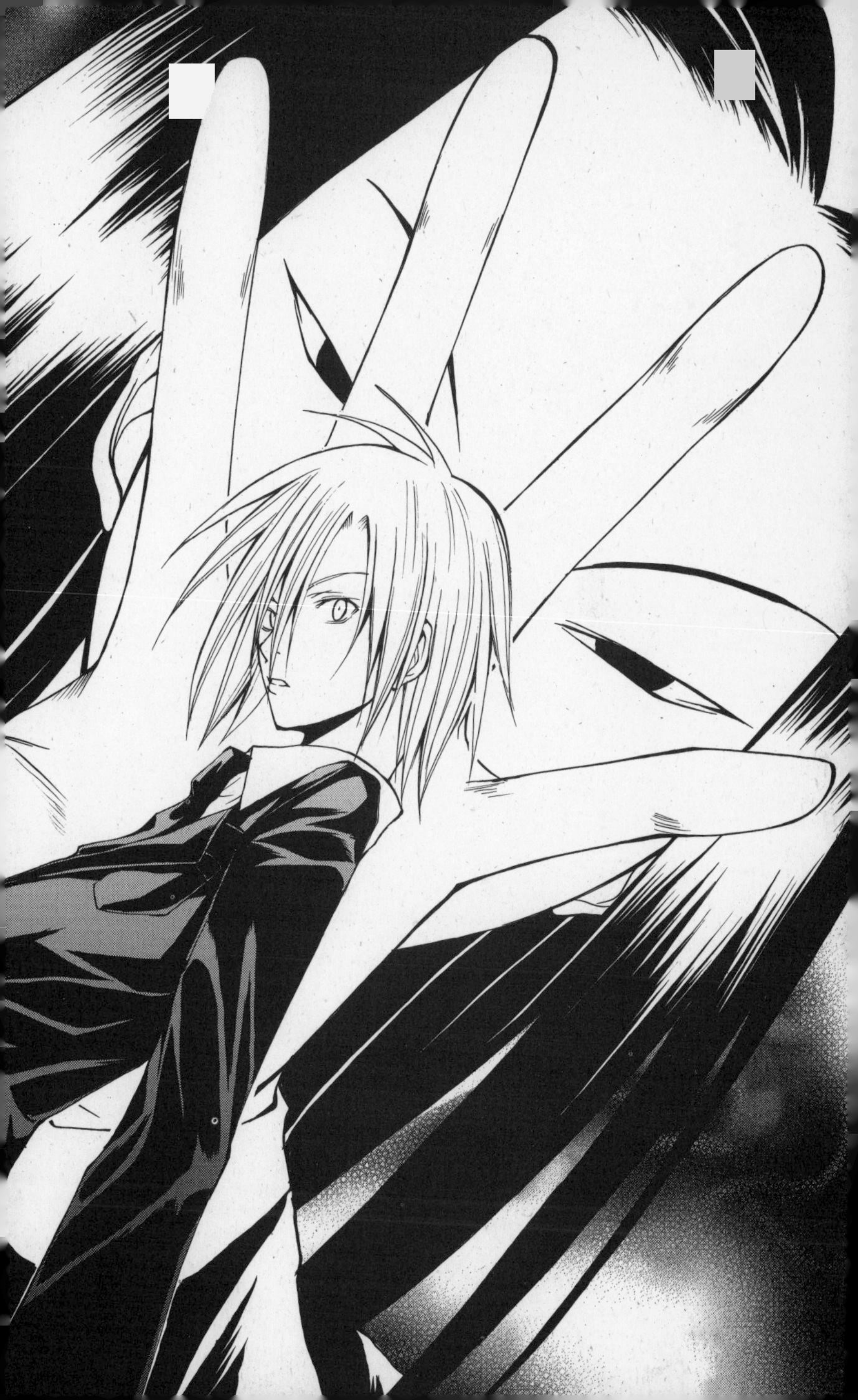

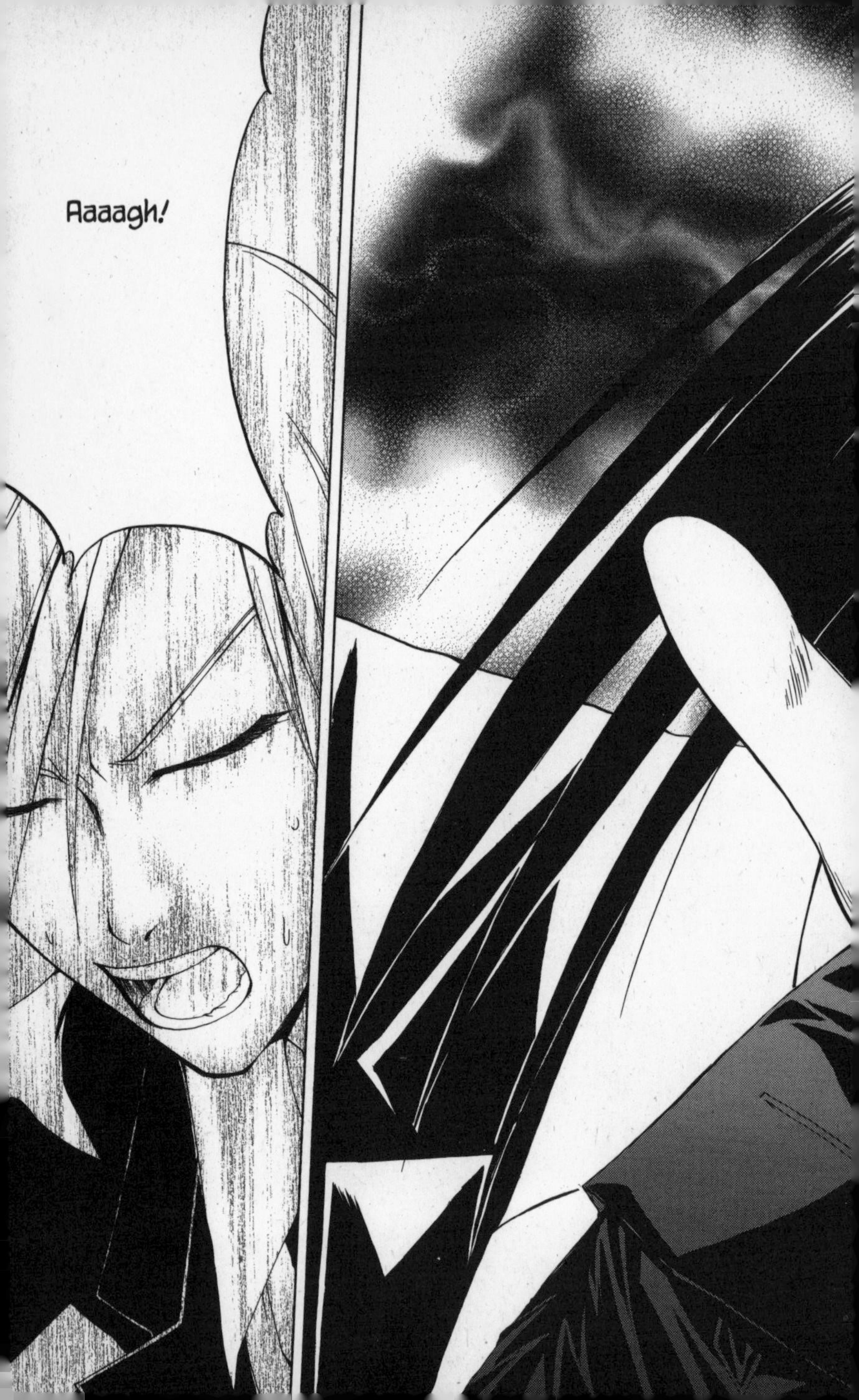
Aaaagh!

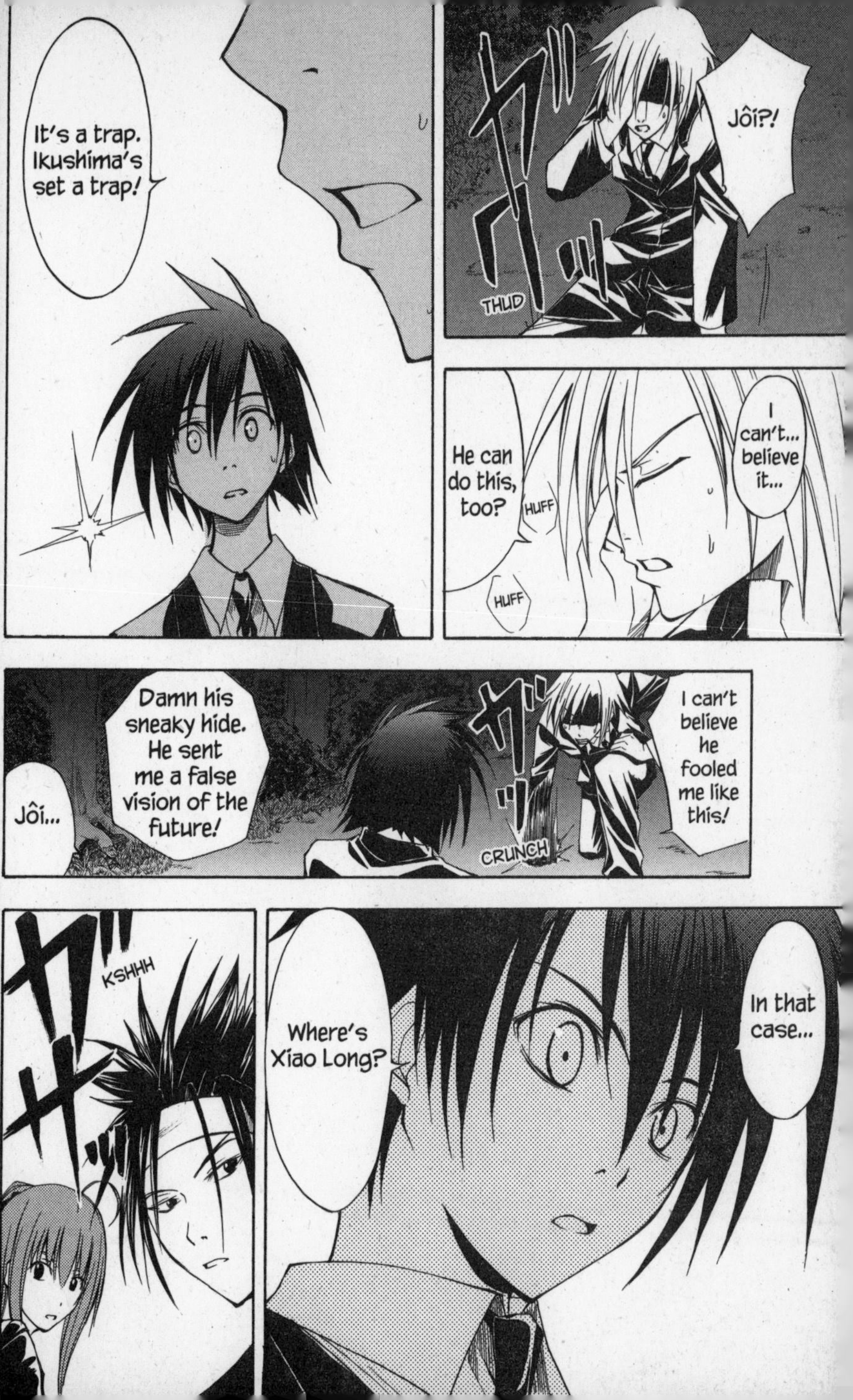

Jôi?!
THUD
I can't... believe it...
He can do this, too?
HUFF
HUFF
It's a trap. Ikushima's set a trap!
I can't believe he fooled me like this!
CRUNCH
Damn his sneaky hide. He sent me a false vision of the future!
Jôi...
In that case...
Where's Xiao Long?
KSHHH

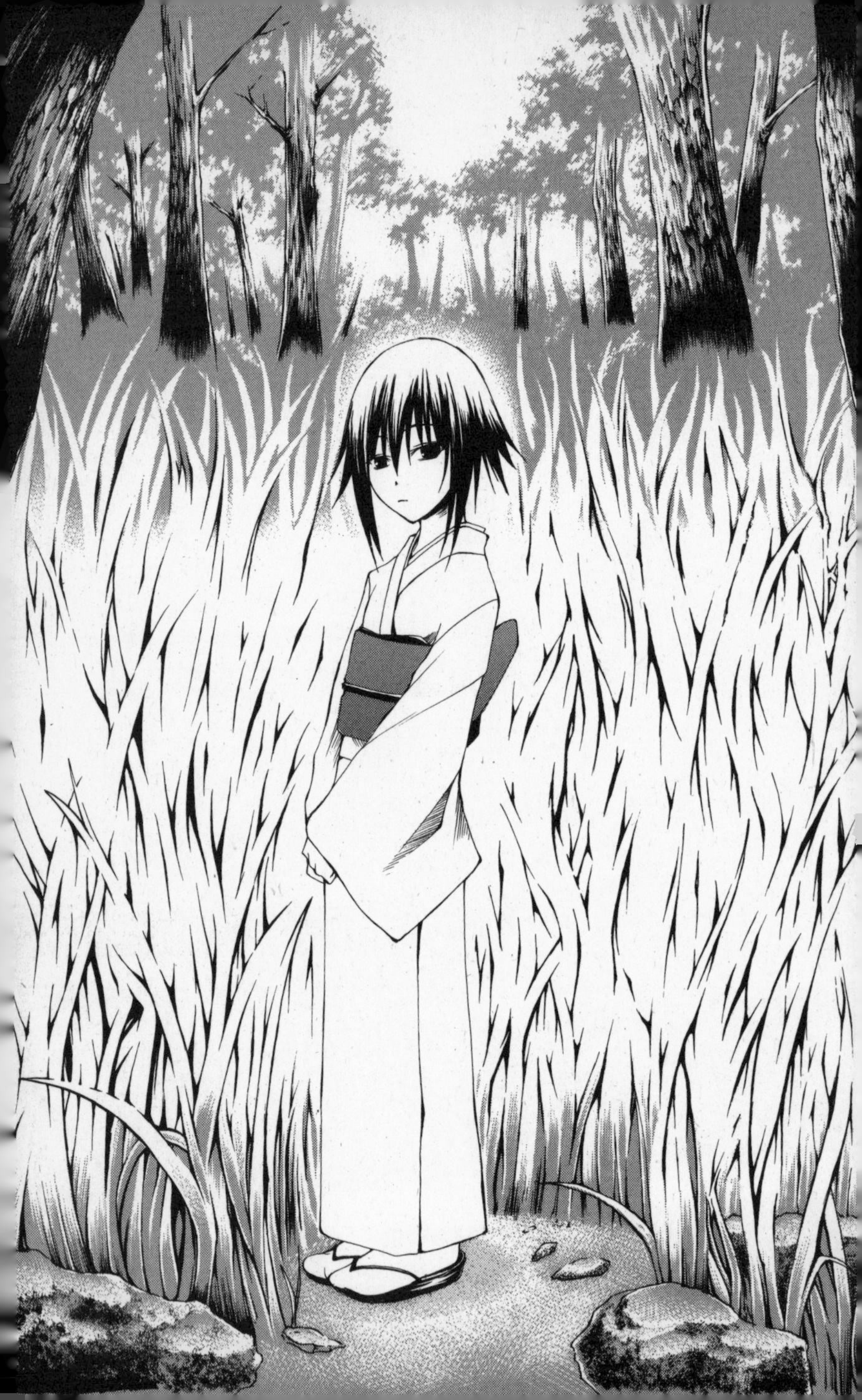

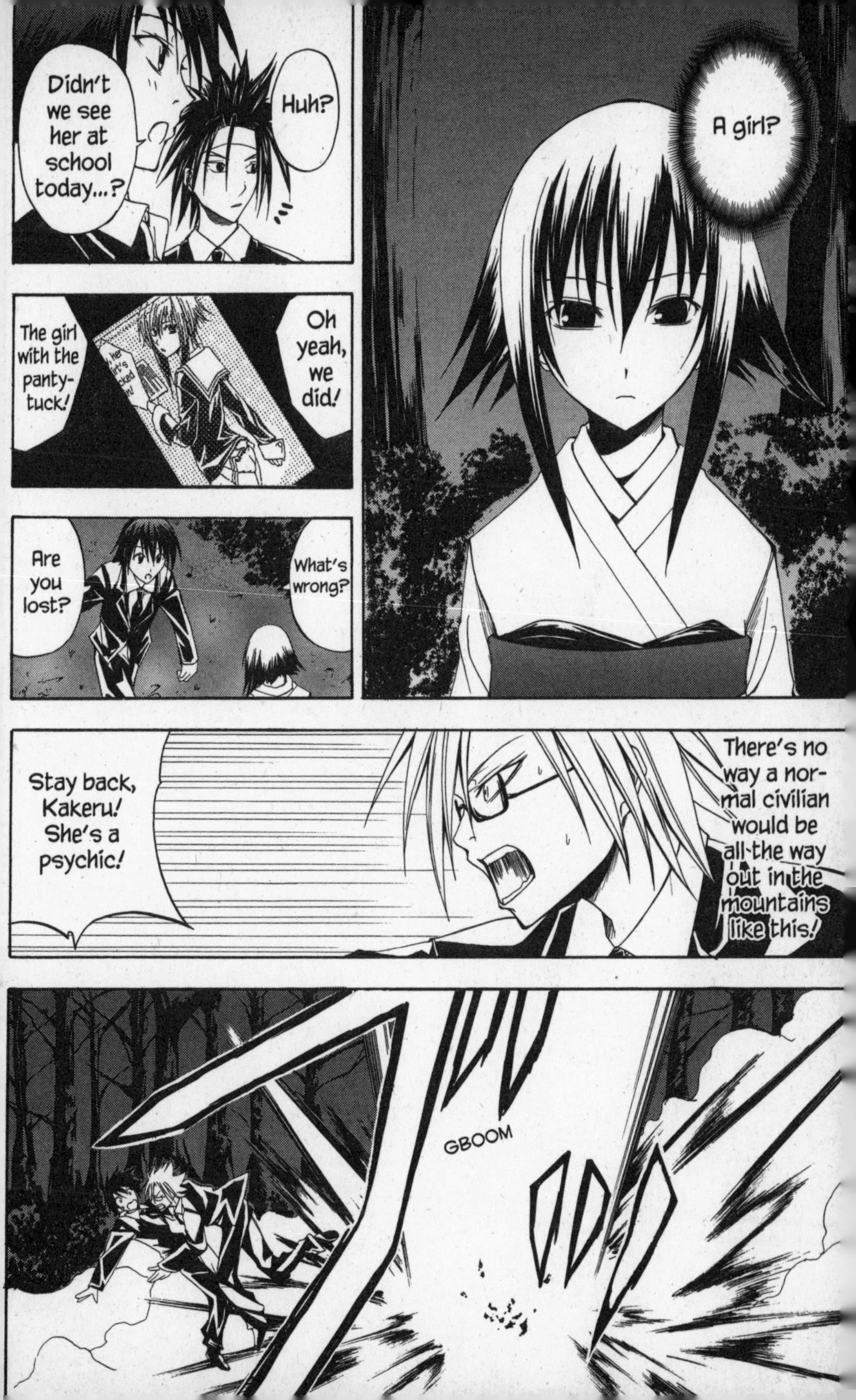
A girl?
Huh?
Didn't we see her at school today...?
Oh yeah, we did!
The girl with the panty-tuck!
What's wrong?
Are you lost?
There's no way a nor-mal civilian would be all the way out in the mountains like this!
Stay back, Kakeru! She's a psychic!
GBOOM

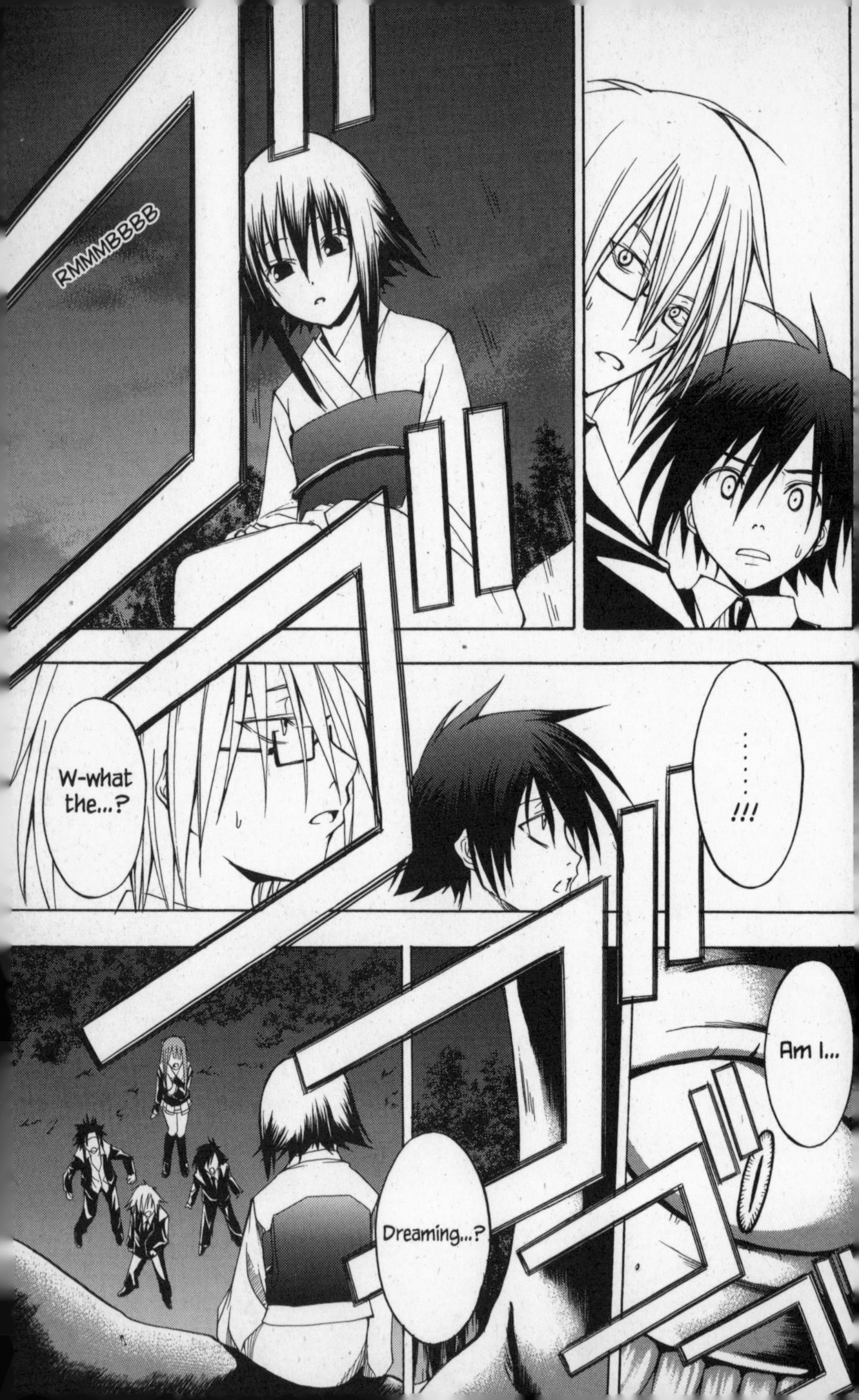
RMMMBBBB
......!!!
W-what the...?
Am I...
Dreaming...?

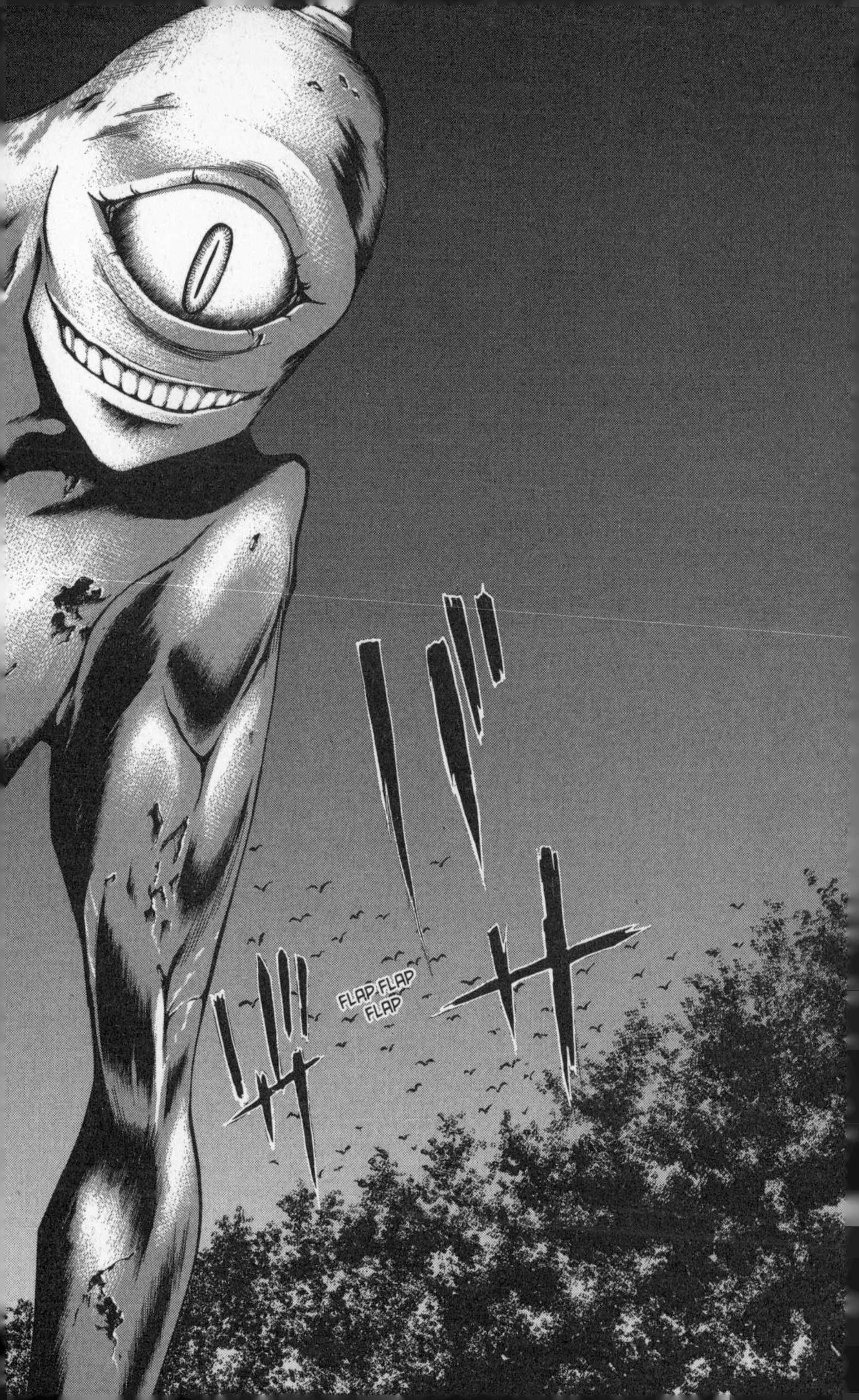
FLAP FLAP
FLAP

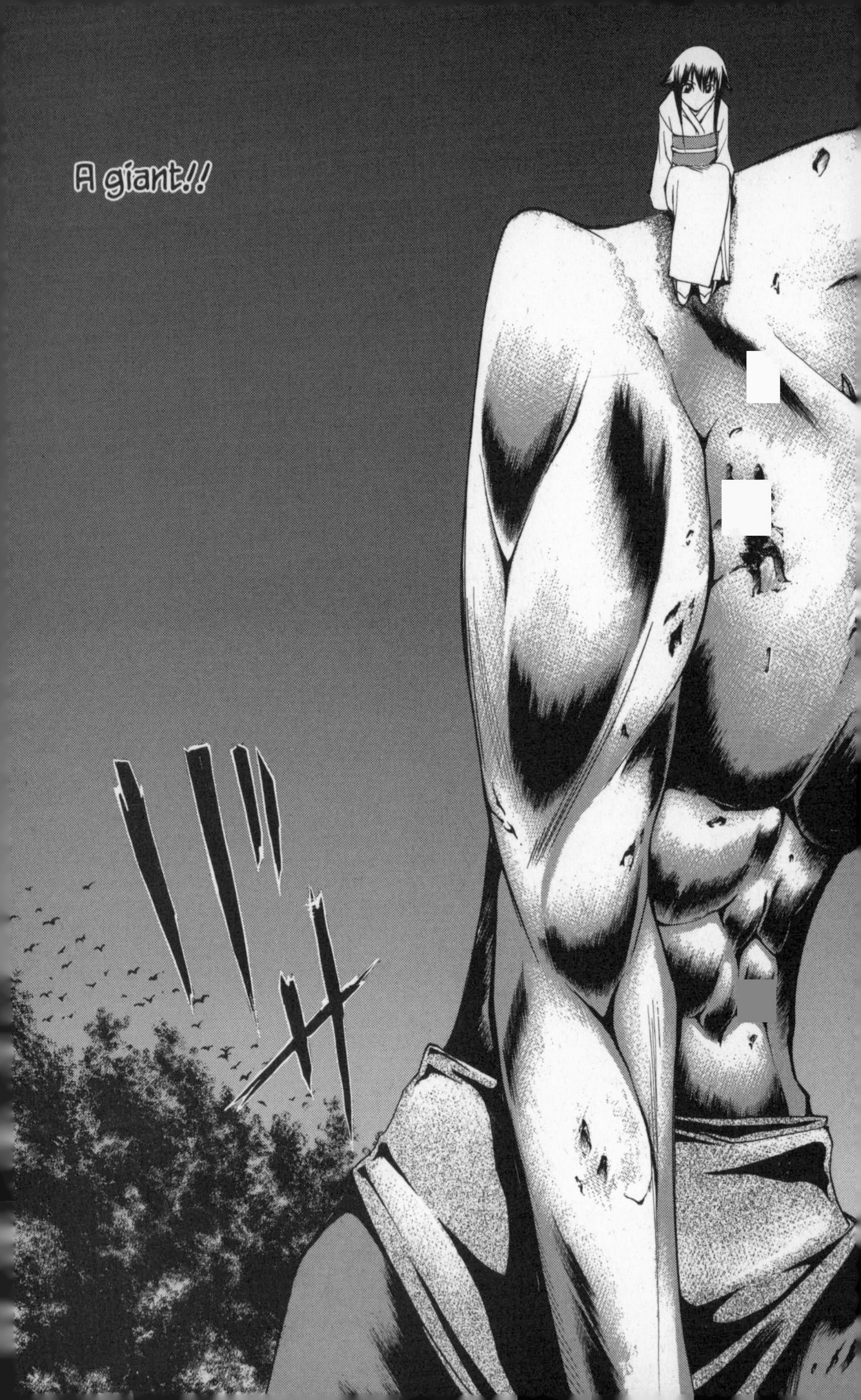
A giant!!

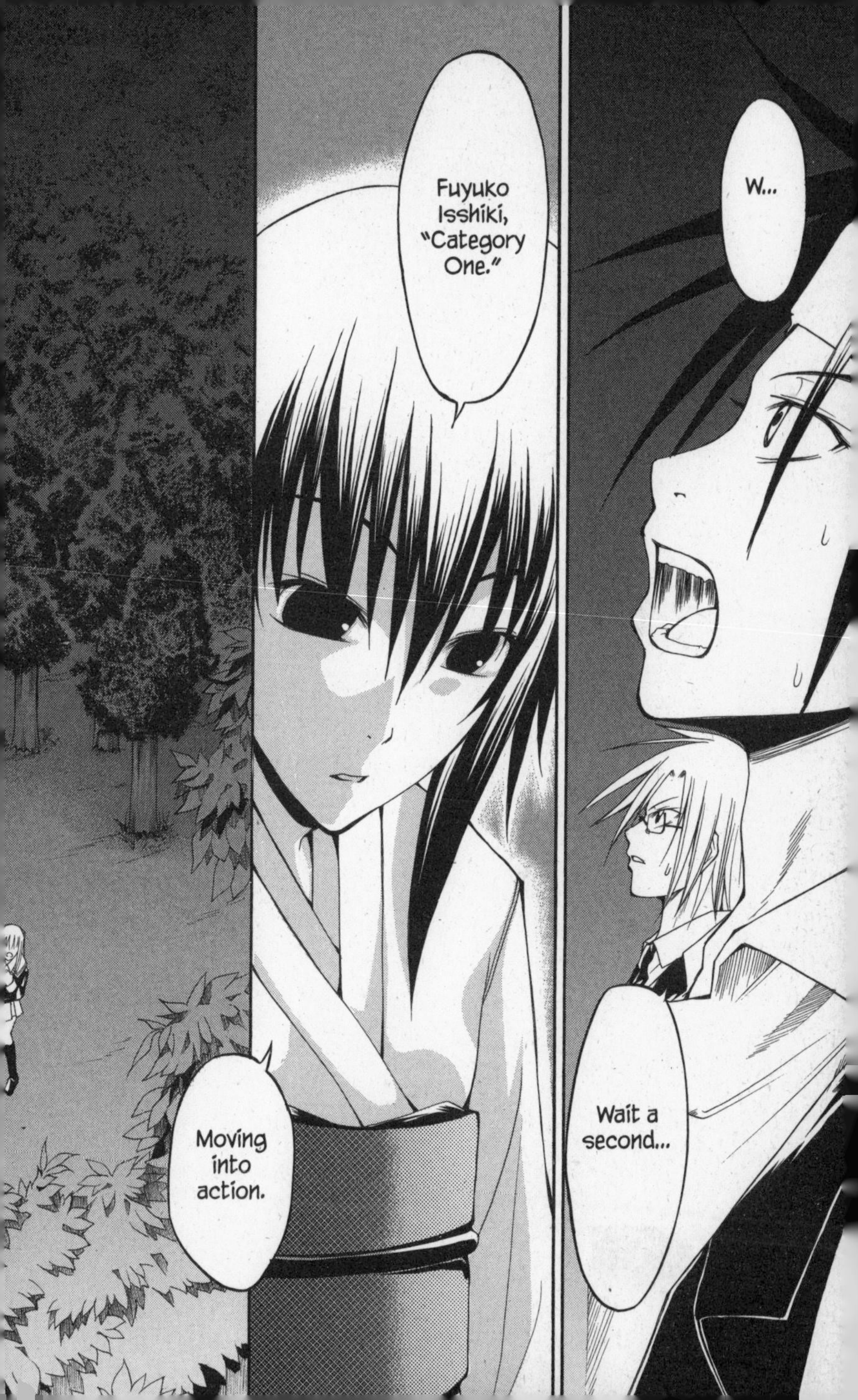
W...
Wait a second...
Fuyuko Isshiki, "Category One."
Moving into action.

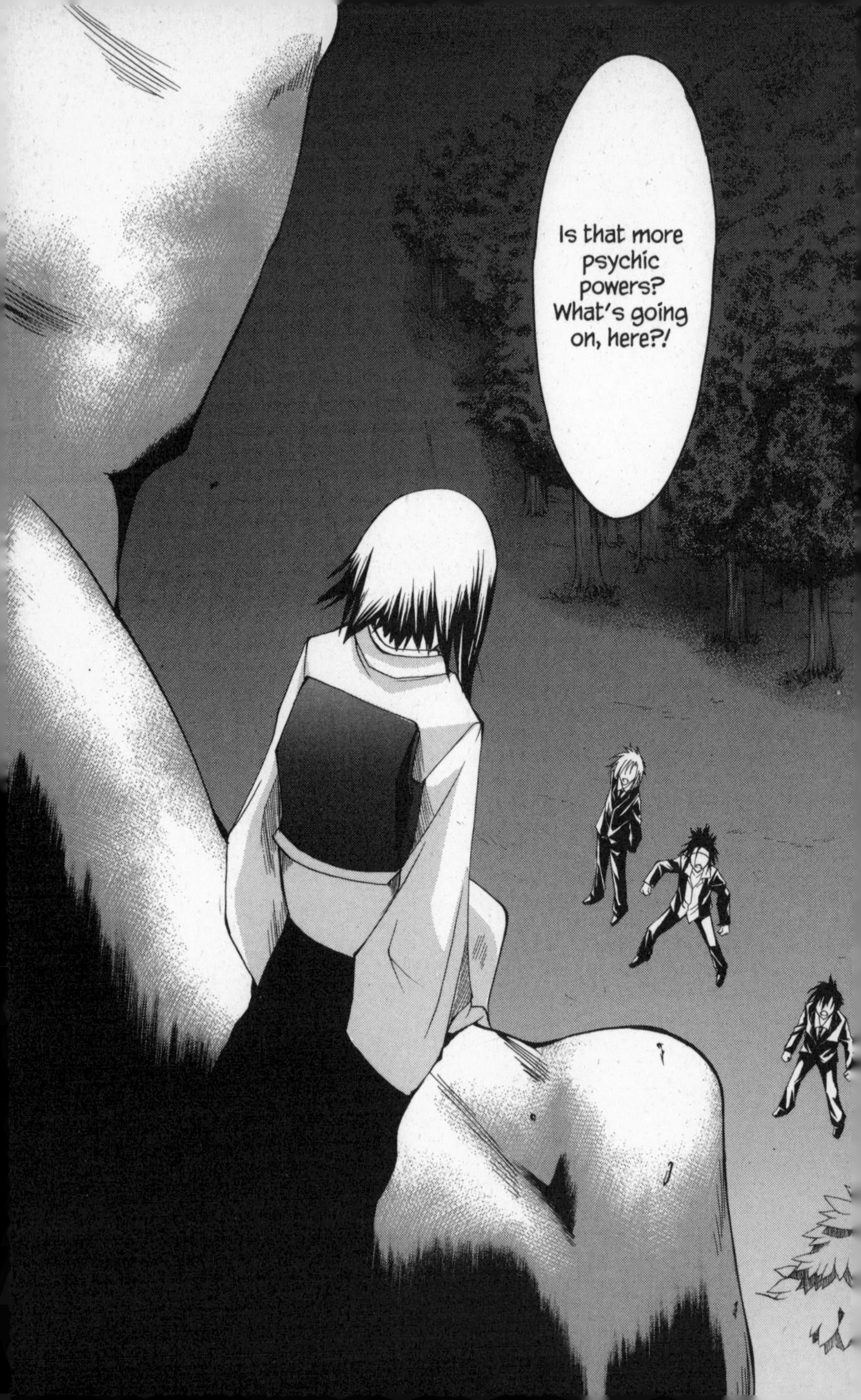
Is that more psychic powers? What's going on, here?!

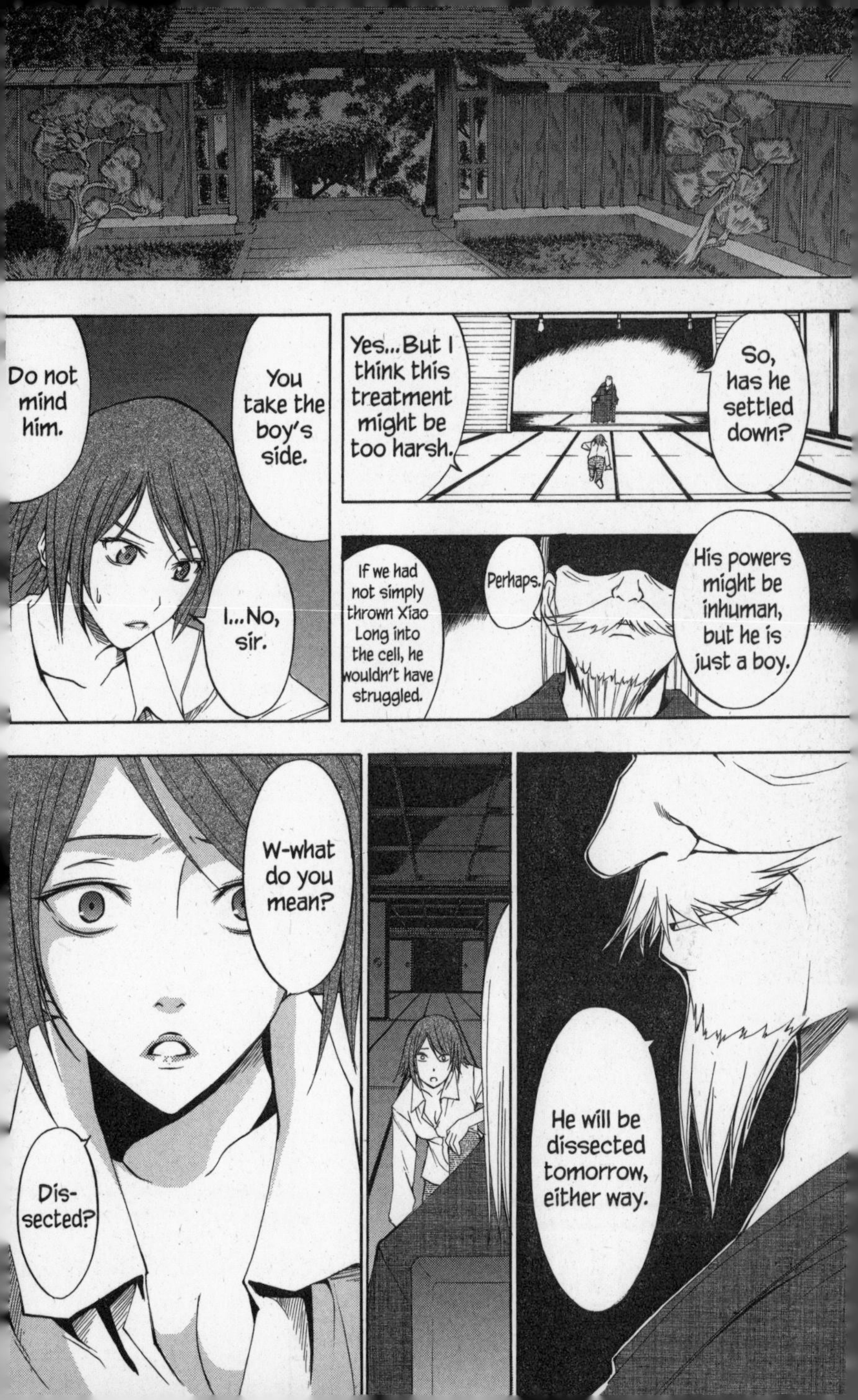
So, has he settled down?
Yes...But I think this treatment might be too harsh.
His powers might be inhuman, but he is just a boy.
Perhaps.
If we had not simply thrown Xiao Long into the cell, he wouldn't have struggled.
You take the boy's side.
Do not mind him.
I...No, sir.
He will be dissected tomorrow, either way.
W-what do you mean?
Dis-sected?

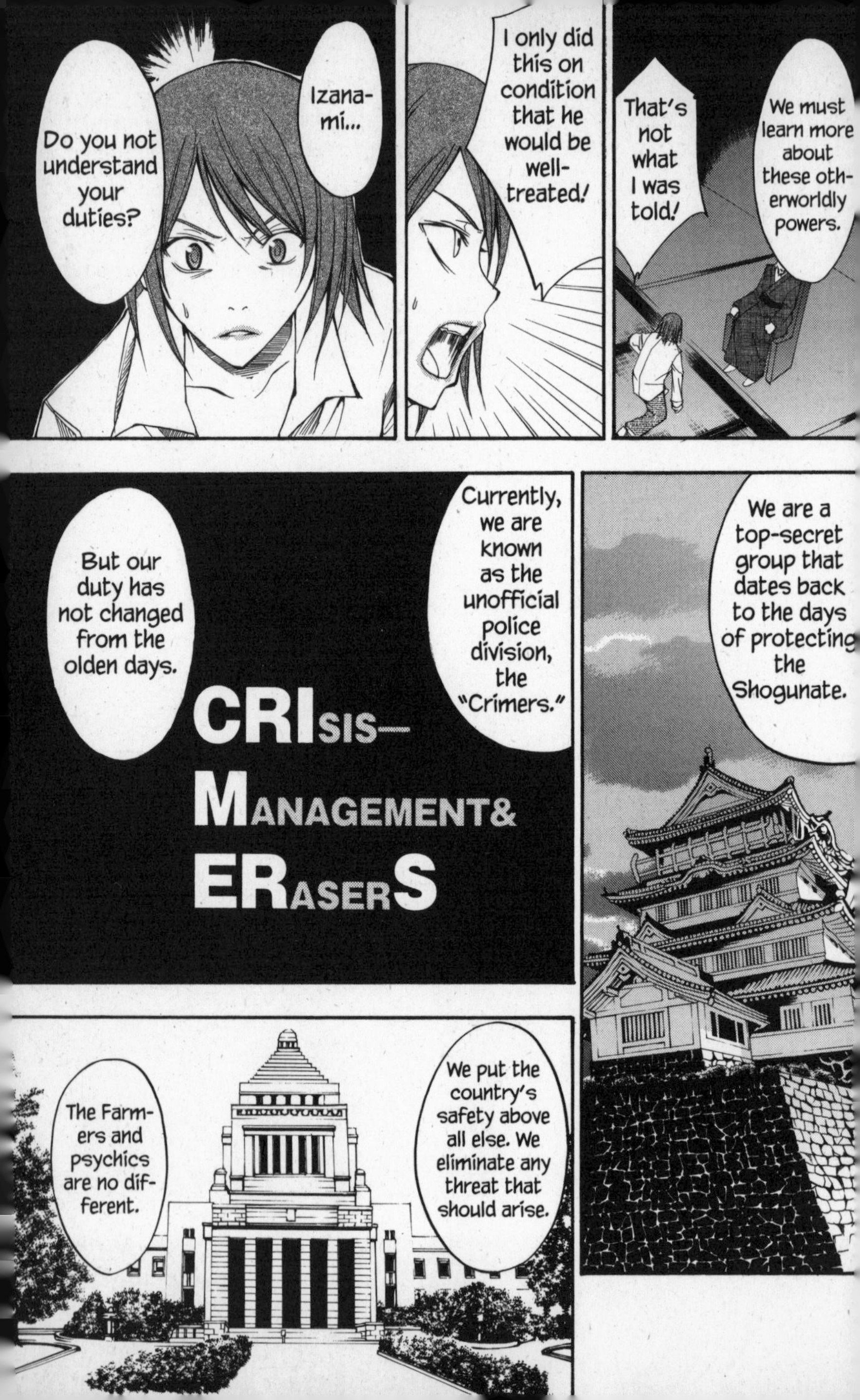
We must learn more about these oth-erworldly powers.
That's not what I was told!
I only did this on condition that he would be well-treated!
Izana-mi...
Do you not understand your duties?
We are a top-secret group that dates back to the days of protecting the Shogunate.
Currently, we are known as the unofficial police division, the "Crimers."
CRIsis—MANAGEMENT& ERaserS
But our duty has not changed from the olden days.
We put the country's safety above all else. We eliminate any threat that should arise.
The Farm-ers and psychics are no dif-ferent.

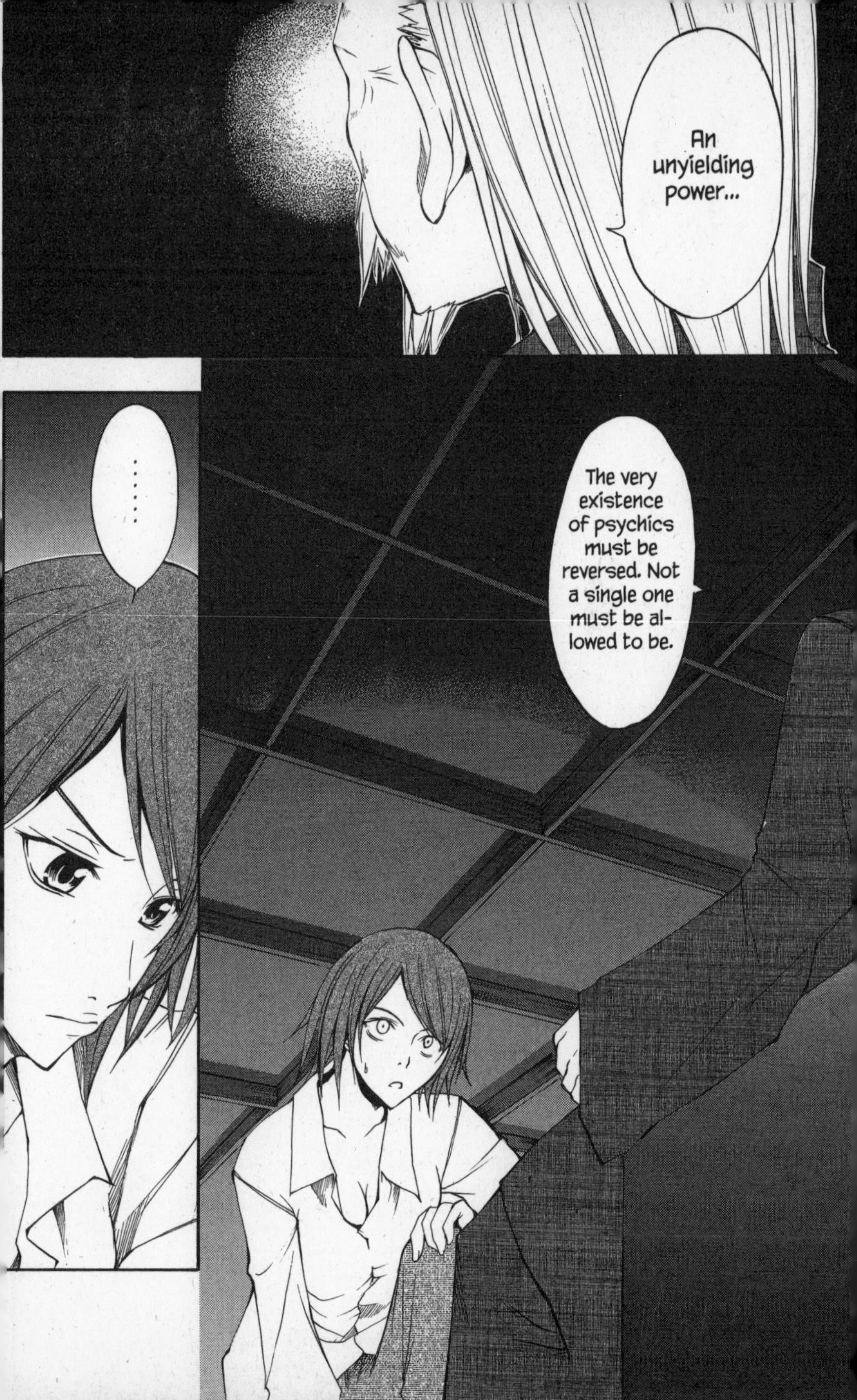
An unyielding power...
The very existence of psychics must be reversed. Not a single one must be al-lowed to be.
......

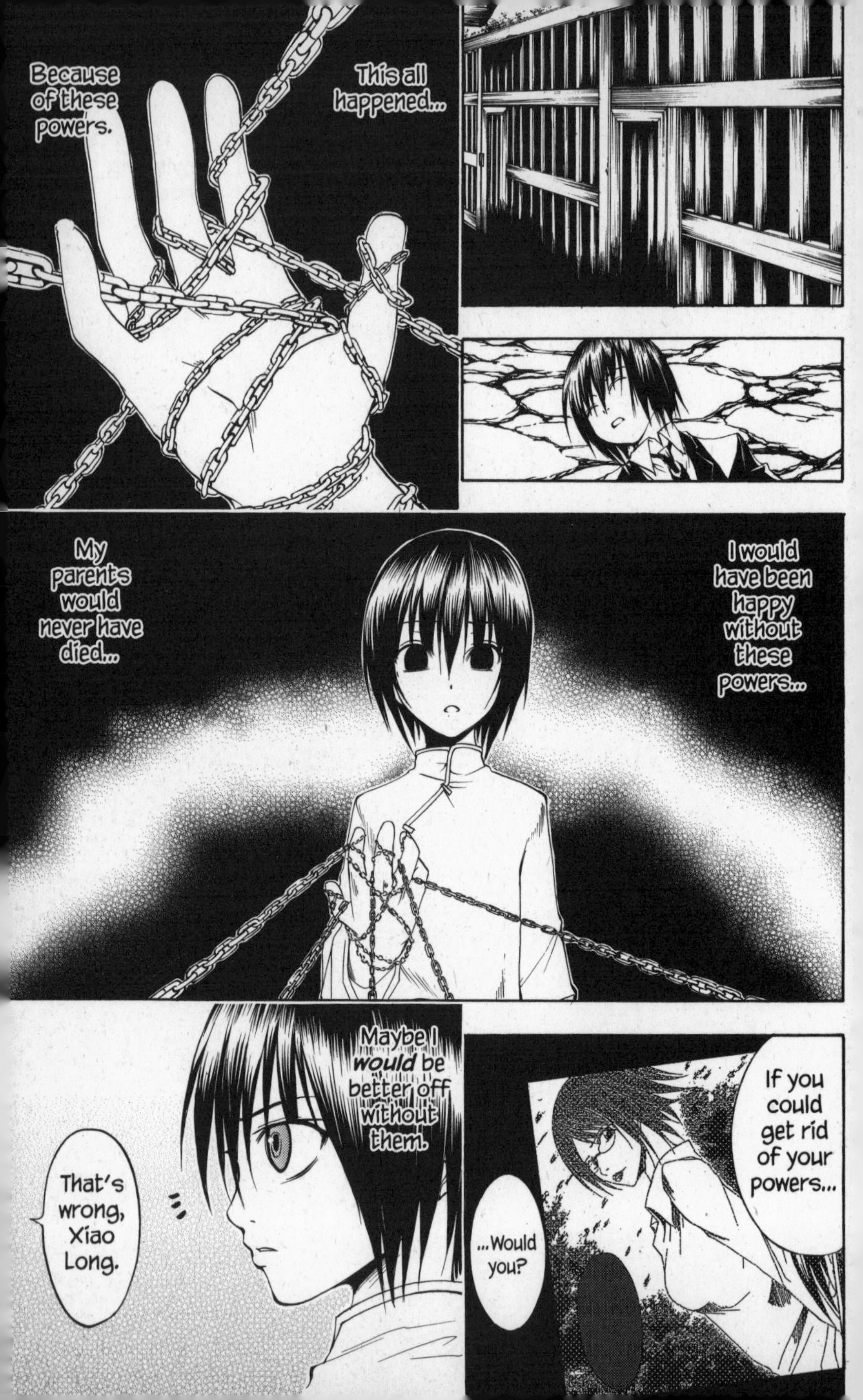
This all happened...
Because of these powers.
I would have been happy without these powers...
My parents would never have died...
If you could get rid of your powers...
...Would you?
Maybe I *would* be better off without them.
That's wrong, Xiao Long.

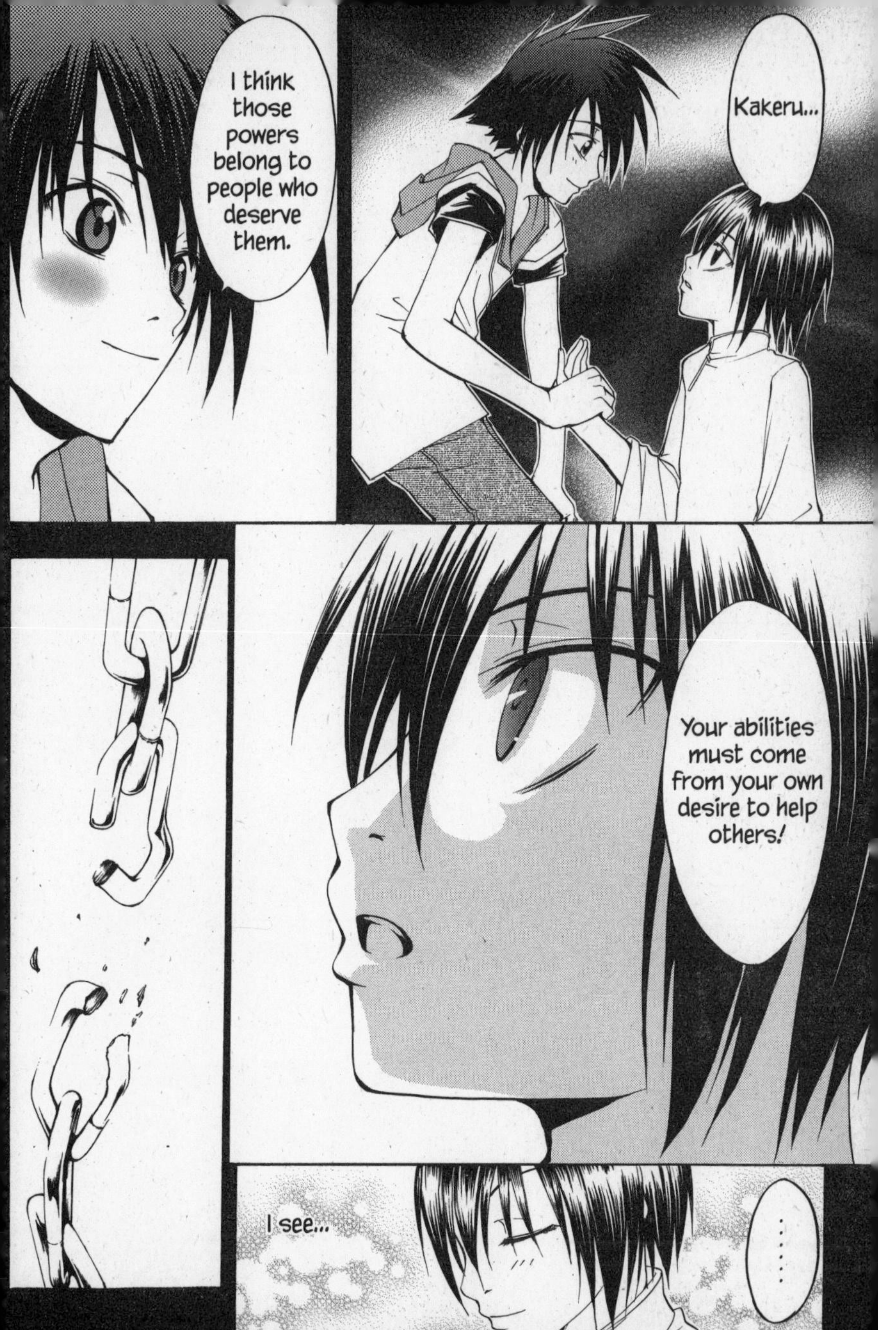
Kakeru...
I think those powers belong to people who deserve them.
Your abilities must come from your own desire to help others!
......
I see...

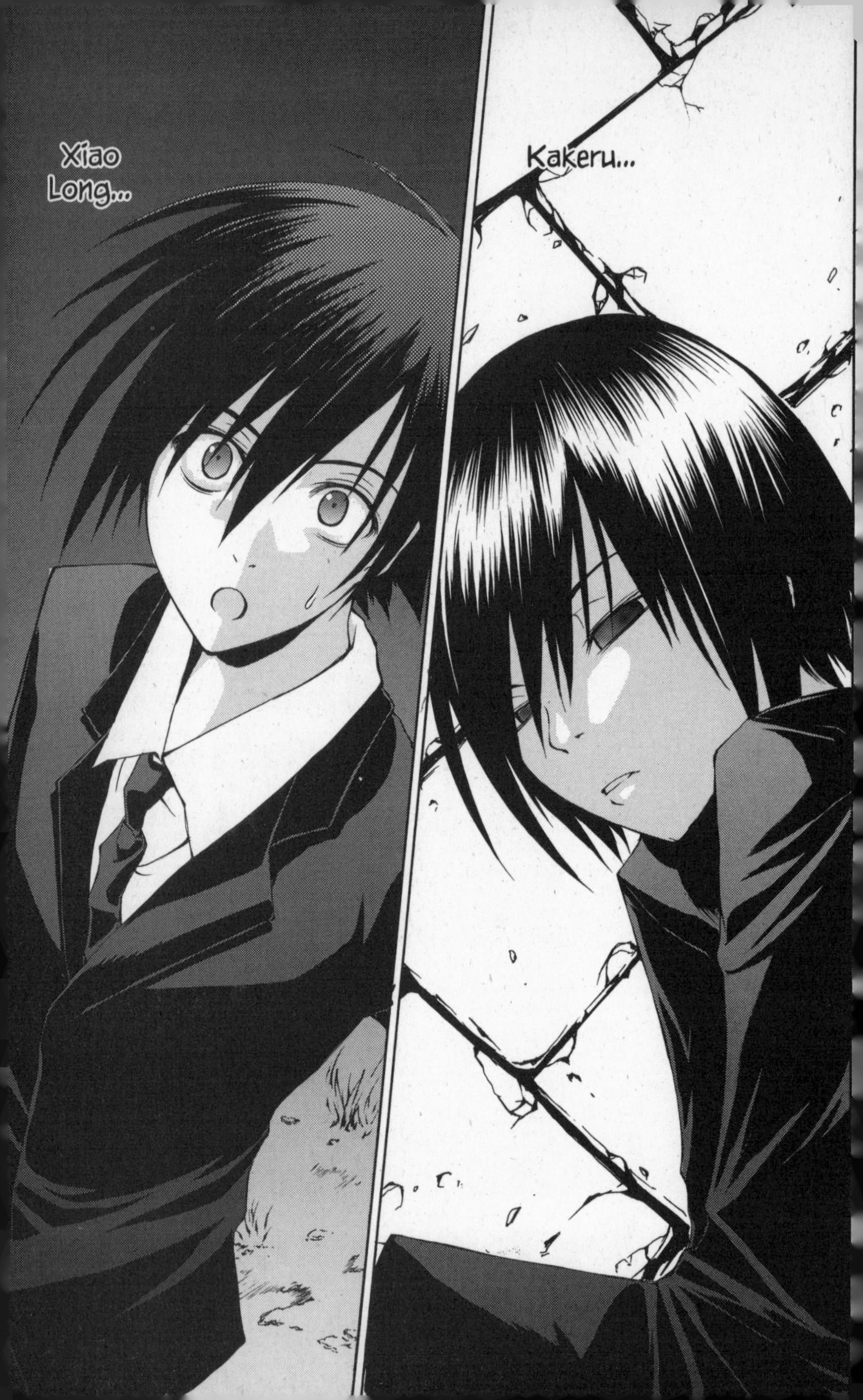
Kakeru...
Xiao Long...

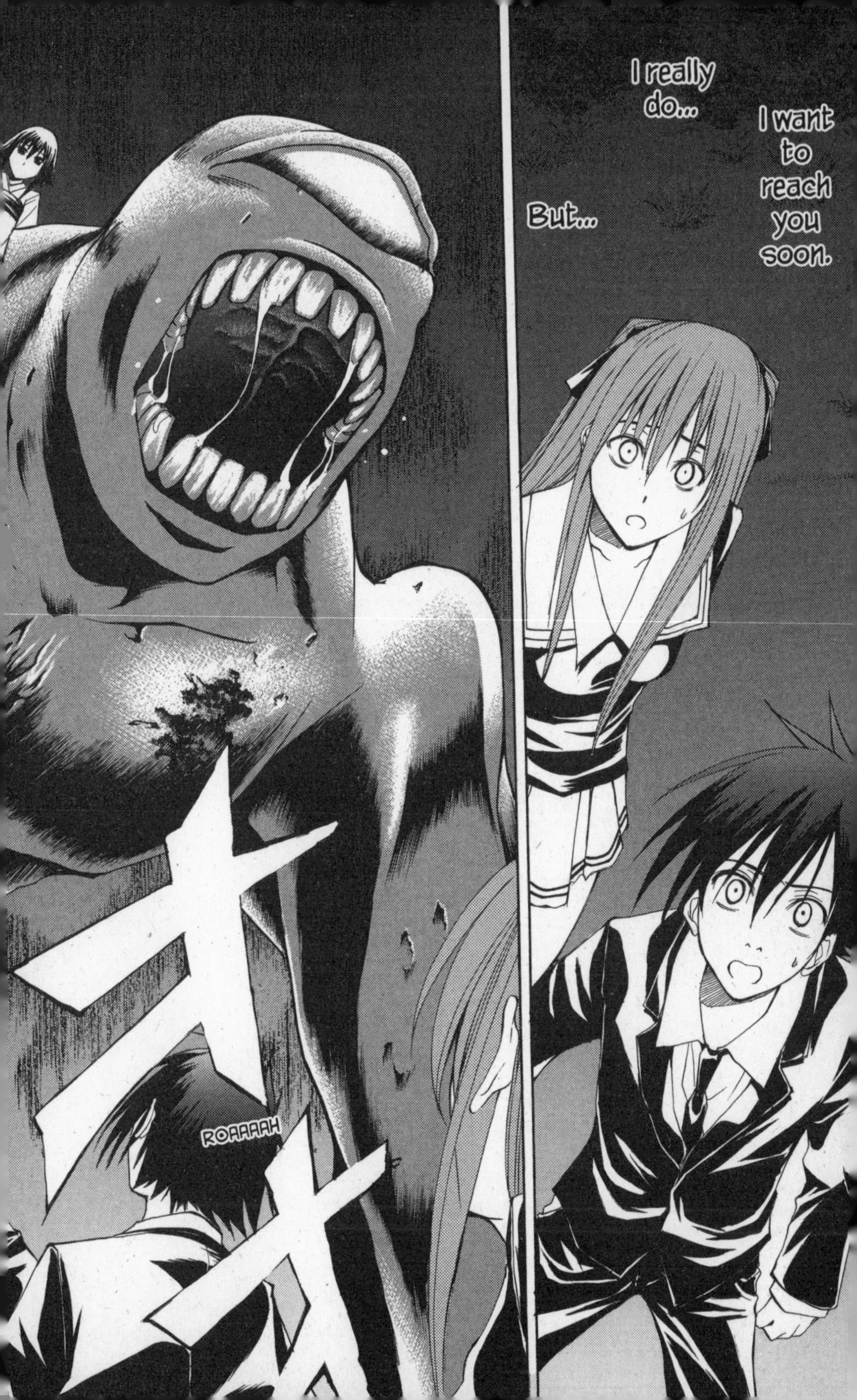
I want to reach you soon.
I really do...
But...
ROAAAAH

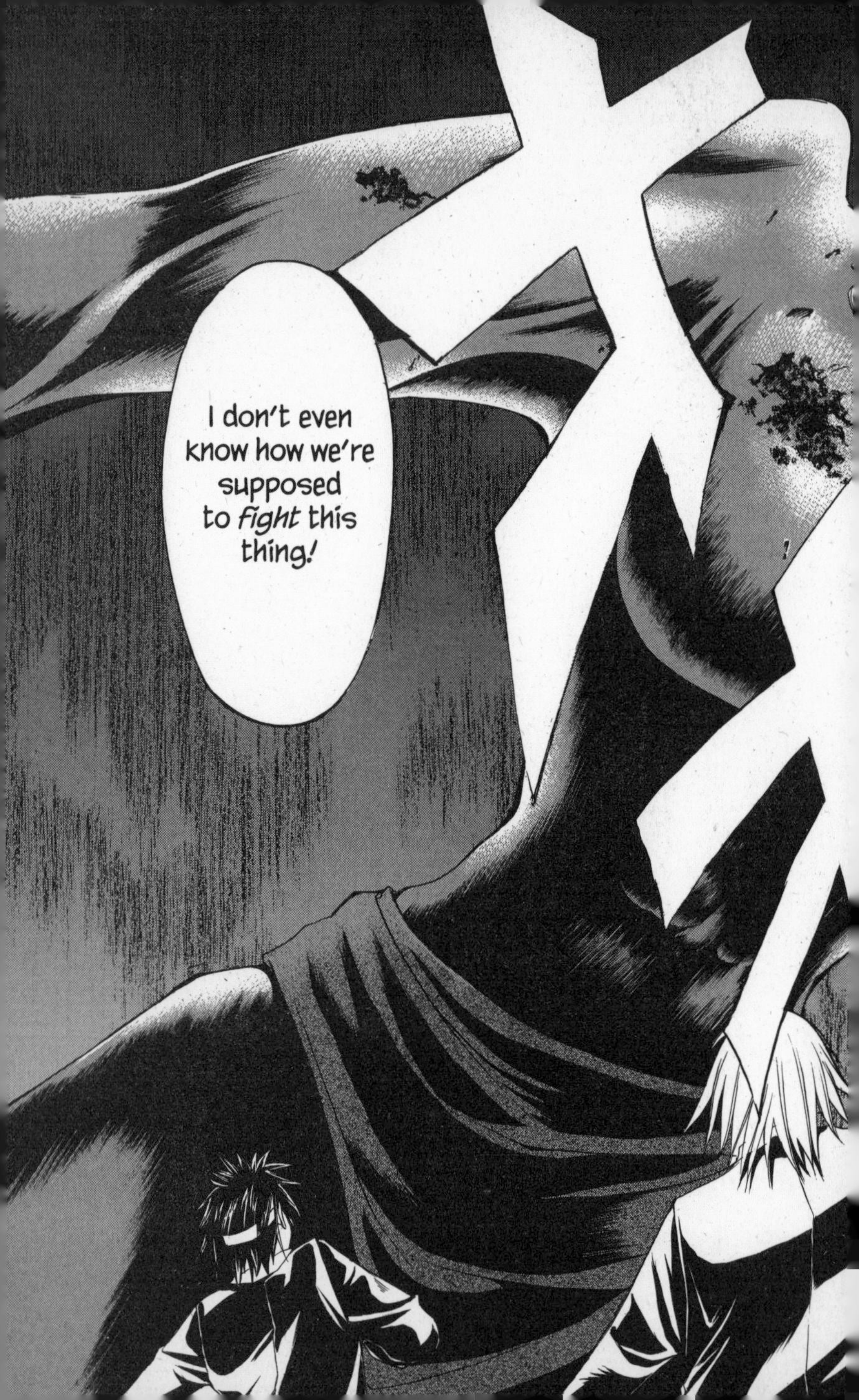
I don't even know how we're supposed to *fight* this thing!

## Omake Four-Panel Manga

# Psycho Busters

## Daily

### Extra-Large

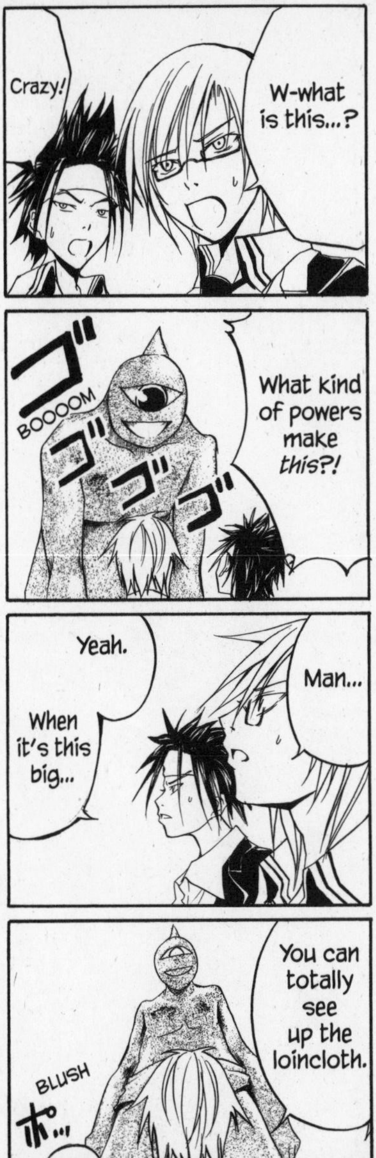
W-what is this...?
Crazy!
What kind of powers make this?!
ゴ
BOOOOM
ゴゴゴゴ
Man...
Yeah.
When it's this big...
You can totally see up the loincloth.
BLUSH
ポ...

# Present

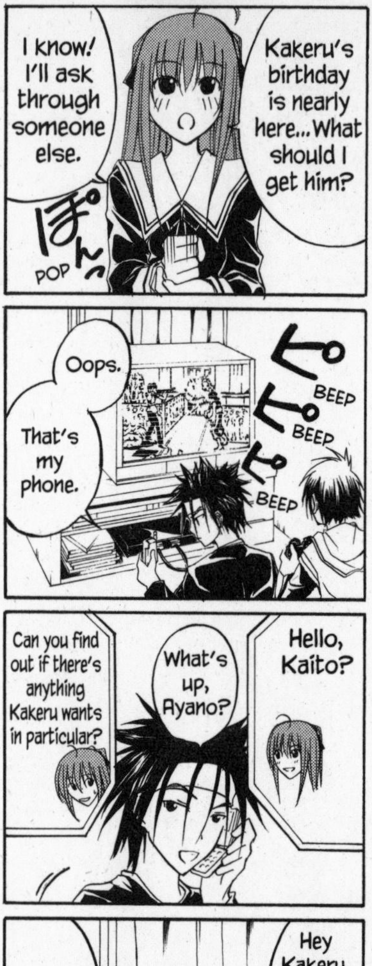
Kakeru's birthday is nearly here...What should I get him?
I know! I'll ask through someone else.
ぽんっ
POP
ピ
BEEP
ピ
BEEP
ピ
BEEP
Oops.
That's my phone.
Hello, Kaito?
What's up, Ayano?
Can you find out if there's anything Kakeru wants in particular?
Hey Kakeru, whad-daya need right now?
A rocket launcher.

# Present 2

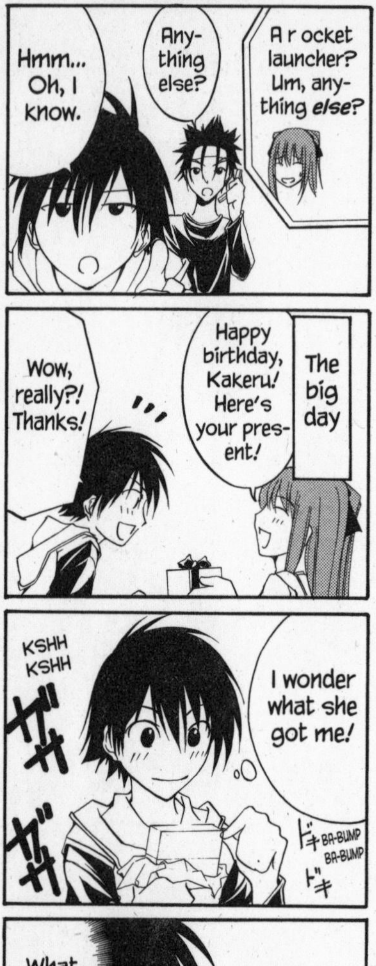
A r ocket launcher? Um, any-thing *else*?
Any-thing else?
Hmm... Oh, I know.
The big day
Happy birthday, Kakeru! Here's your pres-ent!
Wow, really?! Thanks!
I wonder what she got me!
ドキ
BA-BUMP
BA-BUMP
ドキ
KSHH
KSHH
ガサ
ガサ
What the—?!
Ink Ribbon

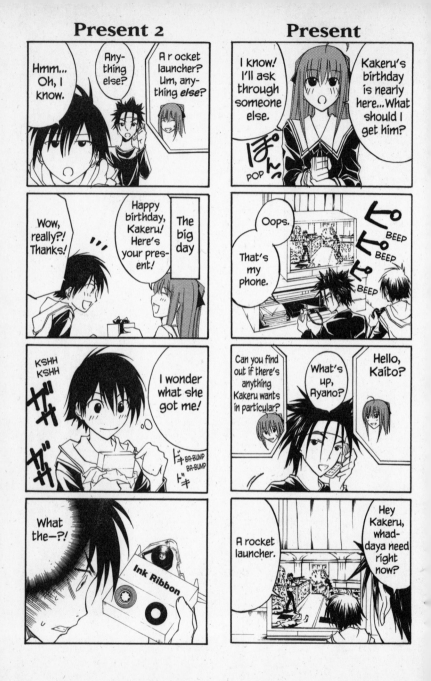

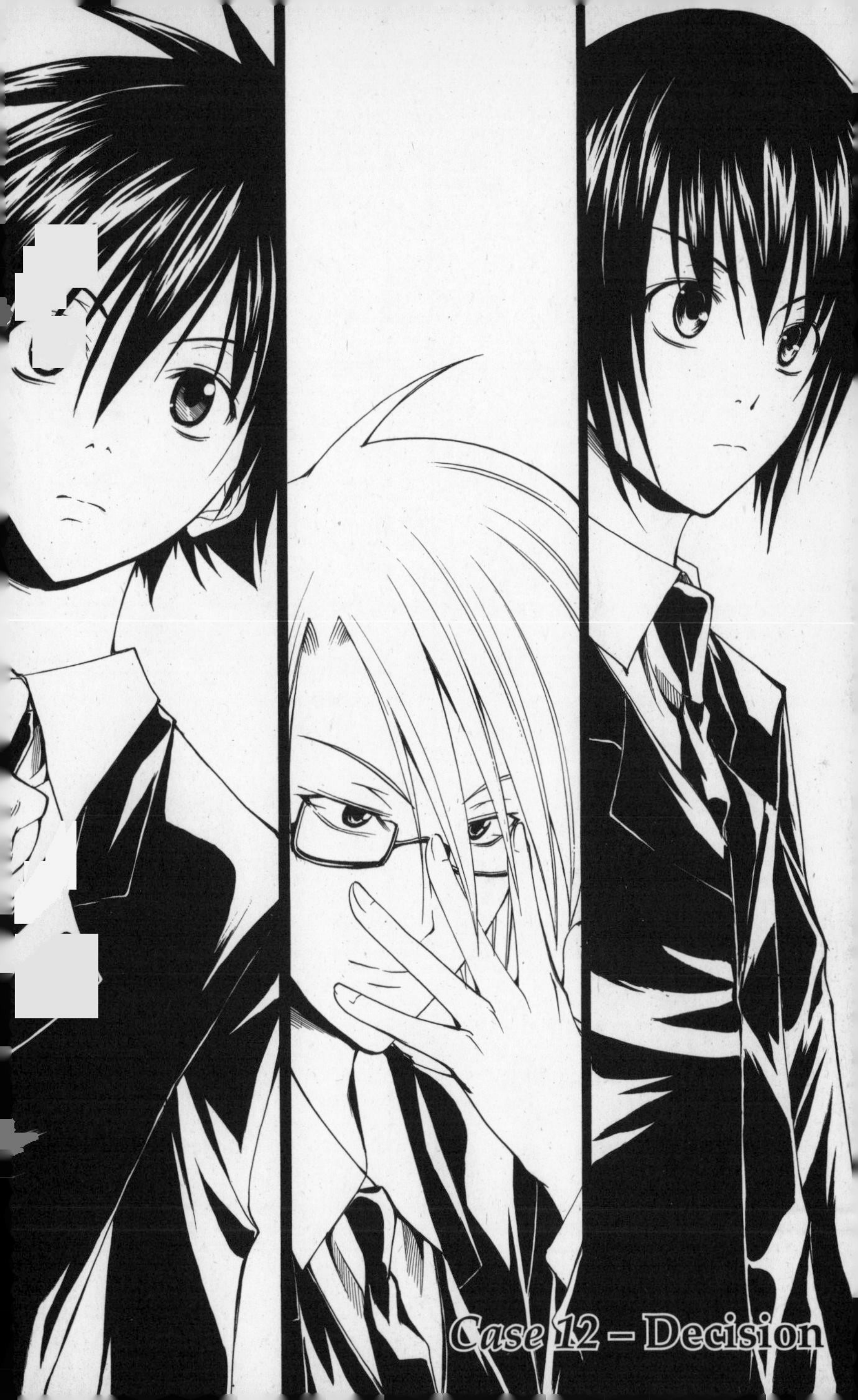
Case 12 – Decision

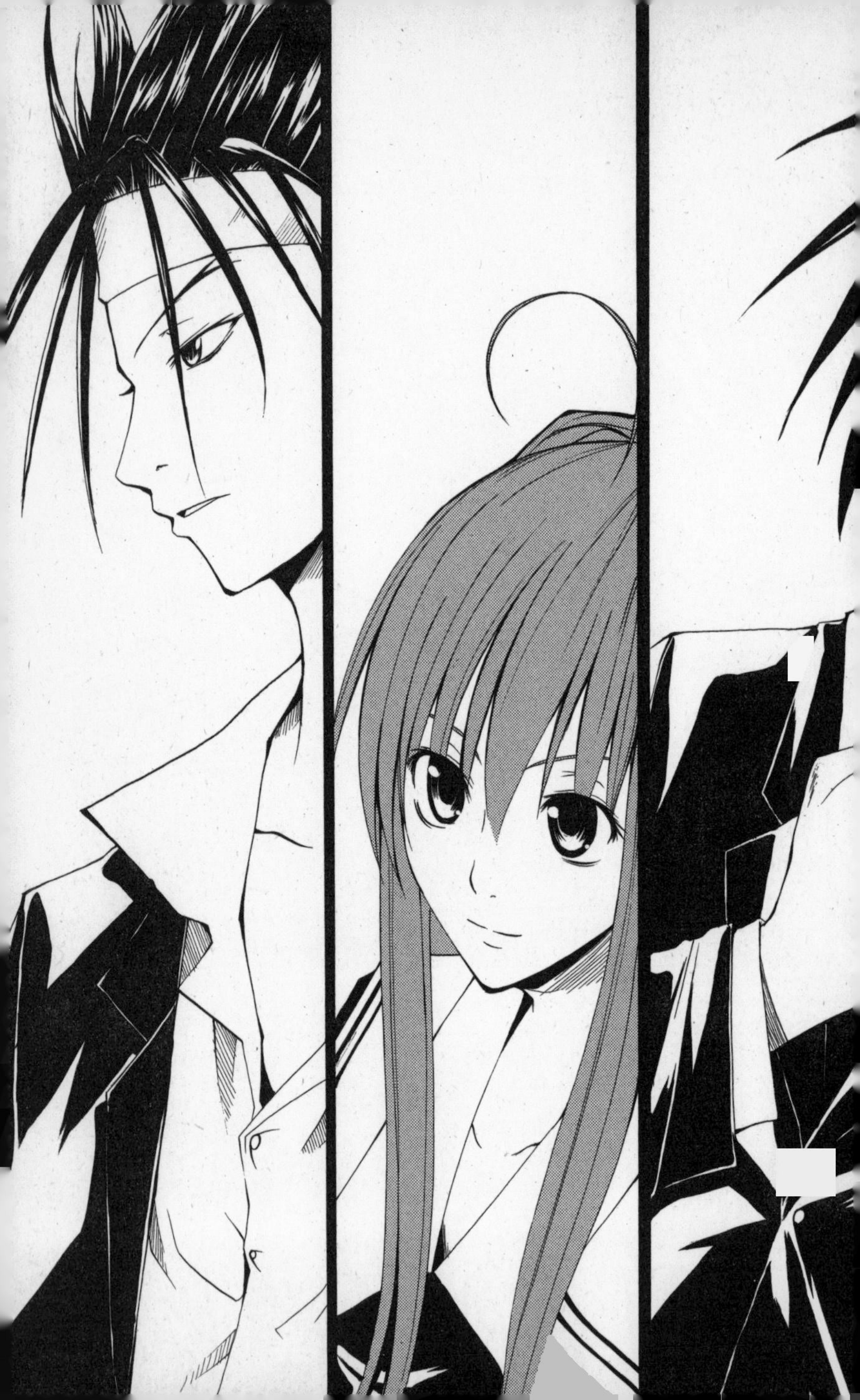

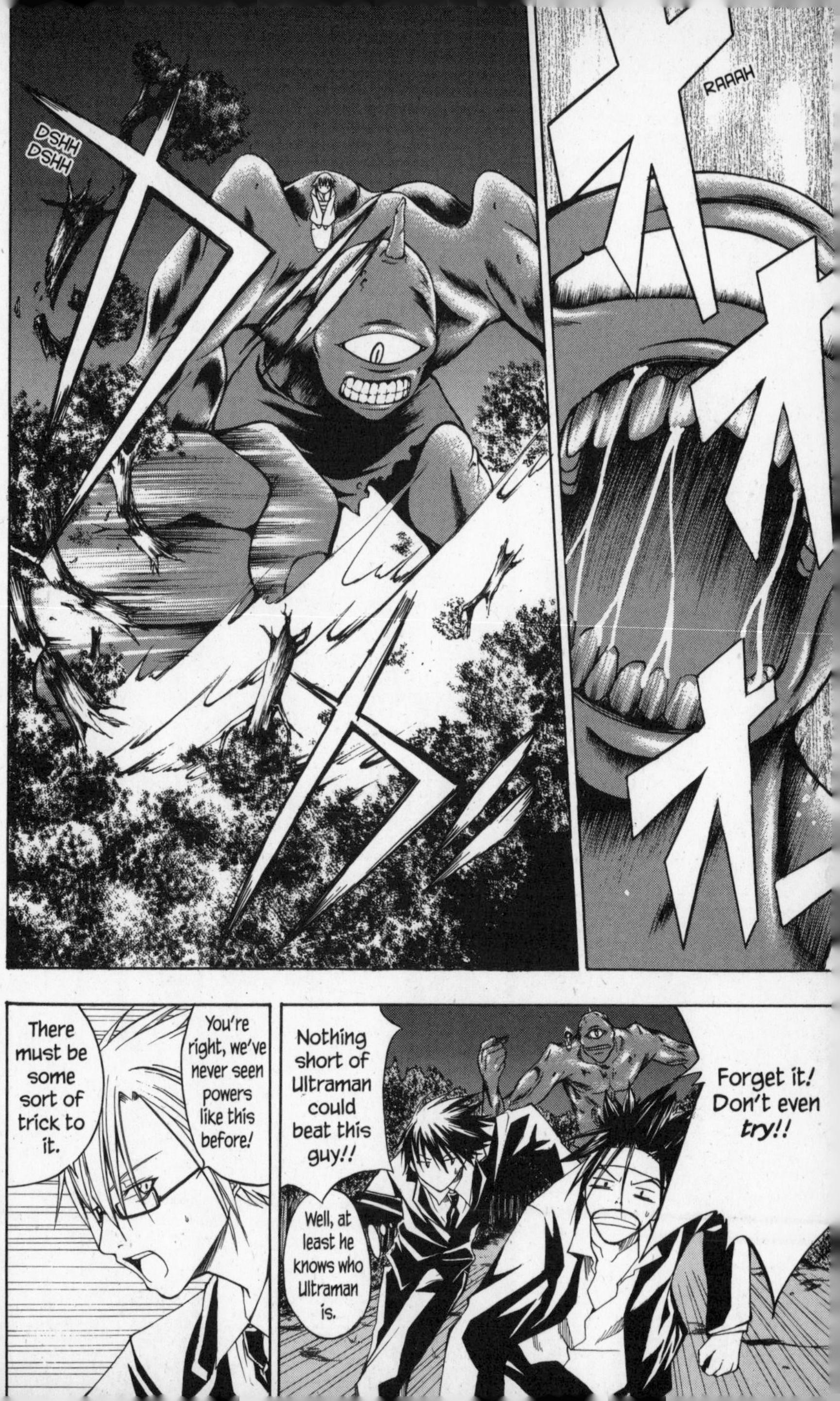
RAAAH
DSHH DSHH
Forget it! Don't even try!!
Nothing short of Ultraman could beat this guy!!
Well, at least he knows who Ultraman is.
You're right, we've never seen powers like this before!
There must be some sort of trick to it.

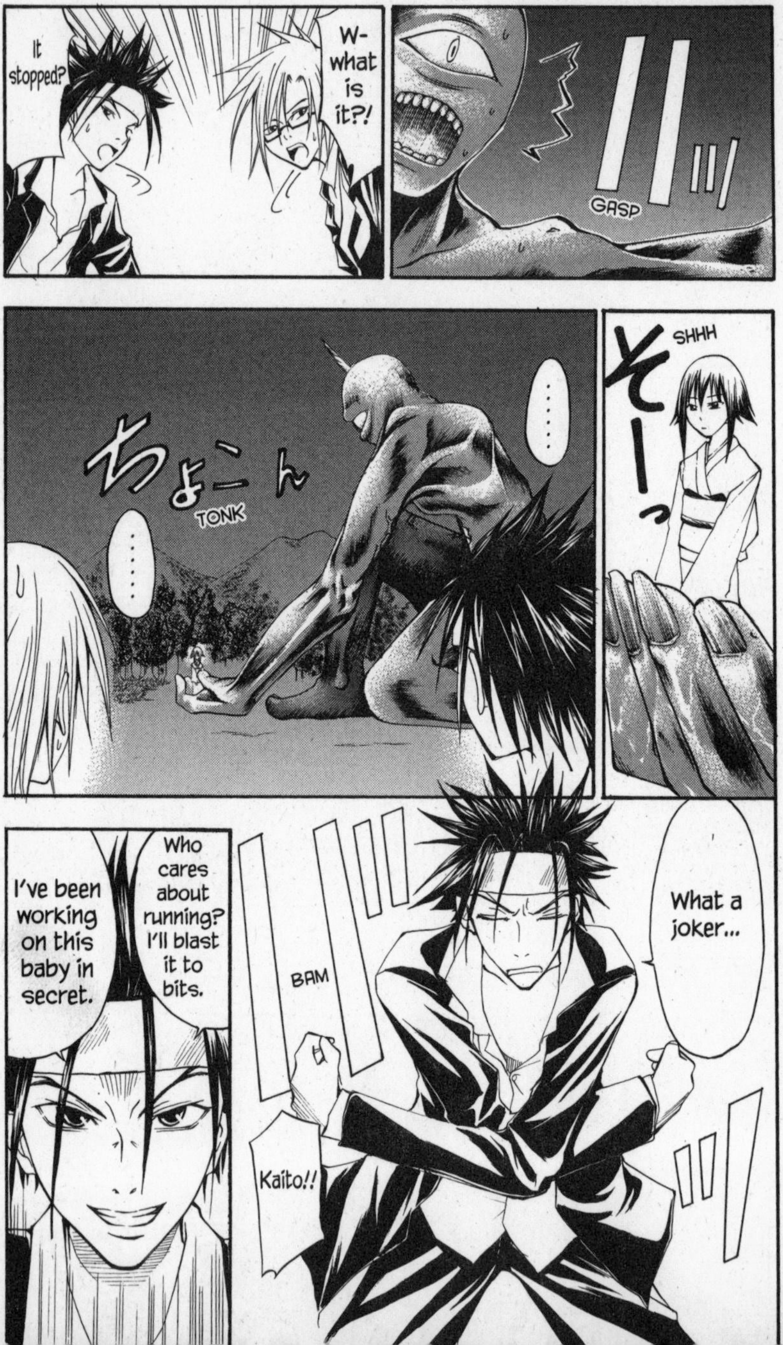
GASP
W-what is it?!
It stopped?
そーっ
SHHH
......
ちょこん
TONK
......
What a joker...
BAM
Kaito!!
Who cares about running? I'll blast it to bits.
I've been working on this baby in secret.

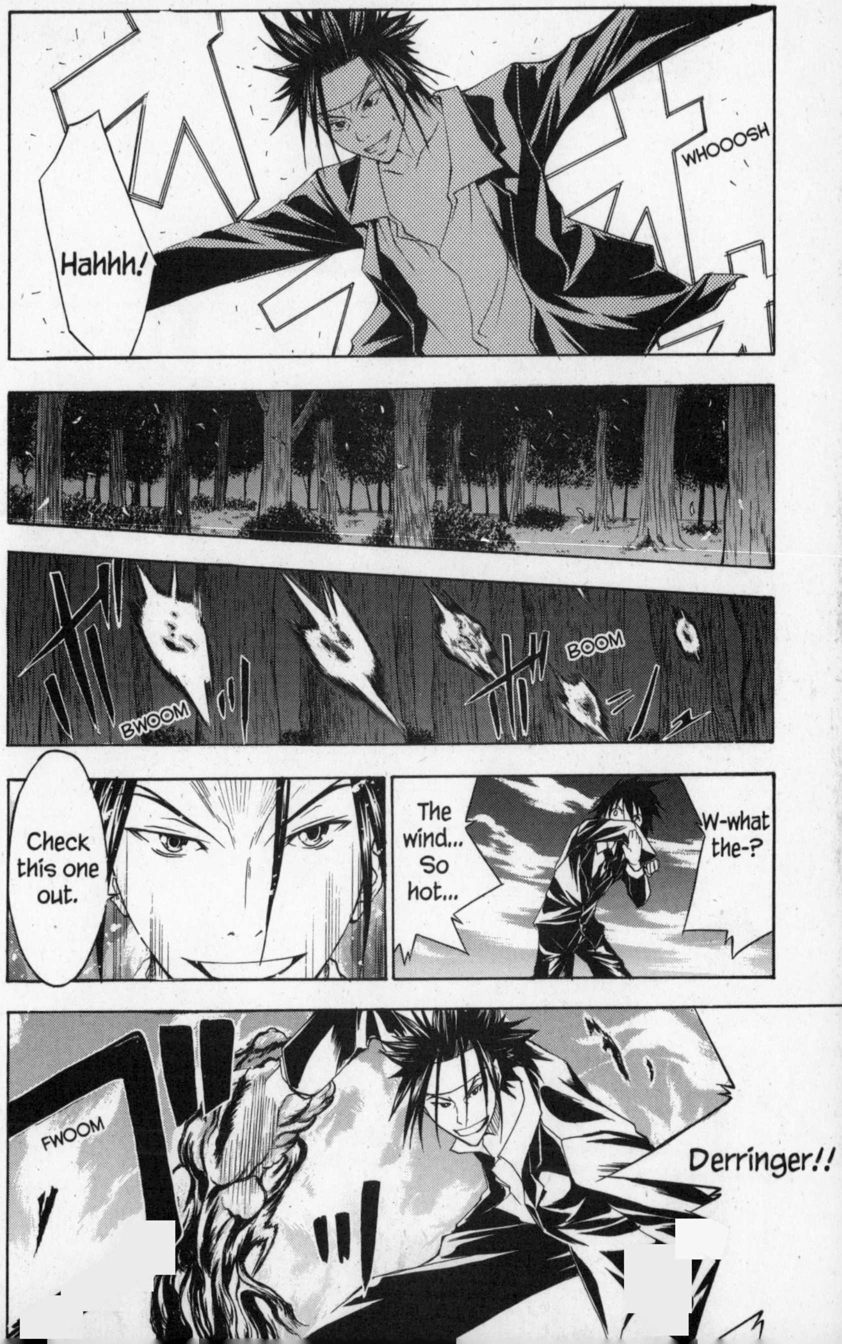
WHOOOSH
Hahhh!
BOOM
BWOOM
W-what the-?
The wind... So hot...
Check this one out.
Derringer!!
FWOOM

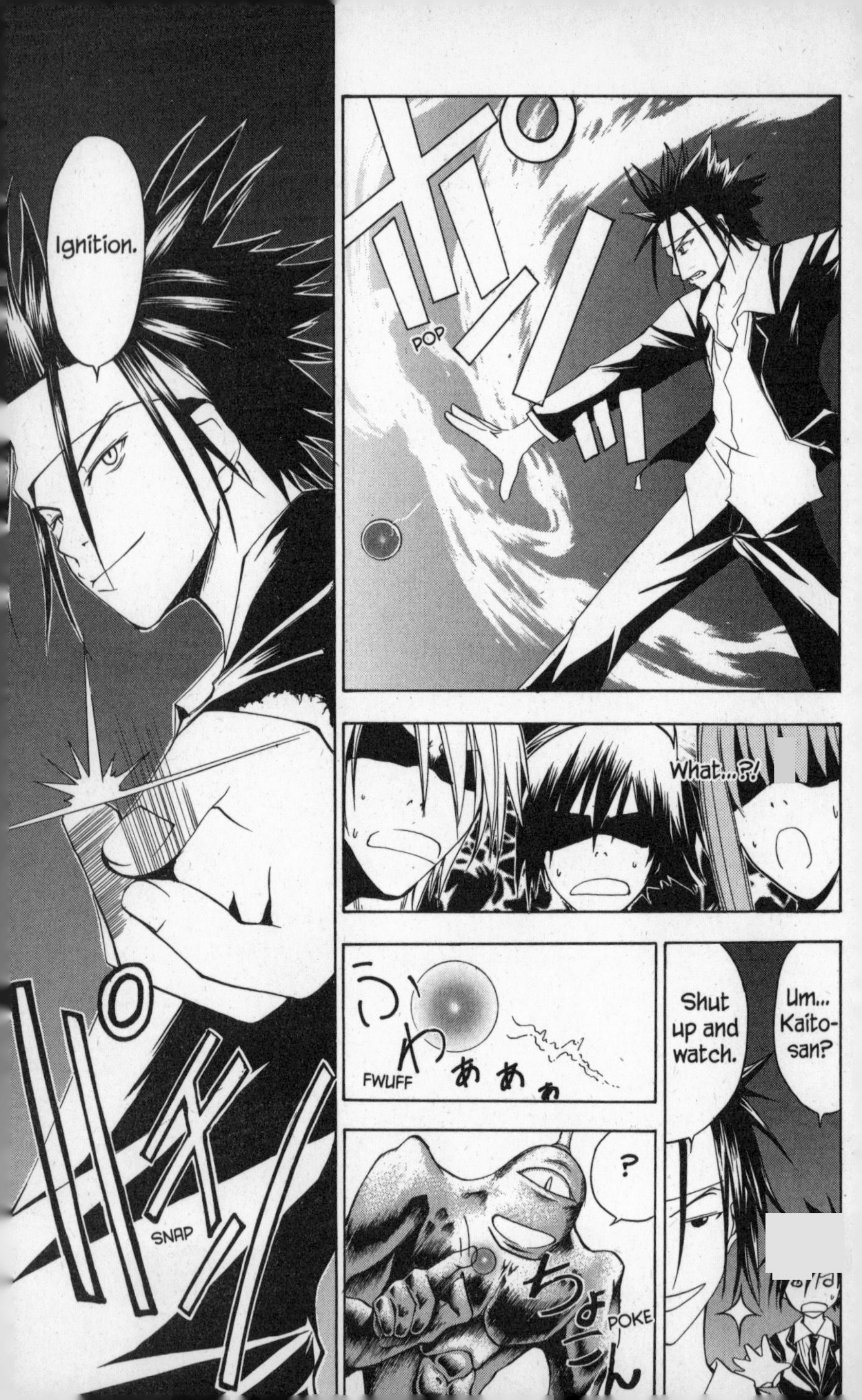
POP
What...?!
Um... Kaito-san?
Shut up and watch.
FWUFF
?
POKE
Ignition.
SNAP

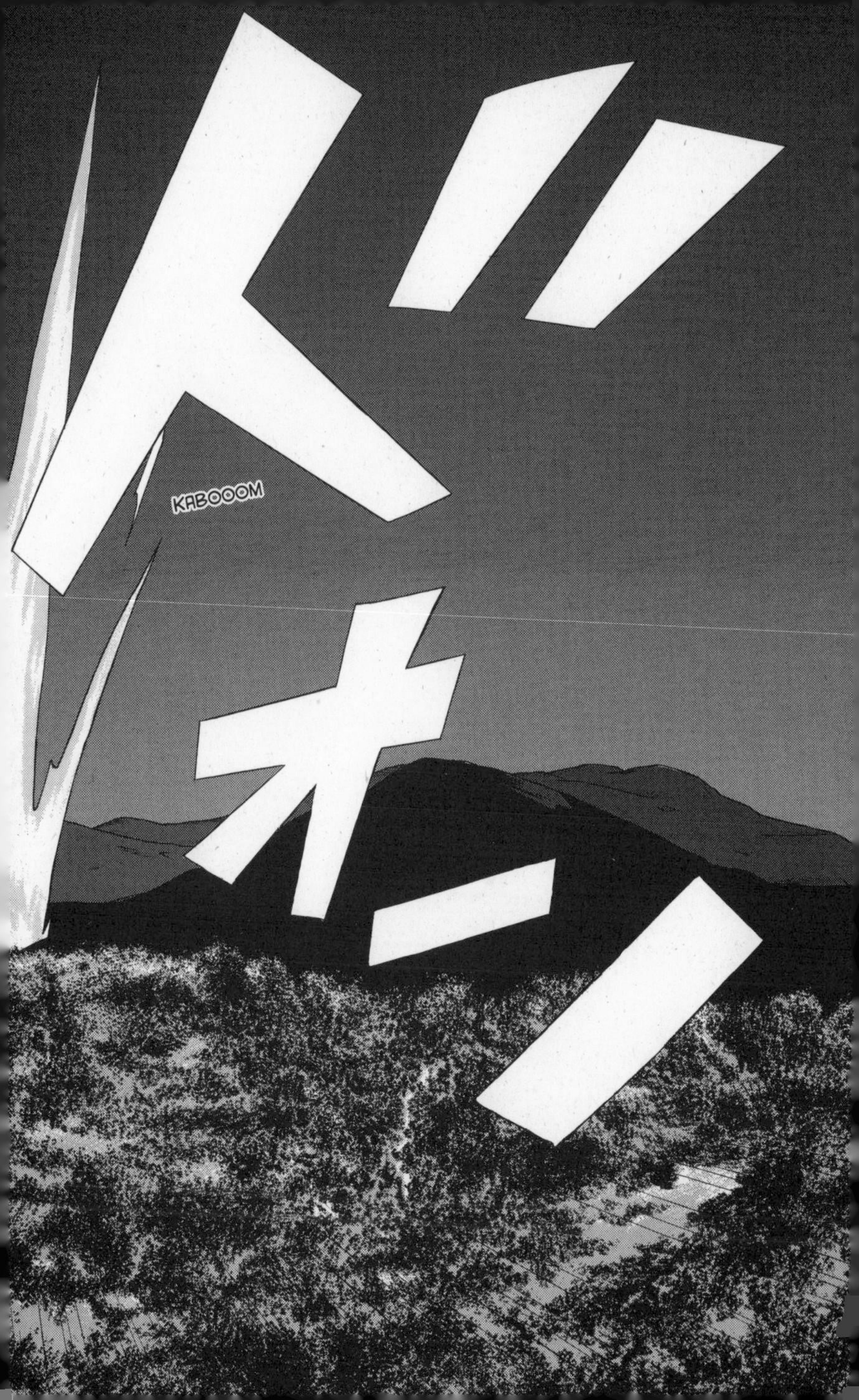
ドドーン
KABOOOM

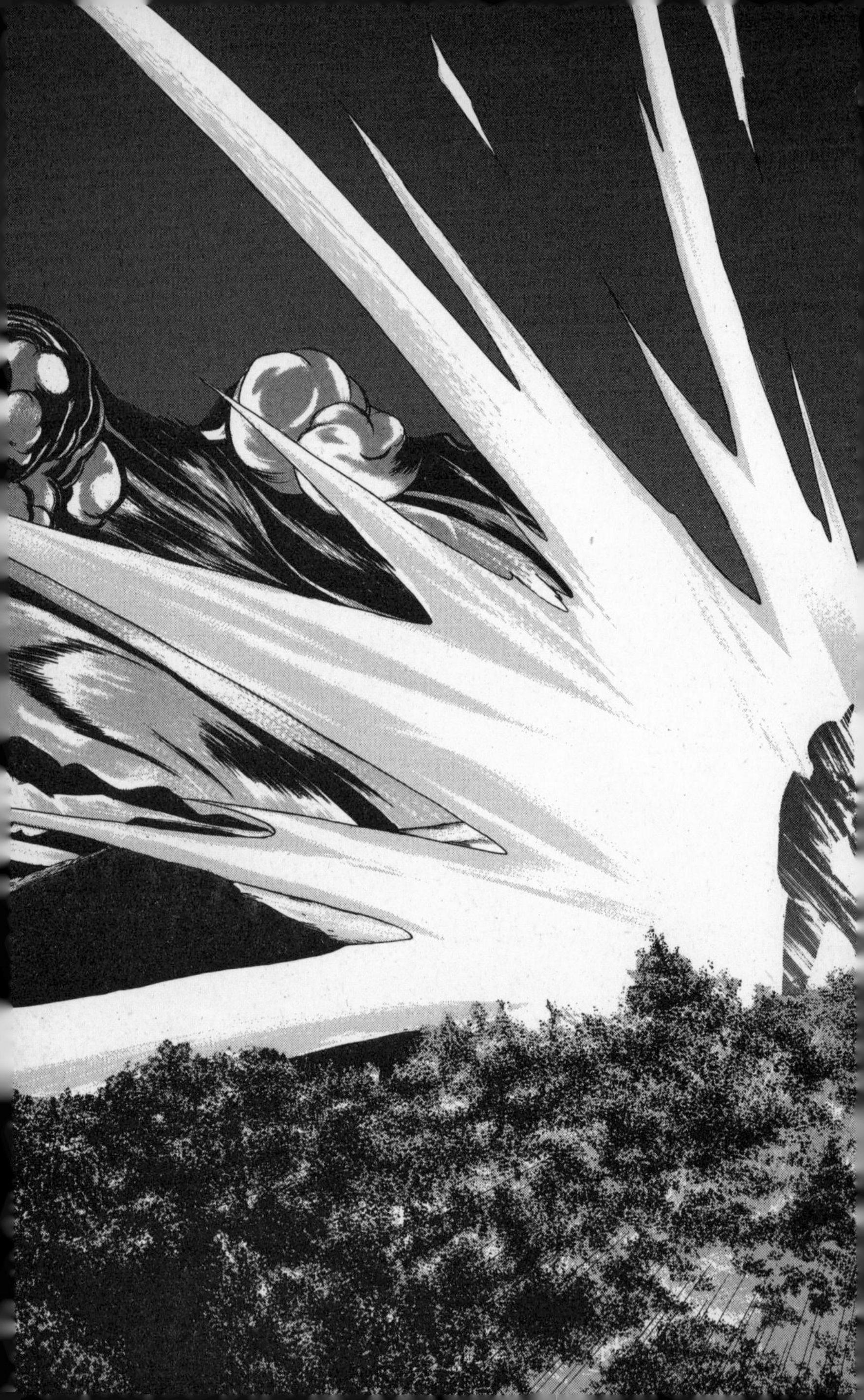

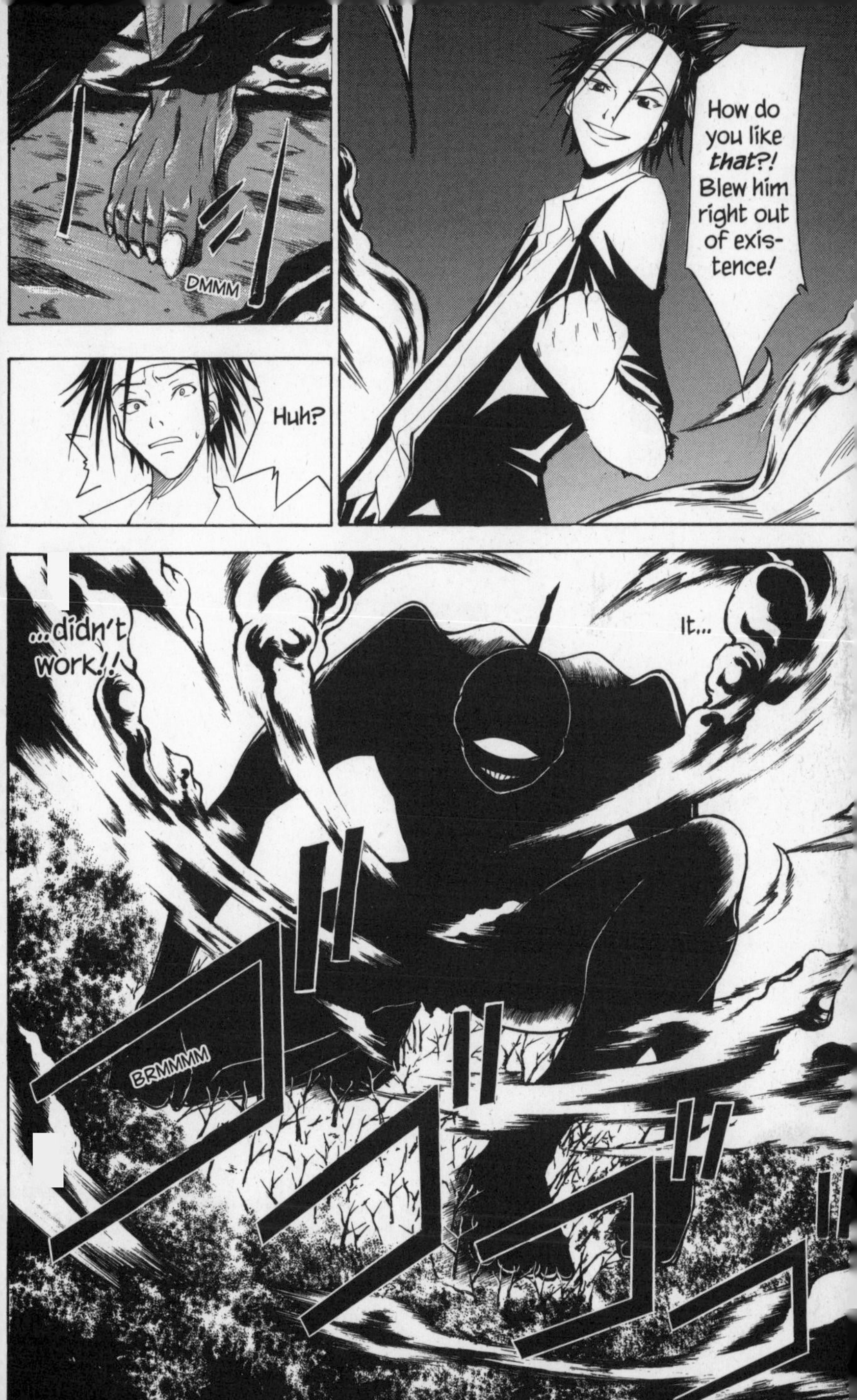
How do you like ***that***?! Blew him right out of existence!
DMMM
Huh?
It...
...didn't work!!
BRMMMM

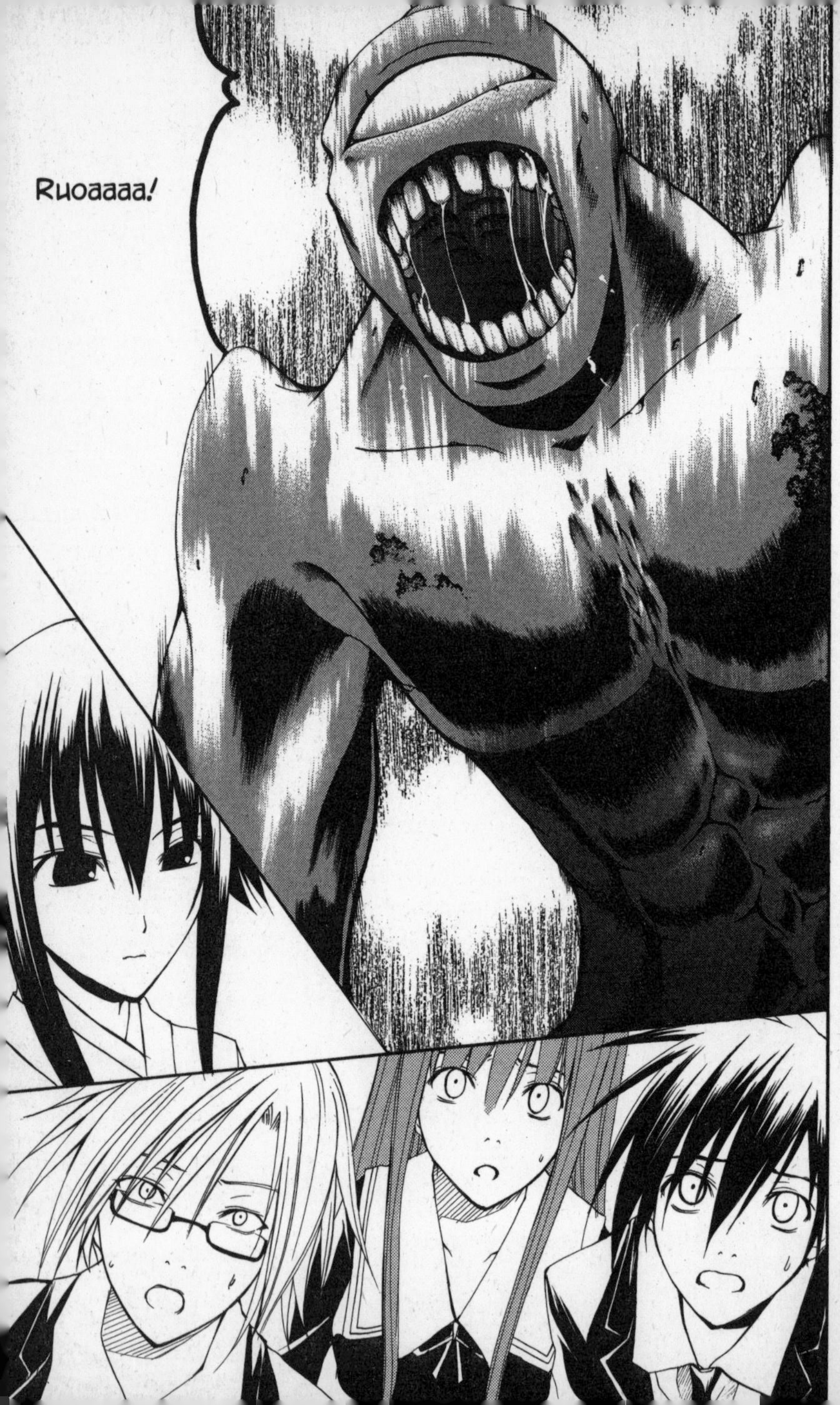
Ruoaaaa!

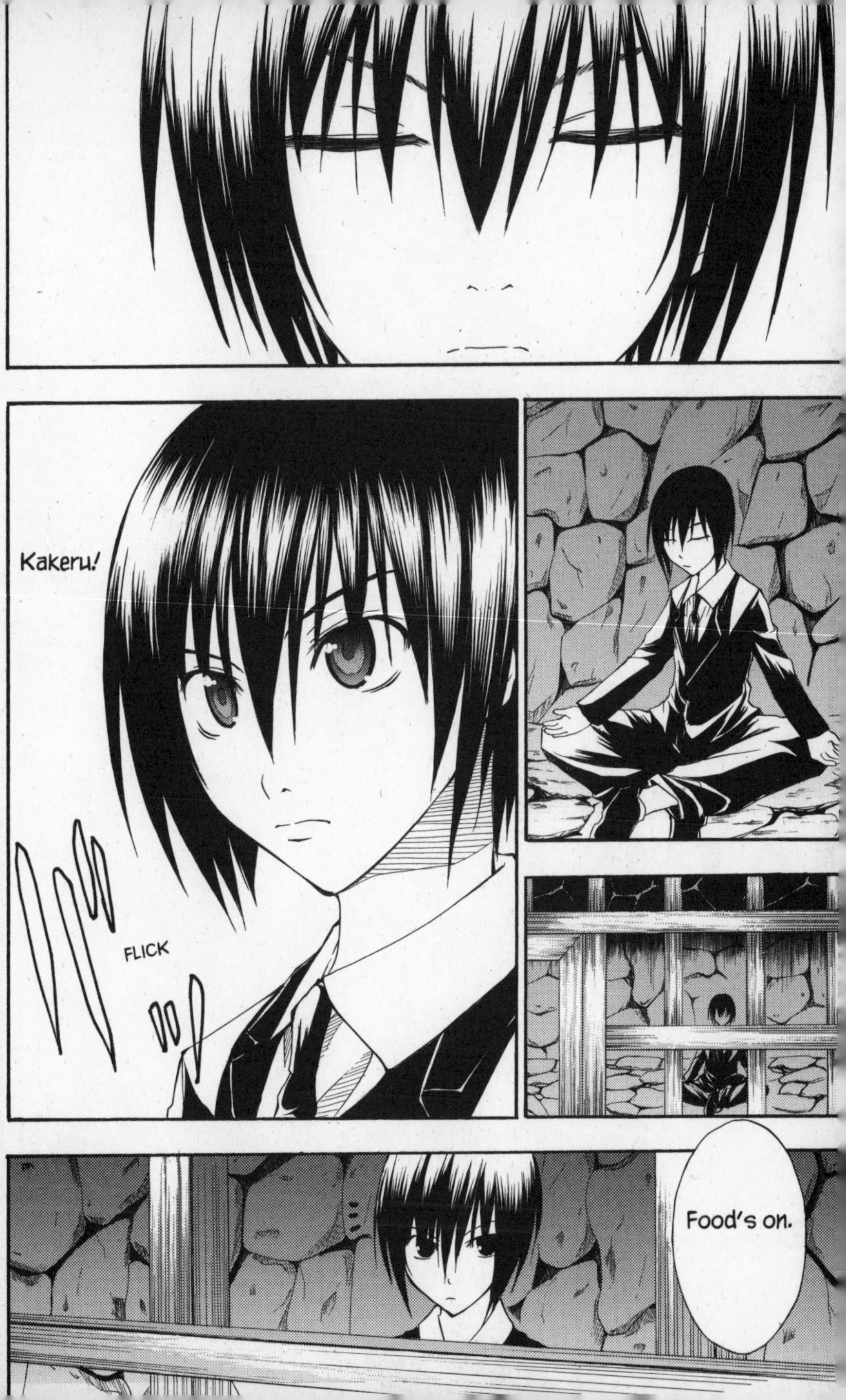
Kakeru!
FLICK
Food's on.

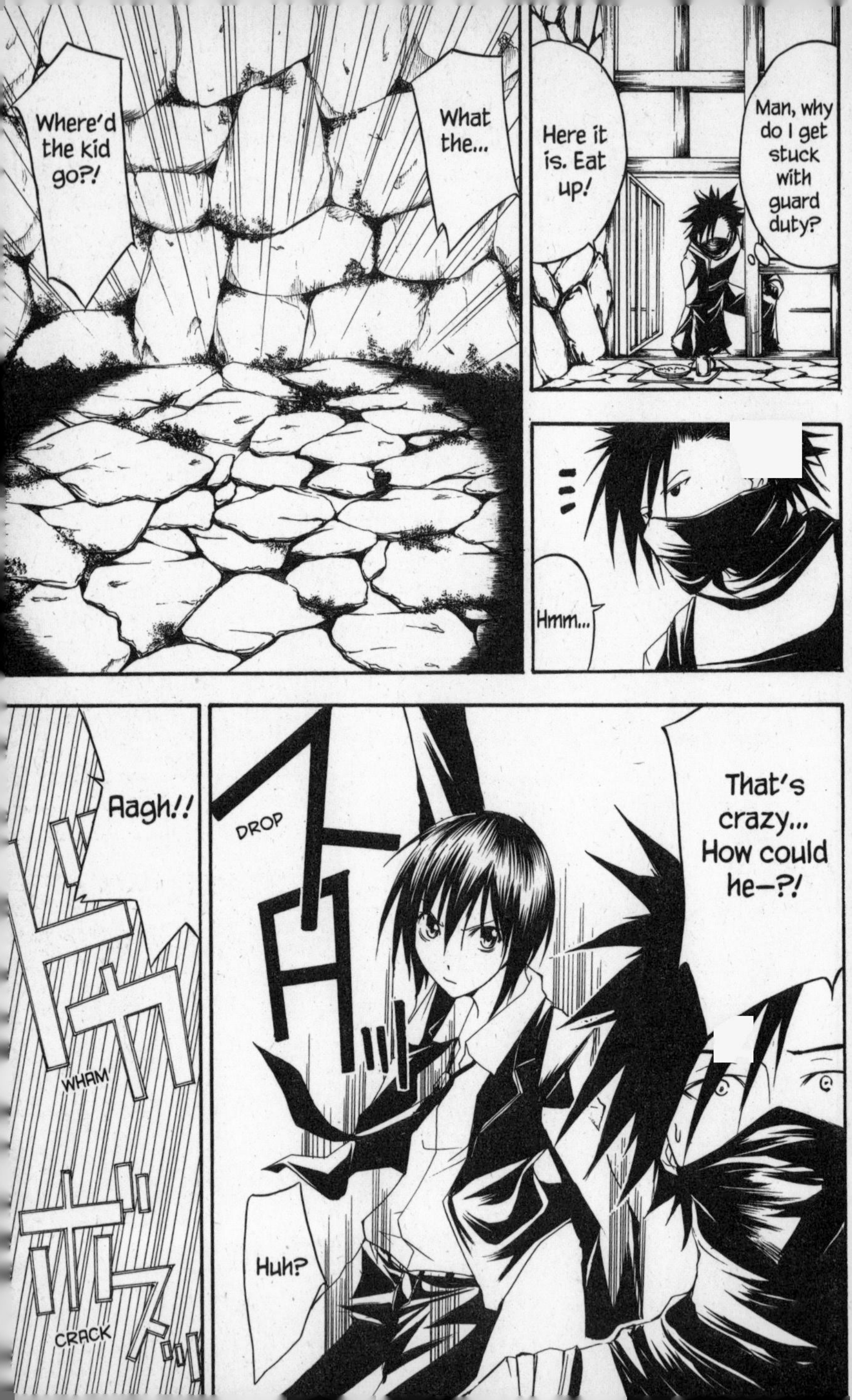
Man, why do I get stuck with guard duty?
Here it is. Eat up!
Hmm...
What the...
Where'd the kid go?!
That's crazy... How could he—?!
DROP
Huh?
Aagh!!
WHAM
CRACK

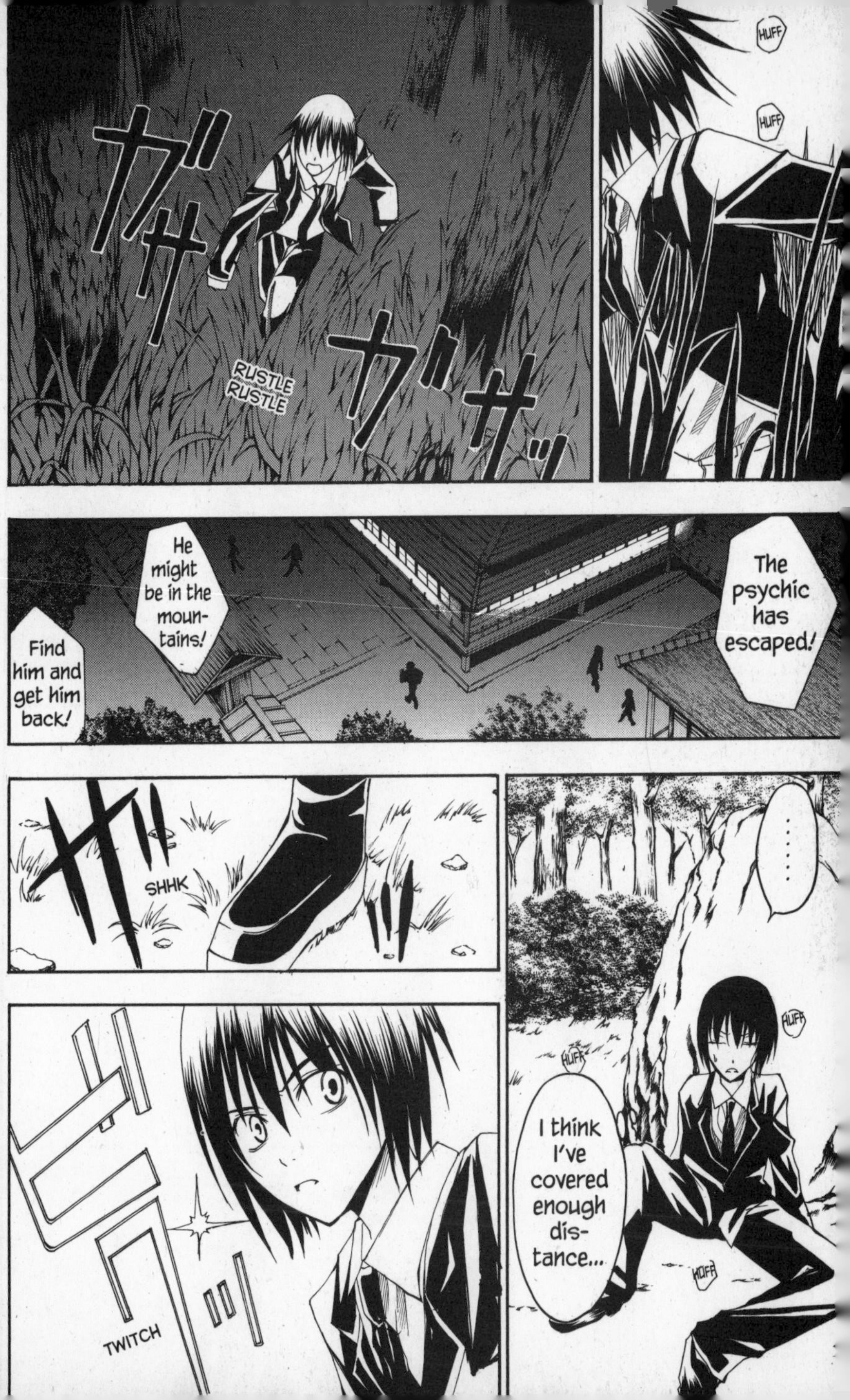
HUFF
HUFF
RUSTLE RUSTLE
The psychic has escaped!
He might be in the mountains!
Find him and get him back!
......
HUFF
HUFF
I think I've covered enough dis-tance...
HUFF
SHHK
TWITCH

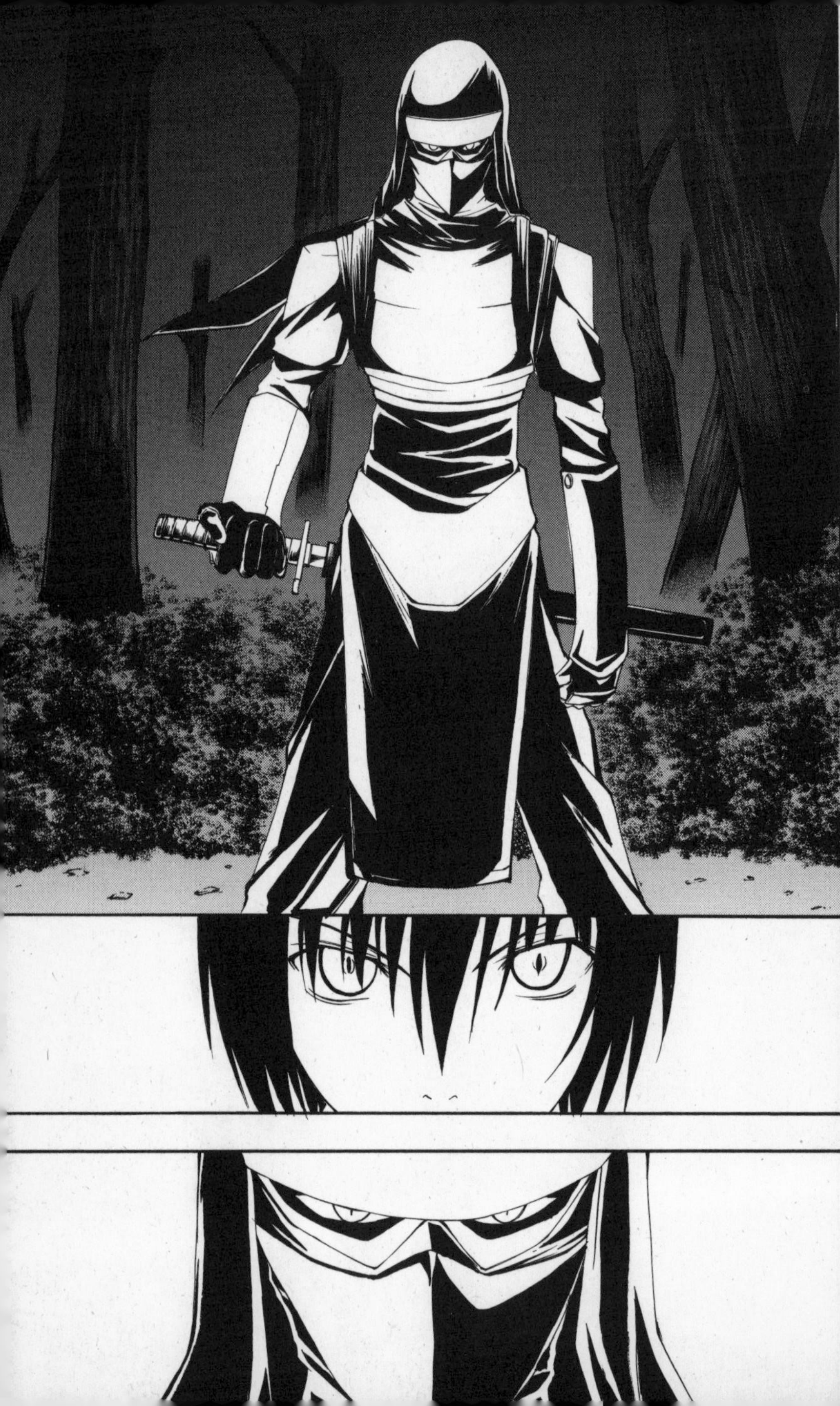

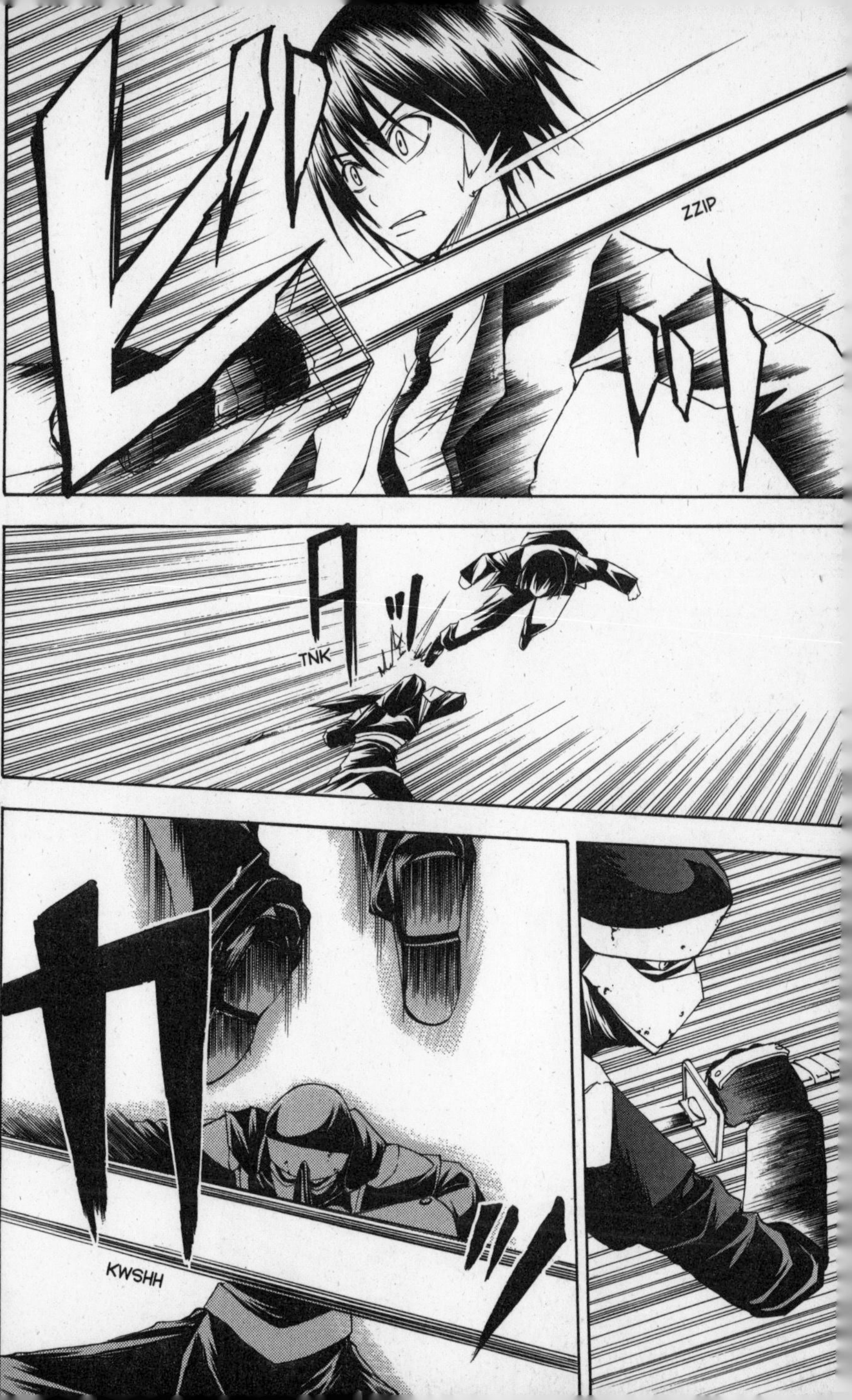
ZZIP
TNK
KWSHH

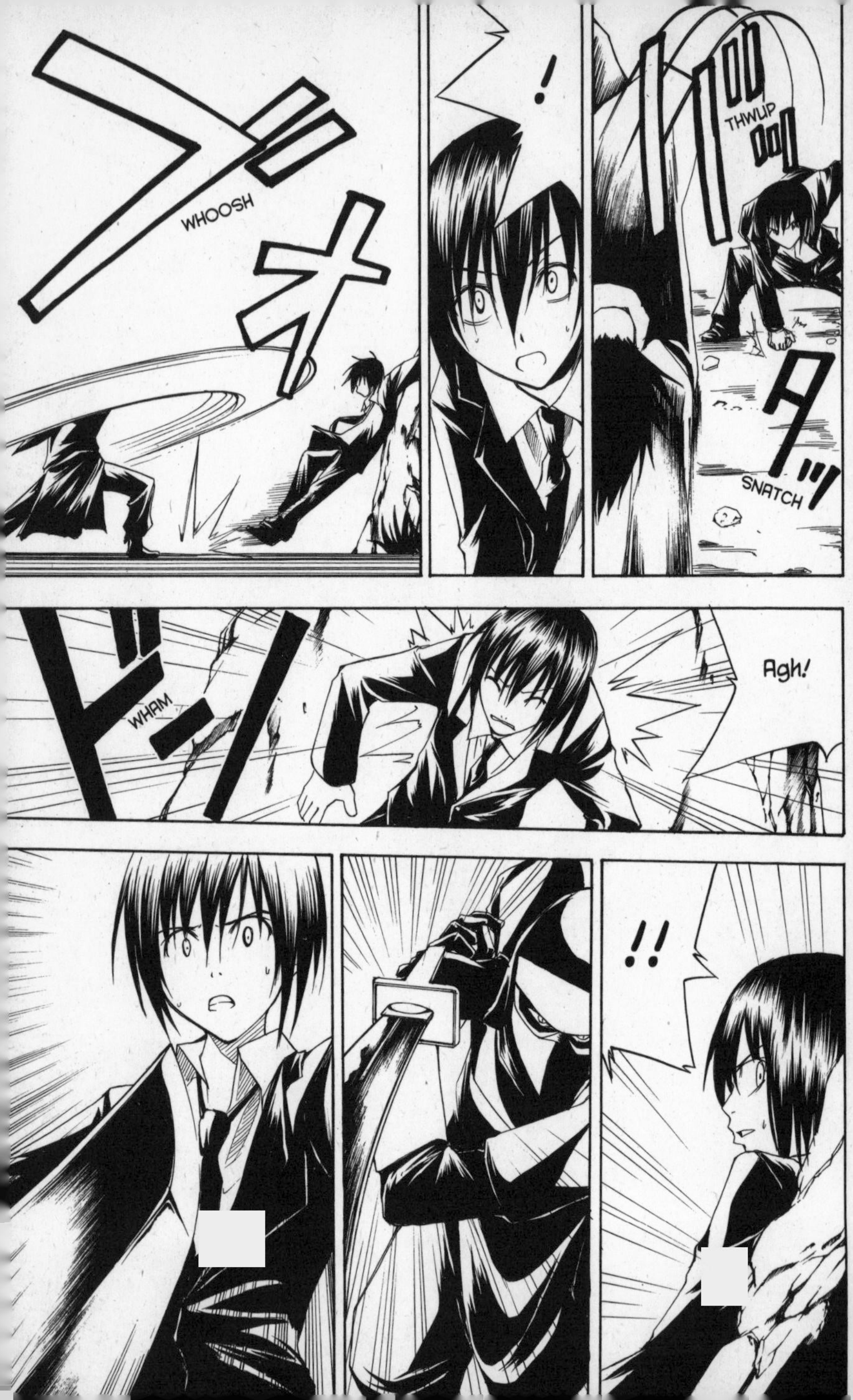
THWUP
SNATCH
!
WHOOSH
Agh!
WHAM
!!

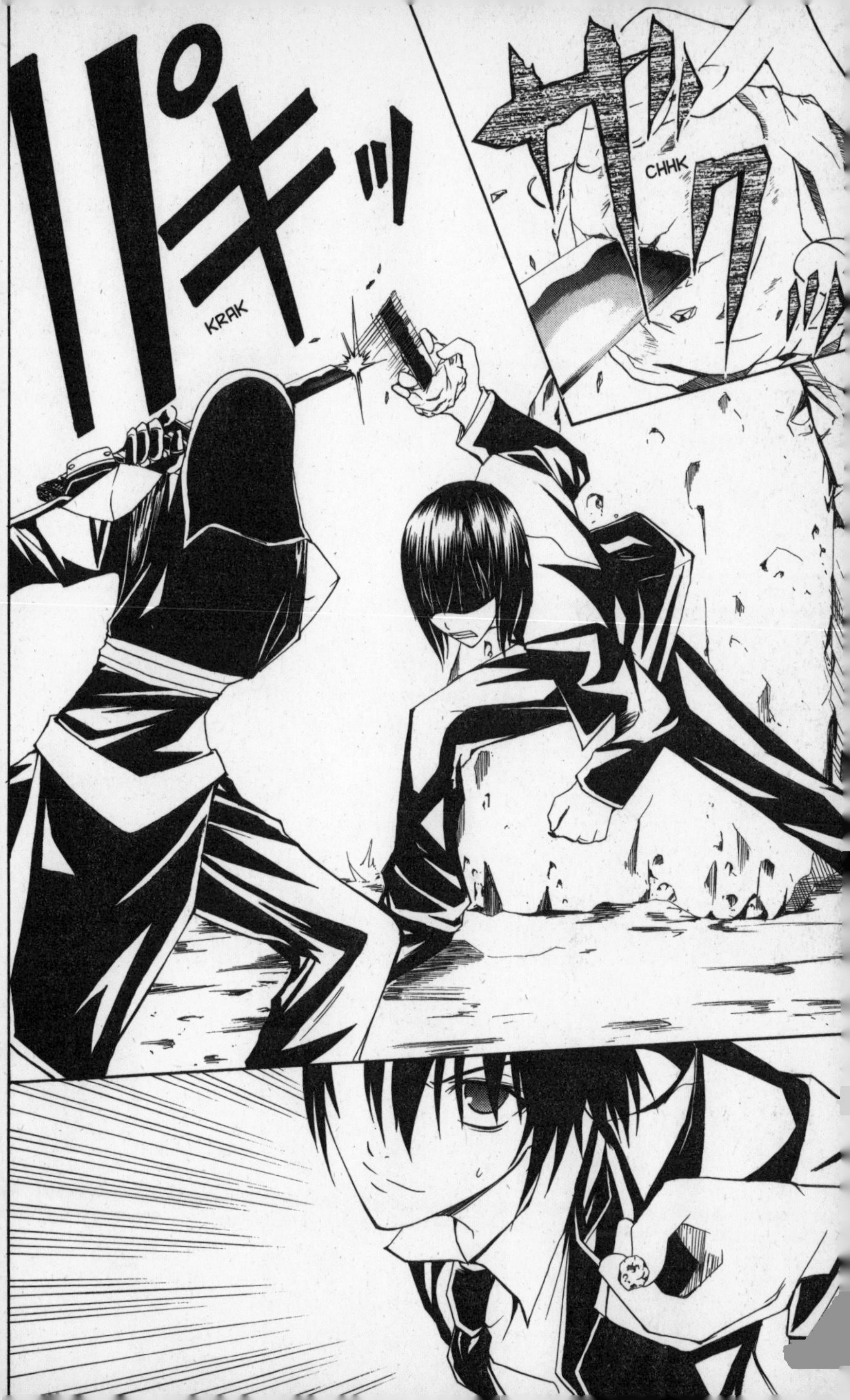
CHHK
KRAK

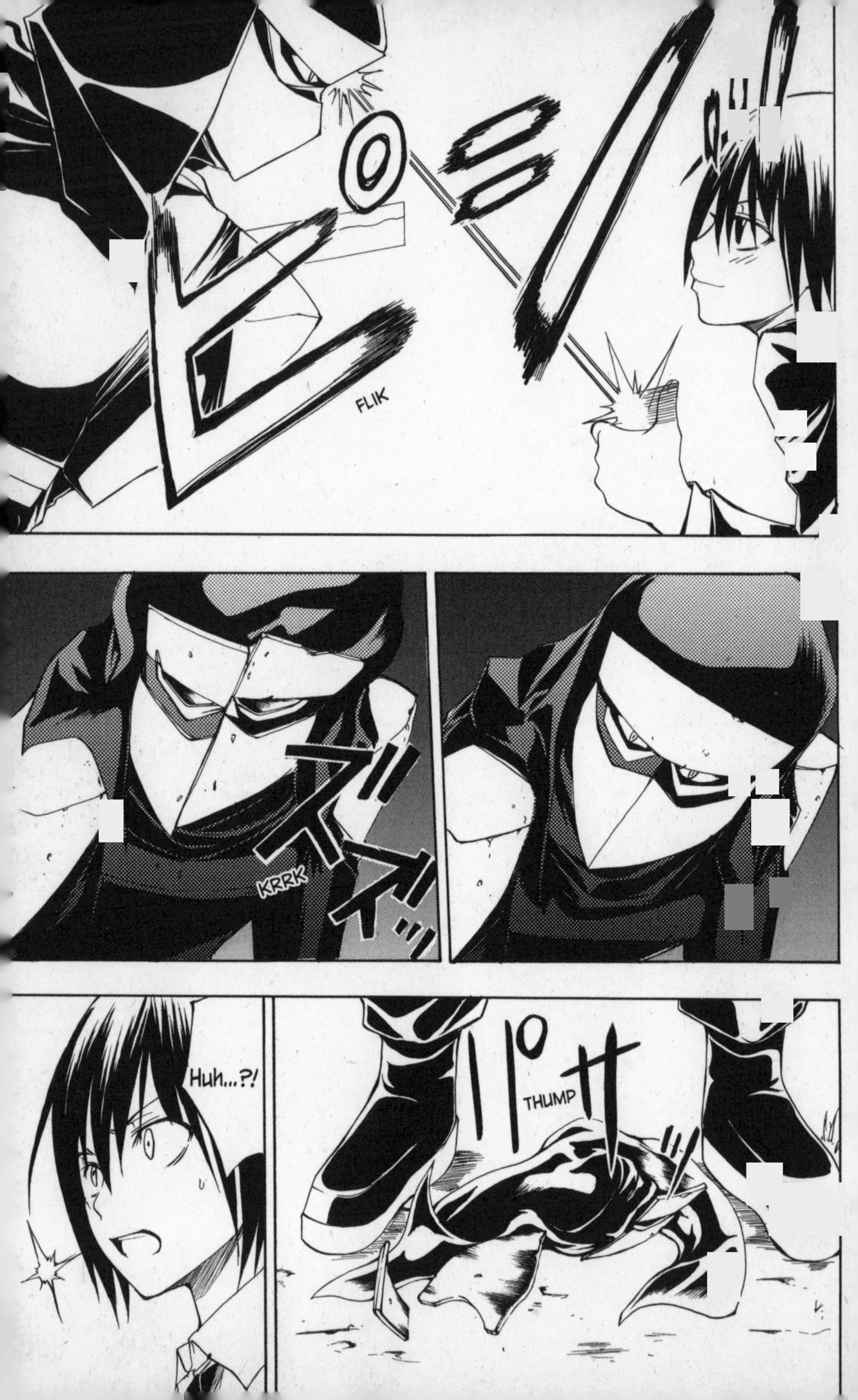
FLIK
KRRK
THUMP
Huh...?!

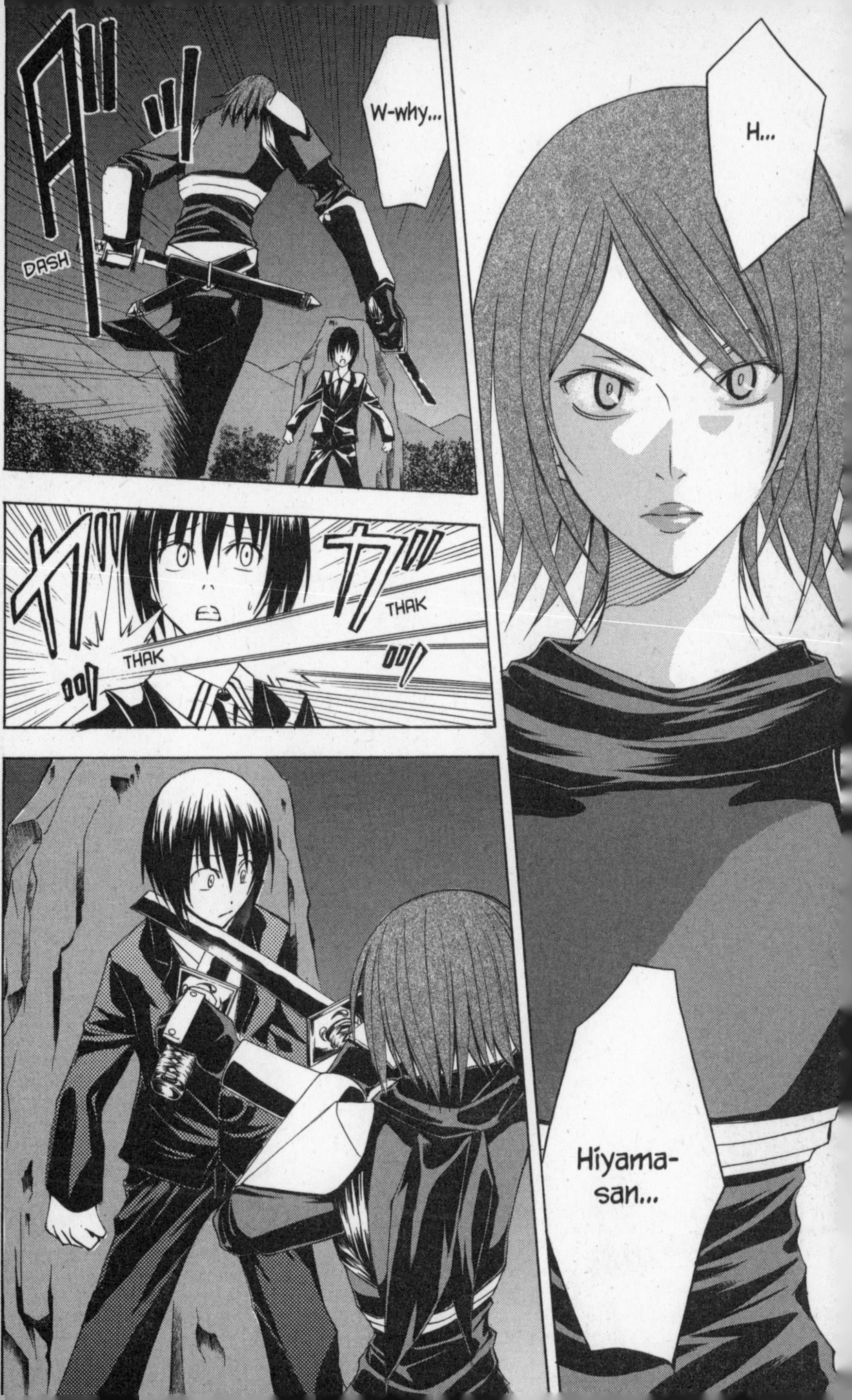
W-why...
DASH
THAK
THAK
H...
Hiyama-san...

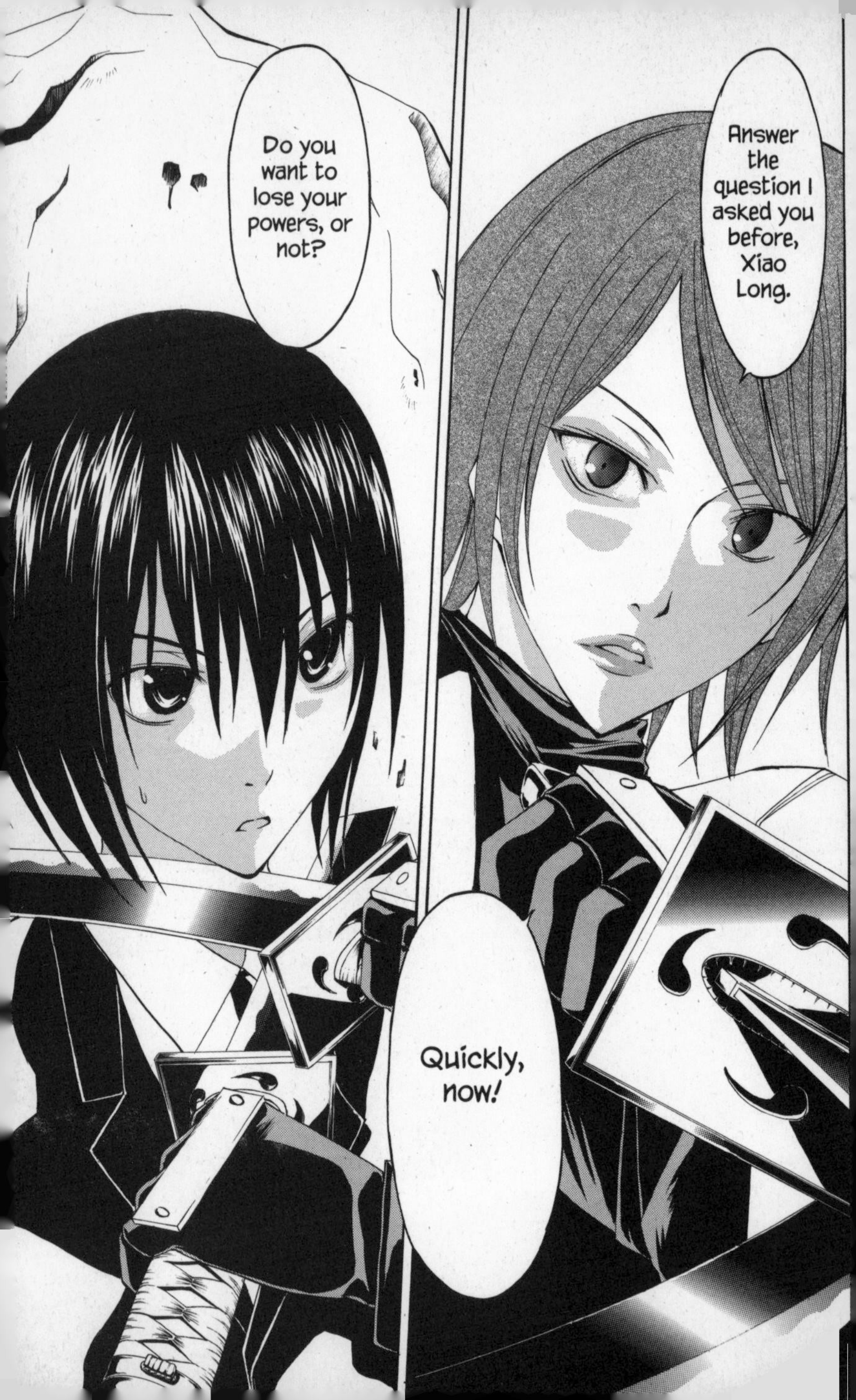
Answer the question I asked you before, Xiao Long.
Do you want to lose your powers, or not?
Quickly, now!

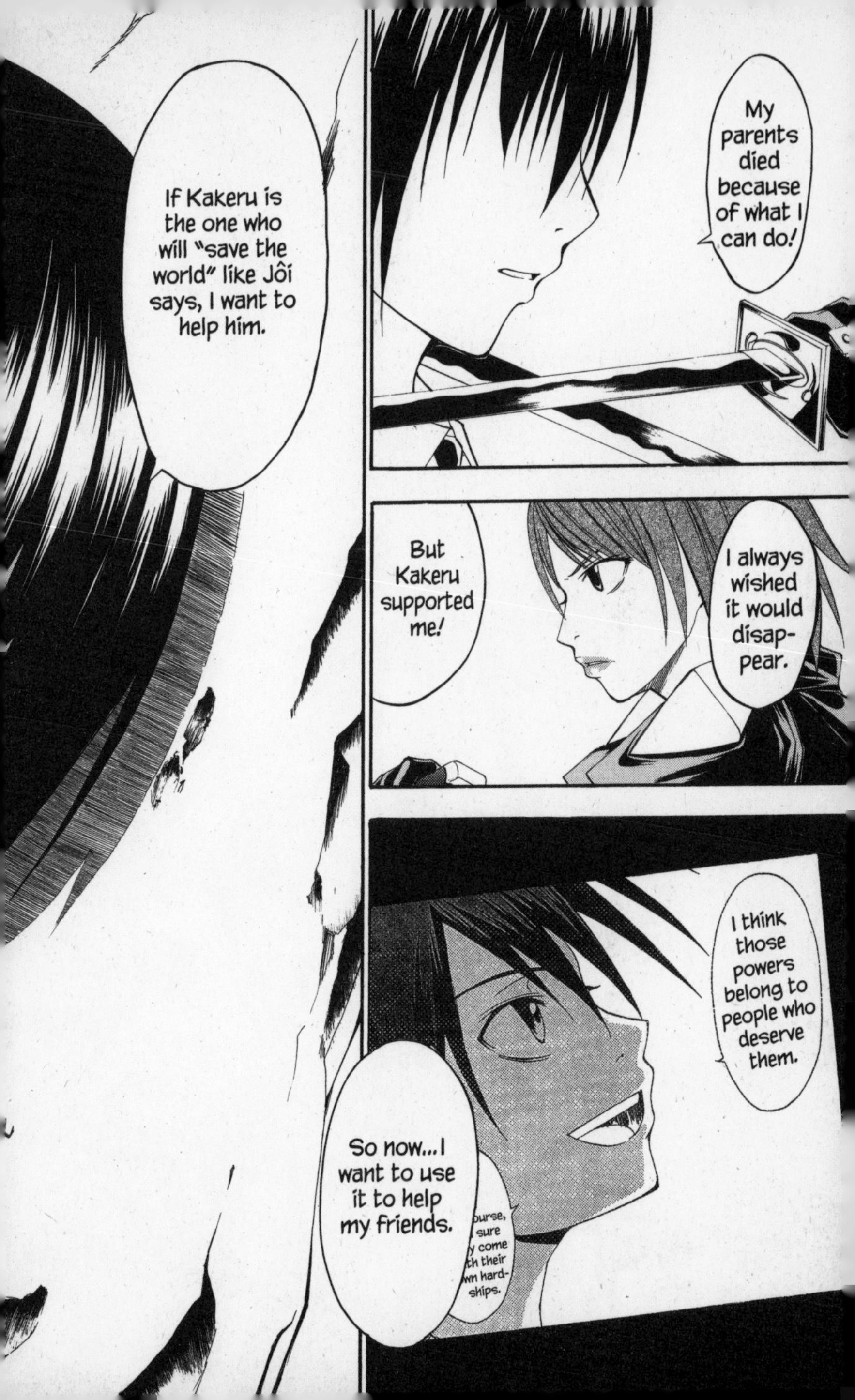
My parents died because of what I can do!
I always wished it would disappear.
But Kakeru supported me!
I think those powers belong to people who deserve them.
So now...I want to use it to help my friends.
If Kakeru is the one who will "save the world" like Jôi says, I want to help him.

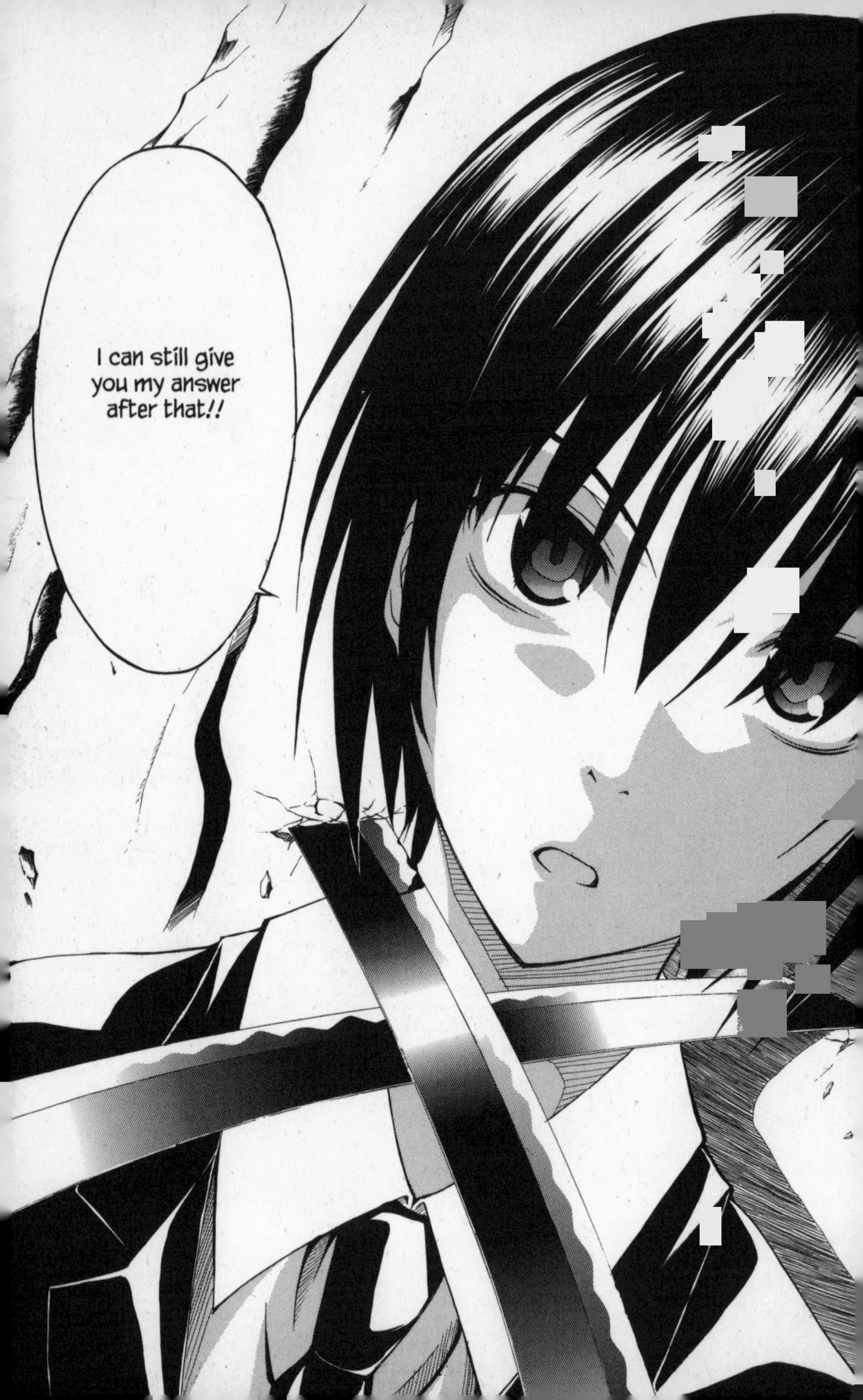
I can still give you my answer after that!!

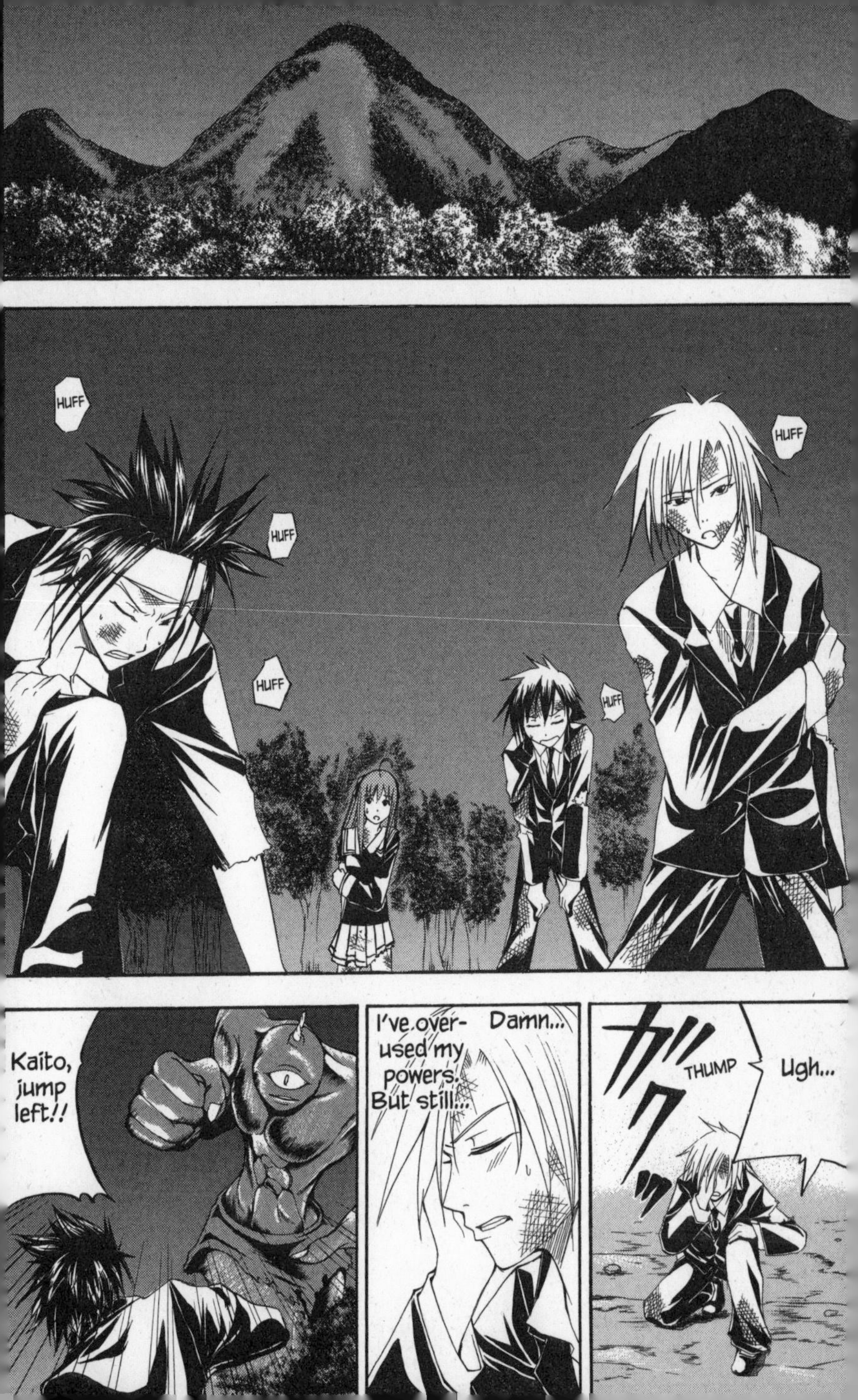

HUFF
HUFF
HUFF
HUFF
HUFF
Ugh...
ガク
THUMP
Damn...
I've over-used my powers. But still...
Kaito, jump left!!

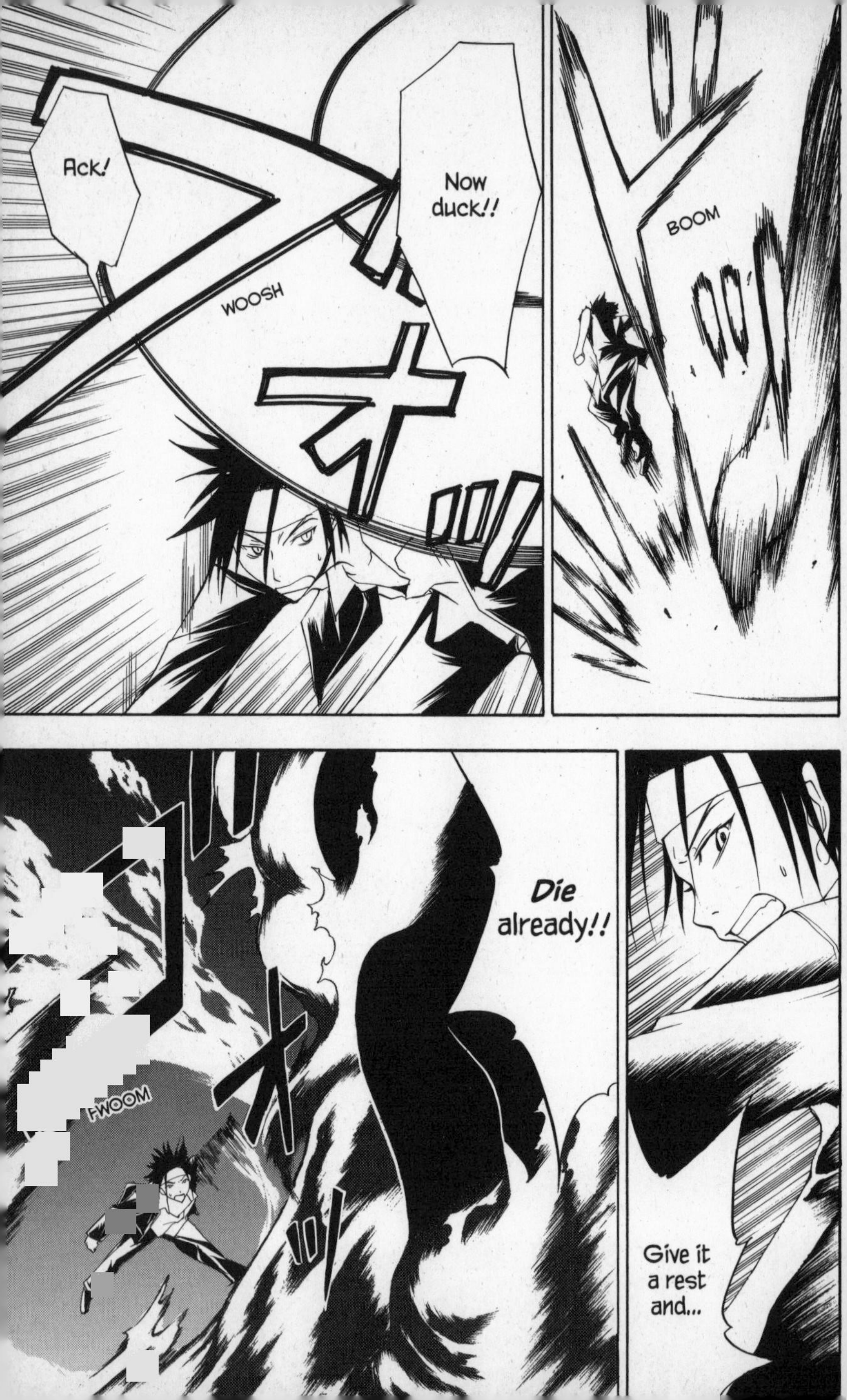
BOOM
Now duck!!
Ack!
WOOSH
Give it a rest and...
Die already!!
FWOOM

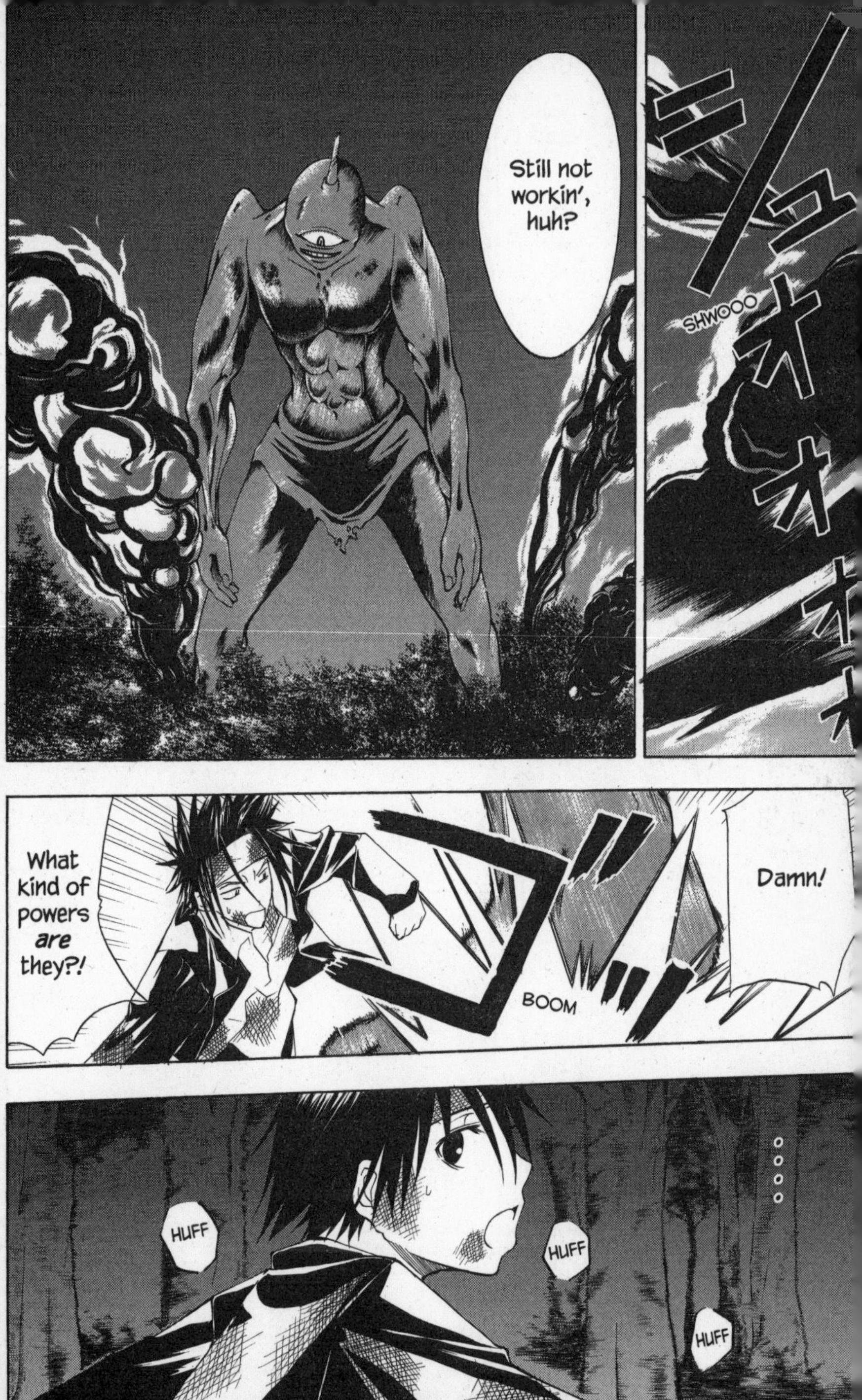
SHWOOO
Still not workin', huh?
Damn!
BOOM
What kind of powers *are* they?!
....
HUFF
HUFF
HUFF

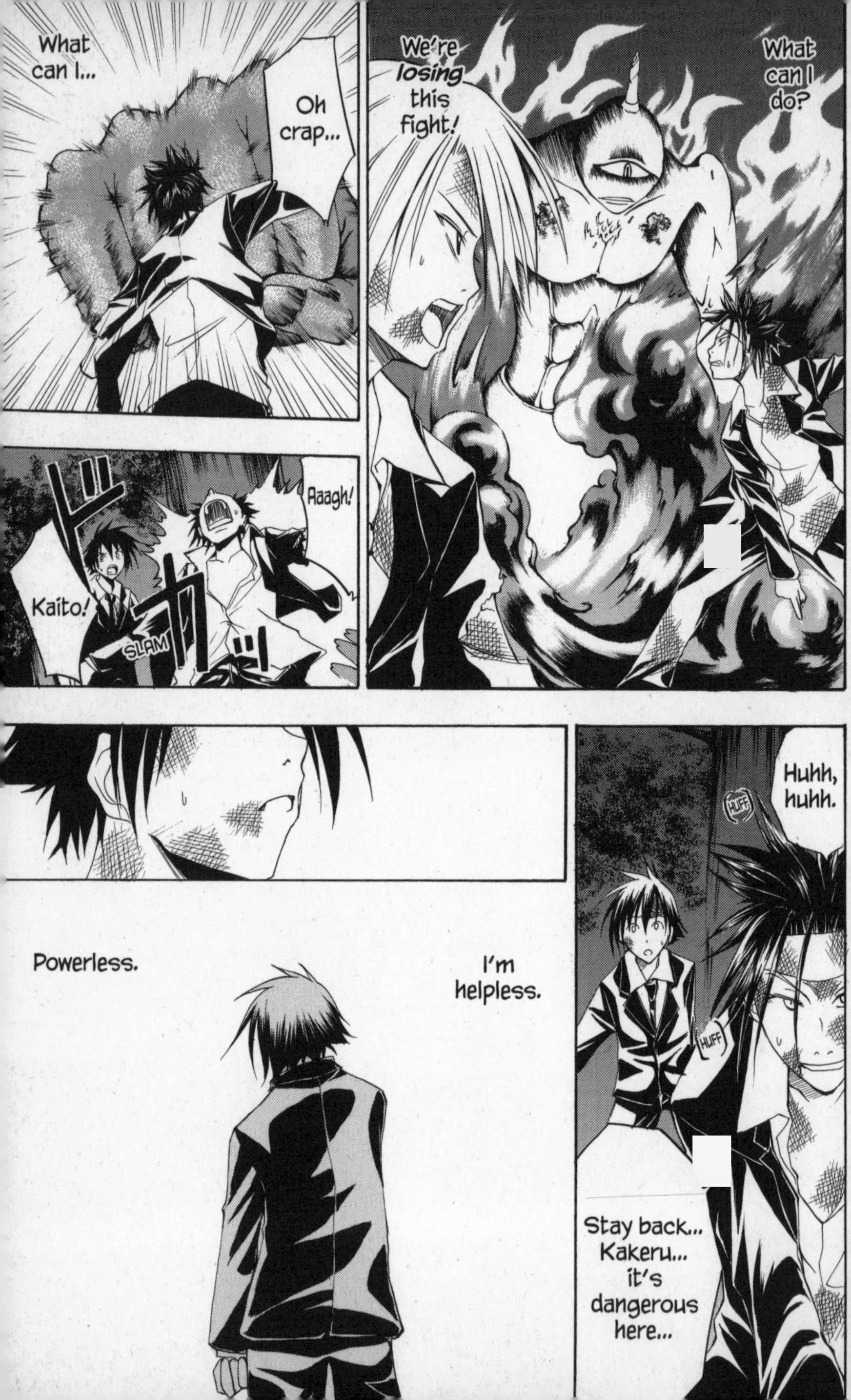
What can I do?
We're **losing** this fight!
Oh crap...
What can I...
Aaagh!
Kaito!
SLAM
Huhh, huhh.
HUFF
HUFF
Stay back... Kakeru... it's dangerous here...
I'm helpless.
Powerless.

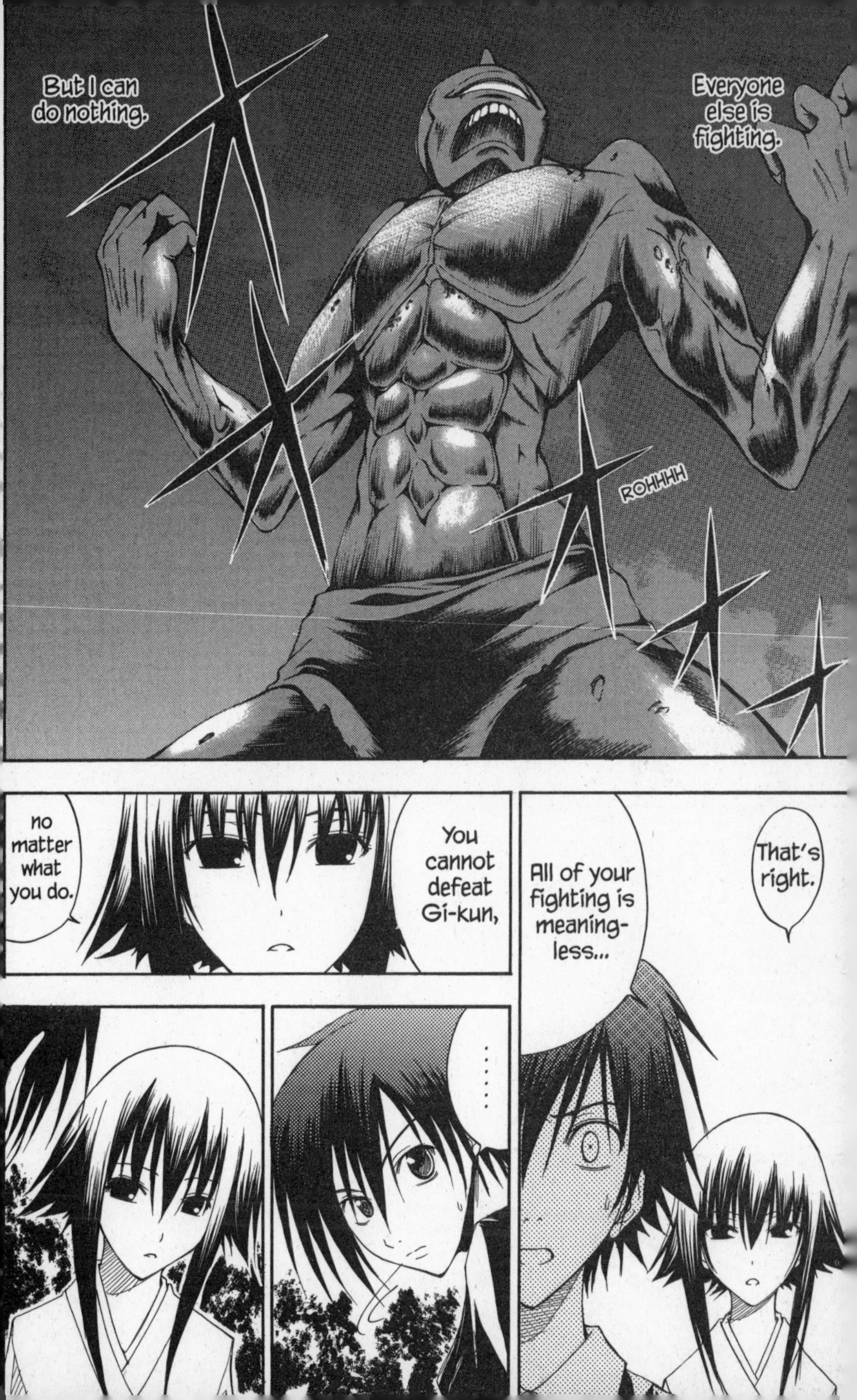
Everyone else is fighting.
ROHHHH
But I can do nothing.
That's right.
All of your fighting is meaningless...
You cannot defeat Gi-kun,
no matter what you do.
.....

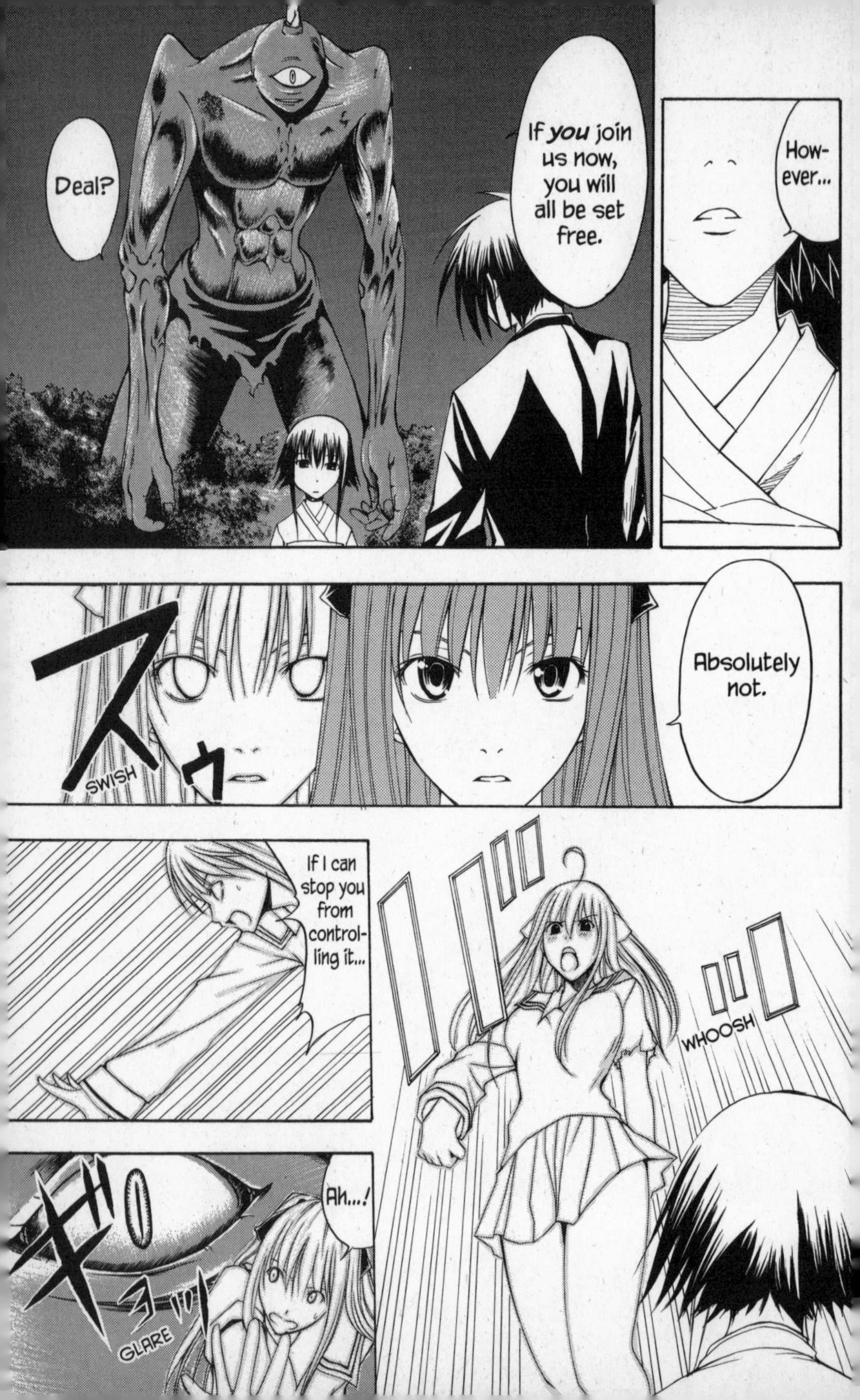
How-ever...
If *you* join us now, you will all be set free.
Deal?
Absolutely not.
SWISH
WHOOSH
If I can stop you from control-ling it...
Ah...!
GLARE

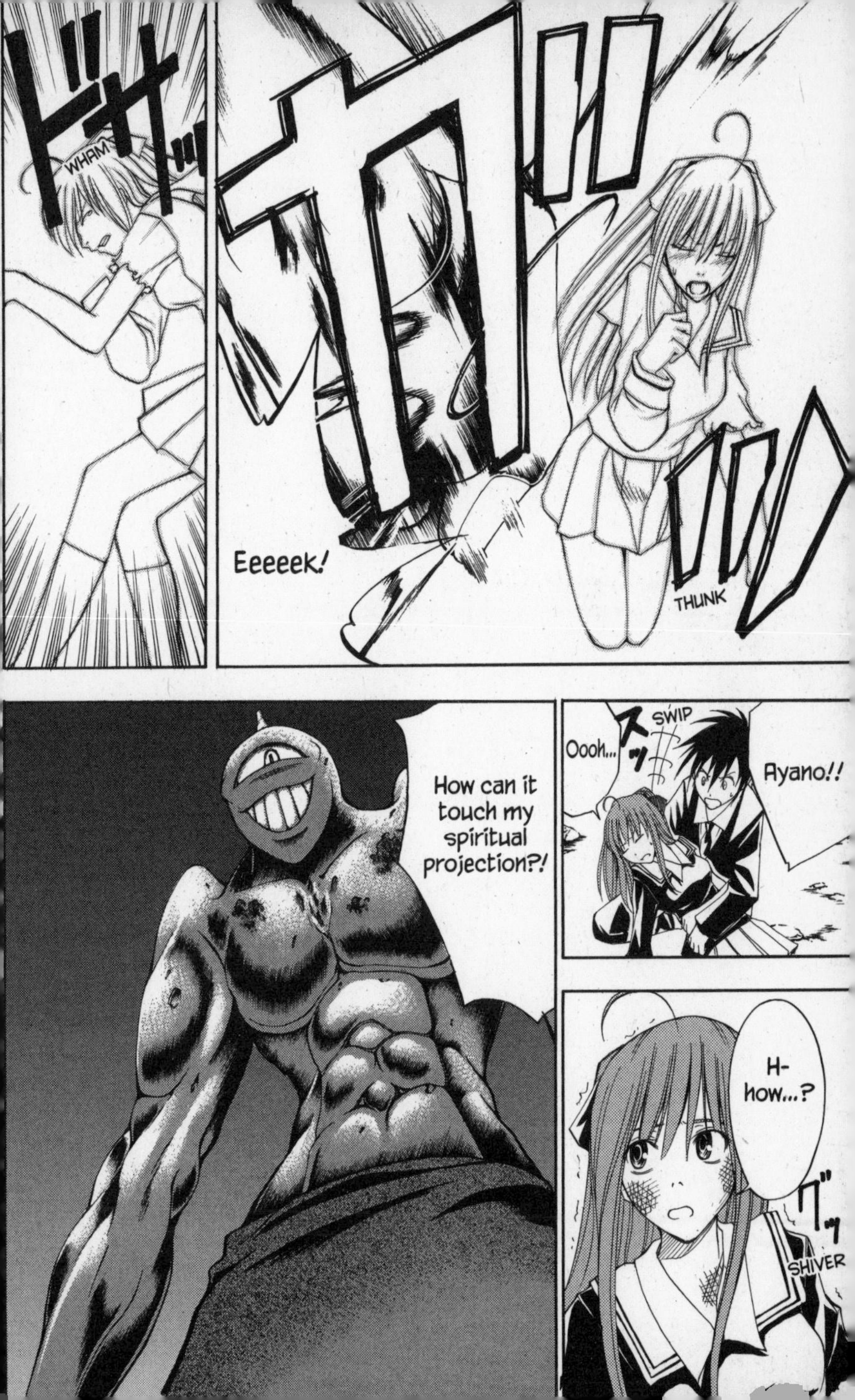
Eeeeek!
THUNK
WHAM
Ayano!!
SWIP
Oooh...
H- how...?
SHIVER
How can it touch my spiritual projection?!

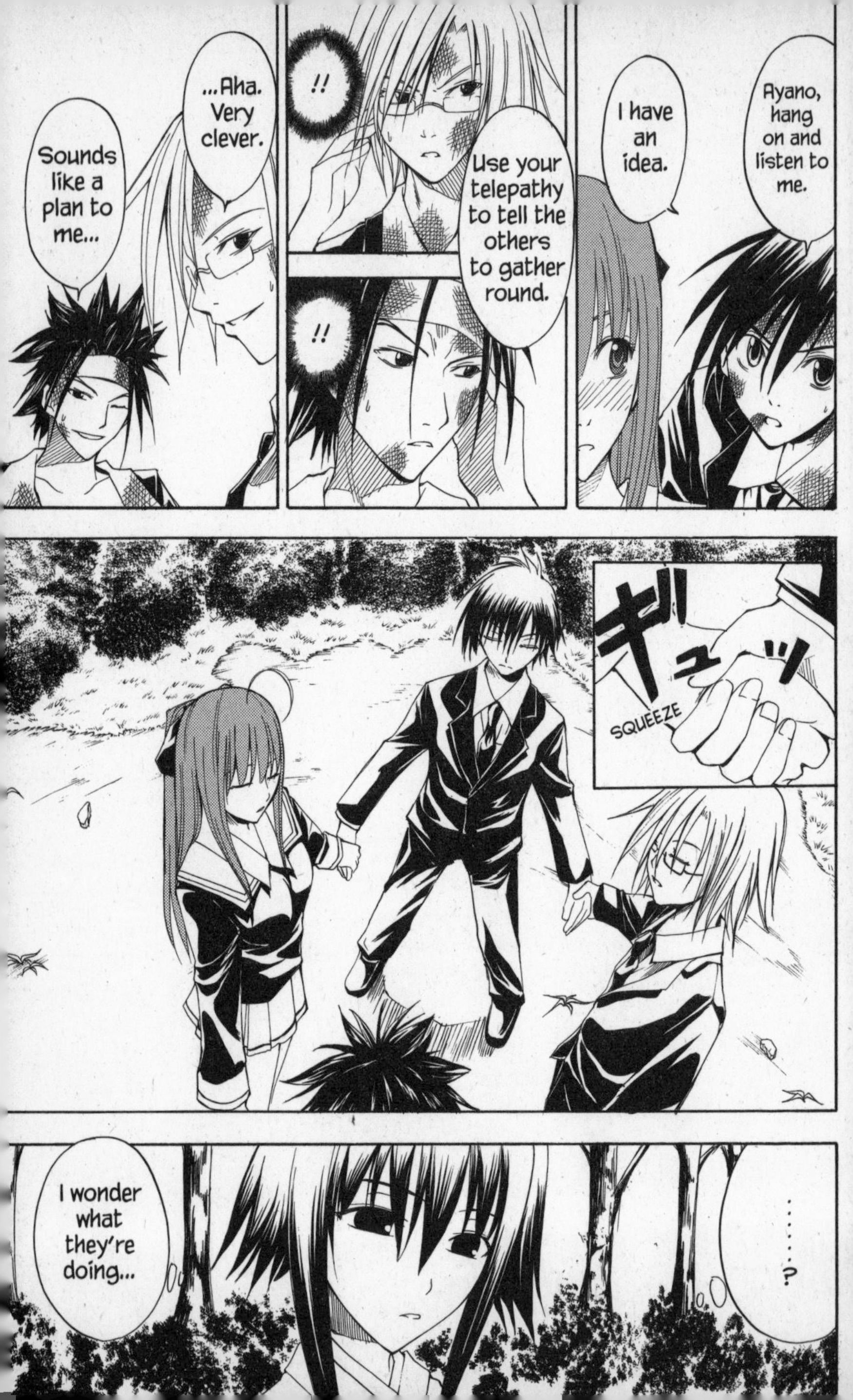
Ayano, hang on and listen to me.
I have an idea.
!!
Use your telepathy to tell the others to gather round.
!!
...Aha. Very clever.
Sounds like a plan to me...
ギュッ
SQUEEZE
......?
I wonder what they're doing...

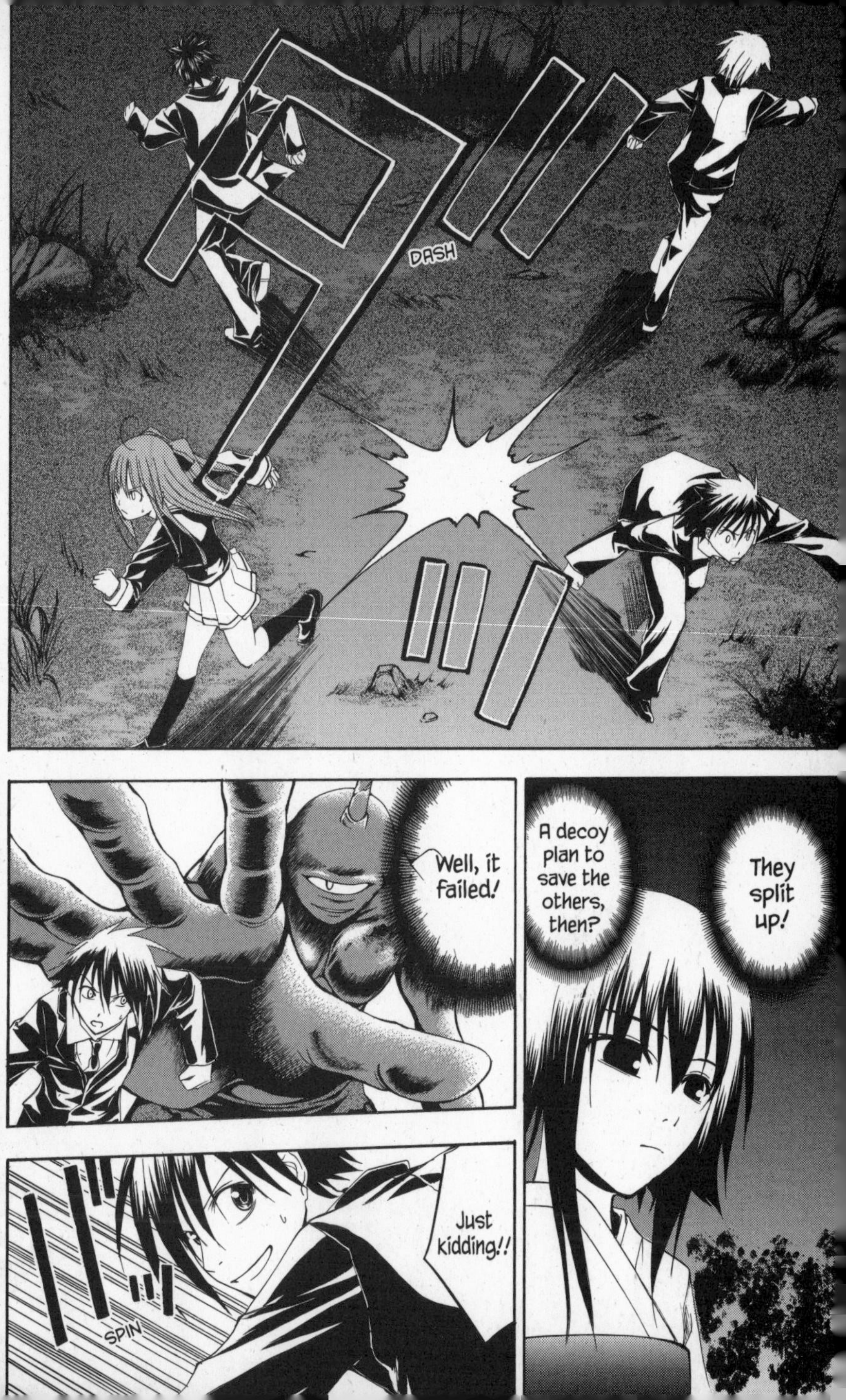
DASH
They split up!
A decoy plan to save the others, then?
Well, it failed!
Just kidding!!
SPIN

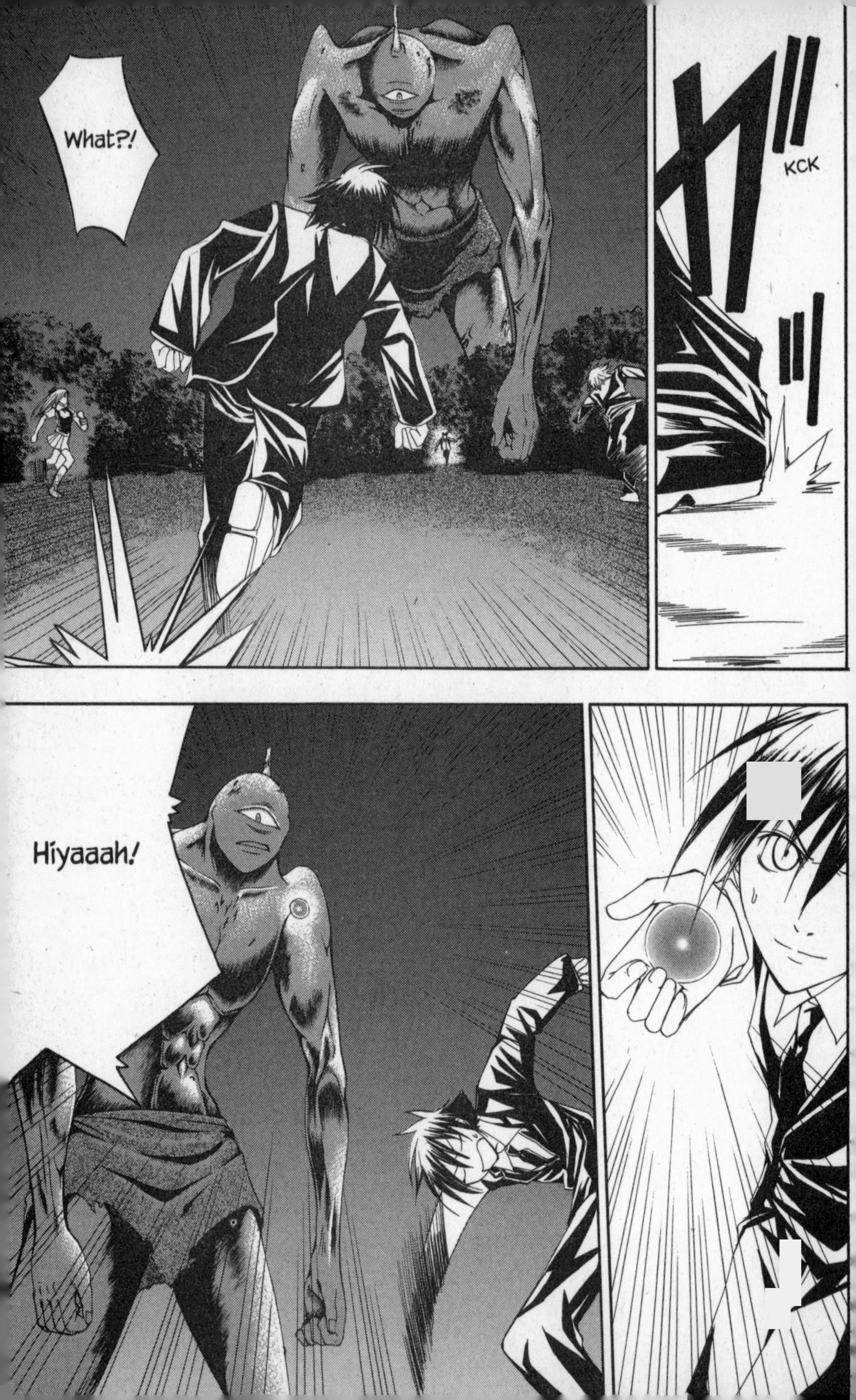
KCK
What?!
Hiyaaah!

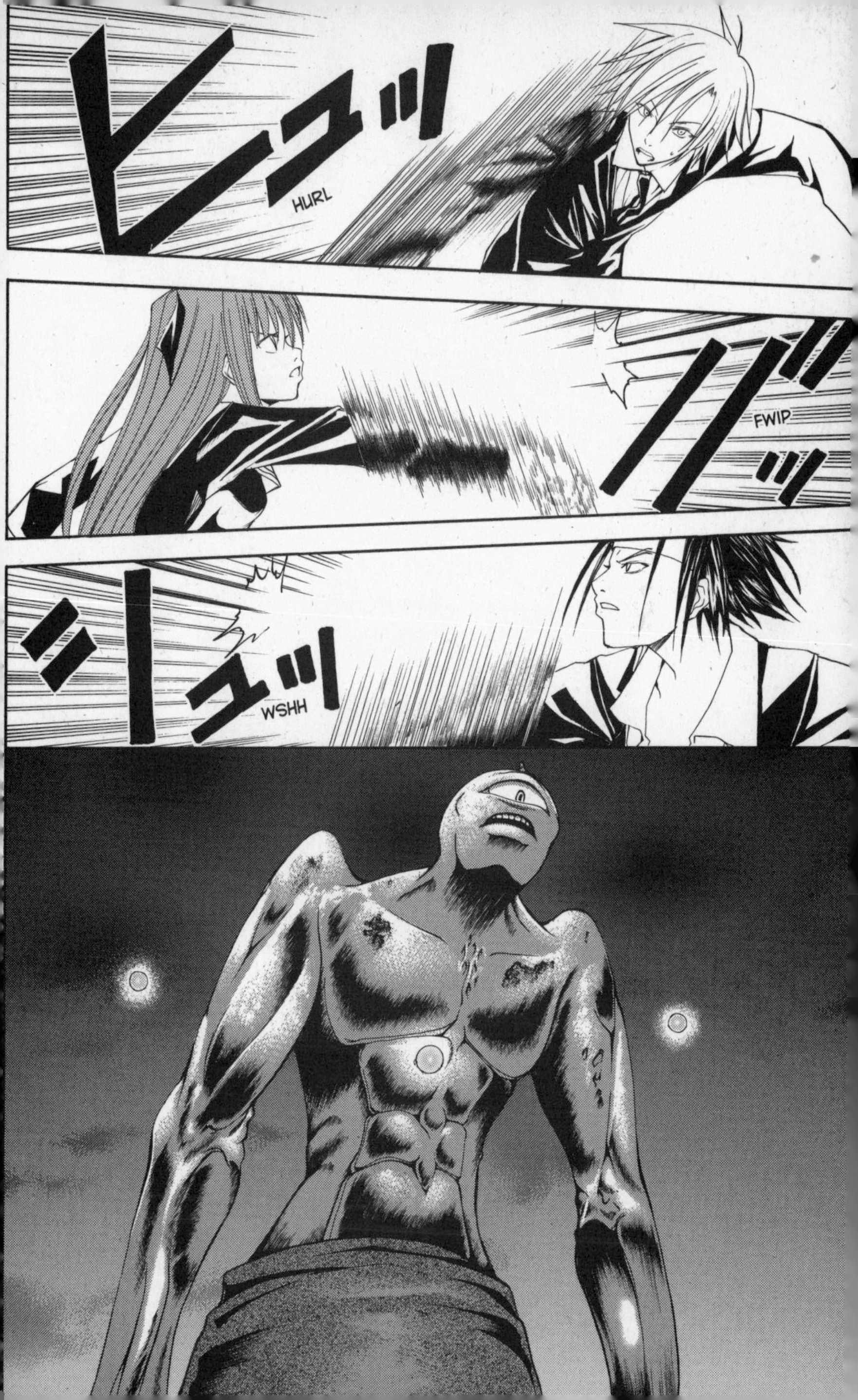
ヒュッ
HURL
ブッ
FWIP
シュッ
WSHH

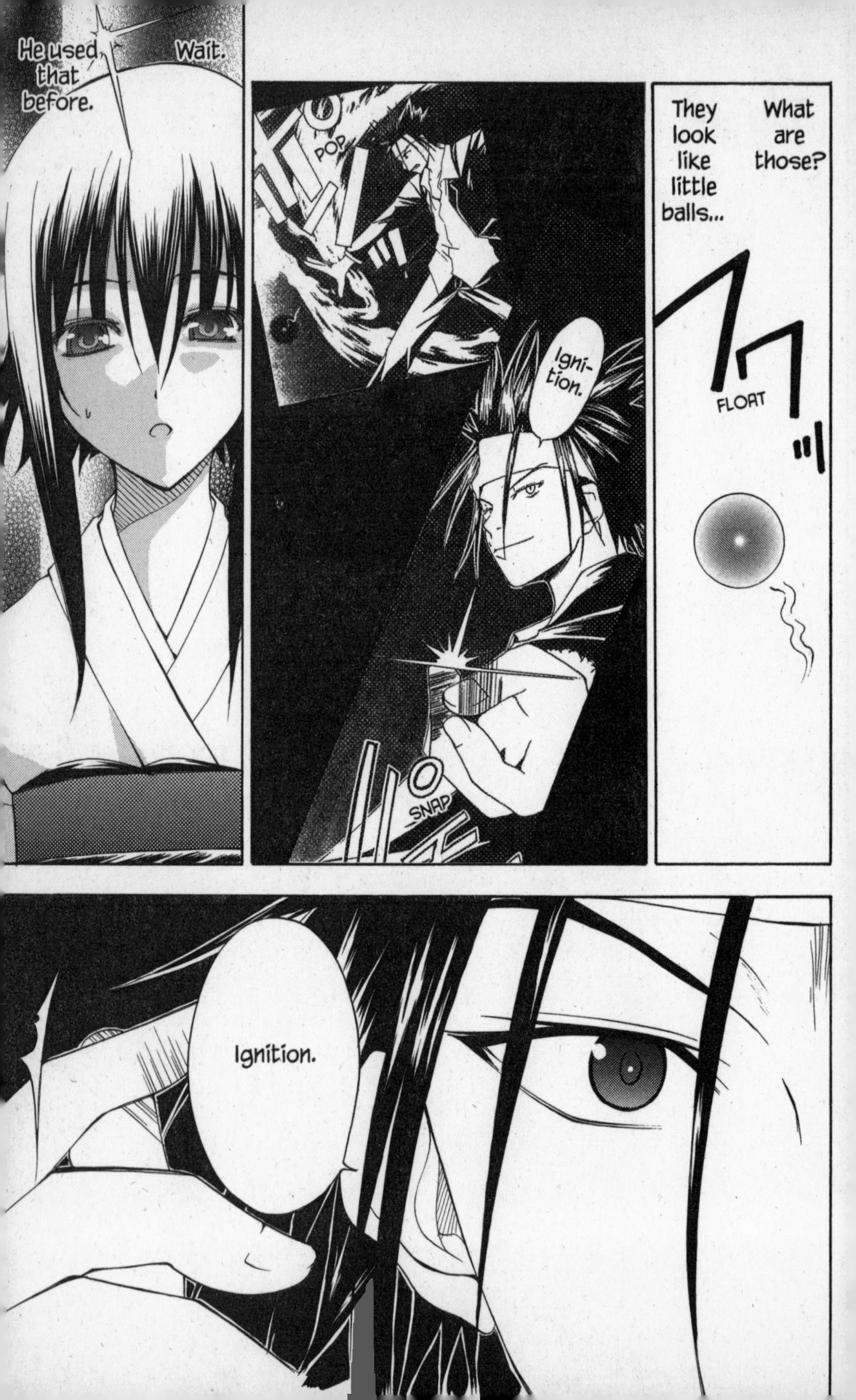
What are those?
They look like little balls...
FLOAT
POP
Igni-tion.
SNAP
Wait.
He used that before.
Ignition.

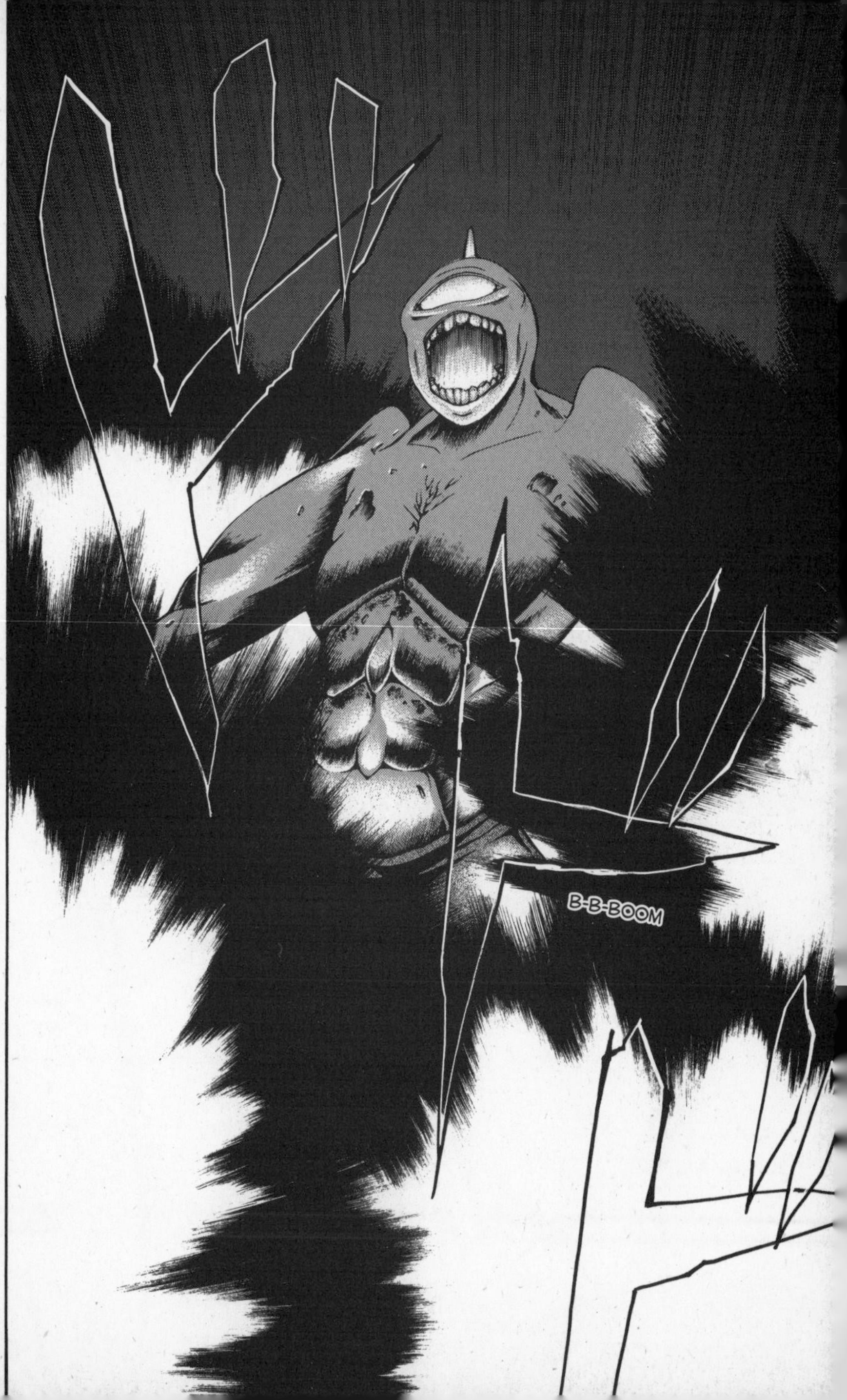
B-B-BOOM

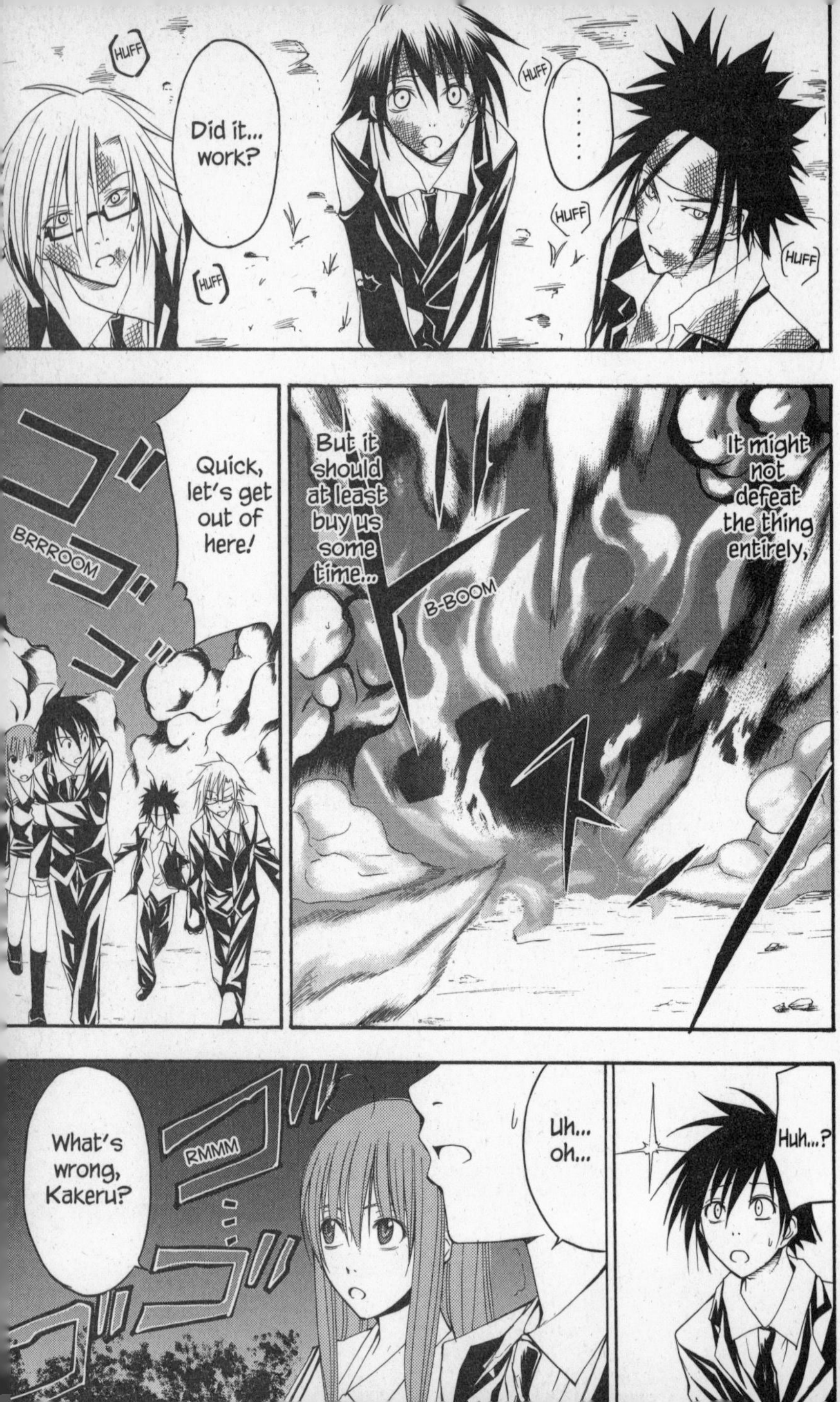
HUFF
......
HUFF
HUFF
Did it... work?
HUFF
HUFF
It might not defeat the thing entirely,
But it should at least buy us some time...
B-BOOM
Quick, let's get out of here!
BRRROOM
Huh...?
Uh... oh...
RMMM
What's wrong, Kakeru?

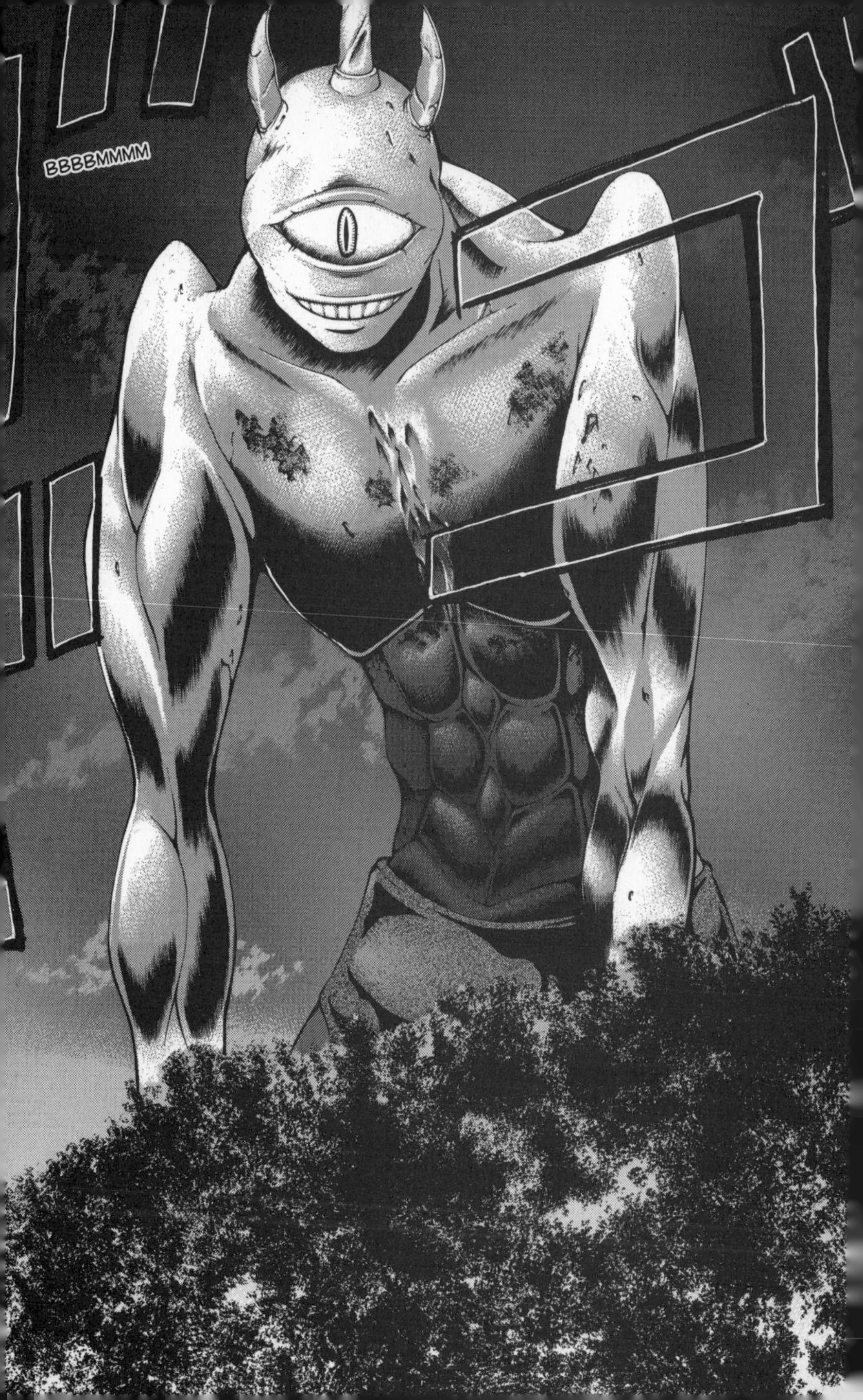
BBBBMMMM

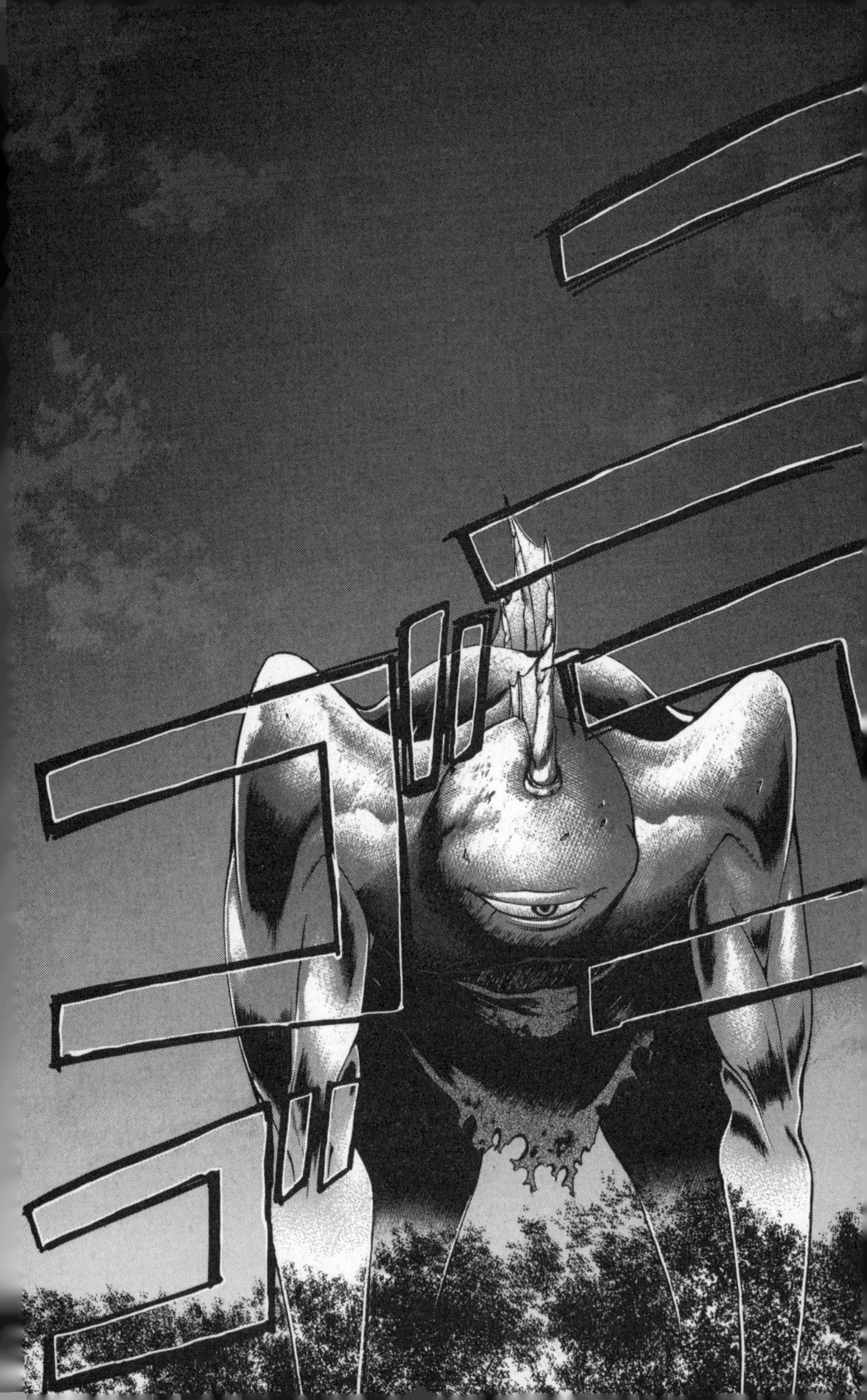
ゴゴゴゴ

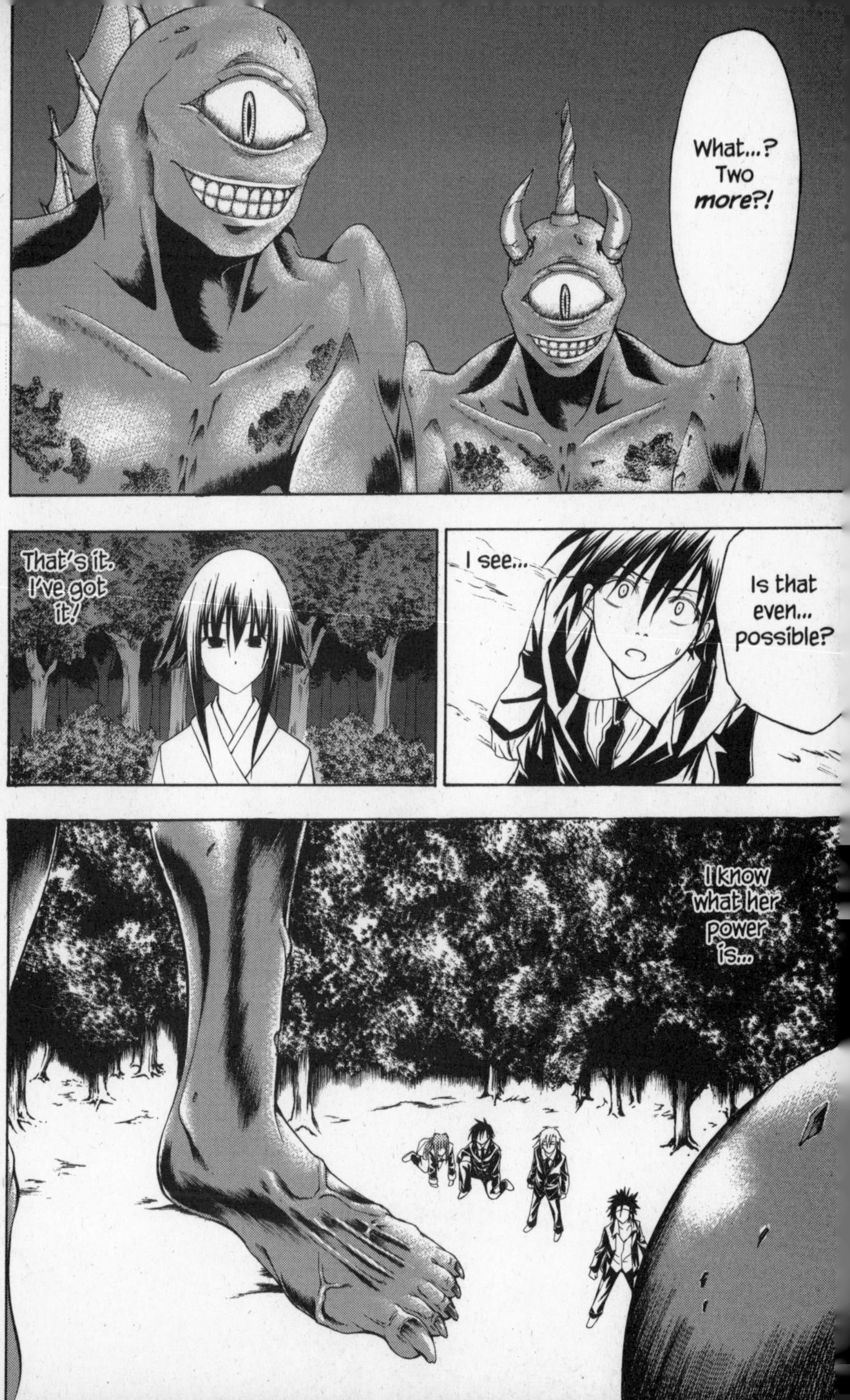
What...? Two more?!
Is that even... possible?
I see...
That's it. I've got it!
I know what her power is...

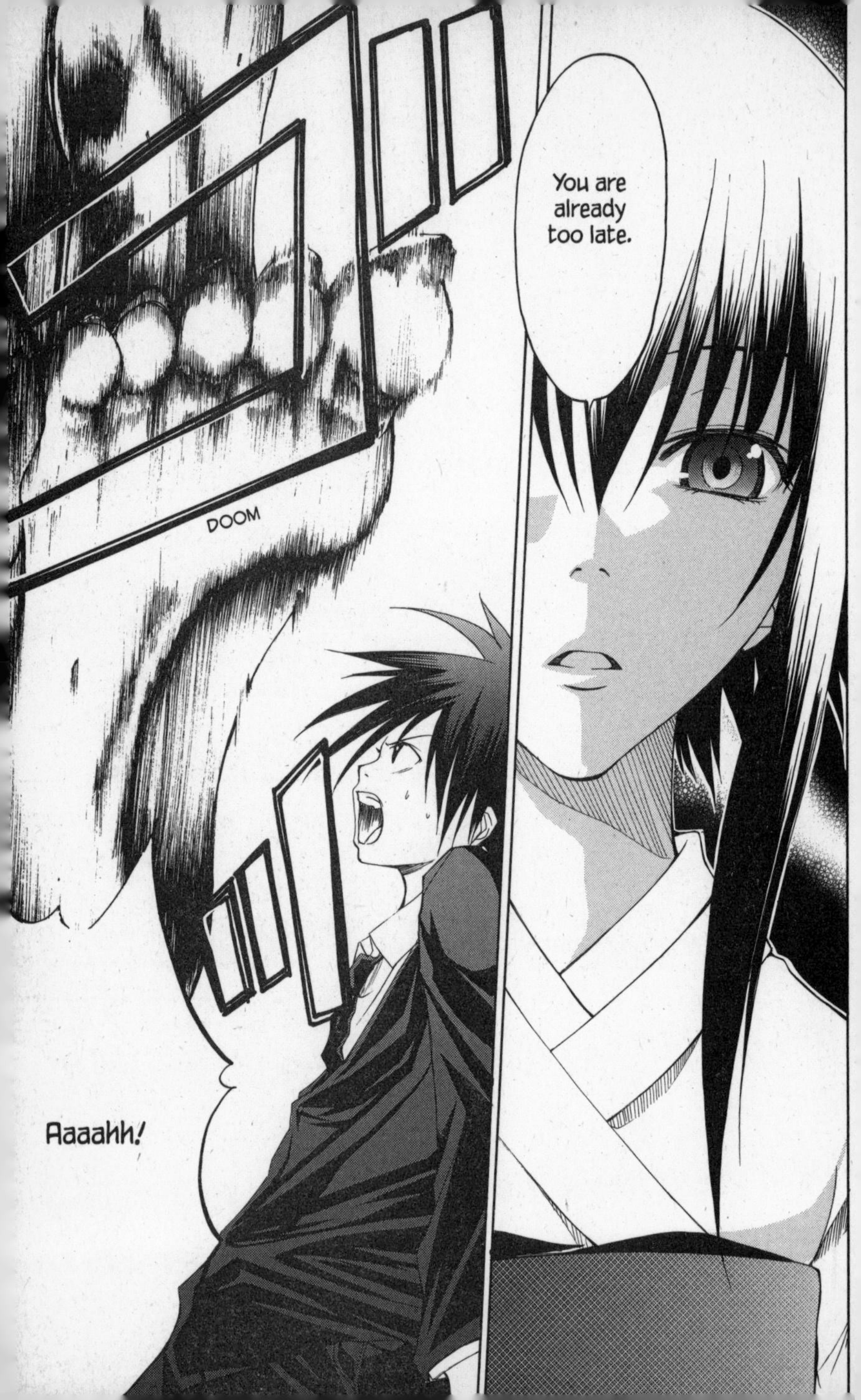
You are already too late.
DOOM
Aaaahh!

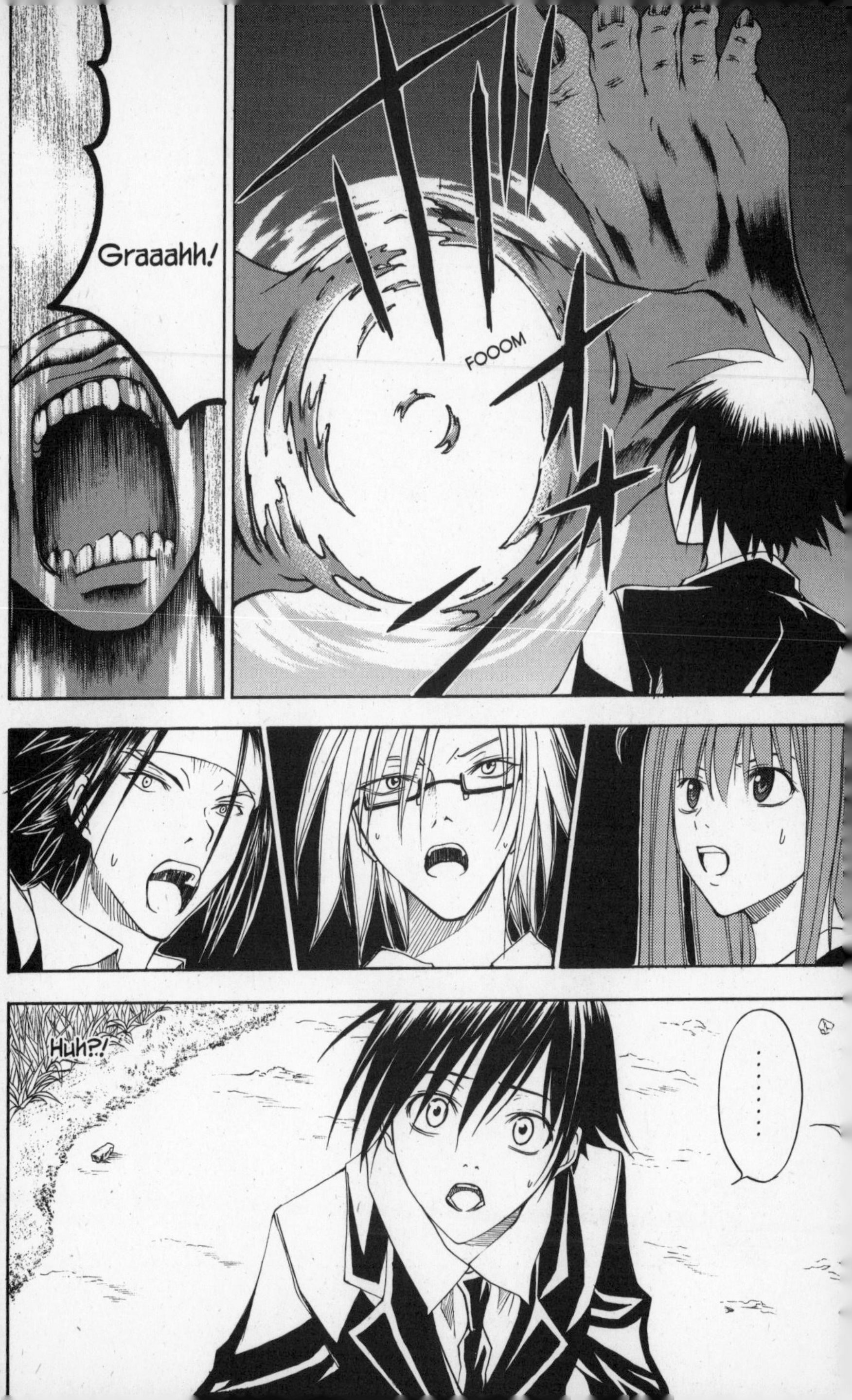
FOOOM
Graaahh!
......
Huh?!

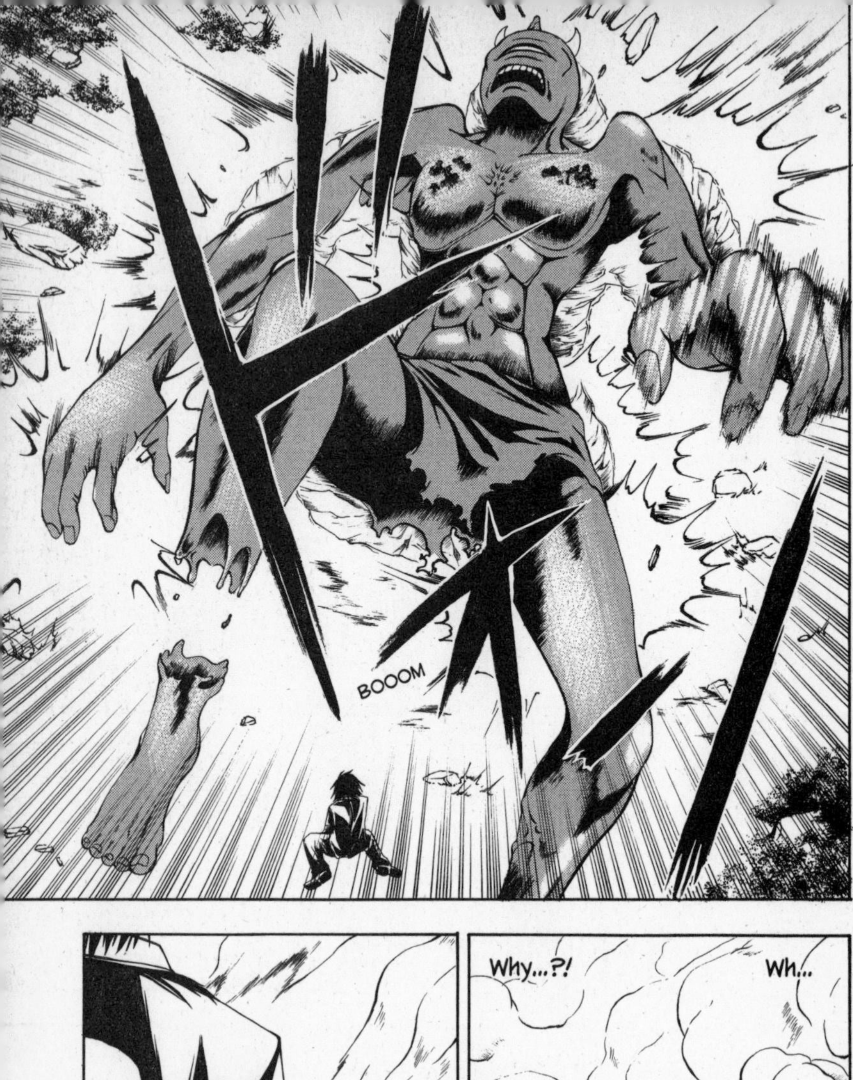
BOOOM

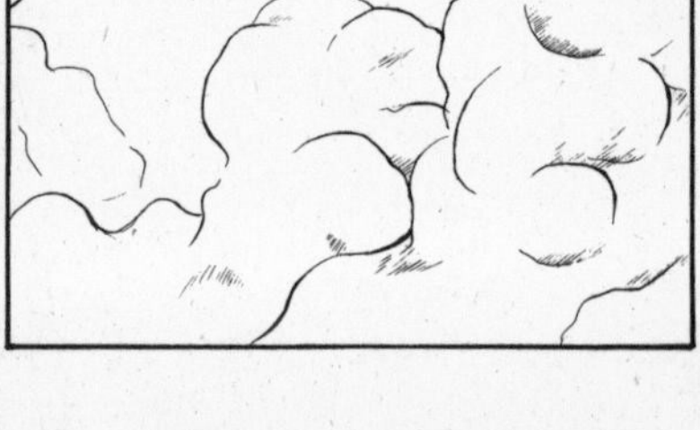
Wh...
Why...?!

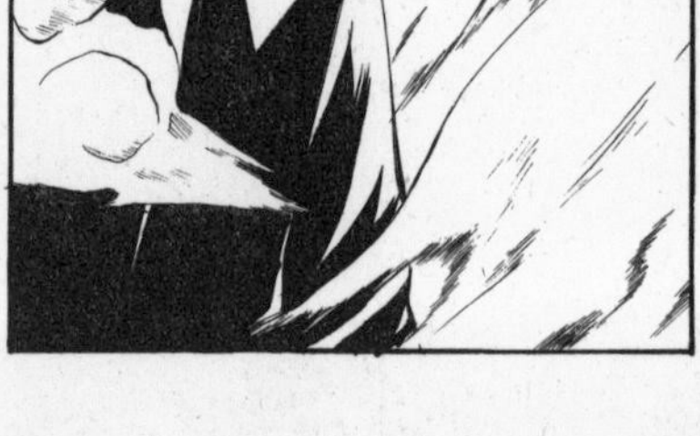

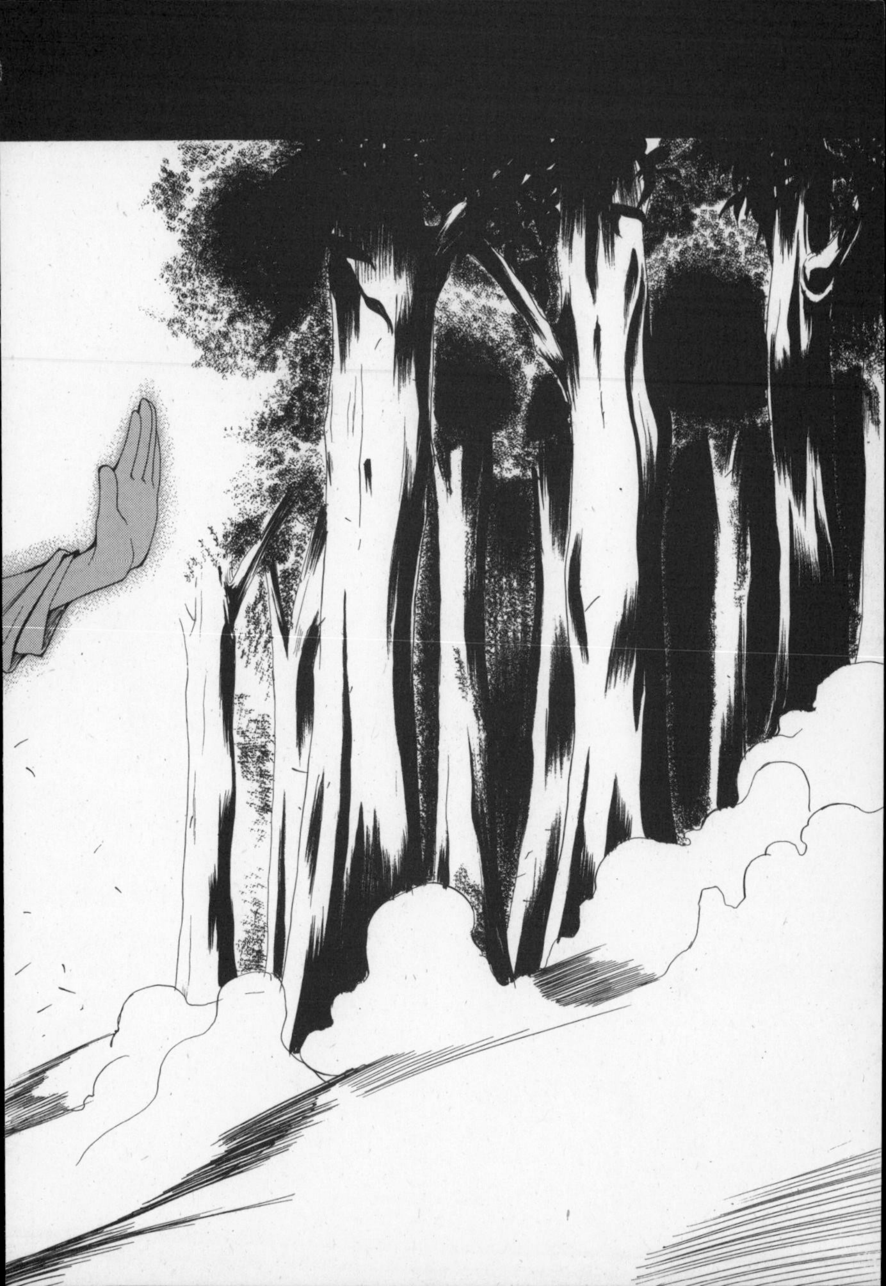

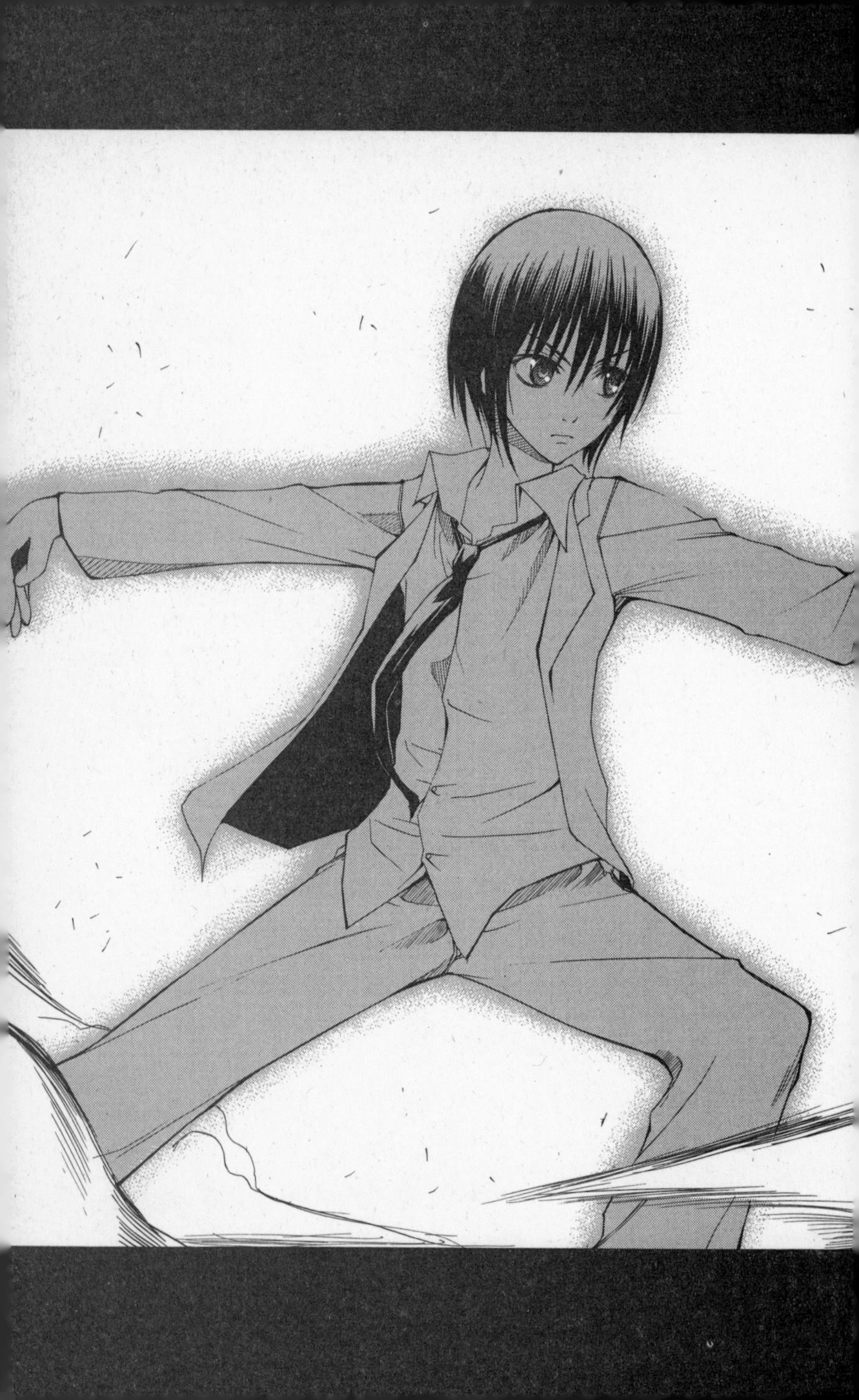

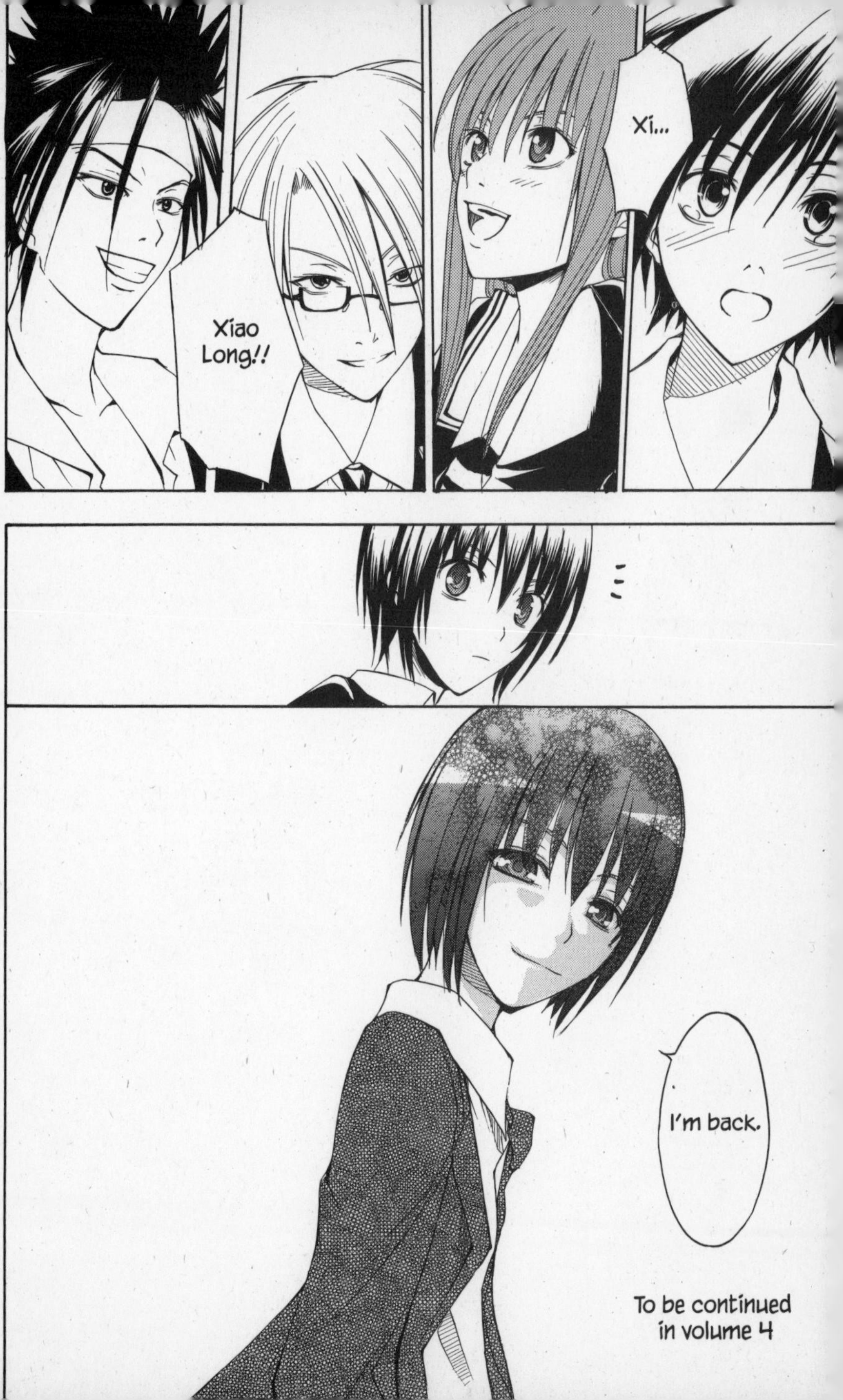
Xi...
Xiao Long!!
I'm back.
To be continued in volume 4

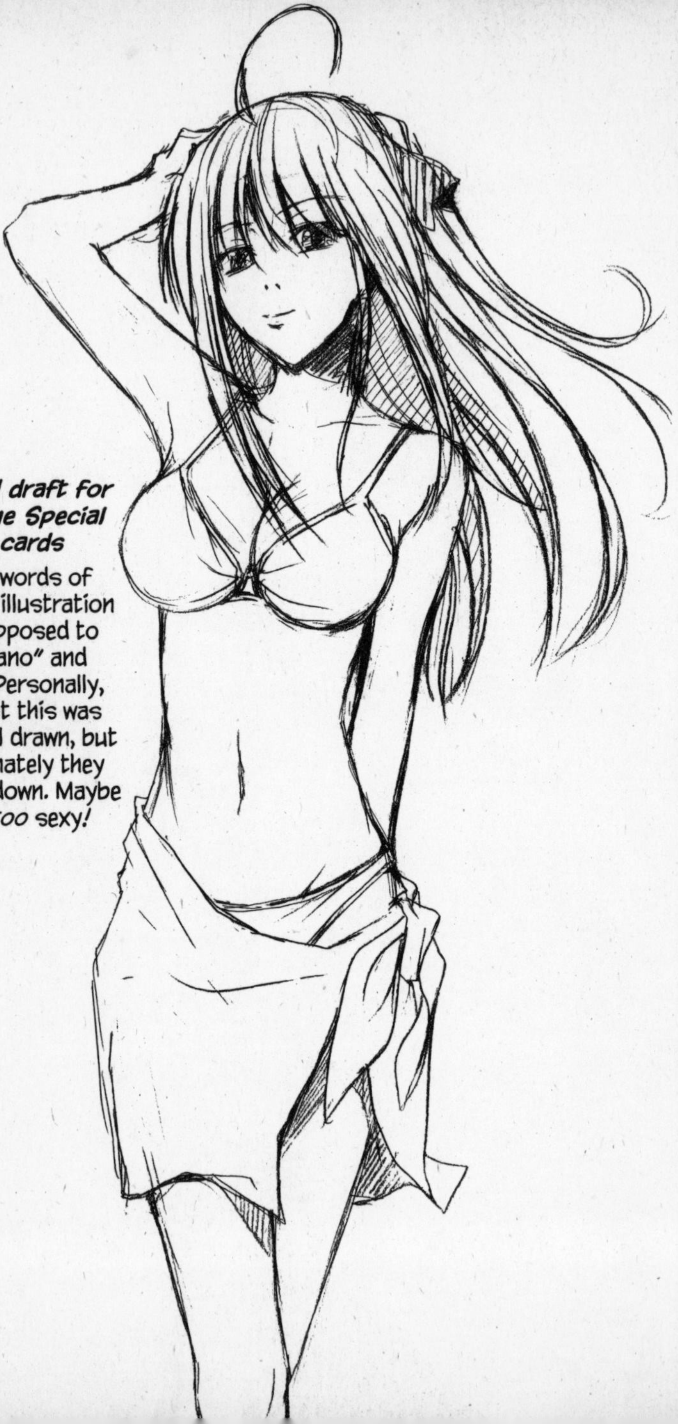

***Rejected draft for Magazine Special gift cards***

The keywords of this card illustration were supposed to be "Ayano" and "sexy." Personally, I thought this was rather well drawn, but unfortunately they turned it down. Maybe it was *too* sexy!

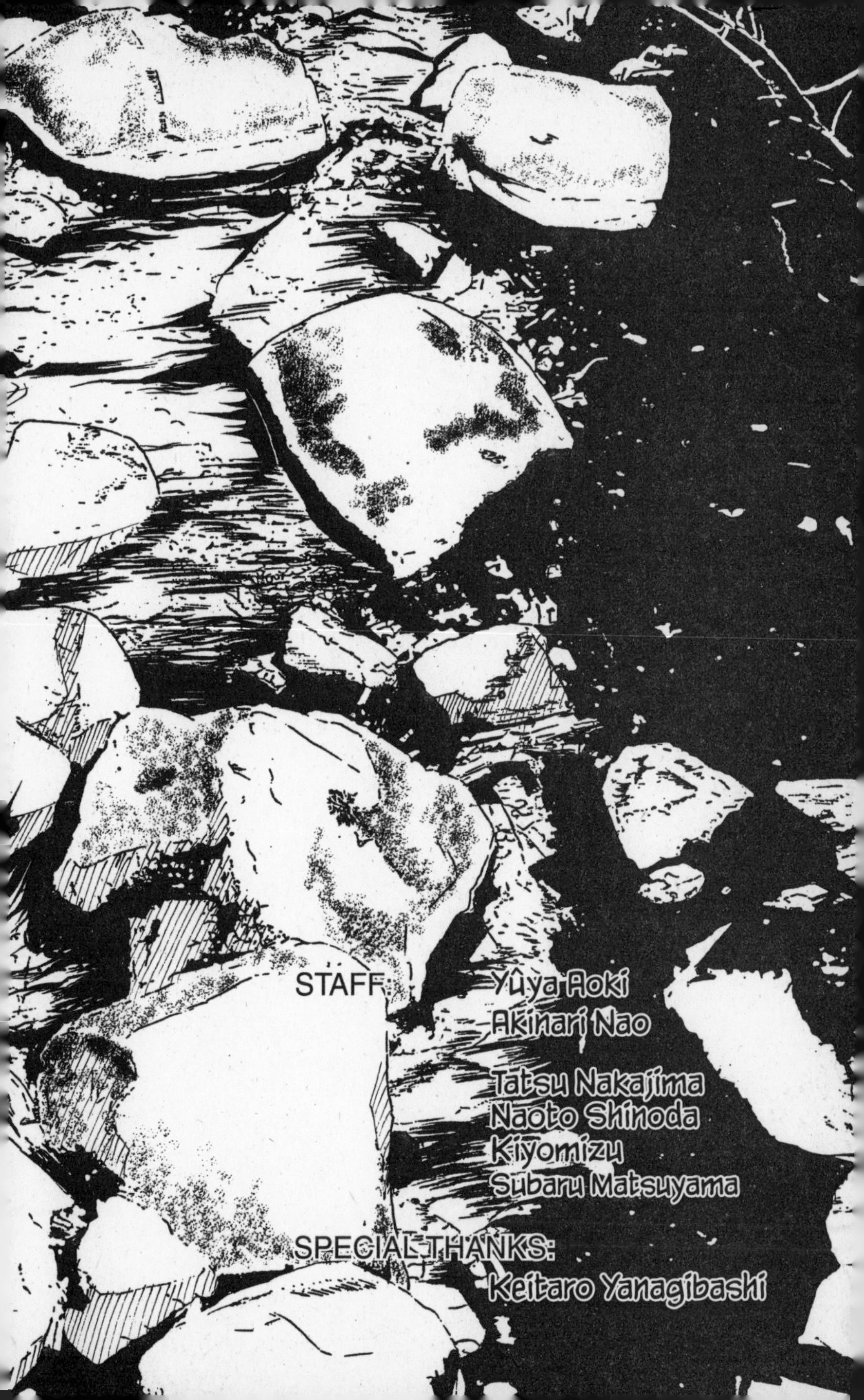
STAFF:
Yûya Aoki
Akinari Nao
Tatsu Nakajima
Naoto Shinoda
Kiyomizu
Subaru Matsuyama
SPECIAL THANKS:
Keitaro Yanagibashi

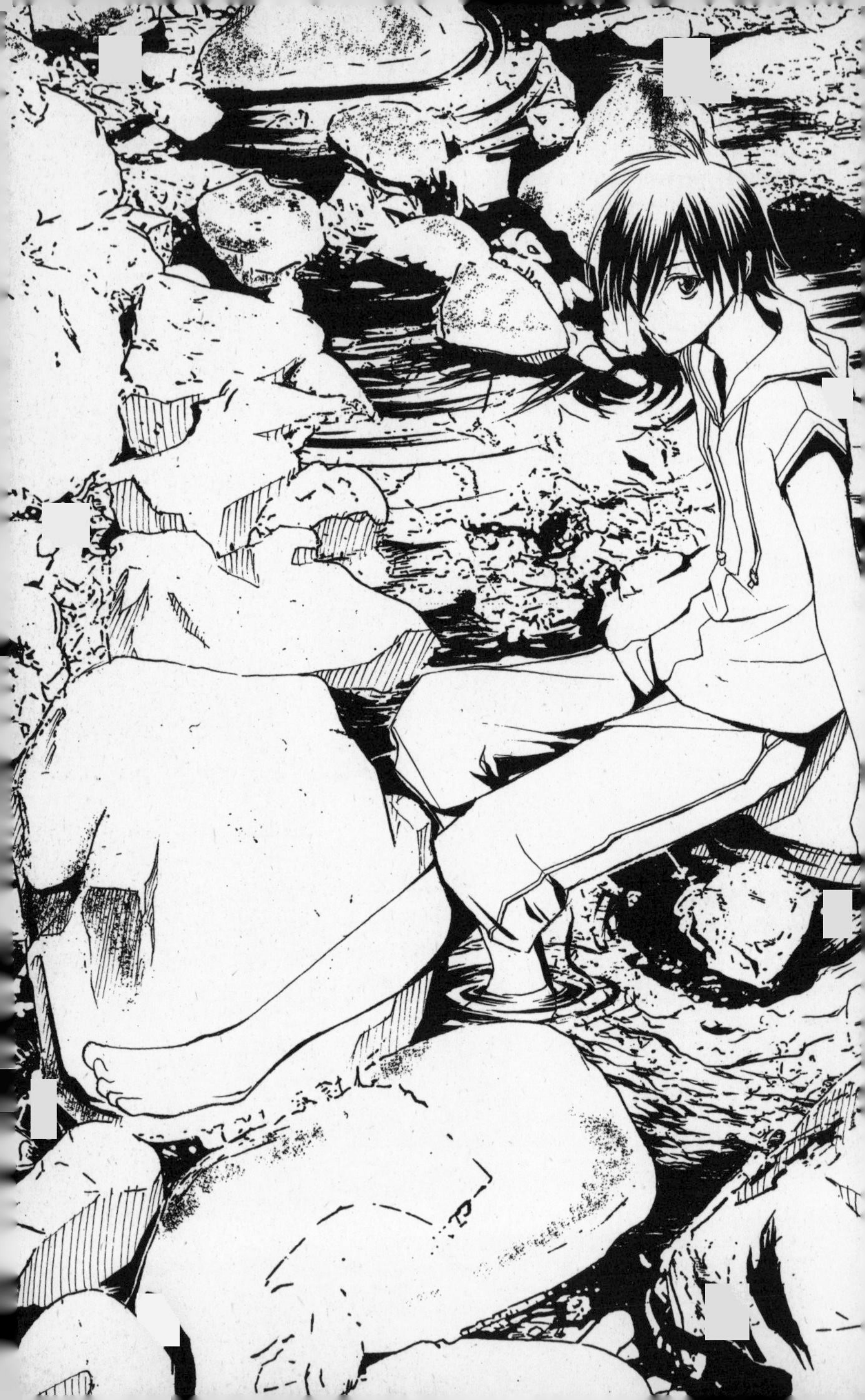

# Translation Notes

Japanese is a tricky language for most Westerners, and translation is often more an art than a science. For your edification and reading pleasure, here are notes on some of the places where we could have gone in a different direction, or where a Japanese cultural reference is used.

## Class duty, page 43

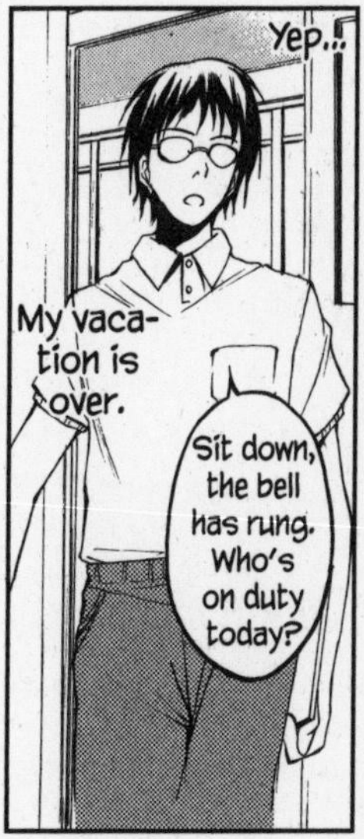
Yep...
My vacation is over.
Sit down, the bell has rung. Who's on duty today?

In Japanese classes, there is typically a "daily duty" position that one or two students perform, consisting of tasks like calling roll or reading school announcements. The student(s) changes every day, hence the name.

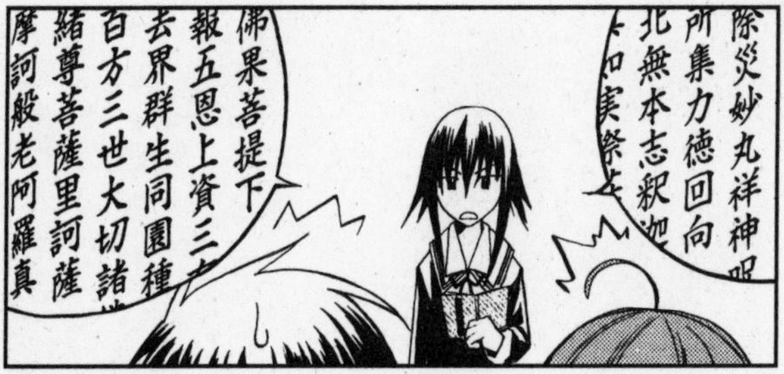
除災妙丸祥神呪
所集力徳回向
北無本志釈迦
佛果菩提下
報五恩上資三
去界群生同園種
百方三世大切諸
緒尊菩薩里訶薩
摩訶般老阿羅真

## Chinese characters, page 60

This character is speaking Chinese. We've left her dialogue in Chinese, to preserve the effect of the scene as the character's speech is incomprehensible to the boys.

## Ink ribbon, page 141

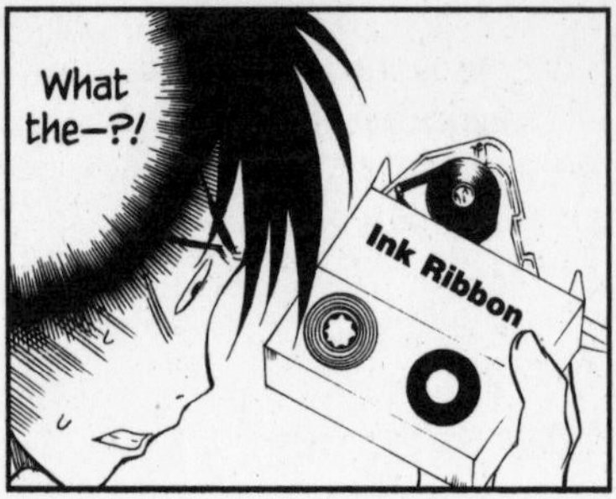
What the–?!
Ink Ribbon

The ink ribbon is a reference to the video game Resident Evil, which Kakeru can be seen playing when he says he wants a rocket launcher. In Resident Evil, the player saves his or her progress in the game by using ink ribbons—an item that comes in limited supply—on a typewriter.

## Ultraman, page 144

Ultraman is the hero of the classic live-action kids' TV show of the same name, originally aired in the 1960s. A superhero who grows in size to fight giant monsters, he is the closest thing to Superman for the Japanese and is so recognizable that even Kaito knows who he is after years in the psychic facility.

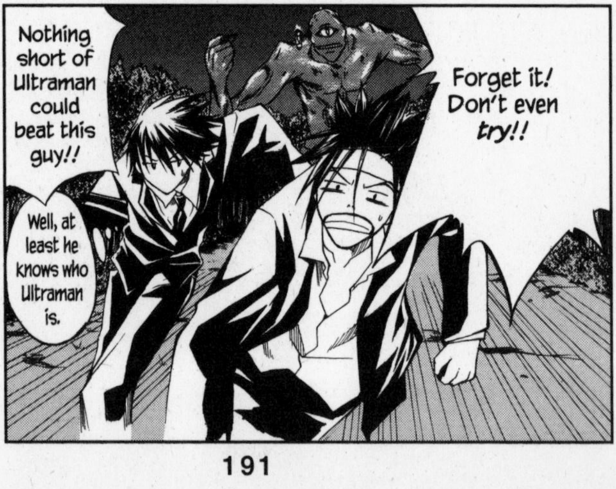
Forget it! Don't even *try!!*
Nothing short of Ultraman could beat this guy!!
Well, at least he knows who Ultraman is.

# Preview of Volume 4

We're pleased to present you with a preview of volume 4. Please check our website (www.delreymanga.com) to see when this volume will be available in English. For now you'll have to make do with Japanese!

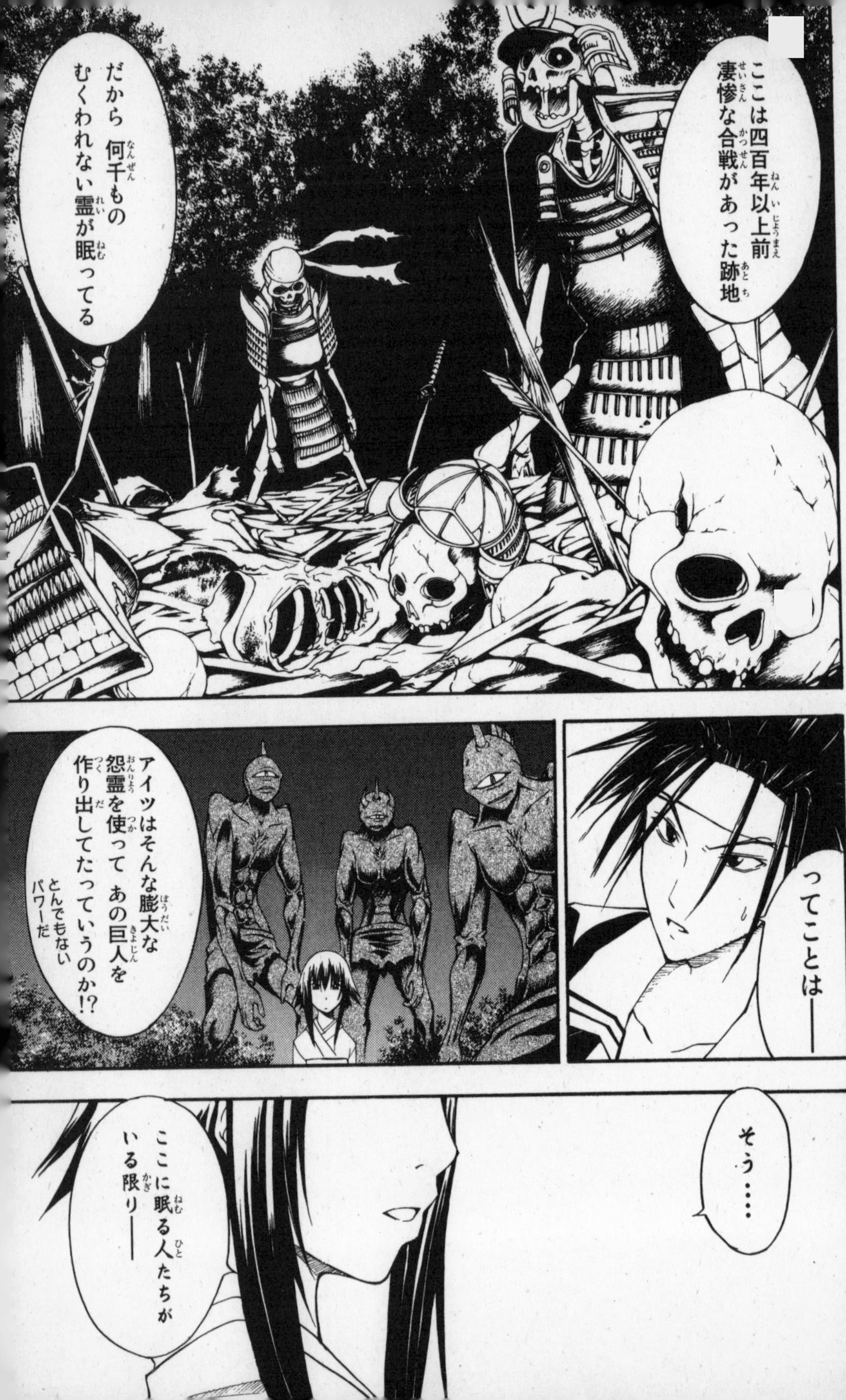
ここは四百年以上前凄惨な合戦があった跡地
だから何千ものむくわれない霊が眠ってる
ってことは——
アイツはそんな膨大な怨霊を使ってあの巨人を作り出してたっていうのか!?
とんでもないパワーだ
そう‥‥
ここに眠る人たちがいる限り——

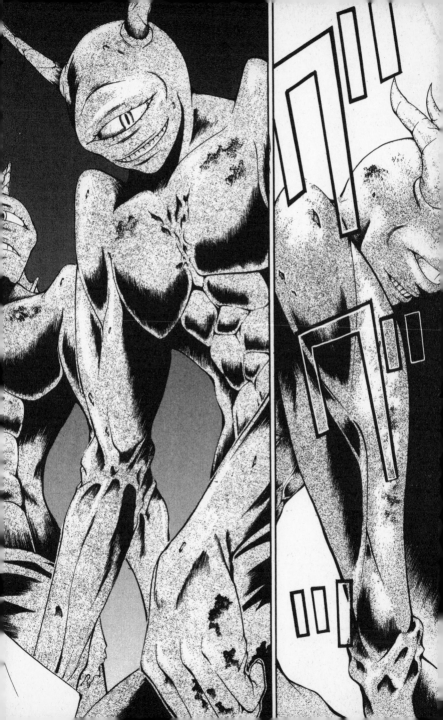

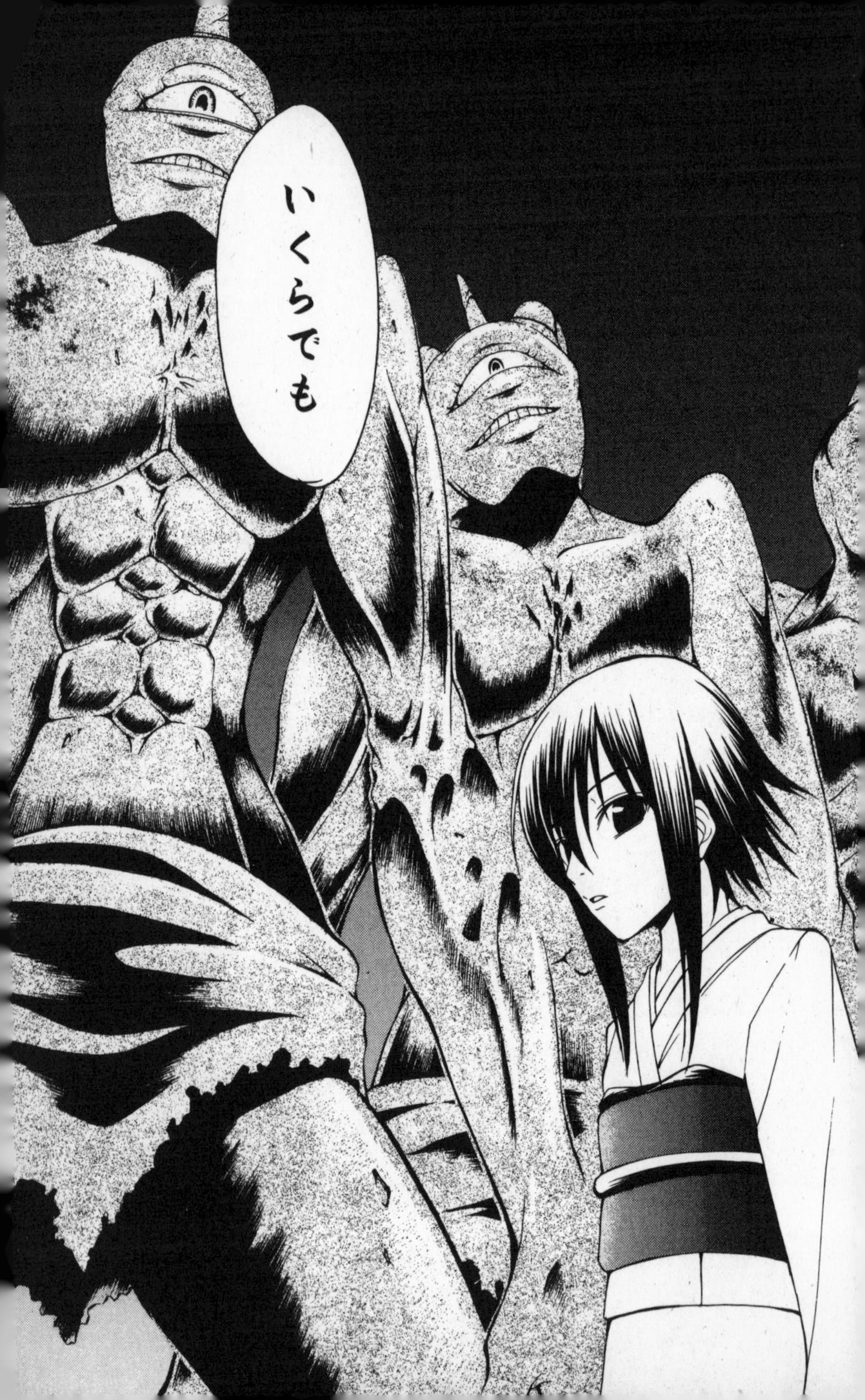
いくらでも

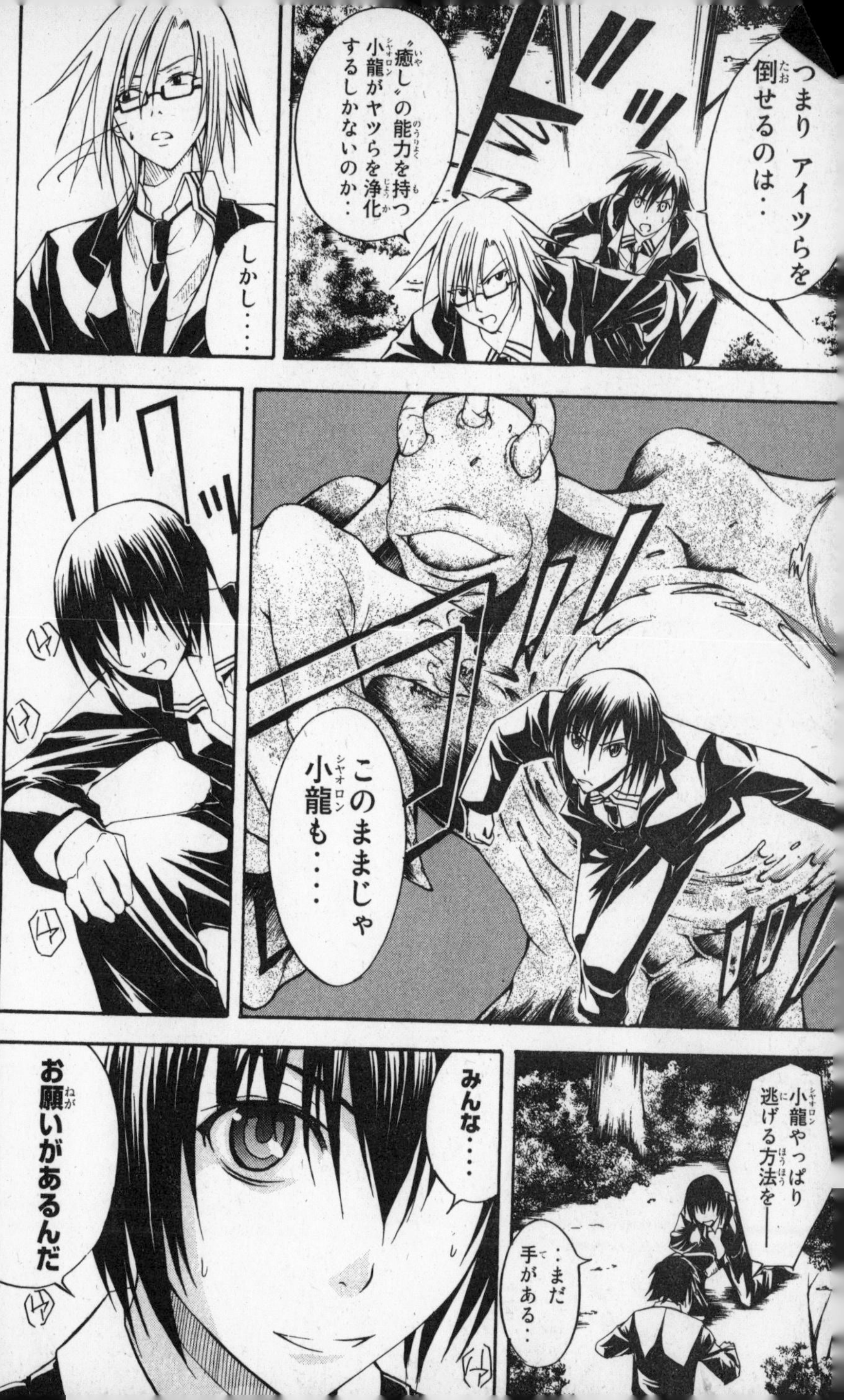

つまり アイツらを倒せるのは‥
〝癒し〟の能力を持つ小龍がヤツらを浄化するしかないのか‥
しかし‥‥
このままじゃ小龍も‥‥
ガクッ
小龍やっぱり逃げる方法を――
‥まだ手がある‥
みんな‥‥
お願いがあるんだ

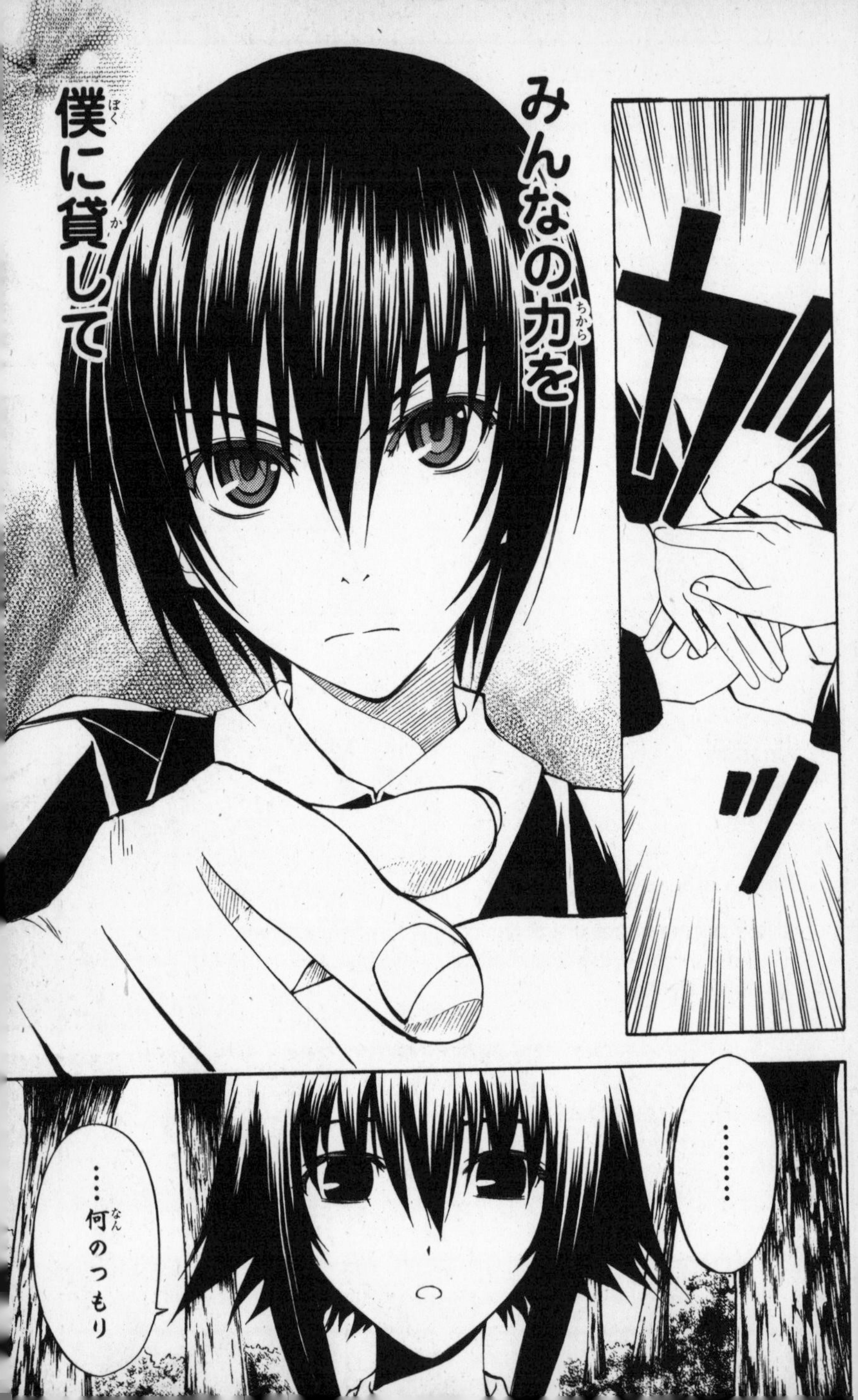

カッ
みんなの力を
僕に貸して
……
……何のつもり

# FROM HIRO MASHIMA,
## CREATOR OF *RAVE MASTER*

Lucy has always dreamed of joining the Fairy Tail, a club for the most powerful sorcerers in the land. But once she becomes a member, the fun really starts!

## *Special extras in each volume! Read them all!*

**VISIT WWW.DELREYMANGA.COM TO:**
- Read sample pages
- View release date calendars for upcoming volumes
- Sign up for Del Rey's free manga e-newsletter
- Find out the latest about new Del Rey Manga series

RATING  T AGES 13+

**DEL REY MANGA** デルレイ

*The Otaku's Choice.™*

# SHIKI TSUKAI

## MANGA BY TORU ZEKU
## ART BY YUNA TAKANAGI

### DEFENDING THE NATURAL ORDER OF THE UNIVERSE!

The *shiki tsukai* are "Keepers of the Seasons"—magical warriors pledged to defend the planet's natural order against those who would threaten it.

When 14-year-old Akira Kizuki joins the *shiki tsukai*, he knows that it'll be a difficult life. But with his new friends and mentors, he's up to the challenge!

*Special extras in each volume! Read them all!*

**VISIT WWW.DELREYMANGA.COM TO:**
- Read sample pages
- View release date calendars for upcoming volumes
- Sign up for Del Rey's free manga e-newsletter
- Find out the latest about new Del Rey Manga series

**DEL REY MANGA**
*The Otaku's Choice.*™

# BY SUZUHITO YASUDA

## A DIFFERENT SET OF SUPERTEENS!

**H**ime is a superheroine. Ao can read minds. Kotoha can conjure up anything with the right word. And Akina . . . well, he's just a regular guy, surrounded by three girls with superpowers! Together, they are the Hizumi Everyday Life Consultation Office, dedicated to protect the town of Sakurashin. And with demon dogs and supernatural threats around every corner, there's plenty to keep them busy!

*Special extras in each volume! Read them all!*

# HARIDAMA
## MAGIC CRAM SCHOOL

**BY ATSUSHI SUZUMI**

MAGICAL FRIENDS

Kokuyo and Harika are a little unusual—and not just because they're sorcery students. They're Obsidians, wizards who must use enchanted swords to help them cast spells. Their fellow students think Obsidians are inferior to "normal" wizards. But Kokuyo and Harika have something that their cohorts don't: the power of friendship!

- From the creator of *Venus vs. Virus*

BY ATSUSHI SUZUMI CREATOR OF VENUS VS. VIRUS
HARIDAMA
MAGIC CRAM SCHOOL

***Special extras in each volume! Read them all!***

VISIT WWW.DELREYMANGA.COM TO:
- Read sample pages
- View release date calendars for upcoming volumes
- Sign up for Del Rey's free manga e-newsletter
- Find out the latest about new Del Rey Manga series

RATING T AGES 13+

DEL REY MANGA デルレイ
*The Otaku's Choice*™

# TOMARE!

## [STOP!]

You're going the wrong way!

Manga is a completely different type of reading experience.

To start at the *beginning,* go to the *end*!

That's right! Authentic manga is read the traditional Japanese way—from right to left, exactly the *opposite* of how American books are read. It's easy to follow: Just go to the other end of the book, and read each page—and each panel—from right side to left side, starting at the top right. Now you're experiencing manga as it was meant to be!